Religion During the R Ukrainian Conflict

MW01034737

This book investigates how the military conflict between Russia and Ukraine has affected the religious situation in these countries. It considers threats to and violations of religious freedom, including those arising in annexed Crimea and in the eastern part of Ukraine, where fighting between Ukrainian government forces and separatist paramilitary groups backed and controlled by Russia is still going on, as well as in Russia and Ukraine more generally. It also assesses the impact of the conflict on church-state relations and national religion policy in each country and explores the role religion has played in the military conflict and the ideology surrounding it, focusing especially on the role of the Ukrainian and Russian Orthodox churches, as well as on the consequences for inter-church relations and dialogue.

Elizabeth A. Clark the Associate Director of the International Center for Law and Religion Studies at the J. Reuben Clark Law School at Brigham Young University, Provo, Utah.

Dmytro Vovk is an Associate Professor and Director for the Center for Rule of Law and Religion Studies at Yaroslav the Wise National Law University, Kharkiv, Ukraine.

Routledge Religion, Society and Government in Eastern Europe and the Former Soviet States

Series Editor Lucian Leustean is Reader in Politics and International Relations at Aston University, Birmingham, United Kingdom.

This Series seeks to publish high quality monographs and edited volumes on religion, society and government in Eastern Europe and the former Soviet States by focusing primarily on three main themes: the history of churches and religions (including, but not exclusively, Christianity, Islam, Judaism and Buddhism) in relation to governing structures, social groupings and political power; the impact of intellectual ideas on religious structures and values; and the role of religions and faith-based communities in fostering national identities from the nineteenth century until today.

The Series aims to advance the latest research on these themes by exploring the multi-facets of religious mobilisation at local, national and supranational levels. It particularly welcomes studies which offer an interdisciplinary approach by drawing on the fields of history, politics, international relations, religious studies, theology, law, sociology and anthropology.

The Making of the New Martyrs of Russia Soviet Repression in Orthodox Memory
Karin Hyldal Christensen

Religion and Politics in the Orthodox World
The Ecumenical Patriarchate in the Modern Age
Paschalis M. Kitromilides

Orthodox Religion and Politics in Contemporary Eastern Europe
On Multiple Secularisms and Entanglements
Edited by Tobias Köllner

Forced Migration and Human Security in the Eastern Orthodox World
Edited by Lucian N. Leustean

Religion During the Russian-Ukrainian Conflict
Edited by Elizabeth A. Clark and Dmytro Vovk

Religion During the Russian-Ukrainian Conflict

Edited by Elizabeth A. Clark
and Dmytro Vovk

Routledge
Taylor & Francis Group

LONDON AND NEW YORK

First published 2020
by Routledge
2 Park Square, Milton Park, Abingdon, Oxon OX14 4RN

and by Routledge
52 Vanderbilt Avenue, New York, NY 10017

Routledge is an imprint of the Taylor & Francis Group, an informa business

First issued in paperback 2021

© 2020 selection and editorial matter, Elizabeth A. Clark and Dmytro Vovk; individual chapters, the contributors

The right of Elizabeth A. Clark and Dmytro Vovk to be identified as the authors of the editorial material, and of the authors for their individual chapters, has been asserted in accordance with sections 77 and 78 of the Copyright, Designs and Patents Act 1988.

Trademark notice: Product or corporate names may be trademarks or registered trademarks, and are used only for identification and explanation without intent to infringe.

British Library Cataloguing-in-Publication Data
A catalogue record for this book is available from the British Library

Library of Congress Cataloging-in-Publication Data
A catalog record for this book has been requested

ISBN: 978-0-367-25575-6 (hbk)
ISBN: 978-1-03-208652-1 (pbk)
ISBN: 978-0-429-28846-3 (ebk)

Typeset in Bembo
by Apex CoVantage, LLC

Contents

List of figures	vii
List of tables	viii
Contributors	ix
Acknowledgments	x
Abbreviations	xi

1 Introduction 1
ELIZABETH A. CLARK AND DMYTRO VOVK

PART 1
Religion, politics, and law 13

2 Civil religion and religious freedom in the Russian–Ukrainian conflict 15
ELIZABETH A. CLARK

3 Dynamics of church–state relations in Ukraine and the military conflict with Russia: political and legal aspects 32
DMYTRO VOVK

4 Come all ye faithful to the Russian world: governmental and grass-roots spiritual discourse in the battle over Ukraine 54
ELIZAVETA GAUFMAN

5 Alternative spiritualities in Russia during the conflict in Ukraine 69
STANISLAV PANIN

6 The United States International Religious Freedom Act, nonstate actors, and the Donbas crisis 86
ROBERT C. BLITT

PART 2
Impact of the Russian-Ukrainian conflict on religious public life and communities   105

7   Ukrainian churches and civil society in the Euromaidan and the Russian-Ukrainian conflict: a sociological analysis   107
VIKTOR STEPANENKO

8   A spatial analysis of religious diversity and freedom in Ukraine after the Euromaidan   128
TYMOFIY BRIK AND STANISLAV KOROLKOV

9   Changes to religious life in Crimea since 2014   144
ROMAN LUNKIN

PART 3
The Russian-Ukrainian conflict and inter-Orthodox relations   157

10   History, ecclesiology, canonicity, and power: Ukrainian and Russian Orthodoxy after the Euromaidan   159
JERRY G. PANKHURST

11   The cause of Ukrainian autocephaly   180
CYRIL HOVORUN

12   Equivocal memory: what does the Ukrainian Orthodox church of the Moscow Patriarchate remember?   192
ANDRIY FERT

PART 4
Interviews   211

13   "The Orthodox identification of militants is an element of their understanding of the *Russkiy mir*": interview with Dr. Ihor Kozlovsky   213

14   "The militants used the Bibles to keep fires going and to cook food": interview with Rev. Dr. Vitaly Sorokun   219

15   Persecutions of Jehovah's witnesses in Russia: interview with Maria Kravchenko   226

Index   235

Figures

8.1   Index of Regulation of and Restrictions on the Majority
      Religion or All Religions (1992–2014), RAS project   133
8.2   Index of Specific Types of Religious Legislation in
      Post-Communist Societies (1992–2014), RAS project   134
8.3   Rate of Change of Communities of the Orthodox
      Churches in Ukraine   136

Tables

5.1   Qualities of the protagonist and antagonist characters in the
movie *Children versus Magicians*   72

7.1   Responses to the question "To which religious confession do
you belong?" (N=1800, %)   116

7.2   Responses to the question "If you are an Orthodox believer,
to which Orthodox Church do you belong?" (N=1800, %)   116

7.3   Aggregate public trust ("fully trust" and "mostly trust"
responses) to different institutions in Ukraine (N=1800, %)   119

8.1   Rate of decline of communities of the Ukrainian Orthodox
Church of the Moscow Patriarchate   137

8.2   Changes in the numbers of denials of registration (absolute
numbers) during 2014–2017   138

8.3   Rate of change of registration of the Ukrainian Religious
Communities from 2014 to 2017, %   141

Contributors

Robert C. Blitt, Professor of Law, University of Tennessee College of Law, USA.

Tymofiy Brik, PhD (University of Madrid), Assistant Professor at the Kyiv School of Economics, Ukraine.

Elizabeth A. Clark, Professor, Associate Director of the International Center for Law and Religion Studies at Brigham Young University, USA.

Andriy Fert, PhD Student, Yuchymenko Family Doctoral School of the National University "Kyiv-Mohyla Academy," Ukraine.

Elizaveta Gaufman, Postdoctoral Fellow at the Institute for Intercultural and International Relations, University of Bremen, Germany.

Cyril Hovorun, Acting Director of the Huffington Ecumenical Institute at Loyola Marymount University, USA.

Stanislav Korolkov, independent researcher, Ukraine.

Roman Lunkin, Doctor of Science (Russian Academy of Sciences), Head of the Center for Religious Studies at the Institute of Europe, Russian Academy of Sciences.

Stanislav Panin, PhD in Philosophy (Moscow State University), Doctoral Student of the Department of Religion at Rice University, USA.

Jerry G. Pankhurst, Professor of Sociology, Emeritus, Wittenberg University, USA.

Viktor Stepanenko, PhD (University of Manchester), Doctor of Science (National Academy of Ukraine), Leading Research Fellow at the Institute of Sociology, National Academy of sciences of Ukraine.

Dmytro Vovk, Associate Professor, Director of the Center for Rule of Law and Religion Studies at Yaroslav the Wise National Law University, Ukraine.

Acknowledgments

The editors would like to thank the BYU International Center for Law and Religion Studies (USA) and the Yaroslav the Wise National Law University (Ukraine) for support of the original conference, "War and Peace and Religion: Religious Freedom during the Russian-Ukrainian Conflict" in April 2018 in Kharkiv, Ukraine, from which many of the chapters arose, and for support of the editorial project.

Our special thanks also to BYU Law students Austin Atkinson, Miranda Cherkas, Athelia Graham, and Kyra Woods as well as Sarah Belliston, a BYU graduate student in English, for editing support and students of the Yaroslav the Wise National Law University for assistance with the April 2018 conference.

We are also grateful to Lucian Leustean, the editor of the Routledge series Religion, Society, and Government in Eastern Europe and the Former Soviet States for his kind encouragement and support of this volume and his valuable advice.

Abbreviations

DPR – the self-proclaimed Donetsk People's Republic
ECtHR – European Court of Human Rights
LPR – the self-proclaimed Luhansk People's Republic
OCU – the Orthodox Church of Ukraine
ROC – the Russian Orthodox Church
UAOC – the Ukrainian Autocephalous Orthodox Church
UGCC – the Ukrainian Greek Catholic Church
UOC-KP – the Ukrainian Orthodox Church of the Kyiv Patriarchate
UOC-MP – the Ukrainian Orthodox Church of the Moscow Patriarchate

1   Introduction

Elizabeth A. Clark and Dmytro Vovk

By 2018, the Russian-Ukrainian conflict, which started in 2014 with the illegal annexation of the Crimean Peninsula and armed confrontation in eastern Ukraine, had seen open warfare that had cost more than 10,000 lives. This conflict between countries which have significant historical, cultural, religious, and political overlap has not only undermined the post-World War II order, but has also brought about dramatic changes in the religious configurations and landscape of the occupied territories, Ukraine, and Russia. It is striking to realize that thanks to the conflict and the aggressive politics of Putin's regime, murder, kidnapping, torture, and expropriation of property of individuals and groups because of their religion exist in Europe of the twenty-first century with high standards and high protection of religious freedom. The conflict has also enhanced the political and geo-political overtones in inter-Orthodox relations within Ukraine and in world Orthodoxy. In an effort to counteract the Russian government's advocacy of a "Russian World" (*Russkiy mir*), a putative sphere of Russian cultural, political, and spiritual influence that includes Ukraine, the Ukrainian state was significantly involved in the establishment of a new, independent Ukrainian Orthodox Church and forced a break with the Russian Orthodox Church.

This book brings together authors from the domains of sociology, law, religious studies, and theology to tease out various aspects of religion's role in the conflict. The chapters reveal that while religious reasons are not the primary drivers and main focus of the clash, which is geopolitical, religion has played significant roles in it. Religious rhetoric and traditions have served as an accelerant and marker in the conflict, but religion has also itself been deeply affected by the conflict, as seen in violations of religious freedom in Donbas and Crimea, changes in church-state relations in Russia and Ukraine, and increased tensions in inter-Orthodox relations both in Ukraine and in worldwide Orthodoxy.

To use Monika Duffy Toft, Daniel Philpott, and Timothy Samuel Shah's (2011) distinction between the peripheral and central influence of religion in violent conflicts and wars, the Russian-Ukrainian conflict has manifested a more peripheral influence, which primarily relates to the identities and loyalties of the players in the conflict, as opposed to a more central influence, which

involves the religious goals of combatant parties. This may seem counter-intu-
itive, given the level of religious-related rhetoric of Russia and its proxies in
Donbas and the stated aims of the Russian World doctrine. Although all parties employ religion as a tool for promoting their internal or external political
agenda, a closer examination reveals that the core goals of the conflict pursued
by Russia, Russia-backed separatists, and Ukraine are primarily secular, rather
than religious.

In his book *The Last Empire: the Last Days of the Soviet Union*, Serhii Plokhy
(2014) shows that Russian officials and politicians discussed the question of
Crimean secession in negotiations with Ukraine in 1991. Hence the proposi-
tion of Crimean secession was rooted in the Russian political mind long before
the *Russkiy mir* doctrine was formulated by the Russian Orthodox Church
(ROC) and employed by the Kremlin. At that time, Russian politicians justified their desire to annex the peninsula by claiming to protect the rights of
Crimea's Russian-speaking population and by accusing the Ukrainian-born
Soviet leader Nikita Khrushchov with arbitrarily transferring the peninsula to
the Ukrainian SSR. Moreover, Elizaveta Gaufman, in her chapter analyzing
the main Russian social network Vkontakte, shows that within the popular
sphere, even now the conflict lacks strong religious connotations; the users of
Vkontakte mostly perceive the conflict as a secular one, where religion, particularly the grant of autocephaly for the Orthodox Church of Ukraine (OCU), is
only one more geopolitical battlefield between Russia and Ukraine or between
Russia and the West.

Similarly, the phenomenon of the Russian Orthodox Army and other Russian or pro-Russian militant groups fighting in Donbas against the Ukrainian government, as well as the religious alignment of the so-called Donetsk
and Luhansk people's republics (DPR/LPR), reflects a peripheral rather than
central religious influence centering on loyalties and identities rather than
goals. The militants have a strong religious identification as defenders of the
Russian Orthodoxy, protecting the faith from "schismatics," "Uniates," "Western sects," and Western immorality. The DPR and LPR authorities also stress
their Russian Orthodox identification and entrench a privileged position for
the church in the pseudo-republics' laws, even though they and the militants
both appear to not have a strong knowledge of Orthodox beliefs and practice (see Ihor Kozlovsky's interview). Their subjective affiliation with Russian
Orthodoxy has been an element of their political motivation to fight against
Ukraine, though not the only element and probably not the crucial one;
their secularly-argued Russian nationalism based on mythologemes of Russians and Ukrainians as "one people" and the Euromaidan as a "fascist coup"
contributed to their willingness to commit violence at least no less than their
religious identification. Additionally, after the collapse of the state order in
Donbas, there have been no religious figures among leaders of the DPR,
LPR, or militant groups: the political order has remained secular, though the
emergence of such religious figures is considered as a feature of inherently
religious conflicts (Otis, 2004).

It is also worth noting that eastern Ukraine, including the area currently under the control of separatists, has been dominated by the Ukrainian Orthodox Church of the Moscow Patriarchate (UOC-MP) – the part of Russian Orthodoxy that these militants came to fight for. Before the conflict there was no evidence of any threats to the dominant position of the UOC-MP in Donbas, and since the conflict began the UOC-MP has continued to enjoy the status of a religious majority in the region, including being favored by local authorities, elites, and communities generally. Russian Orthodoxy serves as a part of the political ideology of the "people's republics," but again it is hard to say that Russia, the DPR and LPR, or militant groups, pursue any real religious ends such as protection or expansion of Russian Orthodoxy.

The use of religion as a marker by the DPR and LPR and the militants here raises a broader problem that can occur when using religious identity in a conflict, even ostensibly to protect a beleaguered group – how counterproductive this can often be in achieving security and influence for the group sought to be protected. Despite the avowed aims of militants to protect the rights of the UOC-MP and an Orthodoxy tied with Russia in Ukraine, for example, the conflict has had a clear negative impact on the interests of the ROC in Ukraine and its position the whole Orthodox World. For instance, social trust of the UOC-MP, the ROC, and its leaders has decreased significantly; up to 500 UOC-MP communities have changed religious jurisdictions and switched to the Ukrainian Orthodox Church of the Kyiv Patriarchate (UOC-KP) or the OCU during 2014–2019; the ROC Patriarch Kirill has in essence become *persona non grata* in Ukraine; and the Ecumenical Patriarchate has legitimized unrecognized Ukrainian Orthodox churches, giving autocephaly to the OCU and challenging the status of Ukraine as a canonical territory of the ROC. Hence, as a result of the Russian-Ukrainian conflict, *Russkiy mir* has not only failed to expand Russia's influence in Ukraine, but has also lost its prominence as an actual political agenda in the country.

Religion of course can not only act as an accelerant or an identity marker, however. Religion's involvement in de-escalating hostility has been most evident in Donbas, where the conflict has taken on the most violent form. Many Ukrainian churches and interfaith organizations have called for cessation of violence and reconciliation, and spoken out against aggressive Russian politics towards Ukraine. In 2014 religious minority communities in the Donbas region established a peaceful initiative, called a Prayer Marathon, in order to prevent Russian intervention in Ukrainian affairs and to decelerate tensions between the Ukrainian government and Russia-backed local groups (see Ihor Kozlovsky's interview). Several Ukrainian and Russian religiously-affiliated institutions have also provided relief and support for people affected by the military conflict (see interview with Vitaly Sorokun) and churches have been involved in prisoner exchanges between the Ukrainian government and the DPR/LPR.

And, certainly not least, the conflict has also had a significant impact on the situation with religious freedom, first of all in Donbas and the Russian-annexed

Crimea. The DPR and LPR have morphed into the territory of probably the most brutal violators of religious rights in contemporary Europe: the authorities of these quasi-republics have banned or severely restricted the activities of all religious minorities, and they violently oppress and stigmatize believers of religions considered "non-traditional for the Donbas." Several religious leaders, priests, believers, and even whole communities have been forced to leave the DPR and LPR or to go underground (Institute of Religious Freedom, 2018). In their interviews, Ihor Kozlovsky and Vitaly Sorokun describe the people's republics as territories of total surveillance and permanent persecution for "unreliable" religious groups. In his chapter Robert C. Blitt argues that the DPR and LPR satisfy features of nonstate actors according to the U.S. International Religious Freedom Act and can be designated as entities of particular concern that have committed severe violations of religious freedom.

Crimea has transitioned from the relatively liberal regulation of religion in Ukraine to the intrusive authoritarian regulation of the Russian legal system. As Roman Lunkin illustrates in his chapter, religious pluralism has significantly decreased in Crimea following the annexation of the peninsula. Several religious leaders left or were deported from the peninsula. Restrictive and vague Russian legislation and court practices have stifled the institutional freedom, missionary work, and public activities of religious minorities. However, as Lunkin shows, the religious policies of the Russian Federation are determined not by religious motivations, but rather by political factors (including the "reliability" of religious groups and their involvement in the Euromaidan protests), national-security considerations (such as alleged religious extremist threats), and geopolitical reasons (e.g., links with mother churches abroad).

Crimea's situation is now similar to that of Russia in general, where the contemporary norm is to view religious issues through the lens of national security, oppression of religious minorities (including those supporting the war with Ukraine, see Stanislav Panin's chapter), and endorsement of the ROC as the de facto official religion, while all other religions are repressed in varying degrees (Sarkissian, 2015, pp. 91–101). During the conflict, the Russian parliament adopted the infamous Yarovaya Law, which put virtually any public religious activity and the private sharing of beliefs in residential locations under full state control. In 2017 the Russian Supreme Court completely banned the Jehovah's Witnesses organization as extremist (see interview with Maria Kravchenko). These and many other cases put together make Russia the worst oppressor of religious freedom among post-Soviet, Orthodox-majority states and one of the worst in the whole post-Soviet space. In 2018, the U.S. Commission on International Religious Freedom recommended Russia be designated a country of particular concern along with three post-Soviet Middle Eastern countries: Uzbekistan, Turkmenistan, and Tajikistan, all three notorious for severe violations of religious freedom.

The conflict has also seriously influenced church-state relations in the territory controlled by the Ukrainian government and in both Donbas and Crimea. The common trend within the Ukrainian state, the two pseudo-states in Donbas, and the Russian regime in Crimea is a strengthening of the positive identification of public authorities with religion. As W. Cole Durham, Jr. (1996) suggests, state identification, towards its extremes (theocratic states at one end or states seeking to abolish religion at the other) correlates with a low level of religious freedom and inequality among religions, whereas various regimes with moderate positive identification or moderate separation of religion and state correlate with a higher degree of religious freedom and higher equality. The move towards greater positive church-state identification in Crimea after annexation and also especially in Donbas and the accompanying loss of religious freedom are significant. The Ukrainian case is different due to several political and social factors: plurality of the religious landscape, a relatively high level of freedom, Ukraine's drift to the West and European integration policies, and the need of support from Western countries. Thus, for now, the gradual rapprochement of the Ukrainian state and the OCU has not yet resulted in serious violations of religious minorities' rights and the establishment of an official or endorsed church as, in varying degrees, is the case in other post-Soviet Orthodox-majority countries.

Finally, the Russian-Ukrainian conflict has also prompted serious transformations in both Ukrainian and global Orthodoxy. The war with Russia popularized the idea of an independent Ukrainian Orthodox Church among both religious and non-religious Ukrainians (see Viktor Stepanenko's chapter). As a result, the state has actively facilitated the unification of Ukrainian Orthodox churches and negotiated autocephaly for the OCU with the Ecumenical Patriarchate. The conflict certainly is not the only reason for the creation of the OCU, as Jerry G. Pankhurst and Cyril Hovorun show in their chapters, but it definitely triggered the process. The ROC and the Russian government have reacted poorly to the establishment of the OCU and its recognition by the Ecumenical Patriarchate, which has provoked new tensions between the Phanar and the Russian Church and created an Orthodox-wide turmoil: every autocephalous Orthodox church now faces the problem of (non)recognition of the new church and, therefore, the question of taking either Constantinople's or Moscow's side in this larger religio-political game.

Meanwhile, because of the conflict, the UOC-MP – the Ukrainian religion with the most followers – is now officially and publicly disfavored. While there is nothing new about the Ukrainian state's taking the side of one of the country's Orthodox churches, this is definitely the first time such a policy has become official and entrenched in legal rules. The Ukrainian government and most of the public perceive the UOC-MP as a threat to their national security because of the Church's ties with the ROC and indirectly with the Russian state and because of the alleged involvement of some of its leaders and clergymen in the separatist movement in Donbas and Crimea. Thus, in post-Euromaidan Ukraine the UOC-MP finds itself in the position of the pro-Russian minority to whom, as Jack A. Goldstone (2014) writes, post-revolutionary societies do not wish to expand formal equality. Hence the state's attempt to force the UOC-MP to change its official name to reflect ties to Russia. In addition,

Ukrainian legislation has regulated the procedures for religious communities to change religious jurisdiction, which previously was left to the charters of individual religions, in an attempt to make it easier for UOC-MP communities to transition to the Orthodox Church of Ukraine.

These efforts raise questions of religious freedom for the UOC-MP and its believers: first, to what extent are national-security concerns a legitimate justification for strengthening state control over religion, and second, whether these measures were proportionate, considering that they targeted the whole church rather than particular leaders, clergymen, or communities involved in illegal activities (see chapters by Elizabeth A. Clark and Dmytro Vovk). Moreover, labeling the UOC-MP as a "Russian church" is more complicated than it may seem. In his chapter, Andriy Fert demonstrates that the UOC-MP has employed two different narratives of self-representation, each of which play to different concepts of identity common over time in Ukraine. One of them focuses on the ecclesiastical unity of the UOC-MP and the ROC, and the other emphasizes the role of the UOC-MP as the Ukrainian national church.

The Russian-Ukrainian conflict itself, the creation of the new Orthodox Church of Ukraine, and the conflict between the Ecumenical and Moscow Patriarchates are still works in progress. Hence, the chapters of this book are only pieces of a complicated puzzle that has yet to be finished. However, we hope that these pieces can contribute to a deeper understanding of the religious dimension of the conflict between Russia and Ukraine.

★ ★ ★

Our book offers the first major analysis of the multiple roles of religion in the Russian-Ukrainian conflict. Krawchuk and Bremer (2016) address these issues thoughtfully, but focus primarily on the events surrounding the Euromaidan and inter-Orthodox issues at the beginning of the conflict. Our authors engage not only the role of religion in the conflict itself from 2014–2018, but also examine the creation of the new Orthodox Church of Ukraine at the end of 2018 and its ramifications in the geopolitical sphere. In addition, in contrast to most of the existing work in the field of religion in Russia and Ukraine, which addresses church-state relations through sociological, historical, and religious studies lenses (see Balakireva & Sereda, 2013; Krawchuk, 2014; Krawchuk & Bremer, 2016; Shlikhta, 2014; Shlikhta, 2016; Plokhy, 2002; Plokhy & Sysyn, 2003; Wasyliv, 2014; Yelensky, 1999), we also offer perspectives from other fields as well, such as law and religion, religious freedom, historical memory, and alternative spiritualties. The volume also contains fresh analysis with novel data from social media, registration of religious organizations, etc.

The book is divided into four sections. The first one is dedicated to religion, law, and politics in the Russian-Ukrainian conflict. **Elizabeth A. Clark**, in her chapter, uses the contemporary understandings of emotional and religious engagement in legal systems and the concept of civil religion to analyze the situation in both Russia and Ukraine, where public displays of religiosity have increased in recent years. Thicker civil religion, however, brings challenges to religious freedom, as minorities become increasingly marginalized and majority religions can lose authenticity. These challenges are particularly salient during wartime, as the emotional and spiritual resonance of religion increases. Clark identifies the increase in the political and symbolic use of religion in Donbas, Russia, and Ukraine during the Russian-Ukrainian conflict and the associated challenges to religious freedom. She argues that religious repressions of minority believers have become particularly acute in Donbas and in Russia, but are also starting to become a concern in Ukraine with legislation targeting the UOC-MP and questions about the use of religious sites.

Dmytro Vovk explores the legal and political dynamics of church–state relations in Ukraine during the Russian-Ukrainian conflict. He demonstrates that the conflict triggered several changes in relations between temporal and spiritual authorities with regard to the military and national-security-related areas and thus contributed to the general shift in Ukraine to a more cooperationist church-state system. According to Vovk, this shift moves Ukraine closer to the church–state approaches employed by other post-Soviet Orthodox-majority countries, including a de facto or de jure multitier system of religions and state favoritism towards the national Orthodox church. However, due to several abovementioned political and social reasons, these tendencies are still significantly milder in Ukraine than in Belarus, Georgia, Moldova, and Russia.

Elizaveta Gaufman analyzes Russian governmental and grass-root discourses of the Russian World (*Russkiy mir*) concept in the context of the conflict with Ukraine. She identifies two main interpretations of this notion: one of them stipulates an affinity to Russian language and culture, and the other is more focused on a geopolitical/civilizational narrative. Comparing statements of Russian politicians and the data of the most popular Russian social network, Vkontakte, Gaufman demonstrates the discrepancies between these discourses. While Russian politicians try to peddle spiritual (Orthodox) links and similarities between Russians and Ukrainians, Vkontakte users seem to perceive the Russian World as a more geopolitical and militaristic doctrine, aiming to expand Russian political influence in the near abroad and globally.

Stanislav Panin examines ideological patterns concerning marginal religious groups and unaffiliated spiritualities in Russia during the conflict in Ukraine. He shows that the Russian media and the ROC tend to impose the image of the enemy on these minorities. Panin argues that this narrative is rooted both in the Soviet criticism of religion and the ideas of the American anti-cult movement brought to Russia during late 1980s and 1990s. In this narrative, minority groups are described as agents of foreign influence aiming to undermine social stability and push Russia into revolutionary turmoil. At the same time, as Panin notes, minority groups hold various perspectives concerning the situation in Ukraine ranging from critical to supportive. However, even a supportive stance towards Russian policies in Ukraine does not reliably prevent these minorities from being considered a threat to the established social order.

The U.S. policies on the protection of international religious freedom is the focus of **Robert C. Blitt's** chapter. Blitt argues that the U.S. State Department has failed to take advantage of an important tool for political action against the self-proclaimed Donetsk People's Republic and Luhansk People's Republics. He argues that the State Department should designate them as entities of particular concern under the 2016 Wolf Amendments to the International Religious Freedom Act. These amendments, designed to allow the U.S. government to impose sanctions on nonstate actors responsible for religious freedom violations, would permit the U.S. to respond to the serious denials of religious freedom in Donbas, while leaving space for diplomacy with Russia.

The second section of the book explores the impact of the Russian-Ukrainian conflict on religious public life and communities. **Victor Stepanenko** analyzes the interrelation between churches and civil society in Ukraine. He argues that although there could be some structural and ideological reservations to understanding churches as civil society institutions, churches can nonetheless play important roles in civil society, particularly by contributing to the process of democratization. According to Stepanenko, this is relevant to the Ukrainian case, where society considers religion as an important social force and major churches were significantly involved in both Maidans – the Orange Revolution of 2014 and the Revolution of Dignity (Euromaidan) of 2013–2014. However, churches' attitudes towards these were markedly different: the Ukrainian Orthodox Church of the Kyiv Patriarchate and the Ukrainian Greek-Catholic Church supported the protesters, while the perception of these events by the Ukrainian Orthodox Church of the Moscow Patriarchate, as well as their believers, was more ambiguous. Stepanenko also tackles reasons for and social consequences of the churches' varied positions in the context of the Russian-Ukrainian conflict, highlights the challenges that Ukrainian churches face in promoting European integration, and delineates promising prospects on closer mutual interaction between churches and civil society.

Tymofiy Brik and **Stanislav Korolkov** provide a spatial analysis of religious diversity and freedom in Ukraine. They explore data on religious communities registered in Ukraine between the Euromaidan in 2013–2014 and the emergence of the new independent Orthodox Church of Ukraine at the end of 2018. They found that the number of registered communities of the UOC-KP increased after the Euromaidan while the number of communities of the UOC-MP remained stable. Thus, the gap between two major Orthodox churches has narrowed. Brik and Korolkov believe that it could be a potential sign of state or local favoritism towards the UOC-KP. However, they have not identified any data suggesting serious repressions of the UOC-MP communities, which, according to them, may pave the way for a gradual transition to the OCU for those UOC-MP communities that choose to join it.

Roman Lunkin's chapter is based on his field research of religious life in Crimea after the Russian annexation of the peninsula. Lunkin has studied institutional and structural changes and ideological shifts which occurred in this period within Protestant, Orthodox, Catholic, and Muslim communities.

He argues that Crimean religious organizations lost almost all religious freedom and freedom of association that they previously enjoyed in Ukraine. The
Yarovaya Law and other Russian draconian legislation provides the state with
powerful tools of controlling religion and oppressing religious communities
that are considered "unreliable." However, according to Lunkin, the Crimean
example shows that, in spite of state attempts to closely control religious life, the
authorities have been unable to thoroughly destroy the religious pluralism that
developed during the Ukrainian period.

The third section of the book is devoted to developments in inter-Orthodox
relations that have been directly or indirectly influenced by the Russian-
Ukrainian conflict and contributes to a nascent scholarly evaluation (Fagan,
2019) of the reasons and consequences of the OCU's autocephaly for Ukraine
and Ukrainian, Russian and Global Orthodoxy. In his chapter, **Jerry G.
Pankhurst** explores relations between Russian and Ukrainian Orthodoxy after
the Euromaidan. He has identified seven historical, political, geopolitical, and
ecclesiastical factors which came together to create conditions that resulted in
the creation of an independent Ukrainian Orthodox Church recognized by
the Ecumenical Patriarchate. These factors include: the establishment of the
Ukrainian independent state and maturing of the country's political elite and
society, Russian aggression, Ukraine's drift to the West, a re-organization in
global Orthodoxy that changed the power equilibrium in relations between the
ROC and the Ecumenical Patriarchate, and the struggle for political leadership
in post-Euromaidan Ukraine, where autocephaly for the OCU was one of the
issues at stake.

Cyril Hovorun describes historical aspects of granting autocephaly by the
Orthodox Church of Ukraine. According to him, the initiative came from the
people and was facilitated by the state, which perceived this issue as both ecclesiastical and political. Hovorun stresses that the Russian-Ukrainian conflict has
catalyzed the cause for OCU's autocephaly, though during the twentieth century there were several attempts to reach this aim. He also argues that current
tensions can be interpreted as a conflict between competing visions of the role
of neo-imperial political projects in the Orthodox Church.

Andriy Fert's chapter explores narratives and the historical memory of
the Ukrainian Orthodox Church of the Moscow Patriarchate that the Church
has employed after the collapse of the Soviet Union, particularly during the
Russian-Ukrainian conflict. He argues that in telling about its past, the Church
employs two basic narratives: the "History of Orthodoxy in Rus'" narrative, emphasizing the unity of the UOC-MP with Russian Orthodoxy, and
the "History of the Ukrainian Church" one, promoting a long-history self-
representation of the UOC-MP and its status as the only true church for all
Ukrainians since the reign of the Grand Prince Volodymyr the Great in the
tenth century. According to Fert, the Church has had to use these two narratives simultaneously, because it permits them to unite communities with different collective memories determined by their political position, attitudes to the
Soviet past, etc.

The fourth part of the book contains three interviews with scholars and experts on religion in modern Russia and Ukraine in the context of the conflict between the countries. Religious scholar **Ihor Kozlovsky**, who was imprisoned for political reasons by the authorities of so-called Donetsk People's Republic during 2016–2017, is interviewed on the role of religion in attempting to de-escalate the war in Donbas, persecutions and violence against religious minorities and activists committed by DPR authorities and Russian and local militants, and links between the conflict and Russian Orthodoxy. **Vitaly Sorokun**, a legal scholar and Protestant minister, talks about repressions against Protestant communities in the "people's republics" and their life in the territories that are not controlled by the Ukrainian government. **Maria Kravchenko**, one of the leading experts on Russian anti-extremism policies, is interviewed on the Jehovah's Witnesses' case in the Russian Federation. She discusses how the Russian state increased pressure on Jehovah's Witnesses and fully banned them in 2017, what legal arguments were employed by the state, the role of the ROC in this process, and the contemporary situation with Russian Jehovah's Witnesses who had to go underground and are prosecuted by law enforcement agencies and courts for illegal religious activities.

Throughout this volume, we have used the BGN/PCGN transliteration system for Russian and Ukrainian because of its ease of reading for English-speakers. We use Ukrainian variants of geographic names (Kyiv, not Kiev) and historical figures (Volodymyr the Great versus Vladimir the Great) which relate to places or figures who lived within the territory of Ukraine's current borders.

References

Balakireva, O., & Sereda, I. (2013). Religion and civil society in Ukraine and Russia. In J. de Hart, P. Dekker, & L. Halman (Eds.), *Religion and civil society in Europe* (pp. 219–250). doi:10.1007/978-94-007-6815-4_12

Durham, W. C., Jr. (1996). A comparative framework for analyzing religious liberty. In J. D. van der Vyver & J. Witte, Jr. (Eds.), *Religious human rights in global perspective: Legal perspectives* (Vol. I, pp. 1–44). The Hague: Kluwer Law International.

Fagan, G. (2019). Between the barricades: The conflicted loyalties of Ukraine's Orthodox. *East-West Church Report, 27*(1), 4–6.

Goldstone, J. A. (2014). *Revolutions.* doi:10.1093/actrade/9780199858507.001.0001

Institute of Religious Freedom. (2018). Religious freedom at gunpoint: Russian terror in the occupied territories of Eastern Ukraine. *Analytical report.* [Adobe Digital Editions version]. Retrieved from www.irf.in.ua/files/publications/2018.10.24-IRF-Report-ENG.pdf

Krawchuk, A. (2014). Constructing interreligious consensus in post-Soviet space: The Ukrainian council of churches and religious organizations. In A. Krawchuk & T. Bremer (Eds.), *Eastern Orthodox encounters of identity and otherness: Values, self-reflection, dialogue* (pp. 273–300). doi:10.1057/9781137377388_18

Krawchuk, A., & Bremer, T. (Eds.). (2016). *Churches in the Ukrainian crisis.* doi:10.1007/978-3-319-34144-6

Otis, P. (2004). Religion and war in the twenty-first century. In R. A. Seiple & D. R. Hoover (Eds.), *Religion and security: The new nexus in international relations* (pp. 11–24). New York, NY: Rowman & Littlefield Publishers, Inc.

Plokhy, S. (2002). State politics and religious pluralism in Russia and Ukraine: A comparative perspective. In P. G. Danchin & E. Cole (Eds.), *Protecting the human rights of religious minorities in eastern Europe*. New York, NY: Columbia University Press.

Plokhy, S. (2014). *The last empire: The final days of the Soviet Union*. New York, NY: Basic Books.

Plokhy, S., & Sysyn, F. E. (2003). *Religion and nation in modern Ukraine*. Edmonton and Toronto, Canada: Canadian Institute of Ukrainian Studies Press.

Sarkissian, A. (2015). *The varieties of religious repression: Why governments restrict religion*. New York, NY: Oxford University Press.

Shlikhta, N. (2016). Eastern Christian churches between state and society: An overview of the religious landscape in Ukraine (1989–2014). *Kyiv-Mohyla Humanities Journal, 3*(3), 123–142. doi:10.18523/kmhj73945.2016–3.123–142

Shlikhta, N. (2014). The Ukrainian Greek Catholic church. In L. N. Leustean (Ed.), *Eastern Christianity and politics in the twenty-first century* (pp. 312–333). doi:10.4324/9781315819037

Toft, M. D., Philpott, D., & Shah, T. S. (2011). *God's century: Resurgent religion and global politics*. New York, NY: W. W. Norton & Company.

United States Commission on International Religious Freedom. (2018). *2018 Annual report*. Retrieved from www.uscirf.gov/sites/default/files/2018USCIRFAR.pdf

Wasyliv, Z. V. (2014). Orthodox churches in Ukraine. In L. N. Leustean (Ed.), *Eastern Christianity and politics in the twenty-first century* (pp. 312–333). doi:10.4324/9781315819037

Yelensky, V. (1999). The Ukraine church and state relations in the post-Communist era. In I. Borowik (Ed.), *Church and state relations in central and eastern Europe* (pp. 146–147). Krakow, Poland: NOMOS.

Part 1

Religion, politics, and law

2 Civil religion and religious freedom in the Russian-Ukrainian conflict

Elizabeth A. Clark

Understanding civil religion's pull

Contemporary movements in economics (Ariely, 2010; Kahneman, 2013), law (Sajó, 2011), and philosophy (Nussbaum, 2001) question the primacy of reason in ordering human behavior and regulation. Kahneman earned the Nobel prize in 2002 for his work on the value of non-rationally based decision-making processes, work that has resonated in other fields. We are coming to realize that emotions, as Nussbaum (2001) argues are "not thoughtless surges of affect but value-laden judgments shaped by social norms" (p. 11). Sajó (2011) argues that the choice in constitutional structuring is not between rational justification of state norms or irrational, emotion-laden systems, but that human-driven emotions can be engaged publicly in a way that takes them and protects their expression without abandoning rationality: "The enemy of reason is not passion, it is fanaticism" (p. 3). On the one hand, he argues, emotions can lead to authoritarian manipulation, and on the other, excising emotions can lead to another extreme of restrictions on liberty. At their best, however, constitutional systems do not annihilate or disregard moral sentiments, but contain them so that they will not lead to instability, injustice, or confusion.

Religion, with its ties to the sacred and the profane, shapes social and moral norms and both influences and is affected by emotional responses. These kinds of religious-related ties to the legal and political order have been variously addressed with terms like civil religion (Bellah, 1967), political theology (Schmitt, 1985/1922), civil theology (Shanks, 1995), political religion (Gentile, 2005), civic piety (Hart & Pauley, 2005), and public religion (Barreto, Cavalcante, & Da Rosa, 2017), to name only a few. A nuanced discussion of these terms is beyond the scope of this chapter (for an attempt, see Richey & Jones, 1974). For my purposes, I choose to use the term civil religion to mean the beliefs, symbols, and rituals associated with the public religious dimension of civic life, in part because it ties back to Jean-Jaques Rousseau's thought and also because of its use in the legal field, increasingly at an international level. (see, e.g., Chelini-Pont, 2010; Ferrari, 2010; Steunebrink & Zweerde, 2004).

Religious norms, like emotions, are ambiguous in a legal system. On the one hand, as Sarkissian (2015) documents, they can be used by authoritarian states to manipulate public opinion. Recognition of this power leads some to assert the need for freedom from religion, insisting that states must create a neutral framework that excludes religion. Given the ubiquity of religion as a sociological matter and of religious and spiritual emotions, this effort seems futile at best, and oppressive of genuine individual attempts to manifest freedom of religion or belief. Soviet attempts, for example, only created an alternative system of beliefs, rituals, and symbols in scientific atheism that some have referred to as a form of religion (Guthrie, 1996, p. 413).

Emotions and religion-related emotions cannot be ignored in a legal system and indeed may play a positive role in embedding and entrenching social and moral norms, building deep ties of patriotism that provide meaning in social sacrifice, such as military service, and establishing a space for transcendental reaching in the face of national tragedy and individual suffering. The sense that religion can help embed and ground social norms and "teach a man to love his duty" was first articulated using the term civil religion by Rousseau. Rousseau's work on religion is somewhat ambiguous, but he clearly stressed the public role religion can play. For example, he writes: "Now, it matters very much to the community that each citizen should have a religion. That will make him love his duty." (Rousseau, 1923/1762, p. 121). For Rousseau, the legitimacy of the religious dimension of social bonds comes because it reflects generalized religious conscience (Durham, 1996).

As Casanova (1994) and others have noted, public religiosity in modern life is not waning and is as furiously religious as it ever was (Berger, 1999). This sense of a public role for religion and its value in supporting the national polity has regained salience, though not without its critics. Bellah (1967) provided the classic articulation of civil religion as the "public religious dimension . . . expressed in set of beliefs, symbols and rituals" (p. 4). He argues that "civil religion has been a point of articulation between the profoundest commitments of the Western religious and philosophical tradition and the common beliefs of ordinary Americans" (Bellah, 1967, pp. 15–16). These layers of beliefs, symbols, and rituals can be comparatively minimal, inclusive, and permit individual opting-out, which I would term a "thinner" version of civil religion; or can be highly specific to a single religion, compulsory, and communicate exclusive state identification with a dominant religion that excludes the possibility of full citizenship of those of other faiths, which I would term a "thicker" version of civil religion.

Civil religion is seen by some in cynical terms as useful to the state for manipulation or even merely useful for identity politics. I would argue, however, that at its best, civil religion, particularly a thin one, can be more than a marker or a slogan and has the potential to play a unifying role, providing a sense of belonging or attachment between citizens and the state. The connection with religion opens one form of grounding for the legitimacy of the state, which is particularly valuable in a system that permits multiple conceptual groundings (Lindholm, 2004). Civil religion, at its best, opens a space of respect for individuals to respond to their own consciences. Much like religious freedom, civil religion can be an attempt to connect immanent and transcendent spheres, leaving a place for conscience, for reverence, and for virtue that strengthens citizenship. Virtue ethics philosopher Paul Woodruff (2014), for example, has described how the virtue of reverence evokes room for moral striving and forms a check on the power of the state. He describes that "reverence has more to do with politics than religion. . . . Power without reverence – that is catastrophe" (p. 14).

Civil religion's tensions with religious freedom

For all its value to the state and society, civil religion, particularly a thick version of it, also brings with it significant tensions with modern states' commitments to religious freedom and neutrality. At its worst, a thicker conception of civil religion in a more authoritarian regime can be deeply oppressive, coopting convenient majority beliefs and discriminating against or excluding followers of minority beliefs from public life. Rousseau hints at this in a disturbing statement:

> While [this faith] . . . can compel no one to believe. . . [its dogmas], it can banish from the State whoever does not believe them – it can banish him, not for impiety, but as an anti-social being, incapable of truly loving the laws and justice, and of sacrificing, at need, his life to his duty. If anyone, after publicly recognizing these dogmas, behaves as if he does not believe them, let him be punished by death: he has committed the worst of all crimes, that of lying before the law.
>
> (Rousseau, 1923/1762, p. 121)

In civil religion at its worst, religious symbols and beliefs become enforceable as marks of citizenship. A state's commitment to religious freedom and pluralism falls to the wayside as religious dogmas and practices are institutionalized and enforced by coercion. Grim and Finke (2010) document how "regardless of the world religion involved or the time frame viewed, when a dominant religion forms an alliance with the state, the state's authority can be used to suppress potential religious competitors" (p. 70). Sarkissian (2015) has also tracked how authoritarian rulers in states with majority religions tend to use identification with majority religious beliefs as an attempt to shore up support without resorting to hard power, resulting in discrimination against and oppression of minority religions.

Even short of Rousseau's proposed banishment or death penalty for unbelievers and those who renounce their beliefs or other forms of coercion or suppression by authoritarian regimes, a thick version of civil religion inevitably raises problems for the freedom of minorities. To determine the content of a unifying civil religion, the state naturally looks to the religious beliefs, holidays, and symbols of the majority of its citizens, yet in doing so inherently excludes minorities who do not share those beliefs, holidays, or symbols. If the state uses coercion to impose expression of these symbols and beliefs, it will be the minority believers that will suffer.

The European Court of Human Rights (ECtHR) struggled with these issues in ruling on the placement of crucifixes in Italian state school classrooms in *Lautsi and others v. Italy (2011)*, where a panel's holding that the crucifixes violated the religious freedom rights of the minority was subsequently over-ruled by the Grand Chamber. The case raises the issue at the core of religious freedom concerns in civil religion: When does state expression of majority traditions, often imbued with deep historical and cultural significance, become impermissible coercion of minorities? In the end, the majority of the ECtHR Grand Chamber held that, while it "is understandable that the first applicant might see in the display of crucifixes in the classrooms . . . a lack of respect on the State's part for her right to ensure their education and teaching in con-formity with her own philosophical convictions", the subjective perception alone was insufficient to violate the individual religious freedom rights (para. 65). The court recognized that crucifixes carried Christian symbolism, but held that, just as in previous religious education cases that emphasized the dominant religion of a country, preferring the symbol of a dominant religion "could not in itself be viewed as a departure from the principles of pluralism and objectiv-ity amounting to indoctrination" (para. 71). The court contrasted the crucifixes, which it described as "passive symbols" that are not associated with teaching about Christianity or proselyting in the classes, with the ECtHR's previous decision in *Dahlab v. Switzerland* (2001), which upheld a ban on teachers wear-ing Islamic headscarves while teaching, because those were "powerful external symbols" (para. 72–74). The fine distinctions the court drew between "external" and "passive" public religious symbols illustrate the challenge that protecting the religious freedom of minorities presents in systems with thicker versions of civil religion.

The religious freedom perils of a thick civil religion are not limited just to minorities. As the implications of *Lautsi* would suggest, state support of major-ity symbols can be a double-edged sword. In order to justify these symbols in a modern pluralistic system, courts must emphasize the secular and historical nature of the symbols, undercutting or trivializing their religious content. In the U.S. system, this takes the shape of what has been called the "Santa Claus" rule, requiring that state Christmas displays also have references to the secular meaning of Christmas and/or Hanukkah (see the U.S. Supreme Court cases, *County of Allegheny v. American Civil Liberties Union*, 492 U.S. 573 (1989); *Lynch v. Donnelly*, 465 U.S. 668 (1984)). Beyond state appropriation of religious symbols, state support in a variety of forms can also more broadly lead to encroachments on religious autonomy (Sewell, 2010).

Limits on religious freedom stemming from thick conceptions of civil reli-gion not only compromise the rights of minorities and the majority religions, but also ultimately fail to achieve the beneficial ends of civil religion itself. To the extent that religious displays, symbols, and rituals are adopted or limited to one faith by coercion, they fail to cultivate meaningful choice and conscience and result in increasingly insincere and ineffective professions of regard for civic loyalty and duty, evoking instead cynical disdain for perceived manipulation of belief. Finally, it is worth mentioning that mandatory civic silence on religious matters can also violate religious freedom. The atheistic political religion of the USSR, or to a much lesser extent *laïcité* as understood in France or Turkey can be as intolerant as a mandatory thick civil religion (cf. Chelini-Pont (2010), who argues that *laïcité*, with its myths of republicanism and "eternal France," can be understood as a French civil religion).

Civil religion in wartime

War, with its heightened need for civic loyalty, seems to bring questions of civil religion to the fore. A state's ability to commemorate the fallen and rally those facing the real possibility of imminent death is strengthened, giving a way for its citizens to be able to tap into the power of the transcendent and have a space for public reverence. This need can be illustrated by Stalin's appeal to the Russian Orthodox Church for support during World War II (see, e.g., Corley, 1996, pp. 130–131), the addition of the phrase "under God" in the U.S. pledge of allegiance during the Cold War (Eisenhower, 1960), or the renewed impetus to create a chaplaincy system in Ukraine during the conflict with Russia.

The increased emphasis on civil religion during wartime, however, brings with it the concomitant possibility of its abuse and violations of religious freedom. I suggest that the challenges to religious freedom during wartime typically take the form of increased public opposition to minority religions, especially pacifist ones and challenges to pluralism from inadvertently or blatantly ignoring religious specificities and reducing religious beliefs to mere cultural identity. At the same time, if handled well, increased state attention to civil religion during wartime can reinforce pluralistic norms and become a way to integrate minorities and create a narrative of national unity.

As a basis for comparison, before addressing these concerns in Russia and Ukraine during the Russian-Ukrainian conflict, I address how these elements played out in the example of the United States during World War II. Although initially cautious, reflecting a post-World War I consensus that churches should declare opposition to all future wars (Sittser, 1997, p. 25), religious organizations offered significant support for World War II as the war continued, although the rhetoric never reached the "holy war" levels of WWI. The Federal Council of Churches rejected a proposed statement that "the Christian Church is not at war," instead determining that there should be "no controversial references to the war" (Sittser, 1997, pp. 120–121). Reflecting the views of most Christians, a number of leaders, including Reinhold Niebuhr and major Christian groups, including the United Lutheran Church, the National Association of Evangelicals, and the Southern Baptists, issued statements emphasizing the necessity of the war and calling on their members to support the government's efforts (Sittser, 1997, p. 122).

Religious identification with the cause of the war, however, brought with it some threats to religious freedom. Adherents of pacifist minority religions faced significant social hostilities and discrimination. Jehovah's Witnesses' objection to military service and flag salutes led many to consider them unpatriotic. Over 2,000 Jehovah's Witnesses served prison time because they refused military service and local draft boards did not accept their conscientious objection claims (Sittser, 1997, p. 186).

Beyond hostility to those seen as unpatriotic, the increased civil religion of wartime also brought significant challenges to religious pluralism. At a minimum, the state, in its efforts to mobilize the flood of soldiers, inadvertently ignored religious specificities: it failed to have identity tags for soldiers reflect categories beyond "Jewish," "Catholic," and "Protestant"; it served pork in mess halls, banned beards and turbans, and required Seventh-Day Adventists to perform Saturday guard duty. (Stahl, 2017, p. 11). State outreach to some religions, such as in the new appointment of an ambassador to the Vatican, faced public opposition by majority Protestant groups (Sittser, 1997, p. 186).

The increased involvement of the state in religious civic space, however, also permitted the state to move civil religion into a broader and more pluralistic world. During the course of the war, the military not only moved from Herberg's (1955/1983) "three religion country" towards the diversity of the late twentieth and early twenty-first centuries, but also was able to have an influence in promoting increased religious tolerance and pluralism in society. In a time when discrimination against Catholics and Jews was still extremely common, the military chaplaincy was able to include Catholics and Jews on an equal basis. During the course of the war (Stahl, 2017, p. 17), the chaplaincy became more professionalized and pluralistic; chaplains were required to have advanced degrees and were trained to understand and work with a variety of beliefs. It still took time during the war for the military to understand the need for Orthodox chaplains, the fact that not all Jews shared uniform beliefs and practices, concerns over the labeling of Christian Science and others as Protestants (Stahl, 2017, pp. 82–83), and the value of using civil chaplains to supplement military ones. But the chaplaincy broke ground in many interfaith areas, including the first publication of a tri-faith hymnal (Stahl, 2017, pp. 48, 50). The interfaith solidarity of chaplains became a national symbol of unity when four chaplains – one from the reformed Church, a Jewish rabbi, a Roman Catholic, and a Methodist – together helped evacuate the sinking ship, the USS Dorchester, and, in the end, gave up their life vests for other soldiers and went down with the ship, praying together. This model of unity and sacrifice across religious lines captured the U.S. public's imagination and was later commemorated in a special postage stamp (Sittser, 1997, pp. 159–160).

Pluralism was a key part of the challenges and opportunities of chaplaincy. Acting Secretary of War reported on a "pansectarian" chaplaincy conference, noting that it granted citizens "a better appreciation of all religions. We know that each expresses the common impulses of reverence for and belief in God. . . . Chaplains are commissioned to work for all men without distinction of creed," but "to interpret this as meaning that all creeds are alike, or that creed is of no value, is to impose one's own religious beliefs upon others. This is to offend religious liberty, because religious liberty postulates religious differences. To wipe out all religious differences, and then claim to be tolerant, has no meaning" (Stahl, 2017, p. 54). A commitment to pluralism was stretched to the breaking point for some when it came to finding a Buddhist chaplain to minister to the Japanese-American units that had been formed. Initial attempts were made to find an appropriate Buddhist priest, but then the decisions was made to exclude them as unnecessary because many of the Japanese-Americans were Christian (Stahl, 2017, pp. 98–99). For some, however, the military's efforts to move to increased pluralism were felt as a watering-down of their religious beliefs, turning their religious beliefs into mere cultural symbols. Some Protestants, for example, were frustrated when the state moved to replace the chaplain's cross as a symbol with a more multi-faith emblem (Stahl, 2017, p. 256).

At its best, however, religion during times of war can not only be a source of unity and increased tolerance, but can also create a space for reverence, reflection, and access to conscience and the transcendental during difficult times, both at the level of individual soldiers and at the level of a nation. Some U.S. presidents have been able to tap into this connection with the transcendental better than others (Holland, 2007). Contrast President Eisenhower's statement, "Our government makes no sense unless it is founded on a deeply felt religious faith – and I don't care what it is," with Abraham Lincoln's profound second inaugural address:

> Fondly do we hope – fervently do we pray – that this mighty scourge of war may speedily pass away. Yet, if God wills that it continue, until all the wealth piled by the bond-man's two hundred and fifty years of unrequited toil shall be sunk, and until every drop of blood drawn with the lash, shall be paid by another drawn with the sword, as was said three thousand years ago, so still it must be said "the judgments of the Lord, are true and righteous altogether." . . . With malice toward none; with charity for all; with firmness in the right, as God gives us to see the right, let us strive on to finish the work we are in; to bind up the nation's wounds; to care for him who shall have borne the battle, and for his widow, and his orphan – to do all which may achieve and cherish a just and lasting peace, among ourselves, and with all nations.
>
> (Lincoln, 1865)

As Lincoln's comments suggest, civil religion during wartime can move beyond a merely utilitarian calculus or even an attempt to facilitate the freedom of religion or belief of service members. Invocation of civil religion in the face of war can also be an important way to reflect the humility and reverence that such tragic and devastating events demand.

Civil religion and the Russian-Ukrainian conflict

The benefits and perils of civil religion in Russia and Ukraine, exacerbated by the Russian-Ukrainian conflict, are clearly evident in both countries, particularly the regions where the conflict reigns. In the separatist enclaves in eastern Ukraine, and to a lesser extent in Russia, we see the potential thick civil religion has for abuse and appropriation by the state. Ukraine's attempts at invoking civil religion have expanded significantly during the Russian-Ukrainian conflict and are now at the crossroads of whether state support of civil religion will move in a coercive and discriminatory direction.

The Donbas region

The so-called Donetsk People's Republic and Luhansk People's Republic (DPR and LPR) demonstrate thick civil religion at its most extreme, illustrating Rousseau's suggestion that those opposing state beliefs should be banished or killed (Institute of Religious Freedom [IRF], 2018).

DPR and LPR leaders and fighters identify heavily with Russian Orthodoxy. A number of the separatist groups involved in the conflict have adopted explicitly religious names, such as the Russian Orthodox Army and Orthodox Dawn, and much of the propaganda about the separatist movement centers around the need to protect the ROC and the rights of Russian-speakers in Ukraine (IRF, 2018, pp. 4–5). As in Russia, "traditional" religions have some official state support, but Russian Orthodoxy takes a very distinctive leading role. In May 2015, the then-leader of the DPR, Oleksandr Zakharchenko, stated that the DPR only recognized the Ukrainian Orthodox Church under the Moscow Patriarchate (UOC-MP), the Roman Catholic Church, Islam, and Judaism, claiming that all others, including the Greek Catholics and the Ukrainian Orthodox Church of the Kyiv Patriarchate (UOC-KP), are harmful "sects." The LPR has not established a formal list, but officials have publicly indicated their opposition to "non-traditional religions" or "sects," including Pentecostals and Baptists (IRF, 2018, pp. 6–7). The LPR has refused to register any Baptist, Pentacostal, or Seventh-Day Adventist groups, requiring them to halt public activities and worship (Corley, 2018). The DLR and LPR have expropriated property from non-recognized groups and have banished, imprisoned, tortured, and/or killed many of their leaders, creating a regime significantly more hostile to unofficial religion than even that in most of the USSR (IRF, 2018; Forum 18, 2018–2019).

Russia

A thick manifestation of civil religion and its accompanying perils are, to a lesser but still very significant extent, also manifest in Russia (see, e.g., Agadjanian, 2001). As described elsewhere in this volume, Putin and Patriarch Kirill of the Russian Orthodox Church have described patriotism and national identity in overtly religious terms in a vision of a civil and religious "Russian World" (*Russkiy mir*), which intertwines political and religious history to assert a unity of all Russian speakers and Orthodox believers in the former Soviet space. The idea of a unified Holy Rus' becomes the mythos and origin story of a powerful, unified Russian world that extends in particular to Ukraine. War and perceptions of an ongoing conflict with the West have also been associated with the intensification of civil religion in recent years. Civil religious beliefs and the Russian Orthodox Church's closer ties with the government under Putin's regime have often been justified as opposition to a hostile West seeking to undermine the Russian government. The implicit threat of Ukraine's pro-Western approach following the Euromaidan in 2013–2014 thus formed a part of the rationale behind the Russian government's support of separatists in the Donbas and increasing efforts to stress the spiritual unity of Ukraine and Russia.

The embodiment of patriotism in expressions of Russian Orthodoxy, however, has taken its toll on religious freedom in Russia. Minority religions, especially those considered unpatriotic because of their ties to the West or their pacifist beliefs, have come under intense scrutiny. In 2016, Russia banned proselyting, which is associated primarily with Protestant and other churches seen as Western. Recently, as in the U.S. during WWII, pacifist Jehovah's Witnesses in particular have been the object of persecution. Russia has gone so far as to ban their interpretation of the Bible and their organization as extremist in 2017 and has begun in 2018–2019 to imprison individual Jehovah's Witnesses for extremism- or proselyting-related offenses. As I have suggested elsewhere, these are a part of a trend of deeply troubling violations of religious freedom in Russia (Clark, 2013, 2016, 2017) and have been condemned internationally (e.g., Kravchenko, 2018; UN rights chief, 2019).

The very closeness of the Russian Orthodox beliefs and the state, however, suggests that the ROC risks losing control of the religious nature and autonomy of its beliefs and having them reduced to mere cultural identity dictated by the state. In a 2017 address to the ROC's Bishops' council, President Putin has made clear that he sees the ROC as a junior partner which has, in his words, "inspired people to constructive action and heroic deeds for the Fatherland" (Pertsev, 2017). Putin compared the Church's situation today with that in the Soviet regime, where the Church was useful for propaganda during WWII, but afterwards had to be monitored and used to prevent civil unrest, illustrating "his utilitarian view of the church as a conduit of the Kremlin tasked with maintaining 'stability and unity'" (Pertsev, 2017).

Gaufman's research (in this volume) on the attitudes of Russian social media users engaged on the issue of the Russian-Ukrainian conflict certainly suggests that Orthodoxy has taken a back seat to nationality and language issues in the popular reception of the *Russkiy mir*. Having become one of several markers for a Russian identity, it risks remaining merely a cultural marker and losing religious salience. It is an interesting question, however, whether the historically close identification of Orthodoxy and national identity in central and eastern Europe (Pew Research Center, 2017) will diminish negative public reactions to the thickness of civil religion in Russia (or indeed whether the historical thickness of civil religion in Russia is the cause of this trend to associate Orthodoxy more with national identity rather than a set of beliefs or practices). Popular opinion polls in late 2018 do seem to suggest that so far the ROC has not suffered a loss of popular support, as the ROC enjoys popularity ratings of 65–68%, second only among social institutions to the Russian army (Russian Public Opinion Research Center, n.d.).

Ukraine

Civil religion in Ukraine in recent years has grown dramatically, influenced in large part by the Russian-Ukrainian conflict. As Sorokun (in this volume) and others (Fylypovych & Horkusha, 2015; Kalenychenko, 2017) indicate, religion played a significant role in the Euromaidan, with clergy and believers involved in the protests. Since the start of the conflict with Russia in 2014, Ukrainian politicians have also taken a much more active role in civil and religious life – participating in prayer breakfasts, inviting religious leaders to speak at political events, and especially in advocating autocephaly for a Ukrainian Orthodox Church. In July 2014, the Ukrainian parliament created the order of the "Heroes of Heaven's Hundred" (*Geroyiv Nebesnoyi sotni*) to commemorate the fallen protestors at the Euromaidan. Chaplaincy, an issue that failed to gain political traction before the Euromaidan, took on renewed currency in light of the conflict. In 2017, an enormous banner in English and Ukrainian showing a broken chain and the words "Freedom is Our Religion" was erected to cover a damaged facade in the Maidan Square.

The most dramatic manifestation of civil religion in Ukraine since Euromaidan is the engagement of President Poroshenko and the Verkhovna Rada (Ukrainian parliament) in the process of achieving an autocephalous Ukrainian Orthodox Church. Although Ukrainian government attempts to foster discussions among various branches of Orthodoxy took place throughout the period of Ukrainian independence, it was not until the Russian-Ukrainian conflict that the issue of having a single canonical Ukrainian Orthodox church became seen as an issue of national security and took on renewed urgency. During the course of the conflict, the UOC-MP has become seen by many as a fifth column, aligned with Russian government policies and working against Ukrainian political interests (Roudometof, 2018). *Russkiy mir* conceptions of the unity of Orthodox Slavs in many ways have backfired during the violence of the conflict, causing a Ukrainian reaction to not only Russia as a political entity, but also to Russian Orthodoxy (and by extension to the UOC-MP) as a marker of Russianness. The UOC-MP has thus become a majority religious denomination that not only has the largest number of adherents, but is also simultaneously publicly disfavored. The sheer size of the UOC-MP, its failure to speak out against the Russian aggression in Ukraine, and its ties to the ROC have made it politically difficult for the Ukrainian government to avoid distancing itself from it. In Catherine Wanner's phrase, Ukraine and Russia have become "two countries divided by the same faith tradition" (Wanner, 2018).

In reaction to this sense that the UOC-MP represents an aggressor state and the reality that non-UOC-MP Orthodox in Ukraine are fragmented among several churches, which were not accepted as canonical by other Orthodox churches, President Poroshenko, with the support of the Verkhovna Rada, approached the Ecumenical Patriarch for the *Tomos* granting autocephaly and convened the Unifying Council that selected the new leadership of the new Orthodox Church of Ukraine. Many observers have suggested that these steps would have been impossible without him (Shchotkyna, 2018). In an act that embodies the entrenchment and polarization of civil religion in Ukraine, three days after the Ecumenical Patriarch decided to grant autocephaly to a Ukrainian Orthodox Church in October 2018, in a nationally-televised broadcast, Petro Poroshenko declared that autocephaly was a needed response to the national security problem of the UOC-MP. In his statement, which was timed on a holiday both religious (Intercession of the Mother of God) and official (honoring the Ukrainian armed forces), Poroshenko asserted that the UOC-MP was not patriotic because it failed to support the Euromaidan and refused to condemn the Russian annexation of Crimea and engagement in the war in the Donbas (Fautré, 2019).

Ukraine, however, is not immune to the religious freedom challenges associated with civil religion. Brik and Korolkov (in this volume) suggest that patterns in state registrations of religious communities during the period of 2014–2017 suggest state or local favoritism of the UOC-KP, but do not suggest overt discrimination against the UOC-MP. Latent favoritism, however, seems to be moving towards legal discrimination against the UOC-MP. In 2017, regulations of chaplaincy by the Ministry of the Interior explicitly barred chaplains from the UOC-MP from serving in the National Guard and the State Border Guard Service. In December 2018, the Verkhovna Rada also passed a law that also explicitly discriminates against the UOC-MP, along with other churches with Russian ties. Law No 2662-VIII of December 20, 2018 imposes restrictions on Ukrainian religious associations with ruling bodies in Russia (literally "the aggressor state"), which essentially applies only to the UOC-MP and some small Old Believer communities. Affected religious organizations must change their names to include the full name of the relevant Russian religious organization. The law also formalized and extended the ban on the UOC-MP commissioning chaplains to all the Ukrainian armed forces. It is not yet clear what the penalty for failure to change the name will be and so far there is no evidence that the UOC-MP will comply.

However, overbroad bans on religious organizations from participating in state chaplaincy or requirements to change religious organizations' names, based only on the international ties of a religious organization, violate international norms of religious freedom (see Boothby, 2004). The European Court of Human Rights, for example, has repeatedly held that governments may not attempt to influence internal structuring of religious organizations (e.g., *Serif v. Greece* (1997), *Hasan and Chaush v. Bulgaria* (2000), and *Metropolitan Church of Bessarabia v. Moldova* (2001)). Organisation for Security and Co-operation in Europe/Office of Democratic Institutions and Human Rights Guidelines on the Legal Personality of Religious or Belief Communities (2014) reinforces that "states should observe their obligations by ensuring that national law leaves it to the religious or belief community itself to decide on its leadership. . . [and] the structure of the community and methods of appointment of the clergy" (para. 31). Religious organizations should not be discriminated against because of their structuring or the country of their leadership. The naming of religious organizations can also be a question of religious doctrine, and is one that states should not intrude upon. Chaplaincy is designed to facilitate the religious freedom of members of the armed forces; denying a member of the military access to his or her chosen religious leaders simply because of the organizational ties to a foreign country, even one supporting a conflict with the state, violates international norms. To the extent the state has a pressing need to interfere with the naming of a church (e.g., to avoid fraud) or denying a member of the clergy access to the military (e.g., because of failure to obtain a security clearance), such interference needs to be done in a proportional and measured way, rather than as a blanket ban or requirement.

In January 2019, the Verkhovna Rada waded further into the internal affairs of religious organizations in a move that seemed designed to assist congregations of the UOC-MP in switching their loyalty to the new Orthodox Church of Ukraine. Law No 2673-VIII changed the basis for individual congregations to switch their membership to a different religious organization, an issue which previously had been regulated simply by the charters of organizations as they registered. Under the law, individual communities are permitted to change their church membership if they receive approval of two-thirds of the members of their religious community.[1] The retroactive changing of property rights and internal structures established in organizational charters is a particularly clear infringement on the internal affairs of religious organizations and deprivation of their rights. States are of course permitted to regulate property ownership, but choice of organizational structure and jurisdiction are part of the protected rights of religious communities. The ECtHR, for example, has rejected state attempts to control or sway the organizational structure of religious organizations. In *Metropolitan Church of Bessarabia (2001)*, it stated that

> State measures favoring a particular leader or specific organs of a divided religious community or seeking to compel the community or part of it to place itself, against its will, under a single leadership, would also constitute an infringement of the freedom of religion. In democratic societies the State does not need to take measures to ensure that religious communities remain or are brought under a unified leadership.
>
> (para. 117)

State interference with the jurisdiction of religious communities not only violates the rights of the community to self-structure, but also affects the rights of the community to its property. "One of the means of exercising the right to manifest one's religion, especially for a religious community, in its collective dimension, is the possibility of ensuring judicial protection of the community, its members and its assets, so that Article 9 must be seen not only in the light of

Article 11, but also in the light of Article 6" (*Metropolitan Church of Bessarabia*, para. 118).

The U.S. Supreme Court has similarly refused to uphold legislation attempting to strip property from a church, in that case a cathedral of the Russian Orthodox Church that had been transferred to the Russian Church in America after the 1917 Russian Revolution (*Kedroff v. Saint Nicholas Cathedral*, 244 U.S. 94 (1952)). The New York state legislature's intent to keep the property from infiltration of atheistic or subversive influences and retain its original purposes was insufficient to keep it from violating constitutional protections of religious freedom. The court distinguished between legislative power to punish subversive action and the law at issue in that case where there was no charge of any specific subversive action. A transfer by statute of control over churches, the court held, "violates our rule of separation between church and state." Citing an early U.S. case, *Watson v. Jones* (80 U.S. 679, 727 (1871)), the court explained that appointment of religious leadership and structuring of religious organizations are internally religious "questions of discipline, or of faith, or of ecclesiastical rule, custom, or law," over which the state has no authority.

In Ukraine, one of the theories underlying the law permitting congregations to switch jurisdictions by majority vote is a belief that the properties were built by the community or with the support of private sponsors, not the hierarchical church itself. Under this logic, provisions in the charter of a UOC-MP religious organization that require a ruling bishop's approval violate the rights of the communities to their property. The problem with this is that it requires state assumptions that are not verifiable by the terms of the property's title and are not consistent with the internal religious structuring of the UOC-MP, a traditionally hierarchical church. The legislature can only go behind the terms of the charter and title by taking a position in a religious conflict. As Justice Frankfurter wrote in his concurring opinion in *Kedroff*, the cathedral at issue in that case "is not just a piece of real estate. . . . What is at stake here is the power to exercise religious authority. That is the essence of this controversy. It is that even though the religious authority becomes manifest and is exerted through authority over the Cathedral as the outward symbol of a religious faith" (p. 121).

The increasing thickness of civil religion in Ukraine has led to significant new challenges to pluralism, not only in restrictions on the religious freedom of the UOC-MP and its followers, but also in some interreligious conflict over state-owned facilities. The Cathedral of Saint Sophia, one of the most prominent religious sites in Kyiv, is owned by the state. The OCU was permitted to hold liturgy in the church in January 2019, but after a statement was made by the Ministry of Culture that the Ukrainian Greek Catholic Church would also be permitted to hold liturgy there in April 2019 (Shramovych, 2019), the shadow leader of the OCU, the former UOC-KP Patriarch Filaret, expressed concern about the state permitting Greek Catholics to likewise celebrate mass in the building because it might cause "confrontation" and "disrupt interfaith dialogue" (Filaret asks, 2019). Subsequently, the Ukrainian Ministry of Culture informed the Greek Catholic Church that the Cathedral would be closed after March 18, 2019 for restoration (Uniate Archbishop, 2019). This temporary measure, apparently designed to mollify the OCU while not engaging in overt discrimination, may duck the issue for now, but, assuming the OCU continues to push for exclusive rights in state space, the Ukrainian government will be hard pressed in the future to avoid either continued closeness with the OCU and discrimination against other religious organizations or a public break with support for the OCU.

Conclusion

The Russian-Ukrainian conflict illustrates not only the ambiguous nature of civil religion's relationship with the state and religious freedom, but also the power that war has to increase the need for civil religion and thus also increase the challenges to religious freedom it brings. Eliminating civil religion is neither feasible nor desirable, as it plays a vital role in unifying citizens, building patriotism, creating a space for conscience and religious belief, and providing access to the transcendental in the face of death and tragedy. When the civil religion is thick, however, and tied closely with a single dominant religion or used by an autocratic regime, it raises significant religious freedom concerns, which are already quite evident in Russia and in the conflict region in the Donbas. Challenges from an increasingly thick civil religion are also coming rapidly to the fore in Ukraine. Recent attempts to disfavor the UOC-MP or privilege the OCU by discriminating against other religious groups, if enforced by the coercive power of the state, will cross the line into violations of religious freedom.

Note

1 As Vovk notes in this volume, this is particularly problematic for Orthodox congregations, which do not have a registered membership. This is compounded by a 2018 Ukrainian Supreme Court (Economic Chamber) decision of June 18, 2018, holding that an Orthodox parish is an independent legal entity, not under control of an eparchy, and thus free to change its jurisdiction (case No 905/3377/15). Previously, the High Administrative Court of Ukraine (now the Administrative Chamber of the Supreme Court) ruled in February 10, 2010 that provisions of charters of religious organizations requiring an approval of ruling bishop for amending the charter or changing the name from one patriarchy to another (which is routine for Orthodox parishes) should be respected (case No 6269/06).

References

Agadjanian, A. (2001). Public religion and the quest for national ideology: Russia's media discourse. *Journal for the Scientific Study of Religion, 40*(3), 351–366. doi:10.1111/0021–8294.00062

Ariely, D. (2010). *Predictably irrational: The hidden forces that shape our decisions* (Revised and expanded ed.). New York, NY: Harper Perennial.

Barreto, R. C., Cavalcante, R., & Da Rosa, W. P. (Eds.). (2017). *World Christianity as public religion.* doi:10.2307/j.ctt1tm7hn1

Bellah, R. N. (1967). Civil religion in America. *Daedalus, 96*(1), 1–21.

Berger, P. L. (1999). The desecularization of the world: A global overview. In P. L. Berger (Ed.), *The desecularization of the world: Resurgent religion and world politics* (pp. 1–18). Grand Rapids, MI: Eerdmans.

Boothby, L. (2004). Protecting freedom of religion or belief in restricted or institutional settings. In T. Lindholm, W. C. Durham, B. G. Tahzib-Lie, E. A. Sewel, & L. Larsen (Eds.), *Facilitating freedom of religion or belief: A deskbook* (pp. 407–423). doi:10.1007/978-94-017-5616-7_16

Casanova, J. (1994). *Public religions in the modern world.* doi:10.7208/chicago/9780226190204. 001.0001

Chelini-Pont, B. (2010). Is *laïcité* the civil religion of France? *George Washington International Law Review, 41*(4), 765–815.

Clark, E. A. (2013). Liberalism in decline: Legislative trends limiting religious freedom in Russia and Central Asia. *Transnational Law & Contemporary Problems, 22*(2), 297–342.

Clark, E. A. (2016, August 30). Russian anti-missionary law in context. *Religious Freedom Institute.* Retrieved from www.religiousfreedominstitute.org/cornerstone/2016/8/30/russias-new-anti-missionary-law-in-context

Clark, E. A. (2017, May 5). Will Trump confront renewed religious repression in Russia? *National Review Online.* Retrieved from www.nationalreview.com/article/447363/jehovahs-witnesses-russia-ban-extremist-religious-freedom-trump-administration

Corley, F. (1996). *Religion in the Soviet Union: An archival reader.* doi:10.1057/9780230390041

Corley, F. (2018, October 23). Donbas: Luhansk: Re-registration denials, raids, communities closed. *Forum 18 News Service.* Retrieved from www.forum18.org/archive.php?article_id=2425

Durham, W. C., Jr. (1996). Rousseau's civil religion and the ideal of wholeness. In N. B. Reynolds & W. C. Durham, Jr. (Eds.), *Religious liberty in Western thought* (pp. 161–201). Atlanta, GA: Scholars Press.

Eisenhower, D. D. (1960). Statement by the President upon signing bill to include the words "Under God" in the pledge to the flag (June 14, 1954). In *Public papers of the Presidents of the United States: Dwight Eisenhower, 1954* (p. 563). Washington, DC: National Archives of the U.S.

Fautré, W. (2019, January 19). Russian Orthodoxy, a security issue in Ukraine. *Romfea News.* Retrieved from www.romfea.news/russian-orthodoxy-a-security-issue-in-ukraine/

Ferrari, S. (2010). Civil religions: Models and perspectives. *George Washington International Law Review, 41*(4), 749–763.

Filaret asks Greek Catholic Church to refuse from service in St. Sophia's Cathedral. (2019, February 23). *112UA.* Retrieved from https://112.international/politics/filaret-asks-greek-catholic-church-to-refuse-service-in-st-sophias-cathedral-37274.html

Forum 18. (2018–2019). Donbas. *Forum 18 News Service.* Retrieved from www.forum18.org/archive.php?country=87

Fylypovych, L., & Horkusha, O. (Eds.). (2015). *Maydan i tserkva: khroniky podiy i ekspertna otsinka* [The Maidan and the Church: Chronicles of the events and experts' assessment]. Kyiv, Ukraine: Sumit-Knyga.

Gentile, E. (2005). Political religion: A concept and its critics – A critical survey. *Totalitarian Movements and Political Religions, 6*(1), 19–31. doi:10.1080/14690760500099770

Grim, B. J., & Finke, R. (2010). *The price of freedom denied.* doi:10.1017/cbo9780511762345

Guthrie, S. E. (1996). Religion: What is it? *Journal for Scientific Study of Religion, 35*(4), 412–419.

Hart, R., & Pauley, J. L. (2005). *The political pulpit revisited.* West Lafayette, IN: Purdue University Press.

Herberg, W. (1955/1983). *Protestant – Catholic – Jew: An essay in American religious sociology* (Reprinted ed.). Chicago, IL: University of Chicago Press.

Holland, M. S. (2007). *Bonds of affection: Civic charity and the making of America.* Washington, DC: Georgetown University Press.

Institute of Religious Freedom. (2018). Religious freedom at gunpoint: Russian terror in the occupied territories of Eastern Ukraine. *Analytical report.* [Adobe Digital Editions version]. Retrieved from www.irf.in.ua/files/publications/2018.10.24-IRF-Report-ENG.pdf

Kahneman, D. (2013). *Thinking, fast and slow.* New York, NY: Farrar, Straus and Giroux.

Kalenychenko, T. (2017). Public religion during the Maidan protests in Ukraine. *Euxeinos,* 24, 23–38.

Kravchenko, M. (2018). Inventing extremists: The impact of Russian anti-extremism policies on freedom of religion or belief. *U.S. Commission on International Religious Freedom's website.* Retrieved from www.uscirf.gov/sites/default/files/Inventing%20Extremists.pdf

Lincoln, A. (n.d.). Abraham Lincoln papers: Series 3: General Correspondence: 1837–1897: Abraham Lincoln, March 4, 1865. Second Inaugural Address; Endorsed by Lincoln, April 10, 1865. Retrieved from www.loc.gov/item/mal4361300/

Lindholm, T. (2004). Philosophical and religious justifications of freedom of religion or belief. In T. Lindholm, W. C. Durham, B. G. Tahzib-Lie, E. A. Sewel, & L. Larsen (Eds.), *Facilitating freedom of religion or belief: A deskbook.* doi:10.1007/978-94-017-5616-7_2

Nussbaum, M. C. (2001). *Upheavals of thought: The intelligence of emotions.* doi:10.1017/CBO9780511840715

Pertsev, A. (2017, December 19). President and patriarch: What Putin wants from the Orthodox Church. *Carnegie Moscow Center.* Retrieved from https://carnegie.ru/commentary/75058

Pew Research Center. (2017, May 10). Religious belief and national belonging in central and eastern Europe. Retrieved from www.pewforum.org/2017/05/10/religious-belief-and-national-belonging-in-central-and-eastern-europe/

Richey, R. E., & Jones, D. G. (1974). The civil religion debate. In R. E. Richey & D. G. Jones (Eds.), *American civil religion* (pp. 3–18). New York, NY: Harper and Row.

Roudometof, V. (2018, December 14). 'A hard rain's a-gonna fall': The nationalization of Orthodox Christianity in Ukraine and Russia. *Berkley Forum.* Retrieved from https://berkleycenter.georgetown.edu/responses/a-hard-rain-s-a-gonna-fall-the-nationalization-of-orthodox-christianity-in-ukraine-and-russia

Rousseau, J.-J. (1923/1762). *The social contract and discourses* (G. D. H. Cole, Trans.). London, UK; and Toronto, Canada: J. M. Dent and Sons.

Russian Public Opinion Research Center. (n.d.). Ratings of social institutions. Retrieved from https://wciom.com/index.php?id=123

Sajó, A. (2011). *Constitutional sentiments.* New Haven, CT: Yale University Press.

Sarkissian, A. (2015). *The varieties of religious repression: Why governments restrict religion.* New York, NY: Oxford University Press.

Schmitt, C. (1985/1922). *Political theology: Four chapters on the concept of sovereignty* (G. Schwab, Trans.). Cambridge, MA: Massachusetts Institute of Technology Press.

Sewell, E. A. (2010). State financing and autonomy of religious groups. In M. Moravčíková & E. Valová (Eds.), *Financing of churches and religious societies in the 21st century* (pp. 12–16). Bratislava, Slovakia: Institute for State-Church Relations.

Shanks, A. (1995). *Civil society, civil religion.* Oxford: Blackwell.

Shchotkyna, K. (2018, December 21). Na pivdorohy do khramu [Halfway to the church]. *ZN. ua.* Retrieved from https://zn.ua/internal/na-polputi-k-hramu-303761_.html?fbclid=IwAR3yH0NsQzjTxsiVAqQ0_QJGNXWFM-F9QxODt1EhiNoh_Fzm6c8d76NW_wY

Shramovych, V. (2019, February 23). Hreko-katolyky anonsuvaly bohosluzhinnya v Sophiyi Kyyivs'kiy, Filaret proty: Shcho pro tse vidomo [Greek Catholics announced worship in Saint Sophia, Filaret objected: What is known about this?]. *BBC News Ukraine*. Retrieved from www.bbc.com/ukrainian/news-47343638

Sittser, G. L. (1997). *A cautious patriotism: The American churches and the second world war*. Chapel Hill, NC: University of North Carolina Press.

Stahl, R. Y. (2017). *Enlisting faith: How the military chaplaincy shaped religion and state in modern America*. Cambridge, MA: Harvard University Press, doi:10.2307/j.ctvgd36j

Steunebrink, G., & Zweerde, E. van der. (2004). *Civil society, religion, and the nation: Modernization in intercultural context: Russia, Japan, Turkey*. Amsterdam: Rodopi.

UN rights chief 'deeply concerned' over Jehovah's Witness sentencing in Russia. (2019, February 7). *UN News*. Retrieved from https://news.un.org/en/story/2019/02/1032151

Uniate Archbishop: No divine liturgy shall be celebrated at the Cathedral of Hagia Sofia in April 7. (2019, March 9). *Romfea News*. Retrieved from www.romfea.news/uniate-archbishop-no-divine-liturgy-shall-be-celebrated-at-the-cathedral-of-hagia-sofia-in-april-7/

Wanner, C. (2018, December 14). Divided by common faith: From the battlefield to the altar. *Berkley Forum*. Retrieved from https://berkleycenter.georgetown.edu/responses/divided-by-common-faith-from-the-battlefield-to-the-altar

Woodruff, P. (2014). *Reverence: Renewing a forgotten virtue* (2nd ed.). New York, NY: Oxford University Press.

3 Dynamics of church–state relations in Ukraine and the military conflict with Russia

Political and legal aspects

Dmytro Vovk

In this chapter I argue that, since 2014, the Ukrainian church–state system has seen dramatic changes, even in areas not directly related to the Russian-Ukrainian conflict. I suggest that the Russian-Ukrainian conflict has directly triggered changes in the church–state system with regard to the military and areas considered related to national security (e.g., autocephaly for the Orthodox Church of Ukraine) and, thus, contributed to a general movement towards a more cooperationist system of church and state relations, one that pushes Ukraine closer to the realm of church–state approaches of other post-Communist Orthodox countries. I focus mostly on the political and legal dimensions of church–state relations, addressing their sociological and religious dimensions only where they relate to the main topic. Moreover, I will discuss what is going on in the field of religion only in the territories under the Ukrainian government's control.[1]

Church–state relations before 2014

Church–state relations in Ukraine before 2014 could hardly be described using only one model. Viktor Yelensky defines them as vacillations "between trying to preserve a positive liberal image and secure guaranteed liberties and attempting to preserve the dependable control of the State over religious organizations and to secure greater latitude of influence over the Church" (Yelensky, 1999, pp. 146–147). In fact, I would assert that there are several dimensions of these vacillations: between the separationist and cooperationist models of church–state relations, between the liberal and intrusive legal frameworks for regulating religion, and vacillations over the extent to which the state is willing to accommodate religious needs. Indeed, all these dimensions are interrelated (for example, registration rules that could potentially influence institutional structures of religious associations relate to both the first and the second dimensions). Because of space constraints I will focus my discussion mostly on the first of these vacillations, the separationist/cooperationist model, touching the two other dimensions only occasionally.

At a formal level, Ukraine is a country that adheres to separation of church and state. The Constitution of Ukraine and the 1991 Law on Freedom of

Conscience and Religious Organizations No 987-XII (Law on Religious Organizations)[2] both establish a separationist model of church-state relations. Article 36 of the Constitution guarantees freedom of religion and entrenches that "the church and religious organizations ... are separated from the state, and school is separated from the state" (the same formulation as was used in the Soviet constitutions of 1936 and 1977). The Law on Religious Organizations prohibits state interference into internal religious relations, affairs and polity, as well as public funding of religions and perceives the state as an outside arbiter among religious organizations. According to the law, religious organizations are removed from political life. They are not entitled to participate in political movements, fund political parties, nominate candidates for public offices, be involved in political campaigns, etc.

The law also stipulates that religious organizations enjoy equal status; there are no legal tiers of religions based on the length of their presence in the country, their number of members, and so on. There are no officially recognized "traditional religions" in Ukraine, as is the case in some European and post-Soviet states. Religious organizations do not perform any state functions like registration of marriages; clerics are deprived of any legal privileges or immunities except the right not to be drafted into the army and not to disclose information they receive as confessors. Until recently, the state did not recognize diplomas of religious education and academic degrees awarded by theological institutions and did not expand academic privileges to instructors working in those institutions. Religious communities were not entitled to establish kindergartens, general schools, or universities. All this is in line with a separationist relationship.

However, since independence was gained in 1991, several features of a more cooperationist model of relations between the Ukrainian state and religions have become increasingly visible. In the preface to the volume of the Ukrainian translation of his works, José Casanova writes that Ukraine is virtually the only European country which has moved from the European model of a national church (or two national churches) and religious minorities or "sects" to the American model of denominationalism (Casanova, 2017, p. 10). The idea that Ukraine has reached American denominationalism may sound a bit overstated for me, in particular because major Ukrainian churches are sometimes treated both on the national and local levels in a very different manner than religious minorities and also claim to be national churches. Since the beginning of the 1990s until the establishment of the Orthodox Church of Ukraine (OCU) in 2018, however, four churches claimed the status of a or the national Ukrainian church (three Orthodox churches and the Ukrainian Greek Catholic Church), none of which commanded a majority of the population. In this aspect, the parallel with the American model makes sense.

At the same time, Ukraine differs substantially from the U.S., having no significant tradition of church autonomy and state secularity. Daniela Kalkandjieva (2011) points out that "the post-Communist governments are less strict in observing the principle of church-state separation, especially in the lands previously exposed to militant atheism" (pp. 605–606). This is relevant for Ukraine, and, in combination with a significant increase of the Ukrainian society's religiosity after the collapse of the Soviet Union and the strengthening of the state's positive identification with religion, it presupposes elements of cooperationist relations between the state and churches.

From the very beginning of the post-Soviet history of the country, the major Ukrainian churches – the Ukrainian Orthodox Churches of Moscow and Kyiv Patriarchates (UOC-MP and UOC-KP, respectively) and the Ukrainian Greek-Catholic Church (UGCC) – have been trying to maintain close relations with the government, the main political players, and local authorities. The biggest churches and religious denominations were deeply involved on different sides in key political events and conflicts, including the Maidan or Orange revolution of 2004 and the Euromaidan or Revolution of Dignity of 2013–2014. Similarly, every president of Ukraine was involved in religious affairs in one form or another (Blitt, 2015, p. 168; Ratajeski, 2015, p. 1561), in particular in addressing tensions between the UOC-MP and the UOC-KP, favoring the former or the latter (Bremer, 2016). Local authorities in several regions of western Ukraine enthusiastically supported the restoration of the UGCC, prohibited in the Soviet times.

Thus, pre-2014 cooperation did not imply ties of the state with a particular church or religion. Ukrainian political and economic elites during this period did not associate themselves with a single church or religion. One can find active Orthodox Christians, Greek Catholics, as well as Protestants, Jews, and Muslims among the main Ukrainian politicians and policymakers. On the local level, however, authorities have usually de facto favored local majority churches through easier procedures of registering new communities, obtaining land for building churches, or organizing public events with particular confessions. Hence, in some aspects, formal equality under the law has been adapted by closer actual relations of local public authorities with different churches (with the UOC-MP in Odesa or Kharkiv, the UGCC in Lviv, etc.).

Evolution of the church–state relationship since 2014

I distinguish the following types of changes of the church–state relationship in Ukraine since 2014: (1) military-related changes, (2) national-security-related changes, and (3) indirect changes. For example, the conflict with Russia was a trigger for establishing military chaplaincy in the Ukrainian army. The Ukrainian state has made major contributions in the OCU's obtaining autocephaly and has been employing the churches in promoting European integration, both of which are declared by the state to be crucial elements of national security. At the same time, these changes to the army and national security spheres do not just represent isolated transformations of church-state relations due to military or geopolitical reasons. I demonstrate how the conflict has contributed to more general church-state institutional and symbolical rapprochement in Ukraine and how they are part of a general movement towards a more cooperationist model of church-state relations. Here I understand institutional rapprochement as a strengthening of the cooperation between public-power and state-funded institutions and churches. Symbolic rapprochement is understood as an increased public perception of religion, particularly of some major Ukrainian churches, as a specific partner of the state in resolving problems of security, national unity, and development.

Military-related changes

Some of the institutional and symbolic changes in the Ukrainian church-state relationship amid the conflict relate to the military sphere. Before 2014, the main relevant regulation was the Law on Military Forces of Ukraine No 1934-XII (1991), containing a vague rule that members of the military should be granted opportunities to manifest their religion and to worship. Practically, it meant that commanders were able, at their discretion, to occasionally invite priests or to provide officers and soldiers with a prayer room for praying. Military service was unpopular; the amount of military personnel was being gradually reduced, and in 2013 the draft was canceled. Thus, draft laws on military chaplaincy found support neither in the Verkhovna Rada (the Ukrainian Parliament), nor in society. This situation changed with the beginning of the military conflict with Russia.

In July 2014, when the conflict in Donbas was intensifying, the Ukrainian government decided to establish the Military Chaplaincy Agency in the Army, the National Guard, and other military subdivisions (Directive of the Cabinet of Ministers of Ukraine of July 2, 2014, No 677-r). Clergymen of several religions had been volunteering actively in the army since 2014. Since 2017, however, military chaplains have been able to be hired as military employees and function in military units on a regular basis after completing relevant ecclesiastical, military, and physiological trainings. By orders of the Ministry of the Interior, UOC-MP chaplains are not allowed to be employed by the National Guard and military units of the State Border Guard Service.

However, the Constitution of Ukraine stipulates that human rights and their guarantees are regulated by laws adopted by Parliament (Art. 92). Military chaplaincy is an institution aiming to help soldiers and officers enjoy religious freedom under the specific conditions of military service. By employing chaplains, the state accommodates the religious needs of the military. Therefore, military (and any other) chaplaincy is a matter of human rights. Although military chaplaincy was created at the same time as prison chaplaincy, which is regulated by the Law No 419-VIII (2015), military chaplains are still operating on the basis of decrees of the Ministry of Defense, the Ministry of the Interior, and other agencies. The absence of a law on military chaplains weakens constitutional, parliamentary, and civil society control in this sphere and allows executive bodies to enjoy too much discretion, which could result in violations of religious freedom.

In April 2017, for example, several Ukrainian churches and religious organizations made a joint address to the military. In this address they particularly condemned "isolated incidents of military-church cooperation that caused painful traumas to religious feeling of the military and their families" (Fatulayev et al., 2017), which could be interpreted as an indirect recognition of violations of religious freedom occurring during the "volunteering" period of church-state cooperation in the military sphere. The Facebook account of the OCU Synodic Department of Military Chaplains, which commission the largest number of chaplains in the army, is full of photos of priests and chaplains of this church sprinkling holy water on lines of recruits, soldiers, and graduates from military schools. It is unlikely that every student or military officer in those lines belongs to the OCU or any other church, whose priest blessed those people or led a collective prayer. Perhaps, commanding officers of these students and soldiers could at their discretion secure the right of religious minorities and non-believers not to participate in such ceremonies. However, there is no legally-based reliable guarantee of religious freedom in military context. A law on military chaplaincy and measures of constitutional and parliamentary control would help to enhance the protection of this freedom.

While the military chaplaincy is evidence of institutional rapprochement of the state and churches in the military sphere, intensive mutual visits and public meetings between the heads of the Ministry of Defense, the National Guard, secret services and certain religious leaders, first of all with UOC-KP Patriarch Filaret and since 2019 with Primate of the OCU Epiphany, also indicate symbolic rapprochement focusing on the public image of military-related church-state partnership. During the meeting with the All-Ukrainian Council of Churches and Religious Organizations,[3] the head of the Security Service of Ukraine emphasized the role of religion as a consolidating force and called for the churches' support in counteracting Russia's attempts to destabilize Ukraine (Holova SBU, 2015). President Poroshenko posted on his Facebook account a picture with the slogan "The army protects the Ukrainian land, the language protects the Ukrainian heart, and the [Ukrainian national] church protects the Ukrainian soul." Billboards with similar slogans were set up all over the country in 2018–2019.

However, the state was less ready for a dialogue and cooperation on the issue of alternative service for conscientious objectors. Although the Constitution of Ukraine and the Law on Military Forces guarantee this right to religious believers, there is no such rule in the Law on Mobilization No 3543-XI (1993). In 2014–2015, there were several criminal cases against believers (in particular Jehovah's Witnesses) who opposed their mobilization to active duty. In those cases, courts canceled mobilizations of those persons or found them not guilty of evasion of military service (Vovk, 2015). Yet the law has not been amended.

National-security-related changes

The Russian-Ukrainian conflict arose in connection with the wish of Putin's regime to keep Ukraine under its control and stop its drifting to the West. In this regard, by getting closer to churches, the Ukrainian state tries to employ the legitimacy, social trust, authority, and the unifying and diplomatic potential of churches both for counteracting Russia directly (particularly within Ukraine), and for facilitating the European integration of the country, which is thought by the state to be a process related to the conflict. It is worth mentioning that the indirect changes in the church–state relationship (see the next subsection) or the military-related changes (see the previous subsection) relate, at least potentially, to most Ukrainian religions, which would like to commission chaplains or be involved in church-state joint public events (although that certainly also depends on the demand for these religions in the religious market). However, the national-security-related changes, which I explore here, predominantly concern only the major churches (except the UOC-MP) and their leaders, because they represent a significant number of believers, enjoy some popularity and respect in society as a whole, can influence public mood, and have international contacts helpful to strengthen the state's position. Moreover, these major churches (the UOC-KP/OCU and the UGCC) position themselves as traditional and national churches with a particular interest in and potential to contribute to national security. Thus, in the general logic of rapprochement, the state's wish to cooperate with them in these issues looks reasonable. This also fits the cooperative model of church-state relations, where the state usually differentiates cooperation with different religions, preferring to cooperate with the major and traditional religions.

The UOC-KP has become the main beneficiary of the process of granting the autocephaly to the OCU, initiated by the state, as the new church has been established mostly on the basis of UOC-KP structures and is headed by its former metropolitan, Epiphany. At the same time, on the national level and in many regions on the local level, the state has refused to cooperate in any form with the UOC-MP, considering the latter as a source and a weapon of Russian influence in Ukraine; in the conflict between the two major Orthodox churches, the state has taken the UOC-KP's side. As it was mentioned above, it is not the first time in contemporary Ukrainian history that the state has supported one of the competing Orthodox churches, but it is definitely the first time that such support has taken the form of official policy and has been so effective.

Since Crimea was occupied and the conflict in Donbas was inflamed, the All-Ukrainian Council of Churches has become an active partner in supporting the Ukrainian state in counteracting separatism and the Russian invasion. The Council has made several statements against the violations of territorial integrity of Ukraine and the Russian occupation of Crimea, on the duty to defend the homeland, and on victory in the war (All-Ukrainian Council of Churches and Religious Organizations [AUCCRO], 2016).[4] The Russian aggression against Ukraine is often addressed by UGCC Archbishop Svyatoslav Shevchuk and especially by Patriarch Filaret and other leaders of the UOC-KP and the OCU. These topics are also raised during meetings of religious leaders and the All-Ukrainian Council of Churches with representatives of the EU, the OSCE, and the Council of Europe. The churches, including the UOC-MP, are involved in prisoner swaps between Ukraine and Russia-backed separatist regimes in the eastern Ukraine.

The state also employs the major churches (except the UOC-MP) to promote its European integration policy and Ukraine's view of the conflict with Russia in the EU. However, Ukrainian churches' perception of European integration is ambivalent. They appreciate the idea of European integration as a chance to get away from Moscow and to join an abstract "European home." But they do not find the EU as a concrete institution with its human rights standards and with additional constraints on national states' sovereignty as tempting them.

In May 2018, Patriarch Filaret delivered a speech in the European Parliament (Moskalyuk, 2018b). While saying that Ukraine is a part of Europe, he emphasized that "the genuine foundation and real values" of Europe are Christianity and democracy. According to Filaret, loss of this foundation (which one may interpret as denial of a Christian understanding of the world, human beings, and morality) could undermine the European home. There is nothing new or unexpected in those arguments. Almost all Orthodox Churches in eastern Europe have an ambivalent or skeptical attitude towards the European integration of their countries (Spohn, 2012, p. 45),[5] but they are not important actors in this process. Ukrainian churches, however, actively support and promote European integration. Their doubts about the EU matching the image of a "Christian Europe" do not prevent the churches from supporting the state and promoting European integration as a geopolitical choice in the context of the conflict with Russia (and using this issue to increase rapprochement with the state). But real progress with European integration could result in the churches' increasing skepticism and wariness.

Autocephaly for the OCU is another important example of national security-related changes in church-state relationships. I am not able to discuss all the details of the whole problem in this chapter,[6] but want to stress some key points.

First, the state and President Poroshenko himself initiated and made a major contribution to the creation of the new OCU and the Ecumenical Patriarchate's grant of autocephaly to it. According to Poroshenko, autocephaly is a part of the strategy the state has been implementing since 2014, aimed at "the complete and total decolonization of Ukraine . . . and its getting beyond Russia's control entirely and unconditionally" (President: Autocephaly, 2018). The President and his administration began negotiating the issue with Patriarch Bartholomew in 2015 and in April 2018, Poroshenko and the Ukrainian Parliament officially appealed to him to grant autocephaly to the Ukrainian Orthodox Church.

Between the time the negotiations with Bartholomew became public in April 2018, and when autocephaly was granted to the OCU, the President posted on Facebook and Twitter about 100 times and gave many speeches and comments on this issue. In his posts he repeatedly emphasized the significance of the independent Orthodox church for the national security of Ukraine and national identity of Ukrainians, as well as for counteracting Russia's "imperial illusions and chauvinistic fantasies" and the ideology of the "Russian World" (*Russky mir*). He also compared autocephaly with joining the EU and NATO in spiritual sphere.

The President was also highly engaged in the Unifying Council (*Ob"yednavchyy Sobor*), where the OCU was established. One of the observers writes that Poroshenko had to personally facilitate the dialogue between groups within the UOC-KP competing for the position of the head of the new church and to force one of the candidates to withdraw his candidature in favor of Filaret's right-hand man Epiphany, who finally won the race (Shchotkyna, 2018).

Second, the autocephaly accounts for the split within the Ukrainian Orthodox Church and the complicated relations (or better said permanent conflict) between the UOC-MP and the UOC-KP. The state strongly interfered in this conflict, taking the side of the latter (and then the OCU) as the national church and its partner in the struggle against Russia. In his 2017 annual address to Parliament, the President emphasized the right of Ukraine to have its own domestic church. Following the President's address, the Presidential Institute of Strategic Studies published analytical materials that argued that a Ukrainian Autocephalous Orthodox Church should be established on the basis of the UOC-KP (National Institute for Strategic Studies [NISS], 2017). In social media and public speeches, Poroshenko called the UOC-MP "a non-Ukrainian church" and stated that the OCU is "a church without Putin and without prayers for the Russian army" (Head of the State, 2018). Immediately after the autocephaly was granted, the President visited several regions of Ukraine to officially celebrate it. He participated in public masses lead by Epiphany or Filaret, during which representatives of temporal and spiritual powers thanked each other for this historical achievement; new billboards with him, Epiphany, and the *Tomos* (the document authorizing autocephaly issued by the Ecumenical Patriarch) were set up across the country again.

Shortly after the OCU was established, the Verkhovna Rada adopted Law No 2662-VIII of December 20, 2018, which targeted the UOC-MP and various tiny Russian Old Believer' communities. The law requires all Ukrainian religious organizations ruled from Russia (literally from "the aggressor state") to point out their affiliation with the relevant Russian mother church in their official names. During consideration of Law No 2662-VII, the speaker of the Parliament emphasized that it was being considered "at Patriarch Filaret's personal request" (RPTs v Ukrayini, 2018), encouraging deputies to vote for it.

The law forces the UOC-MP and its communities to reproduce in their name the full name of the ROC, although they are still permitted to add the words "in Ukraine."[7] The law also stipulates that those religious organizations may be banned from sending their priests, preachers, and mentors to the Ukrainian military forces, legitimizing ex post facto the ban of the UOC-MP chaplains, which is in force in the National Guard and State Border Guard Service, and probably making the Army dismiss existing UOC-MP chaplains. Therefore, the law imposes an additional burden on UOC-MP communities and obliges them to identify themselves with the Russian state and the ROC, which the President of Ukraine has called "Putin's church."[8] Thus, the state marks UOC-MP communities as "agents" of an enemy state and by doing so encourages them to transfer to the OCU in order to avoid the status of social pariah.

On January 17, 2019, the Verkhovna Rada adopted Law No 2673-VIII, aiming to simplify religious communities' transferal from one church jurisdiction to another. Previously, the Law on Religious Organizations did not regulate changing jurisdiction, and religious organizations were free to establish rules for changing jurisdiction in their charters. In Ukraine only local religious communities can obtain legal personality. Thus, national religious associations operate as a sort of a cloud of legally independent religious organizations that are canonically linked to each other. Due to this reason, hierarchical religious associations (in particular the UOC-MP) used to prescribe in their standard-form charters that certain actions and transactions (e.g. selling property, amending the statute, etc.) be confirmed or permitted by a higher religious authority (for example, the ruling bishop). It means that a community could transfer to another religious association, make appropriate amendments to its charter, and keep its property only if the ruling bishop gave his approval (which, in the case of a UOC-MP parish moving to the OCU, the UOC-MP bishop was unlikely to do).

According to Law No 2673-VIII, a decision on community's jurisdictional transfer to another religious association is to be made exclusively by the majority of members of the community.[9] Thus, the law enables UOC-MP communities to transfer to the OCU without the approval of their ruling bishops and to retain ownership of their church buildings and other property. During the parliamentary debates around Law No 2673-VIII, it was clear enough that its authors aimed not to guarantee the right of a religious group to change its church jurisdiction in general, but merely to simplify UOC-MP communities transferring to the OCU and to weaken the influence of the UOC-MP leadership on this process.[10]

Hence both Law No 2662-VIII and Law No 2673-VIII reproduce the logic of the state's specific relationship with the OUC and its efforts to counteract the UOC-MP as the main competitor of the new church, a threat to national security of Ukraine and the religious freedom of communities willing to change church jurisdiction. Those laws prove that the state has strengthened its influence on intra-religious affairs, including issues of religious organizations' self-naming and their polity. Autocephaly and its subsequent events have become the paramount point of institutional and symbolic rapprochement of the state and religion in Ukraine and send a clear message that state religious policies have changed.

Indirect changes

In addition to church–state changes in the military sphere and on national security issues, other changes have occurred since 2014 that do not relate to the

Russian-Ukrainian conflict directly. In social, educational, and family spheres, as well as in the field of public religion, the state has stressed its positive identification with religion, strengthening institutional and symbolical rapprochement. At times this process has been controversial, in particular because rapprochement with religion has been accompanied by European integration policies, which cause predictable conflicts in the area of human rights.

This rapprochement has not led to unequivocal success in attempts by churches to establish their ethical doctrines. They are strong enough to stop most initiatives concerning LGBTQ+ rights and some initiatives on gender equality, but their influence is too weak to encourage the state to entrench their moral views in the legal system, although not for lack of trying. For example, during 2014–2016, when the Constitutional Commission was working on amendments to the Constitution of Ukraine, including the chapter on human rights, the All-Ukrainian Council of Churches, its members, and pro-religious NGOs actively and successfully opposed incorporation of a ban on discrimination on the ground of sexual orientation and the right to marry for everyone, which presumably extends to homosexual persons, into the Constitution. Churches and their allies' opposition to these provisions was one of the main reasons why human rights amendments were not even considered in Parliament while some other amendments were approved. At the same time, all the proposals developed by the All-Ukrainian Council of Churches, including the right to life from conception until natural death, the right of religious associations to establish general schools, the state's duty to take care of religious needs of Ukrainians, and a ban on any compulsory ideology[11] (AUCCRO, 2015) were also ignored by the Constitutional Commission.

Churches were similarly successful at counteracting the ratification of the Council of Europe's Convention on Combating Violence against Women and Domestic Violence (Istanbul Convention) of 2011. Ukraine signed this Convention, but its ratification in Parliament was blocked several times. Domestic violence is a highly mythologized topic in the Ukrainian religious milieu. Measures against domestic violence are alleged to be a way of disproportionate interference of the state in relations between spouses and between parents and children. In the case of the Istanbul convention, this skepticism increased because it also contains a ban on discrimination on the ground of sexual orientation and gender identity in Article 3 of the Convention. During the debates in Parliament, deputies of various factions repeatedly mentioned "traditional values" and the "Christian morals" of Ukrainians.

However, recognition of same-sex marriages and a ban on discrimination on the ground of sexual orientation and gender identification are issues highly debated and negatively perceived in Ukrainian society.[12] Evidently, on these issues the churches do not just promote their ethical doctrines, but also reflect their believers' and the majority of society's expectations.[13] The state, for its part, follows a sort of instrumental approach here, wishing to both keep the churches' support and proceed with European integration policies. In December 2018, the President called on Parliament to ratify the Istanbul Convention

(President urges the Parliament, 2018). The action plan adopted by the Government within the National Strategy on Human Rights 2020 includes a draft law on civil partnership that should have been worked out in 2017. However, during his meeting with the All-Ukrainian Council of Churches, Poroshenko said that same-sex marriages would not be legally recognized in Ukraine (Rada tserkov, 2016). The Ministry of Justice responsible for that draft law and several parliamentary committees supported the President's position.

In the educational area, religious organizations won the right to establish general-education institutions in 2015. Although religions have been seeking this right for a long time, the number of religiously-affiliated schools established to date is insignificant. According to the data of the Ministry of Culture of Ukraine as of January 1, 2018, thirteen schools of this kind operate in Ukraine: one Orthodox (the Moscow Patriarchate), three Greek Catholic, one Roman Catholic, five Protestant, and three Jewish (MCU, 2018).[14] Also, the state has begun to recognize educational and academic degrees awarded by theological seminaries and academies. Priests and religious mentors are often invited to public schools and universities to give blessings and conduct worship or to deliver non-curricular lectures on moral issues.[15]

Churches have also significantly strengthened their public image as a partner of the state. Public religiosity of politicians used to be limited to selfies from Christmas masses and photos of Easter baskets on social media; now leaders of major churches, especially Patriarch Filaret, regularly hold public meetings with politicians, members of Parliament, generals, ministers, and judges of the Constitutional Court, who, theoretically, should be sensitive to their impartiality and neutrality. Some top state officials who were also actively engaged in public promotion of autocephaly called its opponents "pro-Moscow agents," and pointed out that appreciation of autocephaly is an element of loyalty to the state.

In 2011, a group of deputies and religious organizations initiated the practice of a national prayer breakfast in Ukraine. Until 2014, prayer breakfasts were led by MPs who would be called "backbenchers" in the British Parliament, and took place in Kyiv restaurants; but since 2014, they have been held in the state-owned National Center for Business and Cultural Cooperation "Ukrainian House" and attended by the President, the speaker of Parliament, leaders of the parliamentary coalition and opposition, and influential politicians. Local state administrations and city councils in the Poltava, Volyn, Khmelnitsky, Ternopil oblasts, etc. follow Kyiv's example. They provide organizational and media support for local prayer breakfasts. These public collective prayers with the participation of politicians and religious leaders and activists, as well as high appreciation by politicians of the role of churches, in particular in counteracting the Russian aggression and protecting so-called "traditional values," and demonstrations of religiosity as part of being Ukrainian are social signals of closeness between the state and the church.

These forms of public signaling, together with the changes to military and national-security-related issues, illustrate institutional and symbolic rapprochement between the Ukrainian state and churches and demonstrate that the country has been drifting towards a more cooperationist model.

Post-soviet majority–Orthodox context for Ukrainian church–state rapprochement

This Ukrainian movement toward closer church–state cooperation reflects not only the impact of the Russian–Ukrainian conflict, but also a broader trend. This is particularly noticeable when the Ukrainian trend is seen in light of the context of other post-Soviet Orthodox-majority countries (Belarus, Georgia, Moldova, and Russia). According to the Pew Research Center's survey "Religious Identity and National Belonging," (2017) in these countries Orthodoxy is the religion of the overwhelming majority of believers: 92% of the population of Moldova, 89% in Georgia, 73% in Belarus, and 71% in Russia (compare to 73% in Ukraine); the vast majority of Orthodox Christians in these countries belong to a single Orthodox church (the Orthodox Church of Moldova, the Belarussian Orthodox Church [both of which are the ROC's exarchates], the Georgian Orthodox Church, and the ROC).

While these countries do not have exactly the same model of relationship between the state and church, there are some common features of this relationship. These countries not only share a de jure or de facto multitier system of religions, but also limit religious competition and create a partnership with the dominating Orthodox church, in which the latter plays the role of junior partner to the state. The extent to which these features are in fact present in every country differ to some extent based on political regime, foreign policies, self-identification of churches, factors of Russia and the ROC (which, perhaps, force the Moldovan and Belarus states to keep a certain distance with the ROC's exarchates), etc. While the Ukrainian case is not identical to those countries (the most evident distinctions are that the Orthodox church in Ukraine is still split and that the UOC-MP, disfavored by the state, is still the largest religious group). However, in terms of Ukraine's evident movement towards a more cooperative church–state relationship, this comparative analysis of the countries, where close cooperation between the state and the (Orthodox) church of the majority has already been set up, provides important context for the changes identified in this chapter.

All post-Soviet majority-Orthodox countries (except Russia) have constitutions that entrench the state's positive identification with religion, stipulating that the state supports religious denominations (Moldova), that relations between the state and religious organizations are determined "according to their influence on the development of spiritual, cultural and statehood traditions of the Belarus people" (Belarus Law on Freedom of Conscience and Religious Organizations of 1992), or emphasizing "an exclusive role of the Apostolic Autocephalous Orthodox Church of Georgia in the history" of Georgia (Constitutional Agreement between State of Georgia and Georgian Apostolic Autocephaly Orthodox Church of 2002). In Moldova and Belarus, a reference to the special role of the Orthodox Church is also included in their laws on religious associations. The Russian Constitution establishes a separationist model of church–state relations. However, in the preamble to the 1997 Russian Law on Freedom of Conscience and Religious Associations "an extraordinary role of Orthodoxy in the history of Russia, development of its spirituality and culture" is mentioned.

Another feature of post-Soviet majority-Orthodox church–state systems is a recognition by the state of the extraordinary significance of Orthodoxy and, in some cases, other traditional religions. They establish a multi-tier system of religion, where different religions enjoy a differing legal status and interact with the state in distinctive ways. Georgia and Belarus have concluded concordats with Orthodox churches, and the Georgian concordat has a status of a constitutional agreement.[16] In Russia and Moldova, Orthodox churches have concluded similar cooperation agreements with several public bodies on national and local levels, such as the Ministry of Education or Penitentiary Service. Orthodox Churches de jure and/or de facto enjoy the status of a special partner of the state, as well as various privileges and exclusive opportunities in the field of military chaplaincy, direct or indirect public funding, tax exemptions, obtaining land, restitution of church property confiscated during the Soviet times and state support for its restoration, or recognition of religious marriages (only in Georgia). Top-level Orthodox clerics might enjoy the privilege of legal immunity, as does the Patriarch of the Georgian Church (Zviadadze, 2015, p. 48), diplomatic passports, as do top hierarchs of the Orthodox Church of Moldova (Suveica & Spranceana, 2015, p. 106), state security guard service, as does the ROC Patriarch, etc. Restrictive measures imposed on religions by the state are at times applied differently to the Orthodox Church than to other religious groups, which is especially evident in the case of anti-extremist legislation in Russia, which has been applied exclusively to religious minorities.

A third important feature of these states' church–state systems is that those states legally restrict religious competition and interfere in the religious freedom of individuals and groups in the interests of the Orthodox majority. In Russia, these restrictions result in the most severe infringements of religious rights: draconian legislation (e.g., the infamous Yarovaya Law) on religious manifestations, public worship and missionary work (Clark, 2016); significant limitation of the religious freedom of foreigners; and persecution of religious minorities by means of anti-extremist laws, including the ban on Jehovah's Witnesses in 2017.[17] In Belarus, religious groups cannot operate without registration; religious minorities permanently face denials of registration; local religious organizations are not entitled to establish media; and the religious freedom of foreigners is limited. In Moldova, there is a ban on "excessive proselytism" aiming to reduce activities of new religions; foreigners are prohibited from leading religious communities; registration is de facto more difficult for non-Orthodox communities; and in the dispute between the Orthodox majority (the Orthodox Church of Moldova) and the Orthodox minority (the Metropolis of Bessarabia), the state takes the side of the former (Suveica & Spranceana, 2015,

p. 105). These sorts of restrictions also correlate with a country's level of freedom and democracy. Thus, the situation in Moldova and Georgia is better than in Russia and Belarus. However, there is a common tendency here: religious minorities, new and unknown groups, as well as foreigners, are the main targets of restrictions imposed by the state, and the Orthodox majority benefits from those restrictions in the same way as a monopolist or an oligarch benefits from reduced economic competition and state support.

Finally, these countries share a tandem of the state and the Orthodox church, where one partner is senior and stronger, while the other is minor and weaker. The state determines the framework and closeness of these relations, being guided by political and ideological, rather than religious, reasons. Protection of "traditional values" as previously discussed in the Ukrainian context, is a good example here. These states promote this agenda, if it is popular (e.g., non-recognition of same-sex marriages) within the country or employ it as part of an anti-Western foreign policy and rhetoric, as is the case in Russia. However, when it is necessary to step back from anti-LGBTQ+ agenda, the state can do it. In 2012, the Moldova Parliament adopted the law banning discrimination on the ground of sexual orientation and gender identity. The law was highly criticized by the Orthodox church, but it was an important step towards a visa-free regime with the EU, so the state ignored the position of the Orthodox Church.

In analyzing how the church-state relationship in Ukraine has changed since 2014, despite similarities, it is not entirely clear to what extent Ukraine has reached the level of closeness between the state and the Orthodox church that has developed in Belarus, Georgia, Moldova, and Russia. I address this question in the conclusion.

Conclusion

Since 2014 the Ukrainian state has strengthened its positive identification with religion and, consequently, church-state relations have become more cooperative. Military and prison chaplaincy, religiously-affiliated general education and recognition of educational and academic degrees awarded by religious institutions, the increasing presence of religion in the public sphere, the role of major churches in promoting the European integration policies and Ukraine's view of the conflict with Russia, and the crucial contribution of the state to the OCU obtaining autocephaly clearly show this. The informal, unstable, and decentralized multi-tier system that existed before has transformed into a more official and stable one. On the top of this system is the OCU, consisting of former communities of the UOC-KP, the UAOC and a few former communities of the UOC-MP, then followed by the UGCC, which is also actively supporting the state in the military sphere and promoting Ukraine abroad, and, finally, followed by other religions. The UOC-MP has occupied a position of the state's officially disfavored religion (especially after the law on forcible renaming of churches was adopted) due to its non-patriotic, as the state claims, position.

However, it is still supported by pro-Russian politicians and local elites in some regions where the church constitutes the religious majority.

Under such circumstances, the legal model of the church-state relationship entrenched in the Constitution and the Law on Religious Organizations is definitely inadequate and could cause additional problems. For example, when religion is not legally allowed in public schools, and the state actually permits widespread violations of this ban, such lack of regulation could be dangerous for minorities and non-religious students. In 2017, for example, the Ukrainian media reported that a group of students of the National Pedagogical University in Kyiv had been forced by the University administration to attend a worship service in a UOC-KP church (Studentiv Drahomanova, 2017). The Ministry of Education did not react to that incident. In order to avoid such situations, the state should either enforce the ban on religion in public educational institutions (which contradicts the main trend of rapprochement in the church-state relations) or prescribe to what extent religion can enter public education and protect the freedom of religion (as well as freedom from religion) of all parties involved.

Like in other post-Soviet Orthodox countries, in Ukraine the state plays the role of the senior partner in relations with religion; it develops the framework of these relations, in particular with the OCU, and determines how close they should be. The state has effectively interfered in the inter-Orthodox conflict and succeeded in the autocephaly saga, considering it an important factor of the conflict with Russia. However, the state's positive identification with religion does not prevent it from ignoring initiatives that are important to religions in the field of public morality, family, and gender, where they are politically inappropriate.

The church-state relationship in Ukraine has been moving closer to the models embodied in other post-Soviet Orthodox countries characterized by a de jure and/or de facto multitier system, a special role; benefits and privileges for the Orthodox church as the national church; the state's prevailing in the tandem of temporal and spiritual authorities; and strong links between religion and national security. However, these tendencies are less strong in Ukraine than in other post-Soviet Orthodox countries. In particular, the Ukrainian state is less restrictive than other post-Soviet Orthodox countries (Sarkissian, 2015, p. 19); it does not systematically disfavor or oppress religious minorities, and its favoritism towards the OCU has not reached the level of favoritism towards Orthodox churches in Russia, Belarus, Moldova, or Georgia.

What is next?

There are many interrelated factors influencing the relationship between the Ukrainian state and church (religious structure of the country, political struggle within Ukraine, the conflict with Russia, etc.), which makes it difficult to forecast how this relationship will evolve. However, I can identify some general trends that will probably continue in the short term and middle term.

First, under the conditions of the high religiosity of Ukrainian society and the high level of institutional trust of churches and leaders of certain major churches, the state will continue to develop cooperative relations with the church. The cooperation may be formalized in concordats or agreements[18] regulating relations with major churches, providing legal form for the multi-tier religious system in Ukraine. Beyond this, it is difficult to foresee how the state will response to the initiatives already articulated by churches which imply public funding (for instance, public funding of religiously-affiliated schools, paid positions for chaplains in public medical institutions, expanding religious tax exemptions, etc.). The difficult economic situation in the country and the relatively small number of Ukrainians involved in regular religious life could give rise to the state's skepticism towards such initiatives.

Second, if European integration is successful, the state will have to find a way to reconcile the European political course and the ethical skepticism of the major churches (and their believers) towards the reality of European Union policies and regulations. Moreover, having obtained the status of the recognized Orthodox church and "the most national" religion of Ukrainians, the OCU in coalition with the All-Ukrainian Council of Churches and other religions will probably more vigorously counteract any questionable, in their view, initiatives in the field of human rights, including gender, antidiscrimination, or LGBTQ+ issues.

Third, I predict that the OCU will not be able to enjoy the status of official or endorsed church, like Orthodox churches in other post-Soviet Orthodox states do, until the Ukrainian Orthodox community has been united in one church. For now, I see no reason to say that the majority of UOC-MP communities will transfer to the OCU,[19] which means that the Ukrainian Orthodox community will remain split into two large churches. This factor, along with the phenomenon of the UGCC dominating in several Western-Ukrainian regions and also claiming to be a "national church" (Wanner, 2010, p. 654) or a church of "Kyiv tradition" (Bremer, 2016, p. 15), will probably prevent the OCU from transforming into an analogue of Orthodox churches in Belarus, Georgia, Moldova, and Russia.

Finally, relations between the state and the UOC-MP are unlikely to improve while the conflict with Russia goes on. If President Poroshenko is re-elected in the spring of 2019 to a second term, the state will probably continue to be involved in the conflict between the OCU striving for final victory and the UOC-MP. For example, Patriarch Filaret has said that state-owned historically and spiritually significant Ukrainian Orthodox monasteries – the Kyiv Pechersk and Pochaiv *Lavras* – must be transferred from the UOC-MP to the OCU (UPTs prosytume, 2018). If Poroshenko leaves office, the state might make a step back from this conflict. However, it will not make the UOC-MP's relations with the state noticeably warmer for the foreseeable future because of the extremely negative public image of the UOC-MP. Despite this, it is still a challenge for the Ukrainian authorities to prove that the UOC-MP poses a threat to national security or territorial integrity in order to justify the restrictions imposed on that church. If the state does not provide this justification, it will give arguments to the UOC-MP, the ROC, and the Russian government to claim discrimination against the UOC-MP in Ukraine.

Ukraine will continue to stand out from other post-Soviet Orthodox-majority countries as having more liberal regulation of religion and a clearer separation of the state from the church. However, the Ukrainian state and church have become significantly closer to each other than before, with the Russian-Ukrainian conflict as the trigger and one of the main reasons of their rapprochement.

Notes

1 For the relations between public authorities and religions in the Crimea peninsula – a Ukrainian region occupied by Russia in 2014 – see Roman Lunkin's chapter in this volume. Several aspects of the relations between public authorities and religions, as well as violations of religious freedom in the so-called "Donetsk People's Republic/Luhansk People's Republic" are covered in Ihor Kozlovsky's and Vitaly Sorokun's interviews.

2 Liudmyla Fylypovych observes that the 1991 Law was drafted under the influence of American model of church-state relations (Kutuzova et al., 2014, p. 72). I am not convinced that the drafters of the law were familiar enough with the American constitutional framework, particularly with the US Supreme Court jurisprudence on the First Amendment. Thus, I am inclined to agree with Serhiy Plokhy that the 1991 Law reproduced the Soviet model of full separation, but in much more democratic terms as compared with the previous era (Plokhy & Sysyn, 2003, p. 173). The Law on Religious Organizations contains provisions similar to the Establishment Clause and the Free Exercise Clause. However, the main aim of the law is to protect the state and public sphere from religion, not to protect religion from the state, like in the case of the U.S. Constitution.

3 The All-Ukrainian Council of Churches and Religious Organizations is an association of religions representing more than 90% of believers in Ukraine. The Council serves as a space of interfaith dialogue and facilitates cooperation between the state and religions. See Krawchuk (2014) for more about the Council.

4 The All-Ukrainian Council of Churches adopts its statements on a consensus basis, which means that the UOC-MP, as a member of the Council, also supported them.

5 For how EU religious policies influence EU member-states with Orthodox majorities, see Olteanu and Néve (2013). For tensions between Orthodox churches' positions and European norms on religious freedom, see Fokas (2017, pp. 90–93).

6 See on historical and canonical aspects of the Ukrainian autocephaly: Plokhy and Sysyn (2003); Brusanowski (2016); Brünning (2016), and the chapter by Cyril Hovorun in this volume.

7 The UOC-MP defines itself as an independent church, which is organizationally and legally separated from Moscow, but keeps "ecclesiastical unity" with the ROC. The charter of the latter defines the UOC-MP as a self-governing church "with rights of broad autonomy" belonging to the Moscow Patriarchate. However, the ROC charter requires the UOC-MP charter be approved and that a new head of the church be blessed by the ROC Patriarch. Decisions made by the ROC's Local Councils and Archbishops' Council are binding for the UOC-MP, and its head is a permanent member of the ROC Holy Synod (Moscow Patriarchate's Official Website, 2017). There are ongoing debates whether this is enough to conclude that the ROC rules the UOC-MP. However, Law No 2662-VIII recognizes this type of relations between the ROC and the UOC-MP as a ground for the church being forcibly renamed.

In January 2019, the Ukrainian Ministry of Culture published a 819-page list of religious organizations that must change their names, most of them being religious communities, centers, and monasteries of the UOC-MP (Ministry of Culture of Ukraine [MCU], 2019).

8 In the ECtHR case *Magyar Keresztény Mennonita Egyház and others v. Hungary* (2014), the Court notes that the distinctions in the legal status granted to religious communities must not portray their adherents in an unfavorable light in public opinion, which is sensitive to the official assessment of a religion – and of the Church incarnating it – made by the state in public life (para 92). Of course, the state must address threats to national security, in particular those caused by religious associations. Yet, in the situation around the UOC-MP, some other, less restrictive measures could have been found (for example, criminal prosecution of priests or members of communities involved in separatist activities or violations of sovereignty and territorial integrity of Ukraine, or dissolution of concrete communities collaborating with a separatist paramilitary group or the Russian military in Donbas). These measures would help to avoid stigmatization of the whole church and its believers.

9 In contrast to Protestant or Jewish groups, Orthodox Christian communities usually do not have registered membership for believers; decisions are usually made by parish councils or other elected bodies. It can be difficult to identify whether a concrete person belongs to an Orthodox community because most Orthodox Christians do not attend church regularly, but still affiliate themselves with a particular community. Due to this, there is a threat that interested parties would stack decision-making meetings with parish outsiders in order to have a decision on the change of church jurisdiction approved or disapproved. Ironically enough, in the past the UOC-MP employed similar tactics to get a religious community under its control (see the ECtHR case *Svyato-Mykhaylivska Parafiya v. Ukraine* (2017)). Thus the Law No 2673-VIII not only interferes with the right of religious communities to freely regulate their internal structure, since not every religious community uses a majority-vote system to make decisions, but has also failed to prevent the danger of tampering with votes in cases where the community does not have registered membership.

10 According to its charter, the official name of the UOC-MP is the "Ukrainian Orthodox Church." In January 2019, the state registered the ruling center of the OCU as the "Kyiv Metropolis of the Ukrainian Orthodox Church (Orthodox Church of Ukraine)", which is identical to the official name of the UOC-MP (except the part in parentheses). In doing so, the OCU is probably trying to strengthen its symbolical position as the only Ukrainian Orthodox Church and expects that the UOC-MP will change its name under the state's pressure.

11 This provision was aimed at preventing implementation of some antidiscrimination measures that churches and their political allies treat as "gender ideology." For example, the All-Ukrainian Council of Churches repeatedly called for cancelling anti-discriminatory (in particular with respect to gender) examination of school textbooks, considering examination of social roles of men and women in textbooks as a form of imposing this "gender ideology."

12 A public opinion poll conducted by the sociological agency RATING shows that 69% of Ukrainians support "an absolute ban" on same-sex relations, and 15% think that these relations must be significantly limited (RATING, 2016). These numbers prove there exists a social consensus on condemnation of homosexual relations and opposition to its legalization in any form.

13 This could serve as a sociological and political answer to Aristotle Papanikolaou's question of why the church stops at one particular moral situation (same-sex relations) and does not "ask for laws against premarital sex, lying, divorce and so on" (Papanikolaou, 2017, p. 240). See also Kristine Stoeckl (2014) about this in the context of political influence of the ROC.

14 It is striking that 12 of those 13 schools are established by non-Orthodox minorities and 9 of those 12 schools by relatively small Christian and Jewish groups.
15 For example, in 2018 a UOC-KP priest delivered a lecture on family morals for students of Bohdan Khmelnytsky Cherkasy National University (Moskalyuk, 2018a). In the lecture he told students of "negative consequences of premarital sex" and "the problem of the so-called common-law marriage" which correlates with the UOC-KP doctrine on these issues.
16 In the official commentary to the constitutional agreement the Georgian Orthodox Church is defined as "official" (Crego, 2014, pp. 143–144).
17 See more in Maria Kravchenko's report (2018) for the United States Commission on International Religious Freedom.
18 It has been proposed by the Presidential National Institute for Strategic Studies (2017).
19 According to the Ministry of Culture of Ukraine (2018), the UOC-MP consists of around 12,000 communities and more than 10,000 priests. The OUC consists of more than 6,000 communities and 4,000 priests. During December 2018 – March 2019, according to an unofficial source, more than 400 UOC-MP communities switched to the OCU, mostly in the Western part of Ukraine (see RISU, 2019 for the current situation with transition of the UOC-MP communities to the OCU). Along with this, several eparchies of the UOC-MP declared their intent to stay with the church. Maybe, if the state succeeds in forcing the UOC-MP to change its name into the "Russian Orthodox Church in Ukraine," the number of transfers to the OCU will increase. However, at this point I see no reason to assume that the UOC-MP will lose its position of the major church at least in the Eastern, Southern, and some central regions of Ukraine.

References

All-Ukrainian Council of Churches and Religious Organizations. (2015, July 10). Propozitsiyi shchodo zmin do Konstytutsiyi [Proposed amendments to the Constitution]. Retrieved from http://vrciro.org.ua/ua/statements/437-uccro-proposals-for-constitution-of-ukraine.
All-Ukrainian Council of Churches and Religious Organizations. (2016, November 2). Zvernennya shchodo utverdzhennya myru i postupu ukrayins'kogo suspil'stva [Address on building peace and developing Ukrainian society]. Retrieved from http://vrciro.org.ua/ua/statements/475-uccro-statement-on-peace-in-ukraine
Blitt, R. C. (2015). Russia's 'Orthodox' foreign policy. In R. Uitz (Ed.), *Religion in public square: Perspectives on secularity* (pp. 145–174). The Hague: Eleven International Publishing.
Bremer, T. (2016). Religion in Ukraine: Historical background and present situation. In A. Krawchuk & T. Bremer (Eds.), *Churches in the Ukrainian crisis* (pp. 3–19). doi:10.1007/978-3-319-34144-6_1
Brünning, A. (2016). Orthodox autocephaly in Ukraine: The historical dimension. In A. Krawchuk & T. Bremer (Eds.), *Churches in the Ukrainian crisis* (pp. 79–101). doi:10.1007/978-3-319-34144-6_4
Brusanowski, P. (2016). Autocephaly in Ukraine: The canonical dimension. In A. Krawchuk & T. Bremer (Eds.), *Churches in the Ukrainian crisis* (pp. 47–77). doi:10.1007/978-3-319-34144-6_3
Casanova, J. (2017). *Po toy bik sekuliarizatsiyi* [Beyond secularization]. Kyiv, Ukraine: Duh i Litera.
Clark, E. A. (2016, August 30). Russian anti-missionary law in context. *Religious Freedom Institute*. Retrieved from www.religiousfreedominstitute.org/cornerstone/2016/8/30/russias-new-anti-missionary-law-in-context

Crego, P. (2014). The Georgian Orthodox Church. In L. N. Leustean (Ed.), *Eastern Christianity and politics in the twenty-first century* (pp. 140–160). doi:10.4324/9781315819037

Fatulayev, R., Ioan (Yaremenko), Mikhayil (Koltun), Volodymyr (Cherpak), Stanislav (Shyrokodyuk), Mykhaylo (Andrashko), . . . Gafuri, R. (2017, April 13). Zvernennya do viys'kovosluzhbovtsiv napepredodni stvorennya u Zbroynyh Sylah kapelans'koyi sluzhby [Address to the military on the eve of the establishment of a Chaplaincy Service in the Military Forces]. Retrieved from www.irs.in.ua/index.php?option=com_content&view=article&id=1793%253A1&catid=50%253Azv&Itemid=78&lang=uk

Fokas, E. (2017). European religious freedom norms as a challenge to Orthodox churches. In K. Stoeckl, I. Gabriel, & A. Papanikolaou (Eds.), *Political theologies in Orthodox Christianity: Common challenges and divergent positions* (pp. 75–96). doi:10.5040/9780567674173.ch-004

Head of the State: The United Ukrainian Orthodox Church means a church without Putin and prayers for the Russian army. (2018, December 15). *President of Ukraine: Official Web-office*. Retrieved from www.president.gov.ua/en/news/glava-derzhavi-obyednana-ukrayinska-pravoslavna-cerkva-cerkv-52062

Holova SBU: Tserkva povynna staty konsoliduyuchoyu syloyu dlya yednannya Ukrains'koho narodu [The head of SSU: The Church should become a consolidating power for uniting the Ukrainian people]. (2015, December 14). *Institute of Religious Freedom*. Retrieved from www.irs.in.ua/index.php?option=com_content&view=article&id=1634%3A1&catid=34%3Aua&Itemid=61&lang=uk

Kalkandjieva, D. (2011). A comparative analysis on church-state relations in Eastern Orthodoxy: Concepts, models, and principles. *Journal of Church and State, 53*(4), 587–614. doi:10.1093/jcs/csr012

Kravchenko, M. (2018). Inventing extremists: The impact of Russian anti-extremism policies on freedom of religion or belief. *The United States Commission on International Religious Freedom's website*. Retrieved from www.uscirf.gov/sites/default/files/Inventing%20Extremists.pdf

Krawchuk, A. (2014). Constructing interreligious consensus in post-Soviet space: The Ukrainian council of churches and religious organizations. In A. Krawchuk & T. Bremer (Eds.), *Eastern Orthodox encounters of identity and otherness: Values, self-reflection, dialogue* (pp. 273–300). doi:10.1057/9781137377388_18

Kutuzova, N., Karaseva, S., Vasilevich, N., Shavtsova, D., Garbus, T., Filipovich, L., & Khromets, V. (2014). *Religioznyye organizatsii v obschestvennom prostranstve Belarusi I Ukrainy: Formirovanie mekhanizmov partnerstva* [Religious organizations in public spaces of Belarus and Ukraine: Developing frameworks of partnership]. Vilnius, Lithuania: European University of Humanities.

Ministry of Culture of Ukraine. (2018). Dani departamentu u spavah relihiy i natsional'nostey pro relihiynu merezhu [Data of the Department of religious and nationalities affairs about religious landscape]. Retrieved from https://risu.org.ua/ua/index/resourses/statistics/ukr_2018/70440/

Ministry of Culture of Ukraine. (2019, January 26). Perelik relihiynyh organizatsiy, yakym neobkhidno vnesty zminy to statutu [List of religious organizations, which to have to amend their charters]. *Uryadovyy Kur"yer*. Retrieved from https://ukurier.gov.ua/uk/articles/perelik-religijnih-organizacij-yakim-potribno-vnes/?fbclid=IwAR2sVpO2E_h6_miRi6UWraI5eJRNorHKMYTvjgTxmL4h0xHeQHweBSmskq4

Moscow Patriarchate's Official Website. (2017). Ustav Russkoy Pravoslavnoy Tserkvi [The charter of the Russian Orthodox Church]. Retrieved from www.patriarchia.ru/db/document/133114/

Moskalyuk, K. (2018a, March 21). Lektsiya dlya studentiv Cherkas'koho natsional'noho universytetu [A lecture for the students of the Cherkasy National University]. Retrieved from www.cerkva.info/posts/lektsiia-dlia-studentiv-chnu

Moskalyuk, K. (2018b, May 3). Dopovid' Svyatishoho Patriarkha Filareta na konferentsiyi u Yevropeys'komu Parlamenti [His Holiness Patriarch Filaret's speech at a conference in the European Parliament]. Retrieved from www.cerkva.info/posts/dopovid-sviatiishoho-patriarkha-filareta-na-konferentsii-u-yevropeiskomu-parlamenti

National Institute for Strategic Studies. (2017). Analitychna dopovid' do shchorichnoho poslannya Presidenta Ukrayiny do Verkhovnnoyi Rady Ukrayiny pro vnutrishnye ta zovnishnye stanovyshche u 2017 rotsi [Analytical Report for the Annual Address of the President of Ukraine to the Verkhovna Rada of Ukraine on internal and external affairs in 2017]. Retrieved from www.niss.gov.ua/public/File/book_2017/Poslanya_druk_fin.pdf

Olteanu, T., & Néve, D. de. (2013). Eastern Orthodoxy and process of European integration. In A. Krawchuk & T. Bremer (Eds.), *Eastern Orthodox encounters of identity and otherness: Values, self-reflection, dialogue* (pp. 179–206). doi:10.1057/9781137377388_13

Papanikolaou, A. (2017). Whose public? Which ecclesiology? In K. Stoeckl, I. Gabriel, & A. Papanikolaou (Eds.), *Political theologies in Orthodox Christianity: Common challenges and divergent positions* (pp. 75–96). doi:10.5040/9780567674173.ch-012

Pew Research Center. (2017, May 10). Religious belief and national belonging in central and eastern Europe. Retrieved from www.pewforum.org/2017/05/10/religious-belief-and-national-belonging-in-central-and-eastern-europe/

Plokhy, S., & Sysyn, F. E. (2003). *Religion and nation in modern Ukraine.* Edmonton and Toronto, Canada: Canadian Institute of Ukrainian Studies Press.

President: Autocephaly of the Ukrainian church and the acquisition of the Tomos is part of our strategy for the final decolonization of Ukraine. (2018, December 16). *President of Ukraine: Official Web-office.* Retrieved from www.president.gov.ua/en/news/prezident-avtokefaliya-ukrayinskoyi-cerkvi-i-zdobuttya-tomos-52078

President urges the Parliament to ratify the Council of Europe Convention on preventing and combating violence against women and domestic violence. (2018, December 7). *President of Ukraine: Official Web-office.* Retrieved from www.president.gov.ua/en/news/prezident-zaklikav-parlament-ratifikuvati-konvenciyu-radi-ye-51866

Rada tserkov zaklykala prezidenta do reformy pravosuddya i borot'by z koruptsiyeyu [The council of churches called on the President to fight corruption and to reform the judiciary]. (2016, April 23). *Institute of Religious Freedom.* Retrieved from https://irs.in.ua/index.php?option=com_content&view=article&id=1684%253A1&catid=34%253Aua&Itemid=61&lang=uk

Ratajeski, E. L. (2015). The changing religious mosaic in Ukraine. In S. D. Brunn (Ed.), *The changing world religion map* (pp. 1555–1576). doi:10.1007/978-94-017-9376-6_82

RATING. (2016, September 9). Expansion of conservative views in Ukraine. Retrieved from http://ratingpro.org/research/poshirennya_konservativnih_poglyadiv_v_ukraini.html?toindex=1

RISU. (2019). Karta peryhodiv do Pravoslavnoyi Tserkvy Ukrayiny [Map of communities' switches to the OCU]. Retrieved from www.google.com/maps/d/u/0/viewer?mid=1XQR0sfHFFiiXyGiVYqI1mNylJ9fFPdnh&ll=50.37875869902123

RPTs v Ukrayini:Verkhovna Rada ukhvalyla zakonoproekt pro nazvu Moskovs'koho Patriarkhatu [The ROC in Ukraine: The Verkhovna Rada has approved the law on the name of the Moscow Patriarchate]. (2018, December 20). *RISU.* Retrieved from https://risu.org.ua/ua/index/all_news/state/church_state_relations/73995/

Sarkissian, A. (2015). *The varieties of religious repressions: Why governments restrict religion*. doi:10.1093/acprof:oso/9780199348084

Shchotkyna, K. (2018, December 21). Na pivdorohy do khramu [Halfway to the church]. *ZN. ua*. Retrieved from https://zn.ua/internal/na-polputi-k-hramu-303761_.html?fbclid=Iw AR3yH0NsQzjTxsiVAqQ0_QJGNXWFM-F9QxODt1EhiNoh_Fzm6c8d76NW_wY

Spohn, W. (2012). Europeanization, multiple modernities and religion – The reconstruction of collective identities in post-Communist Central and Eastern Europe. In G. Pickel & K. Sammet (Eds.), *Transformations of religiosity: Religion and religiosity in eastern Europe 1989–2010* (pp. 29–50). doi:10.1007/978-3-531-93326-9_3

Stoeckl, K. (2014). *The Russian Orthodox Church and human rights*. doi:10.4324/9781315818788

Studentiv Drahomanova vygnaly na moleben' zamist' par: Vony pryyshly z napysamy 'Mene zmusyly' [Dragomanov University students were forced to participate in worship instead of attending classes: They came with signs 'I've been forced']. (2017, September 29). *UP Zhyttya*. Retrieved from https://life.pravda.com.ua/society/2017/09/29/226711/

Suveica, S., & Spranceana, V. (2015). Perspectives on human rights and religion in Moldova. In H.-G. Ziebertz & G. Črpić (Eds.), *Religion and human rights: International perspective* (pp. 103–112). doi:10.1007/978-3-319-09731-2_8

UPTs-KP prosytume parlament uhvalyty zakon pro zminu nazvy UPTs-MP [The UOC-KP will ask the parliament to adopt the law on renaming the UOC-MP]. (2018, November 2). *Radio Svoboda*. Retrieved from www.radiosvoboda.org/a/news-zmina-nazvy-upc-mp/29579753.html

Vovk, D. (2015). Balancing religious freedom in the context of secularity. In P. Szymaniec (Ed.), *The principle of proportionality and the protection of the fundamental rights in the European states* (pp. 269–294). Walbrzych, Poland: Wydawnictwo Panstwowej Wyzszej Szkoly Zawodowej im. Angelusa Silesiusa.

Wanner, C. (2010). Southern challenges to Eastern Christianity: Pressures to reform the state-church model. *Journal of Church and State, 52*(4), 644–661. doi:10.1093/jcs/csq107

Yelensky, V. (1999). The Ukraine Church and state relations in the post-Communist era. In I. Borowik (Ed.), *Church and state relations in central and eastern Europe* (pp. 146–147). Krakow, Poland: NOMOS.

Zviadadze, S. (2015). Georgian Orthodox Church and human rights: Challenges to Georgian society. In H.-G. Ziebertz & G. Črpić (Eds.), *Religion and human rights: International perspective* (pp. 45–60). doi:10.1007/978-3-319-09731-2_4

4 Come all ye faithful to the Russian world

Governmental and grass-roots spiritual discourse in the battle over Ukraine

Elizaveta Gaufman

Introduction

Who counts as a Russian? For most people in the western hemisphere a Russian is anyone from the post-Soviet space who understands Russian, but this question is much more fraught in the post-Soviet space proper. While for many in former Soviet republics being cast as a Russian brings up the memory of political and/or cultural subjugation (Kolsto, 2018; O'Loughlin, Toal, & Kolosov, 2016), in Russia the sense of belonging frequently includes an ethnodoxic (Karpov, Lisovskaya, & Barry, 2012) component, where a "real" Russian is not only ethnically Russian, but also an Orthodox Christian. However, with both the Russian Empire and the Soviet Union having included many ethnic groups and multiple confessions it is hard for the current Russian establishment to promote an integrational project that does not have some identity wiggle room. Consequently, when geopolitics is at stake, the narratives of belonging and exclusion become increasingly important, especially in the case of the relationship between Russia and Ukraine. Despite the two countries having common origins, closely-related languages, and being majority Christian Orthodox, a conflict resolution is not in sight with continued military hostilities in eastern Ukraine and the unrecognized annexation of Crimean Peninsula. Moreover, Ukrainians continue to be on the list of less-desired ethnic groups in Russia, according to public opinion polls (Levada-Center, 2018).

The Russian government has come up with several justifications for integration projects in the post-Soviet space (Kazharski, 2019) that usually run into the accusations of reconstructing the former USSR. One of these projects, "Russian World" (*Russkiy Mir*), has been a staple of Russian foreign policy since 2007. There are two main interpretations of this notion: one of them stipulates affinity to Russian language and culture, and the other is more focused on a geopolitical/civilizational narrative. President Putin has referenced adherence to the Russian world through language and culture, but Patriarch Kirill has also repeatedly emphasized that the Russian world is about spirituality and not territory, including in the orbit of the Russian World Moldova and Kazakhstan apart from the usual Ukraine, Belarus, and Russia triad. Despite the seemingly exclusively cultural aims of the state-sponsored Russkiy Mir Foundation, its agenda is also to a large extent political, just as Batanova (2008) writes that the ethno-cultural identity of the Russian super-ethnos can be strengthened through Russian World's assertion of Russian geopolitical and cultural space. During a press conference in December 2017 President Putin commented on the war in Ukraine referencing "common spiritual foundations" between the two countries, thus seemingly disregarding the existence of a separate, Ukrainian identity.

While Russian authorities try to pedal the religious commonalities between Russia and Ukraine, social network users do not seem to buy this argument. Data from the social network VKontakte shows that Orthodoxy is not considered as a relevant factor in the Russian-Ukrainian reconciliation. Moreover, while restrictions on religious freedom since the Pussy Riot trial point to the neoconservative turn of the Russian government, social network users see the geopolitical resurgence of Russian great power identity as more important than its religious aspect. Both types of rhetoric, however, consider Ukraine as a Russian satellite, whether for geopolitical or spiritual reasons. This chapter analyzes the discrepancies between the governmental and grass-root understandings of the Russian World in the context of the Russian-Ukrainian conflict using the posts made in the Antimaidan group on the Russian social media website Vkontakte between 2014–2016 and 2018–2019.

The concept of the Russian world

As mentioned above, the Russian World can serve as a suitable moniker for geopolitical ambition in the "near abroad" (Toal, 2017), as well as a linguistic-cultural project (O'Loughlin, Toal, & Kolosov, 2016). The concept echoes numerous Russia-centric integration projects based on the assumption of Russia being a "civilization state" (Kazharski, 2019). As Kazharski points out, "civilizationism is, at the same time, an attempt to plug into globally established discourses on civilizations, Huntington's ideas being its constant reference point." Given that Huntington's central civilizational hallmark is religion, it is no wonder that religion plays an important role in the Russian World as well, despite its exclusionary potential. As Laruelle notes, the Russian establishment has tried to play the civilizational religious card since 2002 through the World Public Forum "Dialogue of Civilizations," with the Moscow Patriarchate also "[playing] the card of the 'dialogue of civilizations' instead of that of ecumenism" (Laruelle, 2009, p. 58). Thus, even within the establishment it is understood that Russian foreign policy presupposes the existence of a specific Orthodox civilization (Laruelle, 2015).

In 2007, the Russkiy Mir Foundation was created in order to promote Russian language and culture abroad. Despite the initially-proclaimed exclusively cultural aims of the Foundation, its agenda has become to a large extent political (Batanova, 2008). The website of the Foundation features, for instance the collection "Civil poetry of Donbass," news about President Putin visiting a book exhibit, and Patriarch Kirill meeting with the veterans of the Great Patriotic War, together with news on publications, translations, and cultural events. It shows that the Foundation's agenda is not only cultural, but is also aimed at promoting Orthodoxy, Slavic unity, and a Russian political agenda, thereby potentially excluding from its agenda non-Orthodox, non-Slavic, and politically opposed aficionados of Russian language and culture or even (former) Russian citizens.

Patriarch Kirill is also a vocal supporter of the spiritual foundations for the (Slavic) unity around Moscow (Press Service of the Patriarch of Moscow and all Rus', 2010a, 2010b). Given that the center of spirituality is supposed to be in Moscow, these claims are also often interpreted through a geopolitical lens, even though ultra-nationalistic circles may be uncomfortable with Kazakhstan's membership in what looks like a Slavic alliance. In the religious context, however, the more ubiquitous term is "Holy Rus'" which usually is a reference to Orthodoxy, but given that Metropolitan Hilarion (Alfeyev), the head of Russian Orthodox Church's Foreign Department is also a member of the Russkiy Mir Foundation's Board of Trustees, the idea of Russian World in its expanded version is accepted as well.

The Russian World as an integration project can be viewed through the theoretical lens of a pastorate. According to Carrette (2013), the analytics of pastoral power come from Foucault's understanding of religious power based on the inherited Christian practices permeating the contemporary world. Pastoral power is supposed to represent a shift from feudal to modern society that is not based on physical coercion (Oksala, 2013), which makes it suitable for analysis of illiberal governance where there are no mass-scale repressions. Even though pastorate might seem like a concept unique to western Europe, there is in fact its Russian genealogical twin in the notion of *sobornost* (Ware, 2011): a church community that does not belong to a specific place, but belongs to the whole world (*vsemu miru*) and unites the souls and lives of its members (Khomyakov, 2015/1864). What makes the Russian World as a project similar to pastorate is the fact that it is not exercised over a territory; as Foucault (2007) would describe it, it is a flock, rather than land, and is a beneficent power, "power of care" towards salvation.

Given that Foucault defined religious power as pastoral power in his *Lectures on Security, Territory, Population*, the messianic sense of power should definitely be taken into consideration, especially given the genealogy of the "Moscow as the Third Rome" concept and the Russian Orthodox Church's (ROC) ambition to unite Orthodox Christians around the Moscow and not the Constantinople Patriarchate (von Eggert, 2018). Pastorate is supposed to be transcendental; it is not just about the territorial confines, but is supposed to have some kind of universal appeal, which the Russian World is supposed to do through its culture and language references. Hence, in the discursive struggles that shape a pastoral political system there should be references to trans-border sovereignty, which is particularly relevant for Russian foreign policy. Discursively, the pastorate system is also supposed to present itself as protecting the flock from danger and leading it to salvation. It is still questionable though, whether "the flock" agrees with the governmental framing of spiritual sameness with Ukrainians within the Russian World. Thus, even though the government may strive to create a pastorate, the population might have other geopolitical and secular constellations in mind.

The Russian world in Russian policy

Putin famously referred to the collapse of the Soviet Union as the "greatest geopolitical disaster of the twentieth century," but the potential Russian World "flock" spans well past the borders of the former Soviet Union. One of the first attempts to capitalize on trans-border Russianness was legislation aimed at encouraging the resettlement of former Russian citizens or "compatriots" (*soot-echestvenniki*). The project of promoting the return of former Russian citizens is based on two legal provisions. The first one is the Federal Law on State Policy towards Compatriots Abroad No 99-FZ (1999), which provides a definition of compatriots and describes the governmental policies abroad to promote Russian culture and to support compatriots. The second is the President's Executive Decree on Assistance for Voluntary Resettlement of Compatriots Abroad in the Russian Federation (2006), which lists concrete benefits that are to be provided to returnees (e.g., tickets to Russia, granting of citizenship, reintegration grants, shipping of belongings, housing, jobs, etc.).

The working definition of compatriots in the Federal Law refers to "any person who used to be a citizen of the Russian Empire, Russian Republic, RSFSR, USSR or Russian Federation, permanently living outside Russia and acknowledging their spiritual and cultural connection to Russia as well as direct descendants of the above-mentioned." Such a definition embraces not only the 25–30 million Russians living abroad but approximately 200 million people (e.g., even the descendants of Poles and Finns who used to be nationals of the Russian Empire). In this way, the program can justify its extension to include the "lost generations" of past immigration waves.

Russian foreign policy in the "near abroad" is a clear manifestation of the trans-border sovereignty, whereby the flock is supposed to be protected from the dangers of Russophobic governments (cf. Toal, 2017; Tsygankov, 2009). This was especially visible during the war in Georgia and as a justification for the annexation of Crimea. Russian speakers, or people who used to own Soviet passports, were issued Russian passports in South Ossetia and Abkhazia before and after the 2008 war (Sakwa, 2012). In a meeting with military officers in November 2011, then-President Medvedev insisted that the war in Georgia was justified to save large numbers of our citizens from, as he said, the "threat" emanating from Georgia. The crisis in Ukraine was also a prominent example of the trans-border sovereignty in action: while South Ossetia and Abkhazia remain independent, Crimea has been annexed by Russia, which has de facto control of it. Very telling in this regard is a speech made by a member of the Communist Party in the Russian Duma:

> Our group considers it necessary to officially recognize the Donetsk and Luhansk People's Republics. We demand that the President of the Russian

Federation protect the **civilian** population, provide effective military assistance to Novorossia! Inaction of Russian authorities is fairly assessed by our Ukrainian **brothers** in the southeast as betrayal. . . . Fascism will never be on Russian soil!

(Nikitchuk, 2014, emphasis added)

The excerpt from the speech above is replete with references to trans-border sovereignty, (e.g., calling the Ukrainians brothers, asking the President to protect the civilian population in Donetsk and Luhansk). By employing the term "Novorossia" and promising not to let fascism thrive on "Russian soil," he explicitly doubts the territorial integrity of Ukraine and asserts Russia's "responsibility to protect."

This issue has also been taken up in the Military Doctrine of the Russian Federation (2014) that states under the rubric "use of the armed forces, other troops and bodies of their main tasks in peacetime, during the immediate threat of aggression and war" that Russian armed forces could be used "to ensure the protection of [Russian] citizens outside the Russian Federation in accordance with the generally recognized principles and norms of international law and international treaties of the Russian Federation," which makes the post-Soviet countries with large Russian minorities especially nervous (cf. the media coverage of the Ukrainian crisis in Estonia in Mälksoo, 2014).

President Putin also seems to stress the spiritual connection between Russia and Ukraine. During his annual press conference in December 2017, he responded to a Ukrainian journalist with a tirade about the fraternal nature of Ukrainian-Russian relationship that carried a religious overtone:

Now to the question whether we are far or close. I know that you, probably, will not agree with this, but each person has his own position. The Slavic world had a difficult beginning. . . . In the end, Russia was formed, of which Kiev was the center. And in this sense our historical, **spiritual** and other roots give me the right to say that **we are basically one people** . . .

In the nineteenth century, there were people who began to talk about the fact that Ukraine should be independent, independent. Do they have the right to do this? They have. Especially, perhaps, it was a real issue within the framework of the empire, where, probably, some violent Russification was being made, although for Ukraine this was least important, **because after all Ukraine is an Orthodox country**. Then it was important. The column **"nationality"** was not in passports, I recall, **there was only "religion."** A Ukrainian was no different from a Russian, in no way.

(Putin, 2017, emphasis added)

Putin's quote is a more politically correct version of the online "holy wars" over Ukraine's status in Russian imagination. Very telling in this case are online debates on the use of the preposition "on" (*na*) or "in" (*v*) with the word "Ukraine" and numerous disputes about the etymology of the name of the country,[1] with pro-Russian parties usually putting forward the argument that Ukraine was never an independent state and has always existed as an appendage of the Russian Empire and Poland (Paulsen, 2013). This discussion, however, can also be analyzed in gender categories, as Ukraine's supposedly subordinate role in geopolitical terms is often conveyed through feminization, either as a gay man or a loose woman (Gaufman, 2017). While online commentators emphasize the great-power aspect of the debate, Putin seems to have moved on to the religious one. Moreover, given that Patriarch Kirill is the head of the ROC, the implicit message of Putin's narrative is that Ukraine is supposed to gravitate towards Russia spiritually.

Putin also made a more unusual "spiritual" reference in the context of the Crimea annexation. In 2014, Putin declared that the ancient city of Chersoneses near Sevastopol is for Russian Orthodox Christians as holy a place as the Temple Mount in Jerusalem is for Jews and Muslims. The "cradle of Russian spirituality" framing probably came as a surprise to most Russians, who vaguely remember their history lessons from middle school, but it was supposed to reinforce Russia's claim to the territory beyond the strategic ones (fleet base) and the already-existing narratives of protection of Russian-speakers from fascism. Thus, a "spiritual" basis for Crimea's annexation has hardly created a potential for conflict resolution between the two countries.

Patriarch Kirill, who seems to have been instrumental in prisoner exchange between the separatists and the Ukrainian government, also likes to talk about a brotherly relationship between the two peoples. He is convinced that the Ukrainian Orthodox Church of the Moscow Patriarchate (UOC-MP) is the only real force that can unite Ukraine (Patriarkh Kirill verit, 2017). Just like Putin, he does not seem to distinguish between Russia and Ukraine as entities:

> For me, Ukraine is the same as Russia. My people and my Church are there. . . . This is a reason for sleepless nights and for great enthusiasm that I feel when I think about the people who are so fiercely **fighting** for their beliefs, for their **right to stay Orthodox.**
>
> (Patriarkh Kirill verit, 2017, emphasis added)

The Patriarch's reframing of the armed conflict in southeast Ukraine is remarkable. In his interview, he does not really mention the previously-dominant "fascism" narrative that was ubiquitous on mainstream media. Instead, he frames the conflict in completely religious terms, arguing that a "European way" precludes people from being Orthodox. This framing is far from unusual: this kind of construction is also linked to a more comprehensive Russian uniqueness discourse: a discussion of "who-we-are-not" helps those who, from the time of the debate between Slavophiles and Westerners in the nineteenth century, have been looking for signs of the collapse of the West, which is opposed to truly Russian spiritual values and "bonds."

The connection between the conflict in Ukraine and religion is also visible in a more recent framing proposed by members of the ruling "United Russia" party. Svetlana Khorkina, an Olympic gymnast turned member of Parliament, had the following exchange about the situation in Ukraine:

[Svetlana Khorkina]   And what about Crimea? People have no right to choose how they want to live? Or do you want to be **killed** like in Syria? They want to speak Russian, live in peace and educate children. They do not want to be **burnt**, as in Odessa. They do not want to be afraid to come to **church**, [or] to go to jail because they just go to the streets on **May 9**, wearing a front-line uniform with awards. Moreover, everything was done legally, through a referendum! People are not pigs, they have a right to vote and to live . . . the life they want. Practically the whole Crimea said: "We want to go to Russia." And they are Russia. We gave people the opportunity to speak quietly, otherwise they would have been **killed**.

[Interviewer]   By whom?

[Svetlana Khorkina]   By Banderovtsy [Stepan Bandera's followers]. Do you think Bandera is normal? What are your thoughts on **fascism**?

[Interviewer]   Negative.

[Svetlana Khorkina]   That's great. And you think there is no such thing now? If people cannot go to a **religious procession**? In order to mark the **Baptism of Rus'** the way they want? (Golovin, 2018, emphasis added)

Khorkina, a loyal supporter of President Putin, brings together the issues that concern many in the "Crimea is Ours" camp. She not only equates belonging to Russia with peace and language, but also explicitly emphasizes the importance of religion (going to church, participating in a religious procession) and the purported absence of such freedom in Ukraine. The quote also alludes to the age-long dispute between Russia and Ukraine about the history that starts for both countries in the Kyivan Rus, as Prince Vladimir (Volodymyr), the one who adopted Christianity as a state religion for the ancient Russia/Ukraine in 988, is considered a Russian in Russian history books and Ukrainian in Ukrainian ones. Khorkina's more important concern is related to the mortal danger to Russian Orthodox citizens. Graphic descriptions of death, such as being "burnt" or killed "like in Syria," were a typical refrain common at the height of the Ukraine crisis when Euromaidan was deemed an existential threat to the Russian-speaking population in Ukraine by connecting it with the collective memory of the Great Patriotic War (Gaufman, 2017).

Another important issue in this context is the autocephaly of the Orthodox Church of Ukraine (OCU) that was granted on January 5, 2019. As mentioned before, representatives of the ROC seem to ignore Russian intervention in the east of Ukraine and the annexation of Crimea, blaming the crisis in the "brotherly" country on nationalists and "external forces." Many Ukrainians who resent Russia's role in the conflict prefer to leave the UOC-MP, which is now seen as an arm of the Kremlin's Russian World policy, with approximately 100 communities having joined the Ukrainian Orthodox Church of the Kyiv Patriarchate between 2014–2018 and significantly more after autocephaly was granted. Now that the OCU is no longer dependent on the Moscow Patriarchate, it means a loss of both prestige and authority for the ROC and Patriarch Kirill personally. How can Holy Russia or the Russian World continue if a significant part of it does not want anything to do with Russia? Religion is, however, not on digital Russians' minds.

Russian world online

On February 27, 2015, the anniversary of the "Crimean reunification" that is now commemorated in Russia as "Special Forces Operation Day," a video was posted on YouTube that has been since called "the best video of Russian propaganda" (Cassely, 2015). This video has the features and style of a first-person shooter computer game, which already gives it a very militarized impression (Jansz & Tanis, 2007; Power, 2007). Entitled "I am a Russian Occupier" (*Ya russkiy okkupant*), the video describes Russian military history (i.e., the occupation of Siberia, the Baltic countries, and central Asia) as events that systematically led to modernization and improvement in the quality of life in the conquered territories. In the case of Siberia, "women cannot be sold for a pack of sable skins" and instead live in industrialized cities with kindergartens. The citizens of Baltic countries, "who asked the Russians to leave," are now "cleaning toilets in the European Union," while during the Soviet era they produced electronic equipment and cars. In Ukraine, instead of heavy industry developed in the Soviet era, "they just build endless maidans and dictatorships" [sic]. At the end of the video, the narrator says that he doesn't need your [Western] hypocritical liberty and rotten democracy, illustrating them with photos of Pussy Riot, Conchita Wurst, and Charlie Hebdo caricatures (see Grief de Sun, 2016). Apart from the profoundly xenophobic "*mission civilisatrice*" that reflects current attitudes towards ethnic Others in Russia, this video portrays the vision of peace that presents Russia as a military man and a civilized nation, able to improve the condition of other ethnic groups on Russian territory.

The name of the video is also sarcastic, as even though the narrator is visually portrayed in a military uniform, the message of the video is that Soviet/ Russian conquests have only improved the state of affairs in the conquered nations. Paradoxically, by bringing war (tanks, missiles, etc.) "Russian occupiers" were also supposed to have eliminated elements of structural violence, such as female inequality, access to education, and healthcare, and to have ameliorated economic conditions. It is also indicative that the Occupier literally says that he "builds peace" and "loves peace" and, consistent with Soviet-era rhetoric, accuses the United States and Barack Obama personally of bringing war to the world. This video is extremely indicative of the peace narrative that exists in modern Russia. It is inextricably linked to the notion of "false" European values that contribute to the reign of structural violence in the West. Given that the video, as it turns out, was sponsored by circles close to the Russian Patriarchy, it is no wonder that apart from the great-power narrative, there was also a reference to the false and supposedly atheistic values brought on by "Europe" – exactly what Patriarch Kirill seems to promote.

A famous Russian writer, Zakhar Prilepin, who leads a battalion on the separatist side in Donbas, is an example of the fusion between the religious rhetoric of the Russian government and the militaristic tendencies of social networks. He likes to talk about "fusion of orthodoxy and communism" in Donbas (Melnik, 2017) and how people carry red flags and the "Savior's Image." He seems to be the minority though: even his followers don't seem to pick up on the religious component of his Ukraine-related statement and instead concentrate on the main "Ukraine as a fascist state" narrative.

The Occupier video made quite a splash on Russian social media and garnered about 8 million views before being deleted (and uploaded again by other users), but Russian social networks provide an abundance of material as well. During the crisis in Ukraine, VKontakte, a Russian clone of Facebook with more than 350,000,000 users, served as an uncensored platform for people engaging in debates over the events in Ukraine. VKontakte allows its users to found "communities" (akin to Facebook groups) where users can post statements, photographs, collages, and music that relate to the topic of the community. Communities can be closed (moderators review the joining request and deny it if they want) or open (anyone can join by clicking a button). One of the most prominent platforms in Vkontakte that united anti-Ukrainian statements was the Antimaidan page (https://vk.com/antimaydan) with 545,000 members in its heyday, not to mention other smaller or localized Antimaidan groups with 20,000 to 50,000 members that usually engaged in similar rhetoric and often reposted the material from the original Antimaidan group.

The majority (68%) of the 29,685 images[2] in the Antimaidan group contain text: either quotes of politicians or text superimposed on images. There is also a significant number of images with military paraphernalia. Another "corpus" of images is related to (racist) caricatures of Ukrainian, European, and American politicians[3] that utilize different enmification techniques, such as representing Russia's enemies as animals (mostly pigs) or caricatured as ugly. Personification is a common psychological reaction that urges humans to affix vectors of power to an (anthropomorphized) entity. This technique is especially visible in journalism, where various phenomena are usually described in individualistic terms to establish a connection between a reader and the written material, often visualizing violence and victims (Tenenboim-Weinblatt, Hanitzsch, & Nagar, 2016). As Breton notes, personification "facilitate[s] emotional expression and communication by providing opportunities for identification, fantasy and the communication of anxiety and fear" (Breton, 2010, p. 25).

It is also notable that the Antimaidan images contain several examples of international memes (Börzsei, 2013), i.e., even when indulging in anti-Western propaganda, Antimaidan users employ Western tools (for instance, memes with Willy Wonka or the philosoraptor). Despite the abundance of visual material, there were relatively few images focusing on visions of the Russian World – most visual posts were related to the rather graphic photos of devastation allegedly wrecked by the Ukrainian army in Donbas: dead bodies, scared civilians, destroyed buildings, and soldiers – similar to other Vkontakte groups devoted to the Ukraine conflict (Makhortykh & Lyebyedyev, 2015; Makhortykh & Sydorova, 2017). However, some of the visuals can provide answers to the questions about the place of religion in the understanding of the Russian world. These memes usually show a stereotypical Ukrainian man facing a choice between Europe and Russia. First, Europe is depicted as a collection of homophobic visuals, such as a seemingly transgender naked devil, or a cross-dressed man with makeup, whereas the Russian side is represented by a fully clothed male angel, not to mention the fact that it is a male Ukrainian who is supposed to make a choice. Second, European values are conveyed through images of money, drugs, and gay men kissing, while Russia's spirituality is exemplified by the domes of a church, a nuclear family, and scientific achievements (e.g., the first astronaut Yury Gagarin and Sputnik). Third, European history is associated with Hitler, while Russia is the force that defeated him (the T-34 tank). Thus, Russian Orthodoxy is conceptualized here as an additional positive characteristic of the Russian World that is supposed to attract Ukrainians, but it doesn't seem to grant Ukrainians the right to be Orthodox in their own state. Thus, Orthodoxy is indeed considered an important factor in Russian identity in jingoistic circles, but it comes with a pro-Kremlin political agenda.

Digital Orthodoxy?

The role of Orthodoxy in the solution of the Ukraine crisis is doubtful for digital protagonists. Antimaidan subscribers are too busy denigrating Ukrainians as pigs, foreign stooges, gay men, and loose women. Orthodoxy is only used to describe the Russian World that Ukrainians seemingly do not belong to, while the "Ukrainian World" – similarly to Patriarch Kirill's statements – is described as one of godless gay Europeans (Neumann, 2017). They are eager for the President to protect fellow members of the flock and violate other countries' sovereignty because, for members of the Russian World, borders are irrelevant as long as there are "brothers" to protect. Predictably, when the *Tomos* was eventually granted to the Ukrainian Orthodox Church, Antimaidan subscribers saw in it a purely political decision with financial overtones mired in the existing fascist brutality frame.

In general, the reaction to the autocephalous status of the OCU in the Antimaidan group has been mostly dismissive. Posts ranged from obscene caricatures allegedly from Charlie Hebdo with the Ukrainian Metropolitan holding a giant phallus instead of the *Tomos*, or holding Tom from the *Tom and Jerry* cartoon instead of the *Tomos* (January 18, 2019), to gleeful reports of alleged barring of OCU pilgrims from monasteries on Mount Athos (February 10, 2019). Antimaidan subscribers disregard the spiritual meaning of the autocephalous status and instead discuss *Tomos* as an "electorate excitement tool" (February 5, 2019) that is supposed to ensure a first-round win in the presidential elections and document a "*Tomos* tour" with the OCU Primate Epiphany and President Poroshenko (January 20, 2019 and February 1, 2019). Antimaidan also reports alleged violent attacks on priests who declined to join the newly established Church (February 4, 2019) and the lack of international recognition of Metropolitan Epiphany (February 3, 2019), while the autocephalous Church is derided as "autofecalus."

Thus, apart from the derision, the independence of the OCU has been framed as a completely political decision that plays into the hands of Ukrainian authorities that are concerned with upcoming presidential elections. At the same time, the supporters of the new Church are framed in a similar way as the supporters of Maidan – violent anti-Russians with little legitimacy in the rest of the world. Supporters of the new church were called schismatics who literally want to burn down churches (January 19, 2019) or are engaged in church raiding (January 13, 2019 and January 17, 2019). This type of framing was reinforced through calling the OCU a "so-called church" and posting about alleged attempts to grab (*otzhat'*) the Kyiv-Pechersk Lavra, the first male monastery in the ancient Kyivan Rus', founded in 1051 (January 21, 2019). The lexicon the users employed had notable criminal overtones aimed at constructing a narrative of the OCU as an illegitimate semi-criminal enterprise designed to boost the failing ratings of President Poroshenko. According to Antimaidan users, faith has nothing to do with it.

Why do people not think that Orthodox Christianity and the Russian World project could play a role in the solution of the Ukraine crisis? Despite the concept having a long history and being somewhat familiar to the Russian population, it has several internal contradictions. For one, the Russian World is often viewed negatively by former Soviet republics who consider it a USSR 2.0 type of integration project and cannot get on board even with the Russian language and culture component, as these are also viewed as an attempt to subjugate or infiltrate their countries (cf. O'Loughlin et al., 2016). With the Foundation turning to more political topics such as taking a side in the Ukraine conflict, the Russian World as a project is also considered an arm of the Russian state, which discourages those who disagree with the Kremlin's policies. Moreover, when Patriarch Kirill and sometimes President Putin promote the ethnodoxic component of the Russian World, it antagonizes non-Christian and non-ethnic Russian compatriots from the project. Given that the question of "who counts as a Russian" is still open, even supporters of a Russian World have a hard time with it.

Most importantly, at the height of the Ukraine crisis in 2014–2015, the narrative of fascism promoted both by the Russian government and the mainstream media drowned out most of the attempts to frame the conflict in different terms.

Consequently, the fascism narrative is still visible both on the governmental level – Khorkina's interview is a case in point – as well as on the popular level, where Antimaidan subscribers are still concerned with a neo-Nazi takeover of Ukraine, posting pictures of Bandera supporters, men with tattooed swastikas and further alleged evidence of a "fascist" Ukraine. Even though it fits well with the pastorate's "flock protection" feature, it is not Orthodoxy that is the main target of the threat, it is the survival of the people. Given this narrative's discursive power and the continued hostilities in the east of Ukraine, it is unlikely that it will fade away and give room to alternative hegemonic narratives.

Especially within a conflict setting, it is important to maintain the otherness of the enemy and Orthodoxy would be a factor of similarity that prevents hating the enemy. Hence, the emphasis on the "false European way" promoted by Patriarch Kirill and many online users: Antimaidan subscribers are more concerned with disparaging Ukrainians rather than looking for ways to reconcile. Another issue is related to societal militarization that seems to overwhelm reconciliatory tones that are often connected to the religious discourse. According to the collected social network data, militarism as a topic is particularly dominant in Antimaidan groups, with multiple albums devoted to missiles, tanks, famous Russian military leaders, photos of uniformed veterans, and even children in military costumes. It is primarily related to the discursive connection with the Great Patriotic War and the military victory associated with it, but also plays into the jingoistic daze of the Antimaidan echo-chamber.

Conclusion

Despite the effort from the Russian government's side, the religious narrative has not found a lot of resonance among the Russian population. Even within uber-patriotic digital enclaves, such as Antimaidan, the narrative of "protecting the right to be Orthodox" is hard to find and the schism between Ukrainian and Russian Orthodox churches is viewed entirely as a political game of power with no questions of faith involved. Instead, most social network users are engulfed with militaristic rhetoric and the great-power status fantasies. This phenomenon could have several explanations. First, within a conflict setting, it is important to maintain the otherness of the enemy and Orthodoxy would be a factor of similarity that prevents from hating the enemy. Hence, the emphasis on the "false European way" promoted by Patriarch Kirill and many online users. Second, societal militarization seems to overwhelm reconciliatory tones that are often connected to the religious discourse. According to the collected social network data, militarism as a topic is particularly dominant in the Ukraine-themed groups. Third, at the height of the Ukraine crisis in 2014–2015, the narrative of fascism promulgated both by the Russian government and mainstream media drowned out most attempts to frame the conflict in southeast Ukraine in different terms and has affected the current framing of the conflict as well. Therefore, in the context of substantial anti-Ukrainian sentiment, the Russian (digital) population does not buy the religious similarity narrative offered by the government and only concentrates on the differences. According to governmental officials and high-ranking Russian clerics, the truly faithful need to either join the Russian World or perish in a godless Europe.

Notes

1 Previously, the linguistic norm was "on" (*na*) that somewhat implied that Ukraine was an "edge" of a bigger entity (Russia). Nowadays, "in" (*v*) is a more prevalent norm, even among some Russian officials.
2 At the time of data collection in 2016.
3 Since the end of 2015, there has also been a number of images dedicated to Syria and Turkey, deriding "two-faced" Erdogan.

References

Batanova, O. (2008). Russkiy mir kak real'nost' i global'ny proekt [Russian world as reality and global project]. *Pravo i politika, 12*, 3017–3021.

Börzsei, L. K. (2013, February). Makes a meme instead: A concise history of Internet memes. *New Media Magazine, 7*. Retrieved from https://works.bepress.com/linda_borzsei/2/

Breton, H. O. (2010). Feeling persecuted? The definitive role of paranoid anxiety in the constitution of 'war on terror' television. In B. Brecher, M. Devenney, & A. Winter (Eds.), *Discourses and practices of terrorism: Interrogating terror* (pp. 93–94). doi:10.4324/9780203857342

Carrette, J. (2013). Foucault, religion, and pastoral power. In C. Falzon, T. O'Leary, & J. Sawicki (Eds.), *A companion to Foucault* (pp. 368–383). doi:10.1002/9781118324905.ch18

Cassely, J.-L. (2015, March). 'Salut, Je suis un occupant russe': Meilleure vidéo de propagande pro-russe? [Hi, I am a Russian occupier: The best video of Russian propaganda]. *Slate.fr*. Retrieved from www.slate.fr/story/98587/occupant-russe-video-propagande

Foucault, M. (2007). *Security, territory, population: Lectures at the Collège de France, 1977–1978* (G. Burchell, Trans.). London, UK: Palgrave Macmillan.

Gaufman, E. (2017). *Security threats and public perception: Digital Russia and the Ukraine crisis.* doi:10.1007/978-3-319-43201-4

Golovin, A. (2018, August 20). 'Ya gorzhus' svoey rabotoy v Gosdume': Bol'shoe interv'yu Svetlany Khorkinoy ['I am proud of my work in the State Duma': Svetlana Khorkina's big interview]. *Sports.ru*. Retrieved from www.sports.ru/tribuna/blogs/golovin/1954197.html

Grief de Sun. (2016, June 2). Ya russkiy okkupant [I am a Russian occupier]. [Video file]. Retrieved from www.youtube.com/watch?v=PshC4OE992k

Jansz, J., & Tanis, M. (2007). Appeal of playing online first person shooter games. *CyberPsychology & Behavior, 10*(1), 133–136. doi:10.1089/cpb.2006.9981

Karpov, V., Lisovskaya, E., & Barry, D. (2012). Ethnodoxy: How popular ideologies fuse religious and ethnic identities. *Journal for the Scientific Study of Religion, 51*(4), 638–655. doi:10.1111/j.1468–5906.2012.01678.x

Kazharski, A. (2019). *Regionalism as an identitary enterprise: Eurasian integration and the Russian world in Russia's international self.* Budapest, Hungary: CEU University Press.

Khomyakov, A. (2015/1864). *Tserkov odna.* [The church is one]. Moscow, Russia: Dar, 2005.

Kolsto, P. (2018). *Political construction sites: Nation building in Russia and the post-Soviet states.* doi:10.4324/9780429498220

Laruelle, M. (2009). *Inside and around the Kremlin's black box: The new nationalist think tanks in Russia* (Stockholm Paper). Stockholm, Sweden: Institute for Security and Development Policy. Retrieved from http://isdp.eu/content/uploads/images/stories/isdp-main-pdf/2009_laruelle_inside-and-around-the-kremlins-black-box.pdf

Laruelle, M. (2015). The 'Russian world': Russia's soft power and geopolitical imagination. *Center on Global Interests website*. Retrieved from http://globalinterests.org/wp-content/uploads/2015/05/FINAL-CGI_Russian-World_Marlene-Laruelle.pdf

Levada-Center. (2018). Monitoring ksenofobskikh nastroyeniy, iul' 2018 goda [Monitoring of xenophobic leanings, July of 2018]. Retrieved from www.levada.ru/2018/08/27/monitoring-ksenofobskih-nastroenij/

Makhortykh, M., & Lyebyedyev, E. (2015). #SaveDonbassPeople: Twitter, propaganda, and conflict in eastern Ukraine. *The Communication Review, 18*(4), 239–270. doi:10.1080/10714421.2015.1085776

Makhortykh, M., & Sydorova, M. (2017). Social media and visual framing of the conflict in eastern Ukraine. *Media, War & Conflict, 10*(3), 359–381. doi:10.1177/1750635217702539

Mälksoo, M. (2014, April 24). Estonia – The Ukrainian crisis as reflected in the Estonian media. *Cultures of History Forum*. Retrieved from www.cultures-of-history.uni-jena.de/focus/ukrainian-crisis/estonia-the-ukrainian-crisis-as-reflected-in-the-estonian-media/

Melnik, G. (2017, March 21). Zakhar Prilepin schitayet, chto v Donbasse reshayetsya sud'ba Yevropy [Zakhar Prilepin thinks that the fate of Europe is being decided in Donbass]. *RIA Novosti*. Retrieved from https://ria.ru/world/20170321/1490463594.html

Neumann, I. B. (2017). Russia's return as true Europe, 1991–2017. *Conflict and Society, 3*(1), 78–91.

Nikitchuk, I. (2014, June 17). Speech at the State Duma's session [Transcript]. Retrieved from http://transcript.duma.gov.ru/node/4103/

Oksala, J. (2013). From biopower to governmentality. In C. Falzon, T. O'Leary, & J. Sawicki (Eds.), *A companion to Foucault* (pp. 320–336). doi:10.1002/9781118324905.ch15

O'Loughlin, J., Toal, G., & Kolosov, V. (2016). Who identifies with the 'Russian World'? Geopolitical attitudes in southeastern Ukraine, Crimea, Abkhazia, South Ossetia, and Transnistria. *Eurasian Geography and Economics, 57*(6), 745–778. doi:10.1080/15387216.2017.1295275

Patriarkh Kirill verit v vozmozhnost' ob''yedineniya khristian raznykh tserkvey [Patriarch Kirill believes in the possibility of uniting Christians of different denominations]. (2007, May 21). *RIA Novosti*. Retrieved from https://ria.ru/20170521/1494757232.html

Paulsen, M. (2013). #Holodomor: Twitter and public discourse in Ukraine. In E. Rutten, J. Fedor, & V. Zvereva (Eds.), *Memory, conflict and new media* (pp. 102–118). doi:10.4324/9780203083635

Power, M. (2007). Digitized virtuosity: Video war games and post-9/11 cyber-deterrence. *Security Dialogue, 38*(2), 271–288.

Press Service of the Patriarch of Moscow and all Rus'. (2010a, September 1). Predstoyatel' Russkoy tserkvi prizval ukreplyat' kazach'yu solidarnost' na vsem prostranstve Svyatoy Rusi' [The head of Russian Church called for strengthening Cossack solidarity around Holy Russia]. Retrieved from www.patriarchia.ru/db/text/1265739

Press Service of the Patriarch of Moscow and all Rus'. (2010b, September 1). Svyateyshiy Patriarkh Kirill: Moldova – neot''yemlemaya chast' Svyatoy Rusi [His Holiness Patriarch Kirill: Moldova is an inalienable part of Holy Russia]. Retrieved from www.patriarchia.ru/db/text/1265739.html

Putin, V. (2017, December 14). Annual press conference of Vladimir Putin [Transcript]. Retrieved from http://kremlin.ru/events/president/news/56378

Sakwa, R. (2012). Conspiracy narratives as a mode of engagement in international politics: The case of the 2008 Russo-Georgian war. *The Russian Review, 71*(4), 581–609. doi:10.1111/j.1467–9434.2012.00670.x

Tenenboim-Weinblatt, K., Hanitzsch, T., & Nagar, R. (2016). Beyond peace journalism: Reclassifying conflict narratives in the Israeli news media. *Journal of Peace Research, 53*(2), 151–165. doi:10.1177/00223433156090

Toal, G. (2017). *Near abroad: Putin, the West, and the contest over Ukraine and the Caucasus.* New York, NY: Oxford University Press.

Tsygankov, A. (2009). *Russophobia: Anti-Russian lobby and American foreign policy.* doi:10.1057/9780230620957

Von Eggert, K. (2018). Kommentariy: Nezrimyy boy Patriarkha Kirilla s Petrom Poroshenko [Commentary: Invisible battle between Patriarch Kirill and Petro Poroshenko]. *Deutsche Welle*. Retrieved from www.dw.com/ru/комментарий-незримый-бой-патриарха-кирилла-с-петром-порошенко/a-45296550?maca=rus-facebook-dw

Ware, K. (2011). Sobornost and eucharistic ecclesiology: Aleksei Khomiakov and his successors. *International Journal for the Study of the Christian Church, 11*(2–3), 216–235. doi:10.1080/1474225x.2011.603975

5 Alternative spiritualities in Russia during the conflict in Ukraine

Stanislav Panin

Introduction

The Ukrainian revolution of 2013–2014 influenced life not only in Ukraine, but also in Russia on many levels and highlighted traumas in Russian society that were hidden for two decades after the collapse of the Soviet Union. The actions of the Russian government during this period, although they might seem strange to an external observer, reflected ideological developments that took place during the last two decades and in turn facilitated consolidation of elements of conservative ideology in Russia. These new developments influenced virtually all areas of life.

In this chapter, I will focus on Russian religious minorities during the conflict in Ukraine, particularly, the loosely institutionalized minority communities that exist as networks of individuals who profess different beliefs, including elements of Paganism, Eastern religions, and New Age, to show how conservative Russian political thinkers and the Russian Orthodox Church (ROC) portray the role of religious minorities, and how the actual diversity of responses from minority communities does not fit into this simplistic depiction.

I begin my analysis by discussing a set of ideological assumptions pivotal for contemporary Russian politics that constitute a widespread, almost official conservative ideology with a concomitant view on religion. Its two main sources are elements of Soviet ideology and ideas of the American anti-cult movement of the 1970s and 1980s that Russian Orthodox commentators adopted and developed during the religious revival of the 1990s. A combination of these elements has led to the construction a new ideology closely connected with the ROC.

An important part of this new ideology, and a key to its success, is its effectiveness in the formation of a national identity and an image of the enemy. According to Alicja Curanović (2012), after the break-up of the USSR "the Russian Federation stood before a double challenge: defining its identity and formulating its own vision of the new order," and religion played a pivotal role in developing answers for both questions (p. 106). An image of an ideal Russian, in the eyes of conservative thinkers, is often inseparable from Russian Orthodox Christianity and other "traditional" religious identities as opposed to enemies who, among other characteristics, are identified as connected to "occultism," "magic," "cults," and "sects." In media publications and ideological statements concerning the situation in Ukraine the term "sect," which has a negative connotation in Russian, often applies to the Ukrainian Greek Catholic Church and the Ukrainian Orthodox Church of the Kyiv Patriarchate, as well as the recently-formed Orthodox Church of Ukraine that, from the view of the Russian Orthodox commentators, splintered from the one and only canonical Orthodox Church on Ukrainian territory, i.e. the Ukrainian Orthodox Church of the Moscow Patriarchate.

The reality, however, is more complicated. The views of Russian religious minorities and those with more idiosyncratic religious beliefs concerning the situation in Ukraine differ significantly. While some of them are sympathetic to the Ukrainian Revolution of Dignity, others have elaborated ambiguous attitudes towards the current political situation that might be equally critical of both the Ukrainian and Russian governments and their policies. Contrary to the one-dimensional image presented in the media and ideological publications, there is no consistency among Russian religious minorities with regard to the conflict in Ukraine. A plethora of factors, including a group's origins and previous contacts with Russian and Ukrainian authorities, shape specific doctrinal positions.

Despite the disparity, these political positions are not random. In fact, their motivation is similar, even though it might lead to opposite conclusions. To understand it, we should focus not on a specific position concerning the Russian government and the situation in Ukraine, but rather on their choice of a subversive position that can play out in different ways in the discussion of particular questions. This subversive attitude is an important characteristic of emerging religions and, in a wider sense, of mystically-oriented movements that do not necessarily assume a religious form and might exist as "spiritual but not religious" or "esoteric" groups (Panin, 2019, pp. 69–71). Such a community may support any political force that they see as a source of social transformation that goes against the current established order. Thus, if they perceive the erring social order as dominated by Western culture and values, they might support policies that counteract it; if, however, they perceive the status quo as an authoritarian Russian political regime, they will, on the contrary, support liberalization and Westernization and oppose current Russian policies.

Such subversive positions make these communities foes of ideological projects that act to establish a clear social order and hierarchy. As a result, they are seen as dangerous regardless of their political views. In contemporary Russia, that means that even those groups and individuals who, during the conflict in Ukraine, choose to support actions of Russian government, can still be perceived as dangerous delinquents because they act outside of established social hierarchies.

Orthodox patriots and satanic extremists

A recent case that is illustrative in understanding of how issues of religious minorities and political censorship coexist in contemporary Russia is that of Kristina Snopp, a journalist from the southern Russian city of Tuapse. In August 2018, the Russian human rights activist group OVD-Info published her story of how she, together with her husband, fled from Russia and asked for political asylum in the neighboring country of Georgia.

The story behind this decision began in 2014 when a representative of the Russian security agency, FSB, contacted Snopp and invited her to an informal interview. As she recalls it, the interview continued more than two hours, during which the FSB agent asked her about her political and religious sympathies. Snopp later recalled their dialog, saying:

> I am a very curious person; I am interested in world religions and at the moment have communicated with people of many confessions – Hinduists (Yogis), Muslims, Protestants, and Pagans from our region. FSB agent Denis was very interested in information about people who follow religions other than Orthodox Christianity. He proposed that I collaborate with him in the field of "sects." I refused.
>
> (Rusova, 2018)

Snopp's own religious affiliation is unclear. In her interview to OVD-Info, she described herself as a spiritually curious person who does not belong to any institutionalized religious community – a position sometimes referenced as spiritual but not religious in scholarly publications. Her FSB interlocutor, on the contrary, had a clear picture of how religious life in Russia should look. According to Snopp, "he said that people in Russia should be believers, preferably Orthodox Christians, because it is the 'state religion as well as the true religion'" (Rusova, 2018).

An idea of Russia as an Orthodox Christian state – although it directly violates the Russian Constitution that defines it as secular – is not new inside the FSB. The agency's officials have made statements about this on many occasions. For instance, in 2012, Victor Ostroukhov, head of the FSB Academy, stated during the ceremony dedicated to the beginning of construction of an Orthodox church located near the building of the academy that "in all times in Rus' the Church and the army were united. The academy's employees, together with all citizens, are interested in the future of their country and are concerned about attacks on the Christian lifestyle that happen more and more often. . . . Together we can defend ourselves from contemporary dangers and keep Russia great and indivisible" (Sotrudniki FSB, 2012). The church, in its turn, has taken such calls for unity seriously. Four years later, when the church building was completed and consecrated, Patriarch Kirill of Moscow personally awarded Ostroukhov with a church-issued award of the Order of Saint Seraphim of Sarov for help during the church's construction (Patriarkh Kirill osvyatil, 2016).

Illustrative in these regards is an animated film *Children versus Magicians* (Fond Sergiya Radonezhskogo, 2016) created in 2016 by the Venerable Sergiy Radonezhskiy Foundation and financially supported by the Ministry of Culture of the Russian Federation. The antagonists in the film are magicians and wizards from the "Academy of Occult Sciences," located in Scotland. Together with NATO armed forces, they prepare an intervention into Russia, and, as we learn in the course of the movie, were previously responsible for the conflict in Kosovo, also aimed against an Orthodox Christian nation (Serbians). The only thing that prevents magical intervention in Russia is the so-called "Russian defense" that forms when a person holds a strong Orthodox faith, develops patriotism, and follows a traditional lifestyle. The protagonists that oppose the evil magicians are Russian military cadets directed by an FSB general, who is described as a head of an FSB department created to investigate and counteract "methods of totalitarian sects and occult groups threating Russia's national security."

The animated film is based on a book of the same title published in 2004 by Nikos Zervas – a pseudonym of an unknown author or a group of authors, praised by a conservative wing of the ROC (see, e.g., Shargunov, n.d.). From the point of view of an analysis of a construction of Russian ideology, it is worth summarizing the attributes of good and bad characters as presented in the movie in form of a table.

These characteristics neatly summarize a general sentiment of a new "Russian" identity as that of conservative Orthodox Christians living and dying for their motherland without questions, doubts, or reward. Patriotism and Orthodox spirituality as pivotal tenets of the new Russian ideology are actively promoted from the highest positions of the Russian political hierarchy. In literature that tries to describe contemporary Russian ideology, authors tend to construct a notion of patriotism as closely connected to "a Christian understanding of the meaning of life" (Tovchenko & Matyunin, 2016, p. 26) as opposed to the "destructive spirituality" that develops because of the introduction of "values foreign to Russian society" (Lonskiy, 2016, p. 74).

To return to the case of Kristina Snopp, the close interconnection between her spiritual views (unaffiliated with any mainstream religion) and her supposed

Table 5.1 Qualities of the protagonist and antagonist characters in the movie *Children versus Magicians*

	Protagonists	Antagonists
Spirituality	Orthodox Christians	Magicians and wizards; also "totalitarian sects"
Nationality	Russian, Serbian, Greek	"Western"; Albanians in Kosovo
Civic values	Patriotic	Betray their countries (particularly Russia in favor of the West) to perform magic
Institutional affiliation	Russian Military; FSB; Orthodox Churches	NATO; "Academy of occult sciences"
Sexuality	Heterosexual Family values	LGBTQ+ Sexual freedom

lack of patriotism played a significant role in her story as well, specifically her views on the situation in Ukraine and the events in Crimea. Note that the FSB agent contacted Kristina in 2014 – the year of the Ukrainian revolution and the annexation of the Crimean Peninsula by Russia – and that it was not a coincidence. Being a journalist in a small local newspaper, Kristina could not share her concerns on the newspaper's pages because editorial policy prohibited it. However, she used online resources to share her political opinions. She said, "I was not indifferent, because I thought that Russia's actions concerning Ukraine were foul and unjust. . . . I published messages on my page in VKontakte social network, where I compared Putin with Hitler" (Rusova, 2018).

The combination of her political position and interest in alternative forms of spirituality proved to be a dangerous mix. After a visit of the same FSB agent to an office of a newspaper where Kristina worked, she was fired from her job and labeled as an extremist due to her allegedly anti-Russian stance. Later on, she moved to the city of Krasnodar in an attempt to start her life from scratch, but in early 2018, a group of police officers visited her husband's work and invited him and Kristina for a talk at a police station. During the talk, police officials showed Kristina an entire folder with documents related to her activities, which indicated that everything that she did on the Internet was subject to police scrutiny. That included photos that she published online, as well as other graphical and textual content, including a photo of Kristina with a ceramic skull taken at a cemetery, which the police considered an indication of Kristina's membership in a satanic cult (Rusova, 2018). After these conversations with the FSB and police officials, Kristina and her husband realized that they could face criminal charges of extremism and decided to leave the country, seeking asylum in Georgia.

Although this story is a salient one, its general outline is by no means unique. According to the head of the Supreme Court of the Russian Federation, Vyacheslav Lebedev, approximately five hundred extremism cases based on publications and social networks posts are initiated each year in Russia (Lebedev otmetil, 2018). The federal public prosecutor's office reported that the number of annual cases alleging extremism doubled between 2011 and 2017 following the implementation of legal changes that dramatically expanded the concept of extremism (V Genprokurature otmetili, 2018).

Many recent cases of extremism have been related to both an anti-cult and an anti-Western agenda, and narratives related to the revolution in Ukraine have become an important element in construction of an image of the enemy. In order to understand how Russian conservative ideology depicts events in Ukraine, it is pivotal to look into the logic of the construction of polemics against "cults," which plays an important role in present-day Russia.

The origins of anti-cult ideology in Russia

In contemporary Russia there exists a set of closely interconnected narratives that describe a certain type of normative identity of a Russian Orthodox

Christian patriot, closely connected to imperialist expectations of the restoration of the Russian Empire. According to Alicja Curanović (2012), in present-day Russia, "one of the sources of revival of the idea of Russia-as-empire has its roots in the imperialistic connotation of Russian Orthodoxy and Russia's broader religious tradition. Emphasis is put in rebuilding the might of a state as an empire and a separate civilization" (p. 107).

This normative patriotism is an ideological driver behind many decisions made by Russian officials both in internal affairs and in international policies. Among other applications, this notion is routinely used in propaganda related to the self-proclaimed Donetsk and Luhansk People's Republics. A defense of the ROC as the only true Orthodox community is also a central factor in polemics regarding the contested status of different Orthodox institutions in Ukraine. Therefore, understanding of the roots of this ideological construction might facilitate discussion of issues of religion in Russia during the Ukrainian conflict.

Contemporary polemics against religious minorities inherit, in many regards, argumentation from the Soviet period. Back in the Soviet Union, religious minorities, especially those of foreign origin, were described in press, in governmental offices, and even in academic publications as alien and hostile to Soviet culture. Criticism of religious minorities developed as a part of polemics against religion in general that used Soviet Marxism to confront a bourgeois and capitalistic West. This enterprise was called "scientific atheism" and was considered a necessary part of Soviet ideology, in accordance with which religion was seen as a remnant of the earlier stages of social development that remained in capitalistic societies as, according to famous Marxist formula, an "opium of the people" needed to distract them from real social and economic problems. Thus, religion was described as an attribute of "the Other," either in a temporal or in a spatial sense. In other words, either it was a relic of the past, or it was an instrument of the hostile West. Western religious communities that tried to proselyte in the Soviet Union were therefore considered agents of foreign influence or even foreign spies.

Despite the general critical approach of Soviet authorities to religion, the level of oppression was not equal for all religious groups in the Soviet Union and the focus of governmental repressions shifted over the course of Soviet history, specifically after World War II. After WWII the targets of criticism shifted to reflect the fact that the image of the enemy itself changed at this time. While in the 1920s, it was the Russian Empire and its conservative sympathizers, in the period of the Cold War, the West took its place. Thus, religious minorities of Western origin became more dangerous from the point of view of policy makers than local religions, including Russian Orthodox Christianity, that were now perceived as harmless vestiges of Russian pre-Communist history.

The Soviet state therefore elaborated different approaches to different religions. Local religions that collaborated with the government and accepted governmental control were considered undesirable, but admissible. During the 1940s, the Soviet government facilitated the establishment of several offices to manage major religious communities, such as the regional Muslim Spiritual Directorates for Sunni and Shi'a Muslims and the Buddhist Spiritual Directorate of the USSR. At the same time, the Council for Relationships with the ROC maintained the Soviet government's relationship with the Moscow Patriarchate between 1943 and 1965.

While the ROC was still publicly criticized, it enjoyed some liberty in the decades after WWII – local councils of the ROC took place in 1945 and 1971, and Moscow Patriarchs Alexy I and Pimen received prestigious governmental rewards such as the Order of the Red Banner of Labor. A 1985 edition of the *Atheist Handbook* summarized the position of the ROC within the Soviet society by maintaining that

> The vast majority of hierarchs and clergy of Russian Orthodox Church have accepted the new understanding of socio-political problems, have radically revised their previous ethical views and value orientation of believers, their attitudes towards to work, science, culture, civic duties. . . . In the middle of the 1920s the Russian Orthodox Church abandoned its earlier pro-monarchist orientation and became loyal to the social and political order, and later supported both the internal and foreign politics of the Soviet state.
>
> (Skazkin, 1985, pp. 145–146)

At the same time, religious minorities were usually targets of official criticism, together with different forms of spirituality unaffiliated with established institutional bodies – such as informal Soviet esoteric communities of the 1960s and 1970s. Groups that tried to live more or less independently from governmental control (e.g., the True Orthodox Church and communities of Old Believers) as well as groups and movements of foreign origin (e.g., the Jehovah's Witnesses and Zen Buddhism) were considered hostile to the Soviet regime and thus were under persistent attack from the authorities.

The expansion of Eastern religions and spiritual practices in the West, as well as manifold forms of the search for mystical experience that spread in the twentieth century were, according to Soviet authors, symptoms of the degradation of capitalistic societies and nothing other than a flight from reason. As a book, *Is Mysticism Revived?*, published in 1984 stated, the reasons for the popularity of "mysticism" and the emergence of the New Age movement in Western countries "are rooted in the irrational nature of social relations," which, according to the author, are typical for capitalistic, bourgeois societies, in contrast, of course, with the Socialistic reality of the Soviet Union (Gurevich, 1984, p. 294).

The situation began to change with the launch of Perestroika in the mid-1980s. The late 1980s and 1990s was a period of radical shifts in many aspects of Russian life, including attitudes towards religion. After the dissolution of the Soviet Union, anti-Western ideology became marginal and seemingly disappeared from the academic and media mainstream. Instead, attitudes towards Western countries became more and more positive throughout that period – at least, until the 2000s, when anti-Western narratives reemerged as a part of a new Russian political mainstream.

To understand this trajectory in Russian culture from liberalization to a new type of conservative ideology it might be fruitful to keep in mind that, among other Western imports, Russia adopted some elements of American Christian fundamentalism. Christian apologetics and anti-cultist polemics were transmitted in Russia during the 1990s in various ways. Particularly, as Shterin and Richardson (2000) pointed out, "some evangelical missionary groups from the United States were extremely active not only in getting across their own religious message, but also in disseminating warnings against newer and older New Religious Movements through tens of thousands of copies of literature or through many web sites" (p. 259). Conservative versions of Orthodox Christianity that appeared in Russia at the same period included texts of American Orthodox monk Seraphim Rose and ideas of Soviet émigré Alexander Dvorkin, who lived in the U.S. where he studied at Saint Vladimir's Orthodox Theological Seminary in Crestwood (New York) and later at Fordham University.

The influence of the American anti-cult movement is particularly evident in the biography of Alexander Dvorkin, who is one of the central ideologists of the pseudo-academic "sectology" (*sektovedenie*) movement in contemporary Russia, which represents a radical branch of Orthodox Christian apologetics disguised as an academic enterprise. Dvorkin lived in the U.S. between 1978 and 1991. This time was an apex of the anti-cult movement and "Satanic Panic," a collective fear of dangerous "Satanic cults" in North America. Development of anti-cult polemics during this period was a reaction to the atmosphere of the 1960s with its new spiritual culture that emphasized religious freedom and an individual quest for spirituality as opposed to participation in mainstream religious communities. According to Bromley and Shupe (1981), "it was during the early 1970s, precisely at the point that traditional churches were reaching their low point for church attendance, that the new religions grew most rapidly," and the biggest loss for mainstream churches was young adults who "were drifting away from them in disinterest and . . . were flocking to the 'false' new religions" (p. 71–72). These new developments in religious life provoked fear in mainstream religions and helped to shape the anti-cult movement that was very active throughout the 1970s and 1980s.

The American anti-cult movement definitely influenced Dvorkin's ideas. In one of his lectures, he maintains that "in Western countries, particularly, in America, in the beginning of the 1990s they actively fought against sects; back then, America was a leader among Western countries in a war against sects" (MPGU, 2016). However, by the mid-1990s, the anti-cult movement in the U.S. gradually declined due to failure to provide substantial evidence of the supposedly sinister activities of "cults."

In particular, in 1987 the American Psychological Association indicated that there is insufficient scientific proof for the mind control claims of anti-cult activists, which lead to rejection of mind-control claims in courtrooms. An attempt of mind-control theory advocate Margaret Singer to sue the American

Psychological Association for participation in a cult conspiracy failed in 1994 (Introvigne, 1998), thus putting to an end any serious legal efforts to shut down new religious movements as cults in the U.S. Similarly, Jenny Reichert and James T. Richardson (2012) pointed out, with regards to the case of claims about Satanic cult abuse, that "the concern and subsequent panic about Satanism have subsided substantially since the mid-1990s, as reflected in the decline of media attention and the number of legal cases involving allegations of Satanic practice" (p. 49). Indicative of this shift of attitude was a study conducted by the National Center on Child Abuse and Neglect performed in 1994 analyzing police investigations concerning claims of cult sexual abuse that

> included 6,910 psychiatrists, psychologists and clinical social workers, and 4,655 district attorneys, police departments and social service agencies. They reported 12,264 accusations of ritual abuse that they had investigated. The survey found that there was not a single case where there was clear corroborating evidence.
>
> (Goleman, 1994)

These new developments gradually shifted public opinion about new religious movements, leading to a crisis of the anti-cult movement in the U.S. The active expansion of U.S.-based anti-cult movements in Europe, specifically the Cult Awareness Network, coincided with their challenging domestic situation where "CAN's domestic internal movement economy was suffering from declining revenues and mounting costs of lawsuits directed against it" (Shupe, 2016, p. 138).

The anti-cult narrative as a part of Russian conservative ideology

While in North America the situation for the anti-cult movement was becoming more complicated, Russia was experiencing a religious revival. It included the fast growth of the Russian Orthodox Church as well as manifold new religious movements. After the collapse of the Soviet Union, Alexander Dvorkin decided to return to Russia and realized that anti-cult narratives were in high demand among a Russian Orthodox audience, because Orthodox Christians, both lay people and clergy, found themselves unprepared for real freedom of religion that meant an open and fair competition with other religions without governmental support – a situation completely new for the ROC. In this situation, the experience of the American anti-cult movement became a handy instrument in dealing with the new social context. As Maxim Gordus (2008) pointed out, "the Russian anti-cult movement made its first steps thanks to the support of Western anti-cult organizations. Therefore, during the last decade of the twentieth century both new religious movements and their traditional foe – the anti-cult movement – were exported to Russia" (p. 3).

Religious studies scholar Sergey Ivanenko recalls his meeting with Dvorkin in 1993 in Moscow:

> Dvorkin did not plan to study religious currents and sects that were new to Russia. He thought that as an Orthodox person, an employee of Moscow Patriarchate, he could not talk to "heretics and sectarians." He was proud of his knowledge and was adamant that he knew more about sects than anybody else did. I asked Dvorkin, "How do you get information about new religious movements in Russia?" He answered, "Everything that I need to know has already been published in the West by anti-cultist groups."
>
> (Ivanenko, 2012, p. 12)

In Russia anti-cult ideas successfully merged with elements of anti-Western narratives and Soviet criticism of religion, now very selective in their new context, so arguments that once targeted all religions now aimed at only those that their Orthodox critics considered not traditional for Russia and called "sects" or "cults."

During Russian politics' turn to the right in the 2000s, these ideas became a part of the new mainstream, supporting the rebooted anti-Western agenda in the media, which became especially visible after the 2013–2014 Ukrainian revolution. Anti-cult ideologists associated the Euromaidan with activities of "sects" that, in their turn, were considered agents of foreign, particularly American, influence aiming to destabilize the situation in different countries and to destroy their "traditional values." Alexander Dvorkin, for example, connected the contemporary threat of "sects" as agents of American influence with the International Religious Freedom Act of 1998 that, according to him, permitted the use of religious minorities as "an instrument of international political pressure, an instrument of national division, and an important instrument of influence," particularly by means of organizing "orange and other colored revolutions" (MPGU, 2016). That, of course, includes 2013–2014 Revolution of Dignity in Ukraine.

This idea, promoted by Orthodox Christian speakers, spread in Russian media and political rhetoric about the situation in Ukraine. The usual suspects have included Pagan groups, the Church of Scientology, Protestant groups such as Embassy of the Blessed Kingdom of God for All Nations, the Ukrainian Greek Catholic Church, and the Ukrainian Orthodox Church of the Kyiv Patriarchate, now extended to the newly formed Orthodox Church of Ukraine. Statements on these groups and their activists are often issued from Orthodox clergy and Russian media outlets. For instance, an archpriest of the ROC, Oleg Trofimov, claimed in a 2018 interview that the Kyiv Patriarchate "is a sect and is not a church" (News-Front, 2018). An article in the newspaper *Izvestia* describes the situation in the following manner: "While the canonical Orthodox Christian Church tries to defend itself from heretics and the Patriarchate of Constantinople, influential Ukrainians one by one join non-traditional Christianity, sects, and even paganism" (Podgorny, 2018). Similarly, the newspaper

Vzglyad depicted religious minorities as the archenemy during the revolution in Ukraine: "Almost all non-traditional religious movements, together with Greek Catholics, have participated in the events of the revolutionary Maidan at least at the level of promotion. Representatives of these cults are also helping Ukrainian military and nationalist armed forces in Eastern Ukraine" (Chausov, 2015). This narrative remains persistent in publications about Ukraine and appears consistently during the whole period of the conflict.

The discussion of "sects" in the Ukrainian revolution usually appears as a part of a larger ideological narrative. In 2017, the GTRK Stavropol'ye media company, a branch of the governmental VGTRK media agency, launched a short film dedicated to exposure of "sects." The main expert in the film was Russian Orthodox priest and "sectologist" Antoniy Skrynnikov. He told the audience about a number of supposedly sinister groups including the Jehovah's Witnesses, the Union of Co-creators of the Holy Rus' (*Sojuz sotvorcov Svyatoy Rusi*), Alexey Ledyaev's New Generation Church, and Falun Gong. Skrynnikov underscored in his comments that Protestant denominations and Falun Gong are backed by the U.S. and act as agents of American influence in Russia and China; to support this claim, the film stressed the active participation of Ledyaev's church in the Ukrainian revolution. "Sects," indicated as extremist communities, were then contrasted with "traditional" religions of Russia, specifically the ROC and official Islam (GTRK Stavropol'ye, 2017).

To sum up, the formula of contemporary Russian anti-cult ideology is a merger of Orthodox Christian fundamentalism, the "anti-satanic" narratives of American Christian fundamentalists of the 1980s, and elements of "scientific atheism," which are now applied selectively against "wrong" religions (described as "sects" and "cults" and therefore not real religions). This ideology allowed for construction of a simplistic picture of the world in which Russia is an Orthodox Christian country that develops around a set of "traditional values" promoted, even monopolized, by the ROC and backed by an exclusive club of "traditional religions." Traditionalist and religious Russia is opposed to the non-spiritual, fallen West that tries to undermine Russia in different ways, including through religious "sects" and "cults" promoted to destroy traditional Russian culture and threaten Russia's security.

Subversive voices

This simplistic picture constructed by Russian conservative ideologists can hardly survive empirical verification. Positions with regard to the situation in Ukraine vary significantly in different spiritual communities.

An interesting case, for example, is Marina Tsvigun, also known by her religious names Victoria Preobrazhenskaya and Maria Devi Khristos, a Ukrainian émigré to Russia who created a movement called "JUSMALOS" (an abbreviation for JUpiter, Saturn, MArs, Luna (the moon), Orion, Sirius) in the early 1990s. Tsvigun was born in then-Soviet Donetsk and was a journalist by training. On April 11, 1990, she had a religious experience that led her to believe that she was the Mother of the World, Maria Devi Khristos (Preobrazhenskaya, 2014b, p. 12). She became a spiritual leader prophesizing about the coming end of the world as we know it (referenced as the Apocalypse, the Quantum Leap, or simply the Transformation), and gathered a group of followers around herself. In 1993, they took over Saint Sophia's Cathedral in Kyiv to perform a prayer there (Ukrainian officials later claimed that the group planned to commit a mass suicide in the cathedral, but Tsvigun rejected this accusation). This action resulted in the arrest of Tsvigun, followed by a prison sentence. After release from prison, Tsvigun moved to Russia, where she returned to being a painter, author, and religious leader (Preobrazhenskaya, 2014b).

Not surprisingly, Tsvigun demonstrates little sympathy for the Ukrainian political hierarchy. She describes the 2013–2014 revolution and the following conflict in Ukraine as a result of a rejection of her teaching and what she perceived as persecution of her and her followers by the Ukrainian government. In the late-2014 issue of her journal, Tsvigun wrote that "this year was a year of Retaliation, a year of the beginning of the war. Satan started it, because Old-Kyi Slavs (*Slavyane DrevneKiya*) did not accept Sophia the Wisdom. . . . Now is the time of the cosmic end: everybody will be judged in accordance with their deeds. After that – the entrance of the Beast. And the Final Battle – for the Rus'!" (Preobrazhenskaya, 2014a, p. 2). This narrative develops in Tsvigun's oeuvre as a part of her prophecies about Armageddon, which is interpreted by Tsvigun as a place associated with the river Don and the city of Donetsk (Preobrazhenskaya, 2014b, p. 673). In accordance with the prophecies, we are now witnessing the final battle between the forces of Light, led by Tsvigun, and the forces of Darkness that began their final attack from the territory of the United States and the European Union, which she references collectively as "the monster of Darkness" (Preobrazhenskaya, 2014b, p. 670). Thus, the Ukrainian government established after the Euromaidan appears in Tsvigun's works as related to dark forces of "reptilians," whereas separatist groups in the Donetsk and Luhansk regions are described as opposition to the darkness (Preobrazhenskaya, 2014c).

Tsvigun's ideas, therefore, share a lot of elements with official Russian propaganda – more precisely, they develop from similar popular beliefs that formed during the Soviet era, such as a narrative about the evil West that wants to corrupt Slavic lands that are depicted as the promised land. Thus, Tsvigun equates Zion with Kyiv (Preobrazhenskaya, 2014b, p. 670), while the word Russia (*Rossiya*) she interprets as "The Shine of Ra" (Preobrazhenskaya, 2016, p. 7). However, that does not mean that she thoroughly supports the Russian government. Although Tsvigun and her followers seem to be more sympathetic to Vladimir Putin compared to other political leaders, they maintain that Russia has committed the same sin as Ukraine – libel against Tsvigun – and now reaps the "karmic" consequences of this decision (Preobrazhenskaya, 2014c, p. 674). Furthermore, Tsvigun has little good to say about the ROC. She describes introduction of Christianity to the ancient Rus' as a violent invasion that lead to manifold deaths and destructions (Preopbrazhenskaya, 2018, p. 129). Tsvigun, therefore, separates her idealized image of Rus' as a sacred place and the center of the universe from current political entities and their governments which effectively serve Seth, or Satan, either because of their malevolence or simply because they decided to ignore the truth.

Construction of unconventional belief systems is a convoluted process that is influenced by multiple factors, including personal spiritual experiences, interactions with different political structures, and the cultural and intellectual background of religious leaders. As we can see in the case of Tsvigun, it can share some components of Russian conservative ideology and at the same time reject others. Therefore, the simple fact of sharing of certain political statements does not guarantee a concordance between a religious community and governmental officials. An illustration of that is a story of a self-proclaimed "magister of Voodoo magic" from Yekaterinburg, Anton Simakov, who in 2016 was sentenced to a mandatory treatment in a mental facility after he publicly performed a ritual aimed against the Ukrainian government where he used several Orthodox religious symbols (Chelishcheva, 2016). That was considered a desecration of objects sacred for Orthodox Christians through their use in a magical ritual and became the basis for accusations of "offence of religious feelings" that culminated in a court trial that sentenced Simakov to the treatment. The fact that his symbolic critique of Ukrainian government was in line with official Russian ideology did not help to avoid sanctions provoked by improper utilization of ideological symbols – symbols of the ROC, which plays a pivotal role in Russian ideological narratives and aims at a monopoly in the field of ideological construction in present-day Russia.

The case, therefore, sheds light on some important aspects of the construction of modern Russian ideology. Not only is a person considered obliged to follow a certain set of ideological statements, he or she also should follow them as sanctioned by a proper authority. Despite particular ideological stances, a person who acts outside the hierarchical structures inherently crosses the line and therefore constitutes a possible threat. Political preferences definitely play an important role in determining how severe measures of oppression and control imposed on a specific person or movement would be. However, it is also true that even movements that are neutral or sympathetic to the government, maintain their Russian identity, and develop narratives about the special historical mission of Russia oftentimes face harassment from state-funded federal media and other types of discrimination. The Russian authorities have been developing a variety of legal and ideological instruments to ensure the stability of this hierarchy and avoid the development of independent sources of ideological legitimization. An important role in this picture is reserved for the anti-cult movement which acts as a component of a new ideological discipline – Orthodox Christian theology – largely aimed at becoming a factory for new ideological narratives.

The observation of different reflections on the conflict in Ukraine, as well as relationships between alternative spirituality and mainstream religious and ideological institutions reveals an opposition more complicated than a simple ideological cliché of nice patriots from FSB and the Orthodox Church united in the fight against evil wizards and sectarians backed by NATO. Apparently, alternative spirituality is quite pluralistic and develops different attitudes towards the same political events. If we want to find some common denominator among these different communities, we need to look for some underlying patterns beyond their views on particular political issues.

Do the cases described above have something in common? Kristina Snopp is a punk-rock musician, anarchist, interested in different religious beliefs, critical about Putin, and supportive of the Ukrainian revolution. Marina Tsvigun was born in Ukraine where she acted as a subversive religious leader in the early 1990s. She was condemned to prison, immigrated to Russia, and now is more sympathetic to separatist groups in the eastern Ukraine than to official Ukrainian institutions – or Russian for that matter. Finally, Anton Simakov, who claims to be a Voodoo priest, seems to be critical about Petro Poroshenko – enough, at least, to hang his figure during one of his rituals – even though his performances are mostly of a provocative nature and do not necessarily imply a coherent political position.

Despite the obvious differences, all of their views share one characteristic – their subversive nature, meaning that they oppose on different grounds established social rules of conduct and legitimizing institutions. All of them profess that some deep social changes will come – although they do not agree which actors will bring these changes. For example, for some, Putin and separatist groups in eastern Ukraine symbolize fundamentalism and an absence of progress, while for others they are symbols of opposition to the world establishment and an opportunity to challenge the status quo. This difference in interpretations accounts for the plurality of positions.

What it reveals for us about the nature of these groups is that they are inherently dynamic and, so to say, chaotic. Unlike established religious communities and political ideologies that bring an element of stability and conservatism into society, alternative spirituality acts as an agent of change and perhaps – in the long run – social progress. That reflects its distinctive social functions, equally important for society, but different from the social functions of mainstream religious communities.

Conclusion

The Russian-Ukrainian conflict has highlighted the existence of several well-pronounced poles in Russian spiritual life. One pole tends to consist of conservative speakers who would emphasize "traditional values," Orthodox Christian identity (or identify themselves with other "traditional religions"), and patriotism as conformity to and affinity with the government and the state. Established religious institutions, particularly the ROC, play a pivotal role in a construction of this conservative ideology and attempt in certain respects to monopolize its production.

At the other end of spiritual life, however, there exists a set of movements that are significantly less institutionalized and attract people with multiple spiritual interests. Sometimes these people can identify with a particular religion – perhaps Paganism, some Eastern religions, or unchurched Christianity – but oftentimes they will avoid any religious affiliations. These groups by their very nature tend to oppose established political and religious hierarchies and therefore in the Russian context they are usually critical of the Russian government and the ROC as an ideological institution. They are by their very nature subversive – which reflects a function of these communities as agents of social change rather than social continuity.

It comes as no surprise that conservative political speakers in government, media, and academia are hostile to this kind of spirituality. Conservative literature depicts it as a threat and tends to form conspiracy theories in which religious minorities are represented as Western agents intended to undermine Russia's traditional lifestyle (whatever a particular speaker understands as such). This is particularly so in the case of the Russian-Ukrainian conflict, where minority spiritual communities are described as a factor that ignited the revolution; as far as the revolution in itself is perceived as threatening, that seems to verify the image of religious minorities as utterly hostile to Russia.

The reality, however, is more complicated. Voices from Russian religious minorities addressing the situation in Ukraine demonstrate different interpretations of the Ukrainian revolution and the events following it. Multiple factors, including the religious beliefs of these communities, their history of relationships with the Russian and Ukrainian governments, and the political views of their leaders may play a role in the construction of narratives about the annexation of Crimea and the war in Ukraine. The common denominator of these narratives is their subversive nature that opposes established religious and political structures. The spiritual communities in question will oftentimes be equally inimical to the governments in both Ukraine and in Russia, and demonstrate critical positions to any sort of oppressive political powers. This transcends a simple dichotomy of either pro-Russian or pro-Ukrainian and instead highlights another framework of possible choices based on which government is perceived in a particular moment as more progressive, open to change, and providing opportunities of subversion of the established social order. This role might be just as well assigned to revolutionaries from the Euromaidan as to Vladimir Putin opposing capitalist world establishment – depending on whom you ask.

These sympathies to subversive actors urging change seems to be the most definitive characteristic of the political sympathies of the type of spirituality in question. This leads to, among other things, some non-obvious conclusions. The most interesting one is that even religious figures who are seemingly on board with Russian policies would not necessarily gain the support of Russian officials. Whatever side they choose, unconventional spiritual communities and individuals remain subversive in their nature, which frightens those actors that prefer conservatism and predictability. Therefore, cases of unsanctioned patriotism might be perceived by governmental structures as just as challenging and dangerous as straightforward opposition, as long as they potentially create means of legitimization independent from state hierarchy. In cases where such voices become loud or strange, or demonstrate a behavior that is threatening to certain parts of the state ideology, they are silenced just as readily as any other opposition.

References

Bromley, D. G., & Shupe, A. D. (1981). *Strange gods: The great American cult scare*. Boston, MA: Beacon Press.

Chausov, A. (2015, February 3). Ukrainu zakhvatyvayut sekty [Sects seize Ukraine]. *Vzglyad*. Retrieved from https://vz.ru/society/2015/2/3/727485.html

Chelishcheva, V. (2016, September 6). Oskorblenie chuvstv verujushchih: Kogo v Rossii sudyat za obryady vudu i napadeniya na Buddu [Offending religious feelings: Who is taken to court for Voodoo rituals and attacks on Buddha in Russia]. *Meduza*. Retrieved from https://meduza.io/feature/2016/09/06/oskorblenie-chuvstv-veruyuschih

Curanović, A. (2012). *The religious factor in Russia's foreign policy*. doi:10.4324/9780203133279

Fond Sergiya Radonezhskogo. (2016, September, 6). Animatsionnyy film 'Deti protiv Volshebnikov' [Animated film 'Children versus Magicians']. Retrieved from www.youtube.com/watch?v=M0HEwEhpaZQ

Goleman, D. (1994, October 31). Proof lacking for ritual abuse by Satanists. *The New York Times*. Retrieved from www.nytimes.com/1994/10/31/us/proof-lacking-for-ritual-abuse-by-satanists.html

Gordus, M. (2008). *Novyye religioznyye dvizheniya: stereotipy i real'nost'* [New religious movements: Stereotypes and reality]. (Abstract of the dissertation for a degree of Candidate of Sciences, Southern Federal University, Rostov-on-Don, Russia). Retrieved from https://dlib.rsl.ru/viewer/01003171891#?page=1

GTRK Stavropol'ye. (2017, September 14). Kak sekty prevrashchayut lyudey v rabov [How sects make people their slaves]. Retrieved from www.youtube.com/watch?v=67c8yxLtV-o

Gurevich, P. S. (1984). *Vozrozhden li mistitsizm?* [Is mysticism revived?]. Moscow, USSR: Politizdat.

Introvigne, M. (1998). 'Liar, liar': Brainwashing, CESNUR and APA. *CESNUR*. Retrieved from www.cesnur.org/testi/gandow_eng.htm

Ivanenko, S. I. (2012). *Obyknovenniy antikul'tizm* [Banal anticultism]. Saint Petersburg: Drevo Zhizni.

Lebedev otmetil rost chisla ugolovnykh del iz-za repostov [Lebedev noted the growth of criminal cases based on reposts in the Internet]. (2018, September 25). *RIA Novosti*. Retrieved from https://ria.ru/20180925/1529258362.html

Lonskiy, Y. A. (2016). Patriotizm kak glavnaja sostavljayushchaya ideologii v bor'be s destruktivnoy dukhovnost'yu [Patriotism as a primary component in the fight against destructive spirituality]. *Gumanitarnyy Vestnik Voennoy Akademii Raketnykh Voysk Strategicheskogo Naznachenija, 4–2*(4), 74–75.

MPGU. (2016, May 16). Dvorkin A. L.: Total'nyye sekty i 'tsvetnyye revolyutsii' [A. Dvorkin: Totalitarian sects and colored revolutions]. Retrieved from www.youtube.com/watch?v=4iyX1hDx4mY

News-Front. (2018, October 11). Protoirey Oleg Trofimov, UPC KP ne yavlyaetsya tserkov'yu, eto sekta, ikh zayavlenie feyk [Archpriest Oleg Trofimov: The UOC KP is not a church, it is a sect, their claim is a fake]. Retrieved from www.youtube.com/watch?v=dmXsla_qqsI

Panin, S. (2019). *Filosofiya ezoterizma: Ezoterizm kak predmet istoricheskoy i filosofskoy refleksii* [Philosophy of esotericism: Esotericism as an object of historical and philosophical reflection]. Moscow: Novoe Literaturnoe Obozrenie.

Patriarh Kirill osvyatil khram pri Akademii FSB [Patriarch Kirill consecrated a church building for the FSB Academy]. (2016, April 10). *Interfax-religion*. Retrieved from www.interfax-religion.ru/?act=news&div=62538

Podgorny, N. (2018, October 26). Kakoy veroyu otmereno: Adepty netraditsionnykh religiy vo vlasti Ukrainy [In the way you judge, you will be judged: Adepts of non-traditional religions gain power in Ukraine]. *Izvestiya*. Retrieved from https://iz.ru/804260/

Preopbrazhenskaya, V. (2014a). Dorogie zemljane [Dear earthlings]. *Victoria RA*, *6*(26), 2.

Preobrazhenskaya, V. (2014b). *Zemnoy put' Materi Mira* [Mother of the world's path on the earth]. Retrieved from https://victoriara.com/files/pdf/ZPMM_2015.pdf

Preobrazhenskaya, V. (2014c, May 31). RAdnoj Donbass [My native Donbass]. Retrieved from https://victoriara.com/modules.php?name=Poetry&pa=showpage&pid=239

Preobrazhenskaya, V. (2016). Prorochestva Materi Mira o Rusi, metke 'Zverya', Preobrazhenii [Prophecies of the mother of the world about Rus, the sign of the 'beast', and the transformation]. Retrieved from https://victoriara.com/files/pdf/PrMM.pdf

Preopbrazhenskaya, V. (2018). Vremja otkryvat' tayny [Time to reveal secrets]. *Victoria RA*, *1*(36), 120–135.

Reichert, J., & Richardson, J. T. (2012). Decline of a moral panic: A social psychological and socio-legal examination of the current status of Satanism. *Nova Religio: The Journal of Alternative and Emergent Religions*, *16*(2), 47–63.

Rusova, S. (2018, August 22). Otkaz sotrudnichat' s FSB i kartinki s Putinym: istoriya pary, poprosivshey ubezhishcha v Gruzii [Rejecting working with the FSB and pictures with Putin: A history of a couple seeking asylum in Georgia]. *OVD-Info*. Retrieved from https://ovdinfo.org/articles/2018/08/22/otkaz-sotrudnichat-s-fsb-i-kartinki-s-putinym-istoriya-pary-poprosivshey

Shargunov, A. (n.d.). Ne zhdite nichego ot XXI veka [Expect nothing from the twenty-first century]. *Obshchestvenniy Komitet 'Za nravstvennoe vozrozhdeniye Otechestva'*. Retrieved from www.moral.ru/ASh_recenzia.html

Shterin, M. S., & Richardson, J. T. (2000). Effects of the Western anti-cult movement on development of laws concerning religion in post-Communist Russia. *Journal of Church and State*, *42*(2), 247–271. doi:10.1093/jcs/42.2.247

Shupe, A. (2016). The North American anti-cult movement. In J. R. Lewis & I. Tøllefsen (Eds.), *The Oxford handbook of new religious movements* (Vol. 2, pp. 117–142). doi:10.1093/oxfordhb/9780190466176.013.9

Skazkin, S. D. (Ed.). (1985). *Nastol'naya kniga ateista* [Atheist handbook]. Moscow, Russia: Izdatel'stvo Politicheskoy Literatury.

Sotrudniki FSB obespokoeny napadkami na RPTs [FSB agents are concerned about attacks on the Russian Orthodox Church]. (2012, July 31). *Grani.ru*. Retrieved from https://graniru.org/Society/Religion/m.199358.html

Tovchenko, R. B., & Matyunin, S. S. (2016). Patriotizm kak natsional'naya ideya i gosudarstvennaya ideologiya [Patriotism as a national idea and state ideology]. *Izvestiya Akademii upravleniya: Teorii, strategii, innovacii*, *1*(17), 24–27.

V Genprokurature otmetili snizhenie chisla del ob ekstremizme v internete vpervyye za vosem' let [Federal prosecutor's office emphasized that the number of trials about extremism decreased for the first time in eight years]. (2018, November 28). *TASS*. Retrieved from https://tass.ru/obschestvo/5850454

6 The United States International Religious Freedom Act, nonstate actors, and the Donbas crisis

Robert C. Blitt

One might reasonably assume that specific provisions for nonstate actors would enhance the executive's ability to confront violations of freedom of religion or belief committed by nonstate actors. However, an examination of the first sets of recommendations and designations of entities of particular concern put forward by the United States Commission on International Religious Freedom and the State Department indicates that International Religious Freedom Act's capacity to successfully respond to such violations is being hampered by both statute-based and implementation-related challenges. These challenges are equally evident in the context of the Donbas conflict, and in turn underscore serious questions regarding the relevancy and effectiveness of the U.S. International Religious Freedom Act provisions on nonstate actors.

Introduction

The ability to violate the right to freedom of religion or belief is not reserved to state actors. In 2016, U.S. Congress's increasing recognition that such violations can and often do occur at the hands of nonstate actors prompted the Wolf Act amendments (2016 Frank R. Wolf International Religious Freedom Act, Public Law No 114–281) to the 1998 International Religious Freedom Act (IRFA). Among other things, these amendments introduced a new mandate for reporting on violent nonstate actors responsible for religious freedom violations.[1] Central to this, the Wolf Act also established a new "Entity of Particular Concern" (EPC) designation for those nonstate actors committing "particularly severe" violations of religious freedom. While this statutory framework bore some superficial resemblance to IRFA's existing process for designating and sanctioning "Countries of Particular Concern," it differed in several significant ways. The first sets of EPC recommendations and designations, issued between 2017–2018 by the U.S. Commission on International Religious Freedom (USCIRF) and U.S. Department of State respectively, underscored these differences while evidencing further problems that may flow from ambiguities in the substance of IRFA's new provisions on nonstate actors.

The following chapter considers the effectiveness of IRFA's new nonstate actor provisions in the context of the Donbas conflict. As part of this discussion, the origins and current implementation of IRFA's provisions on nonstate actors will be examined and used to explore the factors that may have resulted in the self-proclaimed Donetsk People's Republic (DPR) and Luhansk People's Republic (LPR) avoiding scrutiny under the statute. The chapter concludes with several recommendations intended to help advance an implementation of IRFA's new policy tools that better reflects the statute's objective "to promote respect for religious freedom by all governments and peoples."

IRFA's new provisions on nonstate actors

Legislative efforts to direct IRFA's scrutiny to nonstate actors grew out of a sense that violent nonstate actors represented an expanding force responsible for exposing a significant percentage of the global population to severe restrictions on freedom of religion and belief (H.R. 1150, Frank R. Wolf International Religious Freedom Act of 2015 §§ 2, 407). However, the final amendments to IRFA brought about by the 2016 Wolf Act betray two fundamental shortcomings. First, Congressional negotiations resulted in a significant narrowing of IRFA's ability to monitor the full spectrum of potential nonstate actors violating religious freedom. The operative definition for a nonstate actor promulgated by the final Wolf Act clearly retreated from the broader and more encompassing language included in the bill as originally proposed in 2015. This more restrictive definition limited IRFA to engaging only those "nonsovereign" entities determined to be: (1) exercising significant political power and territorial control; (2) outside the control of a sovereign government; and (3) often employing violence in pursuit of their objectives (22 U.S.C.A. § 6402(11)).

On its face, this definition appeared to eliminate the possibility of IRFA examining nonstate actors that merely "tolerate" or finance violations of religious freedom. But more than this, it also established a standard premised on imprecise and vague terms such as "significant," "often," and "control," likely to further complicate the identification of potential nonstate actors violating religious freedom.

Second, while the final Wolf Act created an "Entity of Particular Concern" designation for nonstate actors, its design resembled IRFA's existing "Country of Particular Concern" (CPC) designation only superficially. Most notably, Congressional negotiations over the EPC framework resulted in rejecting obligatory presidential action following an EPC designation. Together with this, Congress dropped the possibility of including nonstate actors falling just short of the EPC standard from IRFA's new Special Watch List (22 U.S.C.A. § 6442(b)(1)(A)(iii)). Thus, in addition to narrowing the overall scope of nonstate actors eligible for scrutiny under IRFA, the Wolf Act amendments ensured that any IRFA-based action taken against nonstate actors would be contingent on an EPC designation, and then still subject to presidential discretion.

In addition to the definitional constraints and executive discretion attached to IRFA's new nonstate actors provisions, an apparent disconnect between USCIRF and the State Department has further hampered the effective implementation of these provisions. USCIRF's 2017 annual report – the first to apply IRFA's Wolf Act amendments – echoed the view from Congress that nonstate actors "are some of the most egregious violators of religious freedom in today's world" (United States Commission on International Religious Freedom [USCIRF], 2017, p. 4). The report proceeded to recommend three nonstate actors – ISIS, the Taliban, and al-Shabaab – be designated as EPCs.[2] Almost one year later, the State Department released its first official EPC designations, which adopted USCIRF's three EPC recommendations but surprisingly added five additional nonstate actors to the list: al-Nusra Front, al-Qa'ida in the Arabian Peninsula, al-Qa'ida, Boko Haram, and ISIS-Khorasan.

Several months after the State Department released its first set of EPC designations, USCIRF's 2018 annual report opted not to reaffirm the State Department's eight EPCs. Instead, USCIRF maintained its original 2017 position and again recommended ISIS, the Taliban, and al-Shabaab as EPCs. In late 2018, the State Department added the Houthis in Yemen (Ansar Allah) to its second set of EPC designations, expanding its original list from eight nonstate actors to nine.

Despite the designation of nine EPCs, to date, the administration has taken no IRFA-specific sanctions action against any of these nonstate actors. Nor have either the State Department or USCIRF seen fit to explicitly assess either the DPR or the LPR under IRFA's new provisions on nonstate actors.

IRFA's provisions on nonstate actors and the Donbas crisis

As noted above, the International Religious Freedom Act establishes a three-pronged test for determining which nonstate actors are liable for scrutiny under the statute. Before a nonstate actor can be considered, it must be found to: exercise significant political power and territorial control; often employ violence in pursuit of its objectives; and be outside the control of a sovereign government (22 U.S.C.A. § 6402(11)). In an effort to better understand the omission of the DPR and LPR from IRFA's scrutiny of nonstate actors, this section applies each of these elements to assess the distinctions and similarities that may exist between currently designated EPCs and the Donbas quasi-states.

Significant political power and territorial control

The Donetsk and Luhansk People's Republics appear to satisfy the first requirement of territorial control and political power. Although these entities lack international recognition, in May 2014, both successfully executed referendums on self-government "as the first step to the creation of a 'Novorossia'" (Office of the United Nations High Commissioner for Human Rights [OHCHR], 2014).[3] This political effort to secure local legitimacy, though conducted in contravention of Ukraine's constitution (OHCHR, 2014), was quickly followed by the successful obstruction of Ukraine's presidential election on territories under DPR and LPR control. In June 2014, the United Nations Office of the

High Commissioner for Human Rights (OHCHR) reported that "representatives of the [the DPR and LPR] and armed men" attacked, seized, or blocked access to district election commission offices and polling stations, "threatening staff and sometimes beating and/or abducting them, often taking away voters' lists, computers and official documents." This systematic interference resulted "in 10 of the 12 election districts in Luhansk region and 14 of the 22 election districts in Donetsk region" being excluded from voting in Ukraine's presidential election (OHCHR, 2014).[4]

Ukraine's abdication of effective control over these territories can be traced back to this point. According to the OHCHR, already by June 2014 "armed groups physically occup[ied] key public and administrative buildings in many cities and towns of the Donetsk and Luhansk regions, and . . . declared virtual 'independence.'" Coupled with this, Ukraine's central government lacked the necessary capacity "to protect residents from the ever increasing acts of violence" in these regions (OHCHR, 2014). Although for a short period it seemed Ukrainian military forces might retake these restive territories, a failed first attempt at a ceasefire and a follow-on second effort cemented a line of contact separating Ukrainian forces from DPR and LPR elements. Articles 9 and 10 of the "Package of Measures for the Implementation of the Minsk Agreements" (Minsk II), negotiated in February 2015, imposed a ceasefire and envisioned a resolution to the conflict by the end of 2015. Parties to the agreement "reaffirm[ed] their full respect for the sovereignty and territorial integrity of Ukraine" and envisioned "reinstatement of full control of the state border by the government of Ukraine throughout the conflict area," the "withdrawal of all foreign armed formations, military equipment, as well as mercenaries from the territory of Ukraine [and] disarmament of all illegal groups" (UN Security Council Resolution S/RES/2202, 2015).

Despite Minsk II's clear objectives, the war – and the cloud of intrigue surrounding it (Goncharenko & Johann, 2018; Neef, 2017) – continues to grind on, further entrenching the DPR and LPR's political power and territorial control. In November 2018, snap elections in the DPR and LPR[5] ostensibly triggered by DPR leader Alexander Zakharchenko's assassination, pushed Minsk II further out of reach and generated widespread condemnation in the West. U.S. Deputy Ambassador Jonathan Cohen condemned the elections as a "sham . . . staged by Russia" (Lederer, 2018).[6] The European Union similarly branded the elections "illegal and illegitimate": "they are in breach of international law, undermine the commitments taken under the Minsk agreements and violate Ukraine's sovereignty and law" (Ukraine rebel regions, 2018).

With the war entering its fifth year, The Economist observed "there is still no end in sight. Large swathes of the Donbas region remain under the control of separatists. A 500-km 'contact line,' bristling with landmines, cuts through it. . . . Talks aimed at resolving the conflict have ground to a halt" (An end to the war, 2018). Left with this status quo, the DPR and LPR both appear to satisfy the requirement of territorial control and political power established under IRFA.

This conclusion is reinforced by measuring the DPR and LPR territorial control and political power against that manifested by designated entities of particular concern such as ISIS-Khorasan and Boko Haram. Neither the State Department nor USCIRF have offered any explicit assessment of ISIS-Khorasan's territorial control. One reason for this may be the fact that ISIS-Khorasan does not maintain control of any significant amount of territory. According to one recent think tank report, ISIS-Khorasan "does not seem to have gained significant territory especially when compared with the Taliban.... Whilst [ISIS-Khorasan] may not seem significant in terms of the conventional measures of control over territory and manpower i.e. numbers of fighters – it is extremely significant in terms of the shifting patterns of violence and militancy" (Ashraf, 2017, pp. 2–3).

Boko Haram similarly appears to lack a meaningful degree of territorial control. Recent studies indicate that although the group's tactical shift has helped it "stay a threat to millions," the Nigerian military has limited Boko Haram's territorial control "to some small villages and pockets of countryside" (Campbell & Harwood, 2018). Other sources confirm this conclusion, observing that during 2015–2016, the Nigerian military successfully "dislodge[ed] the insurgents from areas where they had previously seized control. In response, Boko Haram made a tactical shift [and its] new strategic focus is on disruption rather than territorial control" (SB Morgan, 2017). In May 2018, Nigeria's Ambassador and Deputy Permanent Representative to the UN declared: "Today, Boko Haram insurgents no longer hold any territory in Nigeria" (Olanrewaju, 2018).

From the analysis above, the DPR and LPR readily satisfy IRFA's first requirement concerning significant political power and territorial control based on the statute's plain meaning, as well as its application to other nonstate actors already designated as EPCs.

Violence in pursuit of nonstate actor objectives

Turning to the use of violence in pursuit of a nonstate actor's objectives, here too enough evidence exists to reach a finding that the Donetsk and Luhansk People's Republics qualify for scrutiny under IRFA. According to a high-ranking UN official, the Donbas conflict at the end of 2018 still "remain[ed] an active threat to international peace and security." Over 10,000 people have been killed in fighting between Ukraine and the DPR and LPR, with a recent spike in cease-fire violations and casualties (Lederer, 2018). According to data compiled by Jane's Terrorism and Insurgency Centre in 2015 and 2016, the DPR and LPR ranked in the top ten of global groups most responsible for acts of terrorism, insurgency, and violence. During this period, the DPR's ranking climbed from third to second and the LPR's jumped from seventh to second (IHS Jane's Terrorism and Insurgency Centre, 2016, 2017).

Beyond the military confrontation against Ukrainian forces, the DPR and LPR regions experienced a marked "escalation of violence and violations of international law" with the onset of the conflict. In June 2014, the Office of the

United Nations High Commissioner for Human Rights reported that armed groups in Donetsk and Luhansk, "having gained access to deposits of weapons . . . increasingly started spreading violence." This violence manifested in "abductions of persons not involved in any fighting and related acts of arbitrary detentions, looting, and killings of persons not involved in any fighting and other activities in violation of international law," including targeting civilians for "degrading treatment [and] random shooting and provocations," as well as "intimidation and harassment, torture and killings" (OHCHR, 2014).

Though not all these manifestations of violence may be directly attributable to the relevant authorities, many clearly are.[7] According to Human Rights Watch, DPR and LPR authorities "continued to carry out arbitrary detentions and enforced disappearances . . . local security services operated without checks and balances [and the] overall absence of the rule of law in separatist-controlled areas leaves detainees extremely vulnerable to abuse" (Human Rights Watch, 2017). Similarly, Amnesty International has concluded that the "de facto state security ministries" of the DPR and LPR operate without any checks and balances, and "have arbitrarily detained civilians and in some cases tortured them" (Ukraine: Torture, 2016).

Data from the most recent Global Terrorism Index reinforces the DPR's and LPR's clear reliance on violence to achieve their objectives. According to the 2018 Global Terrorism Index, the DPR represented the second most active terror group in Russia and Eurasia and was "the deadliest terror group in the region in 2017" (Institute for Economics and Peace [IEP], 2017, p. 39). At the same time, despite the separatist conflict in Donbas continuing, the Global Terrorism Index concluded the LPR "has not been responsible for any terror-related deaths since 2015." This latter reality merits additional consideration. While the overt use of physical force associated with such killings may be less pronounced today, other manifestations of violence persist, including in the form of arbitrary and indefinite detentions and disappearances. Moreover, even while the frequency of such acts may be decreasing due to so many opponents of the DPR and LPR fleeing the enclaves, the harm that flows from this violence still lingers. According to one testimony collected by Human Rights Watch, "everyone who stays knows – if you breathe even a word, you're off to the basement and they'll beat you and torture you and no one can save you" (Lokshina, 2016).

The World Health Organization's (WHO) definition of violence provides a helpful framework for better identifying and exposing the full scope of violent practices. According to the WHO, violence is "the intentional use of physical force or power, threatened or actual, against oneself, another person, or against a group or community, that either results in or has a high likelihood of resulting in injury, death, psychological harm, maldevelopment or deprivation" (Krug, Dahlberg, Mercy, Zwi, & Lozano, 2012, p. 5). As the WHO explains, including the term "power" functions to broaden the nature of a violent act and expand the conventional understanding of violence to include those acts that result from a power relationship, including threats and intimidation. The recognition that the exertion of power – separate from physical force – can result in violence is particularly relevant here. For example, one can easily envision a scenario whereby a nonstate actor initially exerts significant levels of physical force, only to scale back such measures after securing territory or introducing an adequate degree of fear in the local populace. From this point forward, the group might shift tactics to rely instead on the threat of harm or manifestations of "power" traditionally associated with the state. In either case, the diminution of actual physical force, however, does not necessarily correspond to a lessening of violence or violations of religious freedom.

Applying this understanding of violence to the Donbas crisis, well into 2018 both the DPR and LPR authorities continued to regularly harass a range of religious minorities (Coynash, 2018), interfere with worship meetings, seize religious literature, fine religious leaders (Corley, 2018a), and confiscate property (Corley, 2018b). Equally alarming – and again, without requiring the use of physical force – an OHCHR report expressed concern over "the further narrowing of freedom of religion or belief in territory controlled by [the DPR and LPR] due to the classification of evangelical Christian denominations as extremist organizations." Among other incidents, the report called attention to the decision by the DPR's "supreme court" to ban the Jehovah's Witnesses as an extremist organization (OHCHR, 2018c). Moving forward, any activity by Jehovah's Witnesses will still be the target of criminal sanction, including the possibility of imprisonment for up to eight years (Corley, 2018c), though the enforcement of such action likely will be contingent on the exercise of power rather than overt use of physical violence.

Even where not criminalized as extremist, other minority religious communities are similarly subject to the growing specter of being outlawed for failing to register under DPR and LPR legislation (Armed militants, 2018)[8] or for contravening other legislative rules prohibiting undesired religious communities. For example, OHCHR has expressed concern over LPR's adoption "of a 'law' which bans all 'religious groups' not directly linked to traditional religions" (OHCHR, 2018a) and the emergence of other directives requiring "religious organizations to obtain a positive 'theological opinion' in order to 'register', act as [a] 'legal entity' and operate" (OHCHR, 2018c). These violations of freedom of religion or belief similarly do not appear to be predicated on the frequent use of physical force. But their perpetuation readily falls within the World Health Organization's definition of violence, inasmuch as enforcement is premised on the intentional exercise of power that is liable to result in psychological harm, maldevelopment, deprivation, or possibly even in injury or death.

While violence unmistakably continues to define the overarching conflict with Ukraine, and remains inexorably tied to the shared DPR and LPR objective of independence, one might still argue that its frequency, scope, or intensity falls short of IRFA's requirement that a nonstate actor "often employ violence in pursuit of their objectives" (22 U.S.C.A. § 6402(11)). Supporting this claim, the 2018 Global Terrorism Index concluded in the narrow context of terroristic violence that until 2017 Ukraine represented "the country in the region most impacted by terrorism. But, deaths ... have decreased by 96 per cent since its peak in 2014 following the rise of separatist activity in the country's eastern states" (IEP, 2017, p. 39). IRFA's text sheds little light on precisely how often a nonstate actor must employ violence before it can be scrutinized under the statute. Moreover, the statutory text fails to opine on the level or intensity of such requisite violence, or whether it legitimately can be directed at military or state personnel or must target civilian populations.[9]

Reliance on the statutory text alone to gauge IRFA's requisite level of violence is insufficient, however, when DPR and LPR violence is held up against emerging IRFA practice. As noted above, DPR and LPR violence was at an exceptionally high level during the period following the introduction of EPC reporting, with both groups ranking among the most violent global nonstate actors. Furthermore, examining the list of designated EPCs reveals a wide interpretation being applied to the frequency, scope, and intensity of violence necessary to satisfy IRFA's violence requirement for nonstate actors.[10] For example, the current EPC listing includes the Taliban, responsible for 77 percent of Afghanistan's 4,653 terrorist fatalities in 2017, with the vast majority of these fatalities impacting police and military personnel (IEP, 2017, pp. 16, 20).

The frequency, scope, and intensity of violence employed by current EPCs provides interpretive substance to the bare statutory language. In turn, this context weighs against any justification for excluding the DPR and LPR as scrutinizable nonstate actors. More accurately, the variety of the violence manifested by current EPCs readily signals that the DPR and LPR – given their track records as violent separatist movements engaged in militaristic conflict and intentionally exerting power to deprive individual human rights – both satisfy the requisite "use of violence" test set by IRFA. To conclude otherwise would effectively endorse an inconsistent application of the statute or risk bringing into question the validity of at least some of the nonstate actors currently designated as entities of particular concern.

If anything can be extracted from the current class of EPCs and the case of the Donbas conflict, it is that the diminution of overt physical force should not by itself operate to disqualify nonstate actors from IRFA scrutiny. While the ability of the DPR and LPR to inflict violations of religious freedom may have been dependent on the initial exercise of physical violence, many continuing abuses – manifested in the form of intimidation, harassment, levying of fines, seizure of property, or the enforcement of registration laws – arguably are not contingent on the ongoing use of such force but rather on more nuanced exercise of power. With this reality in mind, IRFA's requirement for nonstate actors' use of violence should be clarified or interpreted in a manner that does not demand the nonstate actors to sustain regular and ongoing use of violence strictly construed.

The basis for scrutiny of nonstate actors originally introduced in the draft Wolf Act is instructive here. It required that a nonstate actor "engages in, finances, or tolerates violations of religious freedom, terrorism, or violence or discrimination targeting religious minorities" (H.R. 1150, Frank R. Wolf

International Religious Freedom Act of 2015 § 3).[11] Given that Congress ultimately discarded this initial formulation from the final Wolf Act, reading out a requirement for nonstate actor's violence would surely strain the boundaries of statutory interpretation. At the same time, it would seem unreasonable to interpret the current provision as intending to foreclose scrutiny of nonstate actors that violate religious freedom while sidestepping the frequent exercise of violence manifested through physical force. IRFA supports this construction. For example, the statute identifies violent forms of religious persecution as including detention and imprisonment (22 U.S.C.A. § 6401(4)). Further, IRFA's criteria governing particularly severe violations of religious freedom includes measures that are not necessarily contingent on the use of physical force, including inhuman or degrading treatment or punishment and prolonged detention without charge (22 U.S.C.A. § 6402(13)). Against this backdrop, a more purposeful interpretation of IRFA's requirement for nonstate actors' violence should seek to establish only whether a nonstate actor endorses or tolerates violence, or at some point in the past resorted to violence as construed under the WHO's definition as a precursor tool to facilitate subsequent violations of religious freedom. Such an approach would more definitively capture nonstate actors like the DPR and LPR, and prevent discounting other nonstate actors from scrutiny where the use of violence manifested through physical force had become sporadic, whether in the face of nonstate actors' consolidation of power or other factors.

State control

IRFA's third and final requirement for scrutiny of nonstate actors requires freedom from state control. This prong poses the most obvious hurdle to DPR and LPR consideration under IRFA. The United States Commission on International Religious Freedom leaves no room for doubt as to the connection between Russia and these entities. Its 2017 and 2018 annual report chapters on Russia address the DPR and LPR under the heading "Russia's Separatist Enclaves in the Donbas." USCIRF also notes that the "Russian-occupied separatist parastates of [the LPR and the DPR] in eastern Ukraine remain heavily militarized war zones policed by parallel ministries of state security" (USCIRF, 2017, p. 79, 2018, p. 75). With this finding of sovereign government control over the nonstate actors, USCIRF appears to rule out the possibility of assessing the LPR and the DPR under IRFA's provisions on nonstate actors. Its recommendation addressing the conflict in eastern Ukraine is equally pointed and reinforces its position attributing DPR and LPR actions to Russian control. USCIRF simply "call[s] on the Russian government to stop the persecution of religious minorities in the occupied areas of Crimea and Donbas" (USCIRF, 2017, p. 68).

Setting aside the function of Russian government control, USCIRF recognized that DPR and LPR "Ministries of State Security" perpetrated troubling violations of religious freedom, including the intimidation, arrest, torture, and murder of clergy and adherents of various religious minorities, as well as the sei-zure and destruction of property belonging to these religious groups (USCIRF, 2017, p. 75). Carrying out these actions signals the ability of the DPR and LPR to exercise "significant" political power. Further, USCIRF's reporting acknowl-edged that the DPR and LPR demonstrated territorial control by their occu-pation of Ukrainian territory as well their ability to deny individuals reentry into DPR and LPR-controlled territory (USCIRF, 2018, p. 79).

Partly because of religious freedom violations in the Donbas region, USCIRF placed Russia on its "Tier 1" list for the first time in 2017 and rec-ommended that the country be designated a CPC (country of particular con-cern). USCIRF reiterated this recommendation in 2018, observing additionally that the "official ideology" of the "Russian-occupied separatist parastates" of the DPR and LPR is "a mixture of Russian nationalism, Soviet nostalgia, and Russian Orthodoxy, to the extent that the [DPR] constitution recognizes the Russian Orthodox Church as the territory's 'leading and dominant' church." USCIRF further acknowledged that for many religious minorities "the initial phase of the occupation was one of outright terror: kidnappings, torture, and robberies were the norm, in the course of which perpetrators openly expressed their contempt for the victims' religious beliefs." Finally, while it noted that "the worst abuses have declined since 2015," USCIRF concluded that during the reporting period covered, minorities still "remained subject to raids, harassment, fines, and official slander," with "information about religious freedom viola-tions . . . difficult to obtain because communities fear reprisals." Though it came after the end of its 2018 reporting period, USCIRF also took note of the LPR's intention to mirror Russian legislation and require the registration of all reli-gious groups in its territory, a policy used to exclude religious minorities from lawful manifestation of their religious beliefs (USCIRF, 2018, p. 79). USCIRF's sole recommendation impacting the Donbas remained unchanged from 2017.

The State Department rejected USCIRF's recommendation to brand Rus-sia a country of particular concern. Instead, its approach appears to have taken a different tack. Unlike USCIRF, which addressed the DPR and LPR in the context of its reporting on Russia, the State Department restricted its observa-tions on the breakaway republics to the Ukraine chapter of its annual Interna-tional Religious Freedom report. The 2016 report is also less transparent about drawing a clear connection between Russia and the DPR and LPR authorities. Rather than directly attribute DPR and LPR action to the Russian govern-ment, the events in the Donbas fall under the more general section heading "Abuses by Foreign Forces and Nonstate Actors." Here, the State Department reported that "Russian-backed separatists continued to control parts of the Donetsk and Luhansk oblasts." Among other things, these authorities "detained and imprisoned members of the Jehovah's Witnesses as well as other religious leaders," "required all religious groups to register," and seized control of numer-ous places of worship (USDS, 2016).

In 2017, the State Department appeared to strengthen its connection between Russia and the Donbas quasi-states. Rather than merely "backing" the separatists, the State Department reported "**Russia-led** forces continued to control parts of the Donetsk and Luhansk oblasts and to detain and imprison religious leaders," and that "**Russia-led** forces continued to occupy religious buildings of minority religious groups and use them as military facilities" (USDS, 2017, emphasis added). In the same vein, the State Department observed that amendments to DPR laws "empowered **Russian proxy authorities** to abolish religious groups and associations" (USDS, 2017, emphasis added).

Based on this reporting, the State Department and USCIRF readily acknowledge the nature and severity of the ongoing violations of religious freedom confronting religious minorities in the DPR and LPR, as well as the violence associated with such violations. Similarly, both recognize that the DPR and LPR have achieved a measure of political power and territorial control. But neither USCIRF nor the State Department provides any explicit analysis regarding the extent of Russian control over the DPR and LPR (cf. Schofield, 2016). Likewise, neither explains which aspects of that control contributed to DPR and LPR failing to exhibit enough freedom from a sovereign government to be assessed as nonstate actors under IRFA.

The absence of such an analysis may be understandable given that Russia's connection to the DPR and LPR regimes arguably is more direct and controlling than the relationships existing between governments and other designated entities of particular concern. Still, at least some evidence is available to suggest that the Russian government's control is not necessarily absolute in the DPR and LPR. For example, although "Moscow has had a powerful influence" on the DPR and LPR from the beginning, it worked to keep DPR's deceased leader Alexander Zakharchenko "on a short leash because he wanted more autonomy than it was willing to give him" (Miller, 2018). There is even some speculation Zakharchenko's defiance led Russia to play a part in his assassination. As another analyst has concluded:

> To believe that this war is purely a piece of Russian imperialism, with the rebels no more than Moscow's instruments, is to dramatically oversimplify the situation. Of course Russia actively turned local discontents into rebellion in 2014, and continues to provide cover, ordnance and cash to keep the rebel pseudo-states functioning. For all that, though, the D[P]R and L[P]R, their populations and leaders, have their own interests and as much as anything else exploit their patron for their ends.
>
> (Galeotti, 2018)

In the end, what element or degree of Russian control rendered the DPR and LPR disqualified as nonstate actors under IRFA remains an unanswered question. Existing EPC recommendations and designations by USCIRF and the State Department respectively fail to provide an explicit framework for nonstate actor analysis or signal a consistent methodology for including or excluding nonstate actors from IRFA scrutiny, whether due to state control or otherwise. A more systematic and transparent approach here would help clarify and refine relevant factors impacting determinations of nonstate actors and entities of particular concern. Such an approach would also serve IRFA's objective of spearheading an effective response to the challenges posed by nonstate actors violating freedom of religion or belief. Precisely what aspect of sovereign government control operates to disqualify the DPR and LPR from scrutiny of nonstate actors? How consistently must such control be exerted? In the case of the Donbas, how does external control of the DPR and LPR substantively differ from other designated EPCs such as the Taliban, where compelling evidence of "more assertive" Russian support, including "overtly lending legitimacy to the Taliban to undermine NATO efforts and bolster belligerents" (Nicholson, 2017), has failed to disqualify the group as a nonstate actor?

In the same way that a more purposeful interpretation of the requirement for nonstate actor's violence can go a long way to maximizing IRFA's relevance and effectiveness, clarifying the analytical approach used for determining state control can similarly lend itself to taking fuller advantage of newfound policy tools promised under IRFA. Arguably, the DPR and LPR actions risk being diluted or obscured when placed in context of the Russian government's overall hostility towards freedom of religion.[12] To avoid this outcome, USCIRF could have elected to apply a narrower interpretation to IRFA's bar on nonstate actors' manifesting sovereign government control. By imposing a higher threshold for finding state control of a nonstate actor, the DPR and LPR violations could have been delinked from the larger context of Russian actions, thus opening the possibility of issuing EPC recommendations for both nonstate actors. In turn, this decoupling could have enabled the State Department to designate the DPR and LPR as entities of particular concern in response to religious freedom violations, while leaving open a window of opportunity for diplomatic engagement with Russia.

Adopting USCIRF's recommended CPC designation for Russia – a significant blow to U.S.-Russia relations – plainly represented a step too far for the State Department. In contrast, the approach set out above would harness EPC as a narrower targeted measure, opening the possibility of concrete action against nonstate actors who are violators of religious freedom, while communicating a warning to Russia about its extraterritorial conduct. Such an approach would enable the State Department to signal its commitment to promote and protect religious freedom in the Donbas region, while providing room to navigate U.S.-Russia relations, including de-escalating direct confrontation and creating potential momentum for political engagement to avert the possibility of a CPC designation for Russia in the future.[13]

The fact that the Donetsk and Luhansk people's republics have already fallen under U.S. sanctions unrelated to their violations of religious freedom further supports this approach. In March 2014, President Barack Obama issued Executive Order 13660 and set in motion the designation of the DPR and LPR as specially designated entities subject to sanctions. By July 2014, both groups were added to the Specially Designated Nationals and Blocked Persons List (SDN) maintained by the Treasury Department's Office of Foreign Assets

Control (OFAC, United States Department of the Treasury, 2018). By the end of December 2018, OFAC listed 138 entities and individuals subject to sanctions based on executive order 13660, including DPR and LPR leadership.[14]

This reality leaves open the question: if the individual actors that constitute the DPR and LPR and the nonstate actors themselves are already subject to sanctions, why not simply designate the LPR and the DPR as entities of particular concern? Two potential factors may be operating here to validate current policy foregoing such a designation; and both tie back to the State Department's longstanding unease with engaging on the specific issue of religious freedom (Blitt, 2018–2019, pp. 166–167). First, attaching the EPC label to the DPR and LPR would mean putting religious freedom center stage and drawing specific attention to the nature of certain abuses occurring in the Donbas. The historical pattern of a surfeit of USCIRF CPC recommendations and deficit of state-designated countries of particular concern, coupled with the State Department's penchant for avoiding the issuance of standalone IRFA-specific sanctions and waiving the imposition of sanctions altogether, plainly signals the state's discomfort taking direct action based on the promotion of freedom of religion or belief (Blitt, 2018–2019). Second, designating the DPR and LPR as EPCs would be unprecedented insofar as the religious orientation of these nonstate actors differs from all other designated EPCs to date. Currently, all nine designated EPCs subscribe to and advocate some extremist interpretation of Islam. Taking the step of designating the DPR and LPR as EPCs could conceivably upend conventional practice under IRFA by holding openly Christian authorities responsible for severe violations of religious freedom.[15] Tangential to this, such a designation would also be unprecedented because the DPR and LPR would, with one peculiar exception, represent the first EPCs that are not also designated as Foreign Terrorist Organizations. This designation imposes more rigorous sanctions[16] and requires that an organization engage in terrorist activity that "threatens the security of United States nationals or the national security of the United States" (8 U.S. Code § 1189). Currently, all EPCs are also listed as foreign terrorist organizations, except the Taliban, which since 2002 has been subject to sanctions under OFAC's SDN list as a Specially Designated Global Terrorist, and the Houthis.

In the final analysis, the State Department can rightly point to the SDN list to demonstrate concrete action against the authorities in the DPR and LPR. But at the same time, the failure to draw an explicit connection between these nonstate actors and concerns over violations of religious freedom operates to significantly undercut the potential impact of IRFA's new provisions on nonstate actors in the context of the continuing conflict and risks diminishing IRFA's overarching objective of promoting international religious freedom.

Conclusion

This chapter raised the question of whether IRFA's new amendments on nonstate actors might prove relevant for confronting violations of freedom of religion or belief committed by the Donetsk and Luhansk people's republics. The likelihood of harnessing IRFA's newfound powers, however, is decisively reduced by several key factors: first, the final provisions for nonstate actors adopted by Congress appear to significantly limit the range of nonstate actors examinable under IRFA; second, USCIRF and the State Department have moved to implement these provisions without any clear methodology or consistency, leaving their application subject to further ambiguity and uncertainty; and finally, although IRFA urges taking executive action to compel designated EPCs to cease particularly severe violations of freedom of religion or belief, such measures – punitive or otherwise – have not been forthcoming during the Trump administration.

As Donald Rumsfeld has observed, "you go to war with the army you have, not the army you might want or wish to have at a later time" (Schmitt, 2004). In this regard, USCIRF and the State Department must, barring additional IRFA amendments or clarifications, make do with the provisions on nonstate actors that emerged from the legislative process. Their implementation of these provisions to date, however, has failed to map out a constructive path forward. Both institutions have failed to elaborate or clarify the meaning of key terms used to identify nonstate actors. Further, neither institution has demonstrated any consistent methodology for assessing the status of nonstate actors. This is particularly evident in the face of significant disparities between USCIRF EPC (entity of particular concern) recommendations and actual State Department designations.

Nearly all the current entities of particular concern – al-Nusra Front, al-Qa'ida in the Arabian Peninsula, al-Qa'ida, al-Shabab, Boko Haram, the Houthis, ISIS, ISIS-Khorasan, and the Taliban – illustrate inconsistencies in the application of IRFA's provisions on nonstate actors and raise pertinent questions regarding how relevant criteria are being measured and satisfied. The resulting need for clearer methodologies and greater consistency is only confirmed by considering the Donbas crisis and its attendant nonstate-actor-driven violations of religious freedom. Without a concerted effort to remedy these interpretive and analytical gaps, provide greater inter-institutional guidance, and secure concrete responses to particularly severe violations of religious freedom, IRFA's new provisions on nonstate actors risk falling into irrelevancy. This scenario is only exacerbated by the failure of the State Department to date to take meaningful follow-up action in the face of EPC designations. Where EPC designations fail to be accompanied by measures intended to alleviate violations of religious freedom, the administration skirts its stated objective of "push[ing] back against persecution and ensur[ing] greater respect for religious freedom for all" (Pompeo, 2018).

USCIRF and the State Department's Office of International Religious Freedom can begin to remedy at least two of these shortcomings by clarifying reasons underlying the current discrepancies between EPCs recommended and designated. This exchange should include how IRFA's provisions are being interpreted and applied by both institutions. It is evident from the outcome of the first round of designations that, in comparison with USCIRF, the State Department has applied an unusually "liberal" interpretation to IRFA's provisions on nonstate actors, resulting in a greater number of EPC designations than recommended by USCIRF. This outcome inverts the historical pattern demonstrated under the CPC (country of particular concern) process. The State Department's justification for this outcome should similarly be clarified. It may stem from the fact, unlike CPC designations, the current class of EPC designations comes with little political risk attached. All current EPCs are already under U.S. sanctions and none maintain a bilateral relationship with the United States. Moreover, unlike CPC designations, an EPC designation can be issued without having to identify applicable IRFA sanctions or confront the fallout that might flow from a decision to issue a waiver in place of such sanctions.

Whatever the basis for these EPC designation discrepancies, the State Department's Office of International Religious Freedom and USCIRF should rapidly move to identify more common baselines for identifying nonstate actors under IRFA. Adopting a purposive interpretation here can help bridge the emerging inconsistency between IRFA's stated objectives – including promoting the fundamental right to freedom of religion and "standing for liberty and standing with the persecuted" (22 USCA § 6401(b)(1)(e)) – and the vague provisions on nonstate actors that risk reducing IRFA's effectiveness. Such a move can operate to recapture some of the definitional space around nonstate actors lost during congressional negotiations over the Wolf Act. This in turn might enable scrutiny of nonstate actors that arguably fall short on consistent use of violence, waiver in their control of territory, or exhibit certain signs of autonomy but also take orders from a foreign government.

Greater transparency around these standards will also help clarify the current approach to the DPR and LPR. Victims of religious freedom violations at the hands of these groups deserve to know what factors are preventing the DPR and LPR from being scrutinized as nonstate actors or why their actions might fall below the particularly severe violations necessary to trigger an EPC designation. Absent such clarifications, questions will persist regarding whether IRFA's provisions are being selectively applied or adequately enforced.

Whether or not a common baseline can emerge between the State Department's Office of International Religious Freedom and USCIRF, the Commission should move to recapture its traditional policy incubator and watchdog role. Therefore, it should advance a more holistic interpretation and enforcement of IRFA's provisions for nonstate actors, even if some or all of its ensuing recommendations are rejected by the State Department. This approach should apply in the context of the Donbas crisis as well, and include the possibility of taking an unconventional approach to the framing of IRFA's provisions on nonstate actors. While the task of designating EPCs lies with the executive branch, the Commission's job – irrespective of whether it agrees with the State Department's methodology for identifying EPCs – is to provide the government with recommendations that will advance international religious freedom.

More broadly, failure to provide such recommendations – even in the face of divergent standards – risks perpetuating the same lacuna the Wolf amendments originally set out to cure, namely tolerating a permissive environment for nonstate actors to violate religious freedom with impunity.

Notes

1 For a more detailed analysis of the Wolf Act amendments to IRFA, see Blitt (2018–2019).
2 USCIRF's annual report did, however, assert that the Commission would continue "to report . . . on particularly severe violations of religious freedom perpetrated by non-state actors that do not meet the [Wolf] amendments' limited definition because, for example, they do not exercise territorial control" (USCIRF, p. 4).
3 The referendum question was premised on *samostoyatelnost'*, a Russian word the meaning of which could be open to either independence or something "slightly less" (Walker, 2014). According to the OHCHR, the referendum question asked voters: "Do you support the act of self-rule of the People's Republic of Donetsk/People's Republic of Luhansk?" (OHCHR, 2014).
4 "According to figures of the Ukrainian Central Election Commission, 82% of the voters in the Donetsk region, and 88% of voters in Luhansk region were thus deprived of their right to vote" (OHCHR, 2014).
5 According to TASS Russian News Agency, voter turnout was "72.5% in the LPR and 76.2% in the DPR" (Voting at elections, 2018).
6 Russia reportedly was "treating the killing as an act of 'international terrorism'" (Second person dies, 2018).
7 Ukrainian forces are also responsible for violations of international law, including the right to freedom of religion or belief. In one recent reporting period, the UN Deputy High Commissioner for Human Rights concluded that "overall, of more than 200 abuses substantiated by interviews with victims and witnesses, the Government of Ukraine was alleged to have carried out 147 of them" ('Multiplicity' of rights violations, 2018). Perhaps most controversially, the Ukrainian Orthodox Church of the Moscow Patriarchate claimed interference in freedom of religion in the face of government legislation intended to force the Church "to change its name to one that reveals its affiliation with the Moscow-based Russian Orthodox Church" (Ukraine's President, 2018).
8 As the OHCHR has observed, the registration requirement "raises double concerns for many religious organizations. Some parishioners do not want the 'authorities' to know of their participation in a certain religious organization. Some fear facing issues in government-controlled territory if it becomes known that they are registered with the 'republic'" (OHCHR, 2018b).
9 For example, Jane's Terrorism and Insurgency Centre 2017 World Attack Index concluded that nearly 60% of nonstate actor violence targeted security forces rather than civilians (Henman & Barca, 2018).
10 More generally, approaches to quantifying violence are also subject to variation and contestation. For example, see Solomon and Frechette (2017).
11 The draft bill provided no guidance on the meaning to be associated with terms such as "nonsovereign" or "significant political power."
12 At the end of 2018, the State Department added Russia to IRFA's new "special watch list" intended to categorize countries falling short of CPC status but engaging in or tolerating severe violations of religious freedom (USDS, 2018).
13 Of course, opting for this course of action does not ensure the DPR and LPR would be subject to sanction. IRFA requires only that the "President should take specific actions, when practicable, to address severe violations of religious freedom of non-state actors that are designated [EPCs]" (22 U.S.C.A. § 6442a(c)).

14 See https://sanctionssearch.ofac.treas.gov (search under program "UKRAINE-13660"). This number also includes sanctions imposed on individuals and entities relating to Russia's annexation of Crimea. For example, the DPR's prime minister, minister of state security, foreign minister, and interior minister are included.

15 The closest similarity might be Serbia under the Milosevic regime, although the 1990 constitution did not establish an official state religion.

16 While SDN-based sanctions are focused on freezing the financial and property assets of listed persons and groups, FTO (foreign terrorist organization) designations go further by, among other things, prohibiting "material support or resources" including services training, advice, or assistance, and making representatives and members of foreign terrorist organizations, if they are aliens, inadmissible to and potentially removable from the United States. See 18 U.S.C. § 2339A(b)(1) and 8 U.S.C. §§ 1182 (a)(3)(B)(i)(IV)-(V), § 1227 (a)(1)(A)).

References

An end to the war in eastern Ukraine looks as far away as ever. (2018, October 11). *The Economist*. Retrieved from www.economist.com/europe/2018/10/11/an-end-to-the-war-in-eastern-ukraine-looks-as-far-away-as-ever

Armed militants attack Baptist house of prayer in Russian-controlled 'Luhansk Republic'. (2018, September 27). *RISU*. Retrieved from https://risu.org.ua/en/index/all_news/community/terrorism/72809/

Ashraf, S. (2017). ISIS Khorasan: Presence and potential in the Afghanistan – Pakistan region. *The Henry Jackson Society website*. Retrieved from http://henryjacksonsociety.org/wp-content/uploads/2017/10/HJS-ISIS-Khorasan-Report.pdf

Blitt, R. C. (2018–2019). The Wolf Act amendments to the U.S. International Religious Freedom Act: Breakthrough or breakdown? *University of Pennsylvania Journal of Law and Public Affairs, 4*(2), 151–201.

Campbell, J., & Harwood, A. (2018, August 20). Boko Haram's deadly impact. *Council on Foreign Relations*. Retrieved from www.cfr.org/article/boko-harams-deadly-impact

Corley, F. (2018a, August 7). Donbas: Luhansk: Armed raids, worship bans, fines. *Forum 18*. Retrieved from www.forum18.org/archive.php?article_id=2401

Corley, F. (2018b, October 18). Donbas: Donetsk: Places of worship seized, sealed. *Forum 18*. Retrieved from www.forum18.org/archive.php?article_id=2422

Corley, F. (2018c, November 2). Donbas: Donetsk: Jehovah's Witnesses banned. *Forum 18*. Retrieved from www.forum18.org/archive.php?article_id=2428

Coynash, H. (2018, July 2). New wave of religious persecution in occupied Donbas. *Human Rights in Ukraine*. Retrieved from http://khpg.org/en/index.php?id=1530321398

Galeotti, M. (2018, September 4). Zakharchenko's assassination won't bring peace to Ukraine. *The Moscow Times*. Retrieved from https://themoscowtimes.com/articles/war-politics-crime-blowing-up-the-donbass-62764

Goncharenko, R., & Johann, B. (2018, September 2). Alexander Zakharchenko: The latest Ukrainian rebel leader to face an abrupt death. *Deutsche Welle*. Retrieved from www.dw.com/en/alexander-zakharchenko-the-latest-ukrainian-rebel-leader-to-face-an-abrupt-death/a-45323653Henman, M., & Barca, K. (2018, February 18). JTIC 2017 World attack index [Video file]. Retrieved from www.janes.com/article/77899/jtic-2017-world-attack-index

Human Rights Watch. (2018). Ukraine: Events of 2017 (World report 2018). Retrieved from www.hrw.org/world-report/2018/country-chapters/ukraine#

IHS Jane's Terrorism and Insurgency Centre. (2016). 2015 IHS Global attack index. Retrieved from www.janes.com/images/assets/096/48096/JTIC_Global_Attack_Index_2015_14Jan.pdf

IHS Jane's Terrorism and Insurgency Centre. (2017). 2016 IHS Global attack index. Retrieved from www.janes.com/images/assets/165/67165/jtir0370_a.pdf

Institute for Economics and Peace. (2017). Global terrorism index (IEP Report 55). Retrieved from http://visionofhumanity.org/app/uploads/2017/11/Global-Terrorism-Index-2017.pdf

Krug, E. G., Dahlberg, L. L., Mercy, J. A., Zwi, A. B., & Lozano, R. (2012). World report on violence and health. *World Health Organization website*. Retrieved from https://apps.who.int/iris/bitstream/handle/10665/42495/9241545615_eng.pdf;jsessionid=E26C05005BC4FA00A623F37C392D908F?sequence=1

Lederer, E. M. (2018, October 30). Russia and West clash over Nov. 11 elections in east Ukraine. *AP News*. Retrieved from https://apnews.com/73baa978d55f4fd59bdf3d52df1d1ad1

Lokshina, T. (2016, November 28). Raw fear in separatist-controlled Donetsk: Fighting and torture continue to rack Eastern Ukraine. *The Moscow Times*. Retrieved from https://the-moscowtimes.com/articles/raw-fear-in-separatist-controlled-donetsk-56322

Miller, C. (2018, August 31). Separatist leader Zakharchenko was a thorn in the side of both Kyiv and Moscow. *RFE/RL*. Retrieved from www.rferl.org/a/killed-in-a-bomb-blast-donetsk-separatist-leader-zakharchenko-was-a-thorn-in-the-side-of-both-kyiv-and-moscow/29464443.html

'Multiplicity' of rights violations in Ukraine as fifth winter of conflict bites. (2018, December 19). *UN News*. Retrieved from https://news.un.org/en/story/2018/12/1028951

Neef, C. (2017, July 28). Little Russia: Pro-Russian separatists harden split from Ukraine. *Spiegel Online*. Retrieved from www.spiegel.de/international/world/little-russia-pro-russian-separatists-harden-split-from-ukraine-a-1159642.html

Nicholson, J. W. (2017, February 9). Statement for the record for the Senate Armed Services Committee. Retrieved for www.armed-services.senate.gov/imo/media/doc/Nicholson_02-09-17.pdf

Office of the United Nations High Commissioner for Human Rights. (2014). Report on the human rights situation in Ukraine, 15 June 2014. Retrieved from www.ohchr.org/Documents/Countries/UA/HRMMUReport15June2014.pdf

Office of the United Nations High Commissioner for Human Rights. (2018a, March 19). Report on the human rights situation in Ukraine, November 16, 2017 – February 15, 2018. Retrieved from www.ohchr.org/Documents/Countries/UA/ReportUkraineNov2017-Feb2018_EN.pdf

Office of the United Nations High Commissioner for Human Rights. (2018b, September 10). Report on the human rights situation in Ukraine, 16 May to 15 August. Retrieved from www.ohchr.org/Documents/Countries/UA/ReportUkraineMay-August2018_EN.pdf

Office of the United Nations High Commissioner for Human Rights. (2018c, December 17). Report on the human rights situation in Ukraine, 16 August to 15 November. Retrieved from www.ohchr.org/Documents/Countries/UA/24thReportUkraineAugust_November2018_EN.pdf

Olanrewaju, T. (2018, September 5). UN debunks FGs claims that Boko Haram has been defeated. *News Express*. Retrieved from www.newsexpressngr.com/news/53536-UN-debunks-FGs-claims-that-Boko-Haram-has-been-defeated

Pompeo, M. (2018, May 29). Remarks of Secretary of State Mike Pompeo at the release of the 2017 Annual report on international religious freedom. Retrieved from www.state.gov/secretary/remarks/2018/05/282789.htm

SB Morgen. (2017, August 22). Analysis: Scrutinizing the Boko Haram resurgence. Retrieved from www.sbmintel.com/2017/08/analysis-scrutinising-the-boko-haram-resurgence/

Schmitt, E. (2004, December 8). Iraq-bound troops confront Rumsfeld over lack of armor. *The New York Times*. Retrieved from www.nytimes.com/2004/12/08/international/middleeast/iraqbound-troops-confront-rumsfeld-over-lack-of.html

Schofield, M. (2016, October 1). Leaked emails reveal extent of Russia's Ukraine separatist propaganda machine. *The Sydney Morning Herald*. Retrieved from www.smh.com.au/world/leaked-emails-reveal-extent-of-russias-ukraine-separatist-propaganda-machine-20161001-grst7g.html

Second person dies in Donetsk cafe blast that killed separatist leader Zakharchenko. (2018, September 1). *RFE/RL*. Retrieved from www.rferl.org/a/ukrainian-separatist-leader-zakharchenko-reported-killed-in-donetsk-cafe-blast/29464119.html

Solomon, S., & Frechette, C. (2017, July 21). No, al-Shabab is not deadlier than Boko Haram: Here are better numbers. *The Washington Post*. Retrieved from www.washingtonpost.com/news/monkey-cage/wp/2017/07/21/no-al-shabab-isnt-more-deadly-than-boko-haram-here-are-better-numbers/?utm_term=.b0d025ecdfd4

Ukraine: Torture and secret detention on both sides of the conflict line. (2016, July 21). *Amnesty International*. Retrieved from www.amnesty.org/en/latest/news/2016/07/torture-and-secret-detention-on-both-sides-of-the-conflict-line-in-ukraine/

Ukraine's President signs law forcing Russia-affiliated church to change name. (2018, December 2018). *RFE/RL*. Retrieved from www.rferl.org/a/ukraine-s-president-signs-law-forcing-orthodox-church-to-change-its-name/29671193.html

United States Commission on International Religious Freedom. (2017). 2017 Annual report. Retrieved from www.uscirf.gov/sites/default/files/2017.USCIRFAnnualReport.pdf

United States Commission on International Religious Freedom. (2018). 2018 Annual report. Retrieved from www.uscirf.gov/sites/default/files/2018USCIRFAR.pdf

United States Department of State. (2016). International religious freedom report for 2016: Ukraine. Retrieved from www.state.gov/j/drl/rls/irf/religiousfreedom/index.htm?year=2016&dlid=268878

United States Department of State. (2017). International religious freedom report for 2017: Ukraine. Retrieved from www.state.gov/j/drl/rls/irf/religiousfreedom/index.htm?year=2017&dlid=280970

United States Department of State. (2018, December 21). Secretary of State's determination under the International Religious Freedom Act of 1998 and Frank R. Wolf International Religious Freedom Act of 2016. *Federal Register, 83*, 65782. Retrieved from www.federalregister.gov/documents/2018/12/21/2018-27632/secretary-of-states-determination-under-the-international-religious-freedom-act-of-1998-and-frank-r

United States Department of the Treasury. (2018, December 19). Specially designated nationals and blocked persons list (SND). Retrieved from www.treasury.gov/resource-center/sanctions/SDN-List/Pages/default.aspx

Voting at elections in self-proclaimed republics in Donbass over. (2018, November 11). *TASS*. Retrieved from http://tass.com/world/1030318

Walker, S. (2014, May 11). East Ukraine goes to the polls for independence referendum. *The Guardian*. Retrieved from www.theguardian.com/world/2014/may/10/donetsk-referendum-ukraine-civil-war

Part 2

Impact of the Russian-Ukrainian conflict on religious public life and communities

7 Ukrainian churches and civil society in the Euromaidan and the Russian-Ukrainian conflict

A sociological analysis

Viktor Stepanenko

Introduction

The relationship between churches as institutions and civil society as a whole in the "post-secular" world is not only actively debated at a theoretical level (Habermas, 2008), with methodological complexity and a variety of socio-political nuances, but also retains current salience in various national contexts (Kruip & Reifeld, 2007; Welker, Koopman, & Vorster, 2017). This paper analyzes the relationship between churches and civil society in the Ukrainian social, political, and cultural contexts. These contexts involve the increasing importance civil society has had from the Euromaidan (the mass protest movement of 2013–2014 in Ukraine) onwards and during the Russian-Ukrainian conflict, the role and positions of various churches in the country's dramatic social transformation, and the prospects for further relations between religious organizations and civil society.

To understand the relationship between religion and civil society in Ukraine one should note that Ukraine's religious institutional network primarily contains Christian churches, predominantly the two major branches of the Orthodox church, the newly-established Orthodox Church of Ukraine (OCU) and the Ukrainian Orthodox Church of the Moscow Patriarchate (UOC-MP); the Greek Catholic and Roman Catholic churches; and Protestant churches. In this chapter I will use the term "churches" to refer to Christian religious organizations, with a particular focus on the two major Orthodox churches in the country.

The objective of this chapter is to examine the public roles of religious organizations and civil society in the post-Euromaidan transformation. The analysis of the interrelation between these two institutions also implies answering the question whether Ukraine's churches are part of national civil society. In doing this, I am going to clarify conceptual typologies and institutional boundaries between churches and civil society in general and explore the public role of churches in democratization. Then I will focus in more detail on peculiarities of the religious situation in the context of social and political transformations in Ukraine. Using sociological data to provide an empirical basis for the analysis, I will try to demonstrate that the issues of Ukraine's European integration generate challenges for both national civil society and the major Orthodox churches. The varied positions of the churches will be examined in the context of the Russian-Ukrainian geopolitical conflict, particularly with regard to the war in Donbas. And finally, I will explore some of the prospects for closer mutual interaction between the churches and civil society in Ukraine.

Churches and civil society: a conceptual framework

There are many approaches to and definitions of civil society. The concept itself has been at the center of active ongoing theoretical debates since the "rebirth" of the historical concept of civil society in the period of the anti-Communist revolutions in Europe starting in the late 1980s. Since then, the concept of civil society has been enriched with renewed salience and additional interpretations and nuances connected to issues of individual rights and freedoms, solidarity, social justice, and inclusion in the global informational era. John Kean (2010) fairly notes that "the term civil society has become both a master category in the human sciences and a key phrase often used by politicians, corporate executives, journalists, charitable foundations, human rights organizations, and citizens" (p. 451).

The most typical definitions of civil society (Edwards, 2011; Kean, 2010) emphasize that this is the sphere of social activities and relations which exists apart from the state and beyond the market (the so-called "third sector"). Civil society *per se* is also a public (not a private) sphere of social life. The most typical organizational structures of civil society are non-governmental organizations (NGOs) or other civil society organizations (CSOs), which are self-organized institutions acting on the principle of voluntary participation of citizens. An important feature of a normative concept of civil society is its orientation towards civil values and moral virtues. These are the values which make civil society civil.

Churches as institutions share to a large extent (or at least nominally) the vast majority of the typological features of civil society. This is not surprising, because the connection between churches and civil society has deep historical and cultural roots. Despite the stereotypical view regarding churches in Europe as mostly anti-modern and even reactionary powers – the view that is partly based on the history of violent religious wars and of the Inquisition with its cruel persecution of heretics by the Catholic Church in the "dark" Middle Ages –, there is also another part of the story. The churches in Europe historically paved the way for self-governing autonomy from a monarch or sovereign, as self-governing practices were formed initially within the church or in the context of church autonomy, as it was in the Magna Carta in medieval England.

Historically, church autonomy in a way laid the foundations for a democratic tradition of power distribution. The first self-governing practices and historical institutions of civil society, such as free universities, were also formed under church leadership. Additionally, the historical struggle for religious freedom and religious tolerance not only laid to a large extent the foundation for European liberalism and democracy, but also became the core value of the whole liberal idea of civil society. To illustrate, from the time of Alexis de Tocqueville's study *Democracy in America*, the self-organizing activities of Protestant communities were inextricably linked with the very idea of civil society and with the concept of civil religion, at least in the American democratic tradition.

Returning to the typological features of civil society, I attempt to extrapolate them to churches as institutions. In the modern age, and in many contemporary national contexts (such as in Ukraine), both churches and civil society operate outside the state. Thus, churches and civil society as represented in its most typical institutional framework are both nominally NGOs. However, it is an important nuance that civil society is in a non-state sector, and churches, at least in Ukraine, enjoy autonomy from the state, which is based on different premises and historically arose differently.

Like NGOs, churches are formally non-economic institutions, although both civil society and churches provide certain social services and satisfy people's needs, operating in corresponding competitive markets, such as in Ukraine (Brik, 2018). The relationship between NGOs and economics is not unambiguous. Equally, various churches can be seen as large institutional corporations that are competitive in the market for religious services and carry out market-oriented and even profitable activities. However, these activities are supplementary and are not recognized by churches as their main goal and mission. So, from this perspective, churches cannot be considered as profit-seeking business organizations. And in this regard, churches as non-profit institutions also share this typical characteristic of civil society.

Despite these similarities, the interrelation between churches and civil society in their historical transformations and various configurations is a complex and debatable issue (Banner, 2009; Herbert, 2013; Kruip & Reifeld, 2007). In the Christian tradition, this could be traced at least from Augustine's idea on separation (and contrast) of the "Two Cities" – the earthly, mundane city and the City of God. This was perhaps the first conceptual model of the relations between a profane society and the sacred church. And in a similar way, the question whether churches (or rather in our context different Christian churches) are part of civil society is also full of nuances and no less simple. As Gerhard Kruip (2007) argues, answers to the question depend on different perspectives, such as a sociological point of view, a political-strategic perspective, or the standpoint of a faithful believer and committed church member.

The interpretation of the interrelation between churches and civil society also depends on historical and concrete national contexts as well as on one's concept of a civil society, or the "different languages" and "strategic usage" of the term (Kean, 2010, p. 462). According to Keane, the pragmatic approach to civil society, historically traced from Thomas Paine's revolutionary ideas, mostly treats it as an efficient liberal counterbalance to despotic power. The important role of civil society (and of churches in some national cases) in post-Communist revolutions, post-authoritarian transformation, and democratization confirms this. However, as Anne Gathuo (2003) claims, despite the documented success of churches in promoting democracy in transitional countries, "the inherent undemocratic nature of churches has led critics to question its appropriateness as propagator of democracy" (p. 18). This tension is also manifested in the fact that the role of the Catholic Church in the "third wave" of democratization was the result of the "striking historical shift" in doctrines and activities of the Catholic Church, manifested in the Second Vatican Council (1962–1965) and the "subsequent changes in national churches from defenders of status quo to proponents of social, economic and political reforms" (Andersen & Jensen, 2017, p. 2) associated with democratization.

Conversely, the normative approach to civil society mostly focuses on its ethical ideas, stressing the importance of virtues and values in social life. In this framework, churches with their activities in fostering moral values could be considered an important institute of civil society. This idea is mostly supported in the studies examining the interrelation of churches and civil society from theological perspectives (Coleman, 2009; Fergusson, 2004; Welker et al., 2017). However, even in that framework, the positions of different churches on the issues of civil society reflect diverse meanings, contexts, and circumstances. Michael Banner (2009) notes that "there is nothing that can be identified as the Christian answer to the question of civil society" (p. 3). He also argues one should look rather at a certain Christian tradition of social thought "that, in its different versions, is relevant to the questions posed by the modern debate about the existence, character, and qualities of civil society" (Banner, 2009, pp. 3–4).

It is not surprising that the interrelationship between civil society and churches is even more ambiguous and complex from a sociological perspective. In any case, sociologically, churches are usually considered as separate institutions and religion as a special sphere of social activity, both of which are important for civil society. The spheres of civil society and churches often intersect each other in some social activities (for example, charity), as well as in institutional representations (for example, socially oriented NGOs created on the basis of churches, such as Caritas). However, apart from distinct positive patterns of the relationship between churches and civil society, there could be others that are quite destructive. As Donald Miller (2011) fairly notes, "it is also true that religion has the potential to inflict great harm, especially if it becomes an instrument of the state or an uncritical advocate for sectarian or corporate interests" (p. 257).

From a sociological approach, there could also be some other reservations, if not doubts, in affirmatively answering the question whether churches are part of civil society. Some are outlined below, based on primarily typological characteristics of the different Christian churches without going into contextual details, though keeping in mind the case of Ukraine's Orthodox churches. I identify some reservations regarding a special status of churches in their relation to civil society.

First, traditional Christian denominations such as the Catholic or Orthodox churches are in fact large institutional corporations with their own hierarchical structure and system of rule. This rule is carried out from their governing center, guided by the authority of their supreme priests – hierarchs. Such institutional features of some churches may add some methodological inconveniences in considering them as a part of civil society, because the latter is usually interpreted in terms of the network of various grass-roots NGOs in their mostly horizontal and non-hierarchical mutual interactions. Compared to more grass-roots organizations, churches fall under certain methodological "suspicion," which is similar to the problem of whether political parties and trade unions, with their peculiarities of bureaucratic corporate organizations (characterized by Max Weber, and later on by Robert Michels in his "iron law of oligarchy" theory) belong to civil society. In Ukraine, this is certainly the case. Orthodox churches in the country are often criticized for being too close to the state. They are also criticized for being dangerously efficient in gaining political influence and privileges, rather than in operating as social institutions and providing social services.

Despite their nature as hierarchies, the basic self-organizing initiative in churches' affairs is still present, particularly in Protestant religious communities. The Tocquevillian classic model of these communities in the history of American civil society is a good example of that. In Ukraine, the processes of self-organization at the level of local religious communities have been particularly common with the newly established autocephalous OCU from the beginning of 2019. It is still an open question, however, whether the newly established Ukrainian autocephalous church will be able to overcome historical, somewhat conservative Orthodox traditions and transform itself into a more open and democratic church.

Second, although religious belief and practices can involve very mundane things, churches serve as a special institution that primarily cares about the spiritual sphere of life and provides a unique kind of social services. Civil society organizations can also work in a spiritual sphere of life or at least at a high degree of abstraction or at an ideological level, but this is not exactly providing the services that are offered by churches as institutional religious organizations. Church practices often involve a sacred intimacy and engage a person's freedom of conscience in the rituals and ceremonies of his or her dialogue with God such as worship, christening, the sacrament of confession, blessing, the remission of sins, etc. However, it is also true that spirituality is not exclusive to churches; there are increasing numbers of individuals in modern society who claim to be spiritual but not religious (Miller, 2011). But what makes churches unique social institutions is the way they arrange religious spirituality and intimacy through institutional forms. Religious intimacy, even at an institutional level, seems unlikely to be part of the public sphere, even when it comes through collective church ceremonies. In contrast, typical "mundane" NGOs mostly operate in the field of public interactions, determined by communicative publicity and, in fact, forming it.

A final point of reservation regarding a complete compatibility of churches and civil society may come from a conceptual argument on the liberal plurality of civil society as opposed to the somewhat traditional conservatism of churches. This is particularly true regarding Ukraine's Orthodox churches, which remain primarily conservative traditionalistic organizations. For example, Ukrainian Orthodox churches condemn LGBTQ+ communities and civil organizations, considering them as sinners who ruin what they call "traditional family values" (Simonchuk, 2016). But the point is not so much the radical conservatism of Ukrainian Orthodox churches *per se*; the argument on liberal plurality has a much deeper and more ethical character. As John Kean (2010) puts it, normative support for the institutional pluralism of civil society "has no need of so-called Absolutes," but rather implies "suspicion of the moralizing faith in Grand Ideals such as the State, Nation, Progress, Socialism, Free Markets, God, Truth, or Ethics" (pp. 463–464). Institutional religions, particularly those functioning in the post-Communist conditions of persistent practices on monopolizing the truth and undeveloped critical thinking, might also come under such suspicion.

However, religion and churches play important roles in civil society, fulfilling many significant social functions and providing a forum for moral debates and competing social visions about what is good, right, and compassionate (Miller, 2011). Some distinct characteristics of churches as unique social institutions, such as their considerable autonomy, popularity (large loyal membership), high interpersonal trust within the group, and organizational capacity, could be more potentially advantageous when compared with civil society's predominantly secular NGOs (Gathuo, 2003), as many examples of the efficiency of support for collective actions under the wing of churches in developing countries have proved. Moreover, in contemporary "post-secular" conditions, the role and functions of churches have also been changing amidst global contexts of social transformation, modernization, and democratization. In the framework of these contexts, particularly under the third wave of democratization, new arguments have arisen and strengthened the perspective of closer connection between churches and civil society.

The first of such new arguments is articulated in the concept of public religion, which primarily studies the public role of churches in facilitating democratization. José Casanova (1994), who used the concept in his analysis of case studies from Latin America to Poland, showed how modern churches have overcome traditional limitations of the private sphere and have turned into a powerful public factor for social modernization and democratization in close conjunction with local civil society, and, in fact, have become one of the most important institutions of it. Having accumulated the results of many field studies, Andersen and Jensen (2017) also summarized an impressive account of the powerful impact of the Catholic Church in the third wave of democratization worldwide.

> In Brazil the Church vitally empowered civil society through Catholic grassroots organizations, through Church leaders' denunciations of the repression, and through calls for a more democratic order; in Chile the Church kept its compatriots informed about the extent of human rights violations, and it openly challenged the regime when no one else could; in Poland the Catholic Church was instrumental in overthrowing communism through *inter alia* its vigorous moral and psychological support of the opposition movement; in Spain the Church played a crucial role in the demise of authoritarianism, not least by helping the country reach a constitutional compromise on Church-state relations that would avoid a replay of the Spanish civil war.
>
> (p. 2)

Additional evidence of the important role of churches in national democratization processes and in shaping local civil societies comes from Africa (Kruip & Reifeld, 2007; Welker et al., 2017). For example, in Kenya, a coalition of Christian churches campaigned successfully for a multi-party system in the 1980s and facilitated unity among opposition parties in 2002 to bring down an autocratic ruling party that had been in power for 40 years since the country's independence from Britain in 1963 (Gathuo, 2003). The mass protest movement in Ukraine, known as the Euromaidan of 2013–2014, has also actualized the public role of churches in various aspects that I will elaborate on later in the chapter.

The second argument regarding the perspective of the actual connection between churches and civil society involves rethinking civil society as a sphere of civility and practical solidarity (Alexander, 2006). In contrast, this sociological approach to civil society varies from a theoretically reflexive to an often ideologically manipulative vision of it. This approach to civil society focuses on civility as its essential and mostly overlooked aspect (Alexander, 2006; Herbert, 2013). Civility is understood here as a normative value continuum that regulates all spheres of social life, including daily practices (Stepanenko, 2018). It is realized in individual behavioral acts, in various examples of the human ability for nonviolent mutual interactions, and in one's possibilities to overcome individual identities and peculiarities for the sake of collective action in the arena of common interests.

Indeed, modern, predominantly secular society is hardly a community of believers, whether religious or ideological. Such a society is not held together by a faith or political ideology that would be entirely shared by all members of society. However, routine social bonds and peaceful social interactions would be impossible without practical reproduction of civil regulations and norms of human behavior, such as recognition of differences, rules of reciprocity, mutual support and solidarity, recognition and respect to each other, etc. The common perception and observance of basic norms of human coexistence by citizens in a multitude of everyday practices and social interactions create a kind of civil code or a certain regulatory continuum that Jeffrey Alexander (2006) calls a civil sphere.

In these essential practices of maintaining and reproducing civility, particularly in the contexts of conflict and war, churches and religion may actualize their role as a valuable resource and moral potential for real civil society, in its identification of public good, justice, dignity, and other normative ideals. In this regard, it is also worth noting the great experience of cultural combination between practical civility and Protestant religious manifestations that was undertaken in the American cultural tradition. Alexis de Tocqueville defined that specific ethos of American social life as the "habits of heart" and "civil religion." This cultural line is still developing in contemporary neo-Tocquevillian interpretations from Robert Bellah to Robert Putnam.

However, one may argue that American civil religion is a historically unique fusion and experience which could hardly be literally reproduced in other cultural contexts, particularly in post-Communist countries, including Ukraine. In these countries, Communism itself with all its official ideological holidays, celebrations, and symbolic manifestations pretended to be a kind of "political religion." In contrast to civil religion, which mostly describes self-organized activities in the context of liberal regimes (as in the case of the United States), the term "political religion" definitely fits better in describing the ideological practices of totalitarian regimes, such as Communism, Fascism, and Nazism, implying their practices of total political control and indoctrination. The Communist legacy in its many institutional aspects is a historical and cultural burden which will take time to be overcome in Ukraine. Nonetheless, closer communication between religion and civil society in terms of developing practices of democratic civility still remains a promising prospect in any context, including a post-Communist Ukrainian one.

Peculiarities of the interaction between churches and civil society in Ukraine

Ukraine is still undergoing a complex and multidimensional social and political transformation that began with the proclamation of state independence in 1991. The complex configurations of this transformation in its inconsistent and contradictory dynamics combine the processes of economic and institutional modernization, democratization, and the assertion of the European identity of the state with the formation of the modern Ukrainian civic nation. The longer duration and more persistent inertia of the communist institutional legacy (compared to other central and eastern European countries), as well as its long historical subjection within the geopolitical field of (neo)imperial Russia, mostly explain the drama, inconsistency, and contradictory nature of the Ukrainian post-Communist experience, which is often characterized in terms of a hybrid political regime, an unconsolidated democracy, a surface-level or formal Westernization, or a post-colonial institutional dependence.

The country has already experienced three historic attempts at revolutionary breakthroughs from the institutional trap of post-Soviet hybridity: the popular movement for state independence and its declaration in 1991, the Orange Revolution in 2004–2005, and the Euromaidan (Revolution of Dignity) of 2013–2014. However, the process is still incomplete. In addition, attempts for fast and radical reforms for European integration in post-Euromaidan Ukraine face new challenges that appeared after the annexation of Crimea by Russia, the ongoing armed conflict in the Donbas, and all the economic and humanitarian consequences of those actions.

The country's civil society, despite its institutional shortages and risks of right-wing radicalization, was a decisive factor in all three historical attempts of national breakthroughs to modernization, and is still the decisive factor in pushing for reforms. Indeed, consistent and powerful development of civil society is perhaps the only real achievement of the country and an important indicator of its democratization during this period. But one should also admit that Ukrainian civil society has been focused on political activism (up to political radicalism) and has been mostly oriented to the electoral process, aiming to change political configuration at the top levels of the state. At the same time, routine everyday practices in developing civility and strengthening the rule of law in all spheres of social life, activities oriented to developing tolerance and social cohesion, and efforts aimed at conflict prevention have been often overlooked by many NGOs.

The religious situation in Ukraine is no less complex and multidimensional than the country's transformation. Ukraine is a multi-confessional country representing major world religions, and with nine different churches representing the dominant Orthodox tradition. As of January 1, 2018 there were more than 34,000 religious communities of various churches and denominations officially registered in the country (Ministry of Culture of Ukraine, 2018). Among the largest churches on the religious map of the country (in terms of the number of communities) are: (1) the UOC-MP; (2) the OCU, which was created by unification of the Ukrainian Orthodox Church of the Kyiv Patriarchate (UOC-KP), the Ukrainian Autocephalous Orthodox Church (UAOC) and a few communities of the UOC-MP and granted autocephalous status in January 2019; (3) the Ukrainian Greek Catholic Church (UGCC); (4) the All-Ukrainian Union of Evangelical Christian Baptists; (4) the All-Ukrainian Union of Evangelical Christians (Pentecostals).

According to the 2016 nationwide representative survey by the Institute of Sociology of the National Academy of Sciences of Ukraine, the vast majority of respondents (77.6%) profess Orthodoxy, Greek Catholics make up 8%, Protestants 1.3%, and Catholics 1.2%. More than 70% of the population nationwide consider themselves religious believers (Table 7.1).

Table 7.1 Responses to the question "To which religious confession do you belong?" (N=1800, %)[1]

Responses	2002	2006	2010	2014	2016
Non-religious	12.7	12.6	11.7	10.7	11.1
(Christian) Orthodox	74.9	76.3	76.7	78.8	77.6
(Christian) Catholic	1.7	1.2	0.8	1.2	1.2
(Christian) Greek Catholic	7.7	7.4	7.4	7.6	7.9
(Christian) Protestant	1.1	0.9	0.9	0.7	1.3
Islam	0.3	0.2	1.0	0.0	0.1
Judaism	0.2	0.1	0.1	0.1	0.0
Other	1.1	1.3	1.0	0.7	0.5
No response	0.3	0.0	0.6	0.3	0.3

Table 7.2 Responses to the question "If you are an Orthodox believer, to which Orthodox Church do you belong?" (N=1800, %)

Responses	2016
Belong to the Ukrainian Orthodox Church of the Kyiv Patriarchate	37.3
Belong to the Ukrainian Orthodox Church of the Moscow Patriarchate	20.5
Belong to the Ukrainian Autocephalous Orthodox Church	1.4
Belong to another Orthodox Church	1.3
I visit churches, but I do not know which church they belong to	6.8
I am simply an Orthodox Christian, not belonging to any of the churches	28.1
Hard to respond	4.6

In 2016, respondents who described themselves as belonging to Orthodox tradition were also asked about which concrete church they belong to. Up to 40% of those respondents identified themselves affiliated with the UOC-KP, about 20% of the respondents were affiliated with the Ukrainian UOC-MP, and 28% of the respondents responded that they were "simply an Orthodox Christian, not belonging to any of the churches" (Table 7.2).

The surveys reflect a complex (and somewhat confusing) variety of Ukrainian Orthodoxy in popular perception. They also reveal a rather formal religiosity and corresponding manner of individual practice within churches for many people in the country. In a similar way, Catherine Wanner (2014) calls this kind of Orthodox religiosity in Ukraine an "ambient faith," that functions "alongside secularism and not as a direct challenge to it" (p. 433).

In Ukraine, the religious revival in the late 1980s was accompanied by a process of post-Communist transformation that turned a formerly ideologically atheistic country into a society of believers. Although religion (as well as various substrates of magical consciousness) has filled a certain spiritual vacuum after the fall of Communism, the religious revival has also corresponded to democratization and to the formation of civil society in the country. After all, religious freedom as an important part of the whole spectrum of individual freedoms is fundamental to any democracy. From a social and cultural perspective, the real provision of religious freedom also meant a decisive societal transformation from the totality of Communist ideology with its official atheism, and a move from omnipotent state control in all spheres of life to an opening for individual choices in the framework of the post-Soviet experience. In a symbolic sense, this was a deep institutional shift to individual "privatization" of one's own consciousness and will, and since individual freedoms are also essential civic values, this process was no less significant than economic privatization for emerging civil society.

But unlike in neighboring Poland, where the Catholic Church kept its social influence even under the Communist rule and became a powerful actor of democratic transformation from the end of the 1980s, Ukraine did not have a strong national church that could play the role of consolidating civil religion, supporting the country's efforts to strengthen state sovereignty and democratization.

Since Ukraine's declaration of state independence in 1991, many attempts to establish a national autocephalous Orthodox church have been immediately faced with powerful resistance from the UOC-MP and the Russian Orthodox Church (ROC). Official initiatives to obtain autocephalous status for the Orthodox church in Ukraine were reactivated after 2014, and in December of 2018 the new Orthodox Church of Ukraine (OCU) was finally created at the Unifying Council (*Ob"yednavchyy Sobor*).

Even with the entrance of the OCU into Ukraine's religious landscape, the country remains highly poly-confessional and pluralistic. On the one hand, a plurality of churches and denominations is important evidence of a state policy of religious freedom, and an indicator of a rather high degree of the country's democratization in this respect (Brik, 2018), while on the other hand, not all churches in Ukraine could become full allies of national civil society in facing the challenges of the country's European integration that required modernizing reforms in many spheres. The challenge to full engagement of churches in national society primarily stems from the different positions of the major churches, in particular the split within the dominant Orthodox church along the demarcation line regarding Ukraine's geopolitical choice for European integration and the questions of Ukrainian national identity. The UOC-MP, even though it has some pro-Ukrainian representation among its priests, mostly retains a pro-Russian position. The question has also been raised of whether or to what extent the UOC-MP is de facto autonomous (if at all) from its mother church – the ROC, which is one of the most active and powerful ideological institutions employed by Russia in its war against Ukraine. In contrast, the newly established OCU, the previous UOC-KP, and the UGCC are nationally-oriented churches favoring pro-Western positions for Ukraine. This approach makes those churches natural allies of national civil society in supporting some of the reforms[2] associated with the country's European integration.

It should also be noted that the split of the Orthodox church in Ukraine largely coincides with the regional variations in geopolitical orientations and linguistic identification of the country's population. The vast majority of the

OCU parishes (which were inherited from the UOC-KP and the UAOC) are in the west (excluding Transcarpathia), north, and center of the country, while the UOC-MP is strongest in the country's east and south. The UOC-MP also retains control of the major Orthodox centers in Ukraine, such as the Kyiv-Pechersk and the Pochayiv *Lavras*.

However, Orthodox churches in the country have not become a powerful consolidating factor in Ukraine's transformation, and not only because of their disunity. Ukrainian religiosity (with an exception regarding members of small religious groups, and, to some extent, believers of the UGCC) might be considered to be mostly popular ritual practices and religious holidays. That kind of ritual religiosity became fashionable with the lifting of various obstacles on religious activities after the collapse of the Communist atheistic state. Post-Communist mass consciousness is still primarily naïve, magic, and mostly paternalistic, rather than a rational, socially responsible, and consciously religious one. This kind of religiosity presupposes faith not only in God, but equally in astrologers and politicians-populists, a faith in magically simple decisions enabling various kinds of economic or political miracles.

However, even this kind of somewhat-formal religiosity also retains significance in Ukraine's situation of a permanent crisis of institutional trust. Religion and churches as its main institutions play an important social role, and, at least at the level of public opinion, religion and churches have considerable influence in Ukraine. According to a 2018 sociological survey by the Razumkov Center (2018), about two-thirds of respondents (63.7%) recognized the influence of religion on social life in the country. The majority of the respondents of this survey also agreed with the statements that "religion raises people's morality and spirituality" (71.2% agreed), "religion is one among other important factors of a renaissance of national consciousness and culture" (63.7% agreed) and "religion is one of the factors of democratic society" (52.4% agreed). The respondents' opinions on whether religion is a factor in political life in Ukraine were split in this survey, though the majority of the respondents (44.4%) agreed that religion is a factor in politics, and 35% of those being asked disagreed. Ukrainians also want more active involvement of religious organizations in social policy, particularly in dealing with the issues of socially vulnerable parts of population (the poor, disabled, and ill and elderly people). Furthermore, 74% of respondents believe that religious leaders should raise their voices for protecting the poor against the authorities' decisions that lower people's social and economic levels. This also means that in the public mind, churches are seen as an influential social institution that should use its moral authority in helping and protecting people.

Indeed, churches and clergy are steadily among the permanent leaders of public trust in the country. According to a 2017 nationwide monitoring survey by the Institute of Sociology of the Ukrainian Academy of Sciences, about 50% of respondents trusted churches (the question does not specify which church) and the clergy. However, in a similar survey conducted in 2016, almost one-fifth of respondents also trusted astrologers, whose level of aggregate trust was higher in the society than state authorities (the president, parliament, and government) and institutions of justice and law enforcement (police and the courts) (Table 7.3).

Another promising trend of the recent period in Ukraine is the considerable growth of public trust of civil society institutions such as charitable funds, NGOs, and volunteers. In fact, volunteers have even risen to the highest level of public trust, usually attributed to churches and the army. The highest level of public trust of volunteers in 2017 (up to 60%) reflects the public recognition of the valuable social input of the impressive wave of volunteerism that began during the Euromaidan. Voluntarism has developed even further in the post-Euromaidan period, which addressed issues of army supplies and the humanitarian issues of internally-displaced persons after the annexation of Crimea and the continuing military conflict in Donbas. Volunteerism and various forms of charitable assistance are spheres in which churches and civil society could meet each other, more closely interacting and reinforcing a social effect within their mutual collaboration. Another positive fact is that in Ukrainian public opinion, religiosity is not considered as a factor that negatively influences a person's social activity: the majority of the respondents (67.2%) of the Razumkov Center (2018) survey disagreed with the statement that "religion makes people passive and indifferent to social life."

These attitudes are not reflected in actual correlations between religiosity and social activity. Sociological studies demonstrate that the correlative link between religiosity and some characteristics of social activism (such as membership in NGOs, the practice of volunteering, engagement in political actions and support of democracy, confidence, social cohesion, attitudes to transparency, and tolerance and environmental concerns) is rather weak in Ukraine, as well as in Russia (Balakireva & Sereda, 2013), and that religious faith has hardly any impact on a person's life attitudes regarding one's reliance on oneself or on external factors. But there are also some nuances. First, Ukrainian

Table 7.3 Aggregate public trust ("fully trust" and "mostly trust" responses) to different institutions in Ukraine (N=1800, %)

Institution	1996	2000	2004	2010	2014	2016	2017
Churches and the clergy	35.0	38.6	44.0	56.3	47.5	49.7	51.2
Mass media	21.6	28.9	27.9	30.7	25.2	21.2	28.1
Militia/police	13.8	12.4	14.2	13.5	6.5	12.1	22.8
The courts	-	-	15.6	11.6	5.3	6.4	7.9
President	23.4	26.9	15.0	30.8	33.9	10.6	11.2
The parliament	8.7	7.1	8.1	14.2	8.6	5.7	5.3
The cabinet of ministers	13.0	13.7	11.2	19.6	17.2	6.5	7.1
Army	37.1	34.5	34.7	34.2	39.7	41.8	46.0
Political parties	3.3	3.8	8.5	7.7	3.8	4.7	6.0
Charitable funds and NGOs	-	-	15.2	15.5	14.8	31.0	37.5
Volunteers	-	-	-	-	-	47.3	58.1
Astrologists	16.9	15.7	13.6	15.7	11.2	17.2	-

Greek Catholics, mostly located in western Ukraine, are a more active and consolidated religious group than Orthodox Christians. They also demonstrate stronger correlations between their religiosity and orientations to various forms of social activism than average. In addition, as the practice of Ukraine's transformation proves, the social functions of religion and its public and even political role have been and could still be intensified in various complex contexts, such as crisis, conflict, or the war.

The churches at the Euromaidan and in the war

The 2013–2014 Euromaidan was a powerful manifestation of a protest of national civil society against the authoritarian government and was also the most radical public attempt at political change with regard to Ukraine's European integration. These revolutionary events and the dramatic post-Euromaidan development have also brought to the fore the issues of the public role of religion in Ukrainian society. Various churches and their clergy were engaged in the events of the Euromaidan protests in various forms, both direct and indirect.

In fact, the nature of the Euromaidan protests and the Russian-Ukrainian conflict, together with the intra-Orthodox divisions, have further engaged churches in political and civil society spheres and have increased solidarity between civil society and religion in Ukraine. First, churches already had experience in getting involved in political processes, particularly during the political struggle associated with the electoral presidential campaign of 2004 and the following Orange Revolution in Ukraine. The Euromaidan, however, has exceeded the Orange Revolution in terms of radicalism and dramatic events, including a high degree of mutual violence and the loss of human lives. The national scale and international dimension of the conflict, its extreme radical character and bitterness, involving the literal question of life or death for many people, have made it difficult for churches to stay apart from the events. Churches have been unable to avoid mentioning the conflict even during worship services.

Second, the Euromaidan reinforced the latent conflict between two geopolitical courses for Ukraine – namely its aspiration to European integration and its gravitation to the Russian pro-imperial geopolitical field (the so-called "Russian World") – and actualized the issues of Ukrainian national, cultural, and state identity. The churches in Ukraine, particularly Orthodox churches, were already divided and remained in different positions in regard to those issues. During the Euromaidan and particularly in the post-Euromaidan developments, church issues have been politicized and have become an aspect of the country's broader political agenda. The intra-church cleavage within Ukrainian Orthodoxy transformed into a church conflict having not only a national but also a geopolitical character.

In addition, the Euromaidan was per se about values. In its agenda, the protest movement articulated universal social virtues and a moral vision concerning a "good society," justice, solidarity, and human dignity. The concept of dignity became not only the Euromaidan's "primary orienting symbol" that "forged feelings of unity, solidarity and resolve" for the activists (Wanner, 2017, p. 3), but the polysemantic character of the concept of dignity, comprising broad humanitarian, international legal, and historical religious meanings, also provided the protest actions with their multifunctional legitimacy and justified them as the morally righteous pursuit. In a way, the Euromaidan has constructed and developed its own system of "political theology," as Catherine Wanner (2017) puts it. The ideas of dignity; remembrance of the "Heaven's Hundred" (*Nebesna Sotnya*), referring to the protesters killed; and other similar concepts have become part of the new vocabulary of this political theology.

In addition to the function of legitimization of collective actions, a symbolic resource of public (or civil) religion at the Euromaidan was also used for other modes and manifestations. Public religion via its spiritual actors was actively involved in shaping the values for the new public space (Kalenychenko, 2017). It also appeared as a "source of collective duty, when the clergy tried to change or establish the moral rules of life on the Euromaidan" and contributed to "sacralization of the new turn of history, which became a 'revolution'" (Kalenychenko, 2017, pp. 29–31). Public religion in its different confessional forms and its various manifestations, not necessarily always institutionalized, vividly appeared during the protests. According to Horkusha and Fylypovych (2014), the civil church of Ukraine was born at the Euromaidan.

However, the most convincing manifestations of the new public roles of religion were that political deeds and spiritual words were intertwined not only at the level of the Euromaidan's political theology, but also in religious practice immersed in the complex political and social context. In 2013–2014, in Kyiv's streets, a new pattern of practical alliance between the people, not all of whom were religious believers, and churches as institutions that aimed at serving them, was forged. These practices of public religion and the openly engaged churches included the provision of shelters for protesters and medical hospitals for the wounded by the UOC-KP; humanitarian help and donations organized by various churches and religious organizations; regular prayers at the Euromaidan gatherings and meetings; prayers on the front lines of the conflict between the barricades and police; religious services and rituals, including memorial services for the dead; and various forms of spiritual, emotional, and material support provided by the churches to both sides of the conflict.

Another important confirmation of the increasing public role of churches in the conflict was their joint initiatives and activities to mediate the conflict and their attempts to find a peaceful solution. These activities were mostly conducted in the framework of the All-Ukrainian Council of Churches and Religious Organizations, which became a suitable platform for dialogue, negotiations, and discussions among the clerical authorities and politicians from conflicting sides. Even though these initiatives did not entirely succeed and failed to prevent deadly violence on both sides, this was a valuable experience of attempted national reconciliation. It was important not only for confirming the public role of churches, but also for its prospect for development of Ukraine's civil society, with its necessary and largely overlooked agenda.

The role of the churches at the Euromaidan has been already deeply explored in many studies (Fylypovych & Horkusha, 2014, 2016; Kalenych-enko, 2017; Wanner, 2017). An attempt to sum up briefly the main results of these studies can be found in the useful distinction between two dimensions in the public manifestations of religion on the Euromaidan suggested by Tetiana Kalenychenko (2017): (1) the hierarchical (official) presence of religion, including official clerical performance, religious services, and rituals with direct involvement of the highest level of religious hierarchies from different churches and (2) the local (inclusive), a lower level involvement of clergy with believers.

Extrapolating similar distinctions to the issue of engagement of the churches in the conflict more generally one may see some differences. These nuanced differences, particularly between the positions of the Orthodox churches of Kyiv and Moscow Patriarchates, are mostly correlated with the political positions and geopolitical orientations of a majority of their believers at local regional levels. However, in their official and joint appeals, all the churches were unanimous in their wishes for a peaceful solution of the conflict. In a practical way, nationally oriented Ukrainian churches – the UOC-KP, the UGCC, and most of the Protestant communities – have clearly chosen the side of the Euromaidan, which was supported by the vast majority of the faithful of these denominations. The position of the UOC-MP was more complex, since it had to take into account the critical stance of the ROC towards the protest actions against Yanukovych's government. However, many priests of the UOC-MP were on the streets as Ukrainian citizens who sympathized with the protesters. A kind of identity split between a person's prescribed institutional loyalty to the Russian mother church and his personal civic self-awareness as a Ukrainian patriot (as it was in the case of the Farther Heorhiy Kovalenko[3]) appeared to be rather typical for many priests and believers of the UOC-MP at the Euromaidan and the country's post-Euromaidan dramatic development.

The annexation of Crimea by Russia and its support of armed separatism in Donbas starting in the spring of 2014 marked the beginning of the war against Ukraine. Patriotism and the civic duty of protecting the country were actualized as values of a national civil society. In the face of the low readiness of the regular army, it was civil society and its military and civic volunteers who protected the country during the most difficult and dramatic early period of military conflict in Donbas.

With the onset of military conflict, churches and their priests faced a new challenge which demanded their voice and a clear position on the issues of war and patriotism. The UOC-KP and UGCC clearly took a patriotic position, blessing as a holy deed a citizen's constitutional duty to protect the country and its territorial integrity. The UOC-MP again found itself in difficult situation, since its believers and its priests were on both sides of the conflict and because of the position of the

Russian mother church. As a result, the UOC-MP mostly remained silent, trying to avoid a clear official condemnation of Russia as an aggressor.

At the same time, the ROC in its official statements never recognized Russian aggression, but constantly spoke of a "fratricidal war" within Ukraine itself. Moreover, some priests of the Moscow Patriarchate in both Russia and Ukraine blessed the annexation of Crimea and armed separatism in Donbas. Some military units of the aggressor and separatists in that period were also led under names, banners, and symbols of Russian Orthodox Christianity.[4] Many believers and politicians in Ukraine were very sensitive to the ROC's ideological support of the Russian military aggression against Ukraine. In addition, the growing negative attitude toward the ROC was extrapolated to some extent to the UOC-MP. The controversial symbolic gesture by the hierarchs of the UOC-MP, who refused to stand up and honor the soldiers and officers awarded with the order of "Hero of Ukraine" at the parliamentary meeting on May 8, 2015, also reinforced that perception, even though the UOC-MP later explained this as "a protest against any war as such" (Hlava UPTs MP Onyfriy, 2015).

The position of the ROC on the war against Ukraine became both the subject of active public discussions and sharp criticism, and also led some parishes of the UOC-MP, especially in western and central Ukraine, to join the UOC-KP. Furthermore, increasing calls were made in the Ukrainian public discourse to ban the activities of the UOC-MP as a church of "the aggressor state," or, at least, to have its name changed to "The Russian Orthodox Church in Ukraine." In this context, the actualization of the issue of a national Orthodox autocephalous church seemed quite natural, just as it was also predictable that these initiatives would receive a furious rejection from the ROC and active countermeasures by the Russian state via the whole powerful arsenal of its political, diplomatic, and media channels.

Meanwhile, unlike in Crimea and in parts of Donbas under military control by Russia-backed separatists, where no other churches are welcomed outside of the Moscow Patriarchate, the Orthodox autocephaly does not call into question actual religious diversity in Ukraine. At least, the official position of the OCU is promising in this regard. At the official enthronement ceremony for the newly elected Primate of the OCU Epiphany in January 2019, he confirmed that the religious process in Ukraine, including the move of parishes converting to the OCU, should be smooth and that the goal was for it to be "peaceful, calm, and voluntary" (Ukrainian Orthodox Church, 2019).

This principle of peaceful voluntary self-organization could be an important shared value for both religious processes and civil society in Ukraine. It is also symptomatic that the movement towards autocephaly has occurred in parallel with the process of consolidation and institutionalization of civil society in Ukraine. The alliance between churches and civil society as a civic–religious informal association, whose prototype has appeared at the Euromaidan and which would aim at Ukraine's good governance and a society sharing civic virtues and moral values, might be an ideal outcome of these parallel processes.

Conclusion

In responding to the question whether the churches are part of civil society in Ukraine, the answer is not unambiguous. On the one hand, Ukrainian churches are definitely not typical grass-roots civic organizations. All the cautious reservations about churches as peculiar social institutions with their own traditions, hierarchy, and internal rules and procedures seem to be rather compelling in the case of Ukraine. Furthermore, the peculiarity of the religious situation in the country is the diversity of religious denominations and the split of Orthodoxy along the demarcation line for the country's European integration and for the issues of Ukrainian national identity. This division suggests that some vital aspects of the agenda of national civil society are unlikely to be shared by all the churches in Ukraine.

On the other hand, religious institutional plurality and even the peaceful church cleavages in the country might be considered as important and socially valuable indicators of a healthy, though still developing civil society and of institutionalized pluralism reflecting the actual social and cultural diversity and regional variations of Ukraine. This also evidences a high level of the country's democratization with regard to religious freedom.

Current promising prospects for the closer mutual interaction between the churches and civil society have arisen from the Euromaidan. The support of the citizens' protest movement by the nationally oriented churches has meant the formation of new priorities in the configuration "churches – society – the state." The churches, having functioned as influential public actors, have made their choice in favor of serving the people, not the authorities (Shchur, 2013). And as Catherine Wanner (2017) fairly notes, there was the situation in which "religious institutions were against the state as opposed to a collaborative relationship between state and clerical authorities as has been the used historic pattern" (p. 8), referring to the Orthodox religious tradition with its *Symphonia* between the church and state. It is also worth noting that this priority in favor of civil society by the major churches has also remained consistent in their position regarding the issue of the country's territorial integrity in the war in Donbas. After all, in this case, these churches have shared a similar patriotic position with civil society, a position which seemed more consistent than the state policy.

In the current circumstances of Ukraine's challenging transformation, the churches as respected social institutions have already proven their important social function in promoting a public religion agenda combining both religious moral values and civic virtues. An important and still not fully realized public role of the churches in Ukraine could be found in their more active engagement in applying their valuable, even though not entirely successful, experience in conflict mediation and reconciliation. This is an overlooked sphere of public activity that churches' activities could effectively fill, which would also correspond to the task of the actualization of the values of tolerance and civility for civic activists and for Ukrainian society as a whole.

However, both churches and civil society (particularly the NGO network) in Ukraine still need modernization and internal transformation from typically hierarchical bureaucratic structures, which are often engaged in corporative and potentially destructive competition, to active coordinating platforms, local level networks and centers of civic solidarity, volunteering, and mutual support. These similar activities could be motivated by both ideals of religion and civil society: the sincere religious faith in the need to help a fellow citizen and support one's neighbor, and beliefs in civil solidarity, responsibility, and care for the common good.

Notes

1 These sociological data and the following (if not specially indicated) are from the nation-wide representative surveys conducted by the Institute of Sociology of the National Academy of Sciences of Ukraine. The surveys are usually conducted in June and July each year. The sample is 1800 adult (18 years old and older) respondents representing all the regions and socio-demographic groups of the country. Since 2014, the Crimea and parts of Donbas (Donetsk and Luhansk oblasts) are not included in the sample. I will be happy to share our data by request.

2 However, as it was mentioned, there are some reservations regarding traditionalistic positions of Ukrainian nationally oriented churches and their worried skepticism towards some aspects of European integration, particularly concerning the issues of human rights of LGBTQ+ communities, gender identification, etc.

3 In 2014 Farther Heorhiy Kovalenko publicly announced that he did not belong to the UOC-MP, but to the Ukrainian Orthodox Church as a whole. He explained: "I have no problem at all with my patriotism, because I am a citizen of my country. You should be a true citizen, if you are a Christian" (Kostyuk, 2018).

4 See more about this in Ihor Kozlovsky's interview.

References

Alexander, J. C. (2006). *The civil sphere*. doi:10.1093/acprof:oso/9780195162509.001.0001

Andersen, T. B., & Jensen, P. S. (2017). Preaching democracy. *SSRN Electronic Journal*. doi:10.2139/ssrn.2940176

Balakireva, O., & Sereda, I. (2013). Religion and civil society in Ukraine and Russia. In J. de Hart, P. Dekker, & L. Halman (Eds.), *Religion and civil society in Europe* (pp. 219–250). doi:10.1007/978-94-007-6815-4_12

Banner, M. (2009). Christianity and civil society. In J. A. Coleman (Ed.), *Christian political ethics* (pp. 3–21). doi:10.1515/9781400828098–002

Brik, T. (2018, February 18). Religious regulations and Orthodox competition in Ukraine. *The Kennan Institute Blog: Focus Ukraine*. Retrieved from www.kennan-focusukraine.org/religious-regulations-and-orthodox-competition-in-ukraine/

Casanova, J. (1994). *Public religion in the modern world*. doi:10.7208/chicago/9780226190204.001.0001

Coleman, J. A. (Ed.). (2009). *Christian political ethics*. doi:10.1515/9781400828098–002

Edwards, M. (Ed.). (2011). *The Oxford handbook of civil society*. doi:10.1093/oxfordhb/9780195398571.001.0001

Fergusson, D. (2004). *Church, state and civil society*. doi:10.1017/cbo9780511607097

Fylypovych, L., & Horkusha, O. (Eds.). (2014). *Maydan i tserkva: khroniky podiy i ekspertna otsinka* [The Maidan and the Church: Chronicles of the events and experts' assessment]. Kyiv, Ukraine: Sumit-Knyga.

Fylypovych, L., & Horkusha, O. (2016). Holos tserkvy: aksyolohichni vymiry religiynoyi rytoryky na Maidani 2013–2014 rokiv [The Voice of Church: The axiological dimensions of religious rhetoric at the 2013–2014 Maidan]. *Filosofska dumka, 4*, 87–103.

Gathuo, A. (2003). Democracy through an undemocratic institution? The church as part of civil society. *Trotter Review, 15*(1), 9–21.

Habermas, J. (2008). Notes on post-secular society. *New Perspectives Quarterly, 25*(4), 17–29. doi:10.1111/j.1540-5842.2008.01017.x

Herbert, D. (2013). Religion and civil society: Theoretical reflections. In J. de Hart, P. Dekker, & L. Halman (Eds.), *Religion and civil society in Europe* (pp. 13–45). doi:10.1007/978-94-007-6815-4_2

Hlava UPTs MP Onyfriy ob'yasnil pochemu ne vstal v chest' heroyev Ukrainy [Head of the UOC-MP Onufry explains why he did not stand up to honor heroes of Ukraine]. (2015, May 15). Retrieved from www.unian.net/politics/1076337-glava-upts-mp-onufriy-obyyasnil-pochemu-ne-vstal-v-chest-geroev-ukrainyi.html

Horkusha, O., & Fylypovich, L. (2014, May 15). Narodzhena na Maydani: hromadyans'ka tserkva Ukrayiny [Born on the Maidan: The civil church of Ukraine]. Retrieved from https://risu.org.ua/ua/index/studios/studies_of_religions/56419/

Kalenychenko, T. (2017). Public religion during the Maidan protests in Ukraine. *Euxeinos, 24*, 23–38.

Kean, J. (2010). Civil society, definitions and approaches. In H. K. Anheier & S. Toepler (Eds.), *Encyclopedia of civil society* (pp. 451–454). doi:10.1007/978-0-387-93996-4_531

Kostyuk, B. (2018, February 18). UPTs (Moskovs'koho Patriarkhatu) v chas viyny z Rosiyeyu [UOC (Moscow Patriarchate) in times of war with Russia]. Retrieved from www.radiosvoboda.org/a/29039980.html

Kruip, G., & Reifeld, H. (Eds.). (2007). *Church and civil society: The role of Christian churches in the emerging countries of Argentina, Mexico, Nigeria and South Africa.* Berlin, Germany: Konrad Adenauer Stiftung.

Miller, D. E. (2011). Civil society and religion. In M. Edwards (Ed.), *The Oxford handbook of civil society* (pp. 257–269). doi:10.1093/oxfordhb/9780195398571.003.0021

Ministry of Culture of Ukraine. (2018). Dani departamentu u spavah relihiy i natsional'nostey pro relihiynu merezhu [Data of the Department of religious and nationalities affairs on religious landscape]. Retrieved from RISU web-site https://risu.org.ua/ua/index/resourses/statistics/ukr_2018/70440/

Razumkov center. (2018). Osoblyvosti relihiynoho i thserkovno-relihiynoho samovyznachennya ukrayins'kyh hromadyan: tendentsiyi 2010–2018 rokiv [Peculiarities of the religious and church self-identification of Ukrainian citizens: 2010–2018 trends]. Retrieved from http://razumkov.org.ua/uploads/article/2018_Religiya.pdf

Shchur, M. (2013, December 26). Ukrayinski tserkvy na Maydani obraly storonu narodu: interv"yu z relihiyeznavtsem Viktorom Yelens'kym [Ukrainian Churches at the Maidan took the peoples' side: Interview with religious scholar Viktor Yelensky]. Retrieved from www.radiosvoboda.org/content/article/25212456.html

Simonchuk, O. (2016, January 19). LHBT i Tserkva: chy ye mozhlyvist' porozuminnya? [LGBT and the Church: Is there possibility for mutual understanding?]. Retrieved from www.lgbt.org.ua/materials/show_3710/

Stepanenko, V. (2018). Tsyvil'nist': sotsiolohichna aktualizatsiya kontseptu [Civility: A sociological actualization of the concept]. *Sotsiologiya: Teoriya, Metody, Marketyng, 1*, 65–84.

Ukrainian Orthodox Church enthrones Epiphany as leader. (2019, February 3). *RFE/RL*. Retrieved from www.rferl.org/a/ukrainian-orthodox-church-enthrones-epifaniy-as-leader/29748596.html

Wanner, C. (2014). 'Fraternal' nations and challenges to sovereignty in Ukraine: The politics of linguistic and religious ties. *American Ethnologist, 41*(3), 427–439. doi:10.1111/amet.12097

Wanner, C. (2017). The political valence of dignity and the Maidan protests. *Euxeinos, 24*, 3–9.

Welker, M., Koopman, N., & Vorster, J. (Eds.). (2017). *Church and civil society – German and South African perspectives*. doi:10.18820/9781928355137

8 A spatial analysis of religious diversity and freedom in Ukraine after the Euromaidan

Tymofiy Brik and Stanislav Korolkov

Introduction

Religious freedom proliferated in all post-Communist societies after the collapse of the USSR. Yet, over the course of time, researchers have observed significant changes in religious regulations in the region. For example, there is evidence of renewed religious repression in central Asia and Russia (Froese, 2004; Stark & Finke, 2000). Our chapter adds to this literature by examining religious regulations and religious vitality in Ukraine after the Euromaidan.

Religious regulations are discussed further in the text in terms of new legislative proposals as well as in terms of changes in public opinion towards certain religious groups. In this way, we follow the conceptualization of Grim and Finke (2006) who distinguished among governmental regulation, governmental favoritism, and social regulation of religion. Governmental regulation includes official policies implemented by the state; governmental favoritism involves privileges awarded to certain religious groups by the state; and social regulations are cultural restraints on specific religious groups that the state does not enforce but it may appear to tolerate if not encourage.

This chapter studies religious vitality in terms of religious communities at the regional level. We present and discuss data about the number of registrations of religious communities granted as well as those denied. In Ukraine, as in much of the post-Communist world, legal registration is seen as an important gateway for religious groups to be able to function. While in Ukraine, unlike in Russia and Belarus, registration of religious communities is not required for the practice of religion, it does provide an important badge of legitimacy, in addition to creating a legal entity that can hold property, enter into contracts, etc. We chose to study religious communities in order to detect changes in the religious landscape in Ukraine after the Euromaidan. Previous studies have frequently employed religious identities and church attendance derived from surveys in order to achieve the same task. We believe that this approach risks confounding religious and national identities. Religious and national identities are often blurred and intertwined in eastern Europe (Brubaker, 2012). In contrast, our approach detects shifts at the level of formal religious groups that respond to changes in state policies and religious regulation directly.

Another novelty of our analytical approach is that it shifts from a bottom-up to a top-down perspective. We believe our approach renders a better focus on how state policies influence religious organizations in Ukraine. Most of the existing literature about religious organizations in Ukraine emphasizes the bottom-up narrative (e.g., Balakireva & Sereda, 2013; Casanova, 1998; Krindatch, 2003; Mitrokhin, 2001). According to this narrative, civil society, local communities, and regional political actors were the most pivotal actors in shaping religion in Ukraine. These actors influenced religious organizations through supporting, financing, and legitimizing their activities or through simply generating demand for religious services. Moreover, in terms of the supply-side theory of religion, Ukrainian diversity in language and religious traditions has created specific local niches of religious consumers. Consequently, these niches have been catered to by different Orthodox churches (Brik, 2018). Since Ukrainian diversity has influenced religious vitality through stimulating religious demand, this diversity had been conceptualized as one of the bottom-up causes of religion as well.

While the bottom-up approach is very important, it offers only a part of the story. We add to the literature by focusing on the top-down perspective. In this chapter we look at how political changes and state policies at the national level influence regional quantities of religious communities. This top-down approach has rarely been applied to study Ukrainian religious organizations. The only macro-level event which has been unequivocally accepted in the literature as the most significant cause of religious vitality in Ukraine is the collapse of the USSR; after the mid-1990s and before the Euromaidan in 2014 there were no significant events of this kind. Therefore, there was no salient demand to study top-down processes of religion in Ukraine. However, after the Euromaidan, the annexation of Crimea by Russia, and the hybrid war in Donbas, the role of state policies and public opinion has changed. Current Ukrainian religious life at the level of religious communities has been shaped to a large extent by these macro-level processes. Therefore, we choose to address the top-down side of the story in order to more completely describe the religious situation in contemporary Ukraine.

The data we employ describe numbers of religious communities at the regional level. We compare official statistical data published on January 2014 and March 2017. The first dataset includes information about all religious communities that existed in 2013 (the time preceding and during the Euromaidan). These religious communities were permitted to register during the course of 2013; the official data were published on January 1, 2014. The second dataset, with similar types of data albeit from 2016, was published on March 29, 2017. This contrast permits us to compare how the religious market in Ukraine has changed after the Euromaidan.[1]

These data show two types of dynamics. The first one describes changes in the number of registered religious communities. A positive dynamic means that more communities of a given religious group were registered in a region over a particular period of time. In contrast, a negative dynamic means that some of these communities either closed down or decided to leave their religious organization and joined another religious organization. Another possibility leading to a negative dynamic could be that communities lost their official status because they could not comply with Ukrainian laws. Finally, it is also possible that communities vanished with time because of a lack of new member growth or because of poor management. The second dynamic observed in our data describes changes in the number of communities that were denied registration. A positive dynamic of this variable means that a given religious organization experienced more denials from the state when attempting to register.

Our data suggest that the structure of the Ukrainian religious landscape has changed since the Euromaidan. Most of the change reflects an increase in the number of communities of the Kyiv Patriarchate. At the same time, we do not observe severe repression of the Moscow Patriarchate. Instead, we observe a certain stagnation in these communities (in other words, their numbers remain rather stable). There is a difference between losing numbers (decline) and having no growth (stagnation). Although there are other possible explanations for this, one that appears likely given the stagnation of the Moscow Patriarchate and the increase of the Kyiv Patriarchate could signal state and/or local favoritism towards the latter. As some polls suggest, this favoritism towards the Kyiv Patriarchate goes hand in hand with societal acceptance of this religious organization. More Ukrainians see this church as legitimate when compared to its rival, i.e., the Moscow Patriarchate. Having said this, our data do not show repression of the Moscow Patriarchate in terms of a severe decline in number of communities or increase of denials of registrations for these communities.

Our data indicate new trends in the development of the religious landscape in Ukraine. For many years, the Ukrainian Orthodox Church of the Moscow Patriarchate (UOC-MP) has been superior to its rival the Ukrainian Orthodox Church of the Kyiv Patriarchate (UOC-KP) in terms of the number of registered communities. However, we observe that after the Euromaidan the number of registered Kyiv Patriarchate communities increased, and we do not observe the same pattern among the Moscow Patriarchate communities. The gap between these religious groups has narrowed since the occurrence of the Euromaidan. This new trend is likely to have consequences in both political and cultural spheres of Ukraine.

The religious landscape in Ukraine: demand, supply, and regulations

As an initial matter we explore aspects of religious markets, focusing on how these play out in the Ukrainian context. We argue that looking at the supply-side, particularly in the context of post-Euromaidan Ukraine, also provides valuable insights into the Ukrainian religious market and the impact of top-down changes.

Demand

Sociologists often employ the term markets to describe religious suppliers, i.e., formal religious groups. The religious market in Ukraine has been quite diverse and pluralistic for years. In sharp contrast to many other post-Communist countries, Ukrainian religious markets have been compared to the American model in terms of variability (Casanova, 1998). They include a variety of Orthodox and non-Orthodox churches: the UOC-KP, the UOC-MP, the Ukrainian Autocephalous Orthodox Church (UAOC), the Ukrainian Greek Catholic Church (UGCC), the Roman Catholic Church, different Protestant churches, as well as regional minorities that adhere to Islam (mostly Crimean Tatars) and Judaism.

According to surveys conducted in Ukraine in 2018, only 9% of respondents identified themselves as atheists (Kyiv International Institute of Sociology [KIIS], 2018). The overwhelming majority of respondents identified themselves as Orthodox (69%). The second most popular church among respondents was the Greek Catholic Church (9%). There is a significant regional variation (Borowik, 2002; Titarenko, 2008; Yelensky, 2010) – while Orthodox respondents are present in all regions of Ukraine, Greek Catholics are localized in the western macro-region (KIIS, 2018).

Supply

Surveys tap into the demand side of religion. Thus, data are needed to estimate the supply side of religious services. For the latter purpose, we turn to the rich spatial and temporal statistical data on religious communities registered in Ukraine (see Brik, 2018 for more details).

In this chapter, we choose to discuss our data on religious communities for six religious groups which together comprise approximately 79% of the population (KIIS, 2018). These groups are: (1) the UOC-KP; (2) the UOC-MP; (3) the UGCC; (4) the Jehovah's Witnesses; (5) the Evangelical Baptist Union of Ukraine; and (6) all Muslim communities considered together.

The UOC-KP and the UOC-MP are the two major Orthodox jurisdictions in Ukraine and compete with each other for followers. Although they are very similar in terms of their theological principles and ethical doctrines, they often disagree in how they value the national identities, language, history, and culture of Ukraine (Brik, 2018; Krindatch, 2003). While the UOC-KP and the UAOC have exploited pro-Ukrainian historical narratives, their opponents from the UOC-MP have often relied on the "Russian World" (*Russkiy mir*) doctrine, particularly appealing to believers in some regions of Ukraine, and use a narrative of "the truly national Ukrainian Church," which is more attractive in others.[2]

The Jehovah's Witnesses and Evangelical Baptists are two large groups we consider for the analysis as well. While Jehovah's Witnesses do not consider themselves Protestants, they are often perceived as one of the country's "new" religious groups (we do not discuss whether this is true) that, in contrast to Orthodox and Catholic groups, emerged in Ukraine together some new Protestant denominations. They are often considered as part of a large cluster of Protestant and Evangelist organizations regardless of their own views about it. For example, the Ministry of Culture of Ukraine included Jehovah's Witnesses in the statistical data for 2018 in a group called "Other Protestant churches" (Ministry of Culture of Ukraine, 2018). We address the Jehovah's Witnesses and Evangelical Baptists in particular because they have been quite vulnerable in predominantly Orthodox societies. For example, Jehovah's Witnesses were recently banned in Russia,[3] and their communities have suffered oppression in the self-proclaimed Donetsk Peoples' Republic (DPR). Hereafter in our discussion we include Jehovah's Witnesses as a part of the Protestant cluster in Ukraine.

Finally, we present data on Greek Catholic communities and all Muslim communities. These communities used to be concentrated in particular regions of Ukraine. However, after the Russian annexation of Crimea and the hybrid war in Donbas, local Muslim communities have migrated to other regions.

According to these data, the UOC-MP dominated at the national level in terms of religious communities from 1991 to 2015, growing from an estimated number of 5,031 to 12,574. The second largest group of communities, all Protestants (including the Jehovah's Witnesses), grew from 1,823 to 10,038. The UOC-KP demonstrated stable growth over the course of time, outrunning the Greek Catholic communities. The latter did not manage to expand outside of western Ukraine.

As we discussed in our previous studies (Brik, 2018), the data on religious demand (i.e., surveys) and religious supply (i.e., statistical data of religious communities) for 1992–2012 show an interesting discrepancy (we also see this in the data for 2017).[4] The Kyiv Patriarchate has become the most popular religion and yet remains inferior in terms of communities. In contrast, the Moscow Patriarchate is not as popular among respondents and is still superior in terms of communities. In other words, there is a negative correlation between popular support and structural strength. This situation, however, has been gradually changing since the Euromaidan as the number of the UOC-MP's communities has declined. Moreover, since 2018 (a period we do not study here) it appears that more than 400 communities of the UOC-MP have transitioned to the new independent Orthodox Church of Ukraine (OCU).[5]

Regulations

In terms of religious regulations, Ukraine has been quite free and pluralistic when compared to other post-Communist states, based on data from the Religion and State (RAS) project. This project has systematically collected comparative data to investigate religious regulations around the world (see Fox, n.d., 2008, 2011, 2018 for more information). Two indexes based on these data are presented further in the text.

The first index, "Regulation of and Restrictions on the Majority Religion or All Religions," is based on 29 items describing various restrictions that may exist in a society, such as restrictions on religious political parties, public religious speech, access to places of worship, and so forth. The second index, "Specific Types of Religious Legislation," is based on 51 items, such as restrictions on the production, import, sale, or consumption of specific foods or alcohol, restrictions on interfaith marriages, tithing requirements, various restrictions on women's public appearance, and the like.

Figures 8.1 and 8.2 show these two indexes for post-Communist societies from the early 1990s to 2014. The darker shades indicate higher values of the index while white indicates an absence of data (for instance, former Yugoslavian countries like Bosnia or Montenegro, or Ukraine in 1990). As can be seen, most of the religious regulations in post-Communist places have been instituted in central Asian countries. At the same time, Ukraine has witnessed lower rates of regulation, with levels comparable to those seen in Romania, Moldova, Bulgaria, and Russia.

Figure 8.2 shows the distribution of the index of religious legislations. In terms of this index, Ukraine had one of the most relaxed legislative systems among all post-Communist societies.

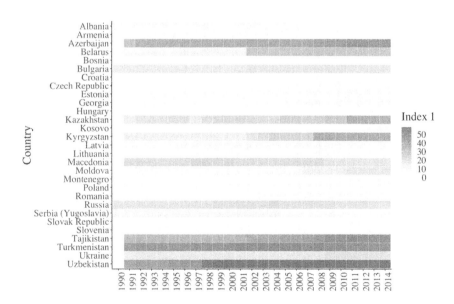

Figure 8.1 Index of Regulation of and Restrictions on the Majority Religion or All Religions (1992–2014), RAS project (Fox, n.d., 2008, 2011)

Figure 8.2 Index of Specific Types of Religious Legislation in Post-Communist Societies (1992–2014), RAS project (Fox, n.d., 2008, 2011)

Changes after the Euromaidan

Although Ukraine has been known to be quite pluralistic with respect to religious groups, this has changed recently. The Euromaidan, the annexation of Crimea by Russia, and the hybrid war in Donbas influenced Ukrainian politicians and the Ukrainian public to be less tolerant of Russian influence on religion. Religion has become increasingly seen as a matter of national security and cultural influence from Russia.[6] For instance, in terms of public opinion, in 2015 many respondents reported a loss of trust in the Moscow Patriarchate. For example, 37% of respondents answered that the Kyiv Patriarchate is the church of the Ukrainian people, 12% said the same about the UGCC, and none of the respondents said this about the Moscow Patriarchate. Moreover, 19% of the respondents agreed that the Moscow Patriarchate is the church of the aggressor state (Democratic Initiatives Fund [DIF], 2015).

In terms of legislative efforts and policies, President Petro Poroshenko has emphasized the importance of having one united Orthodox church of Ukraine. At the same time, Ukrainian legislators have debated imposing new restrictions on churches that are headquartered in Russia. In 2017, members of the UOC-MP marched in protest against such legislative initiatives (Pid Radoyu, 2017). Quite recently, on December 20, 2018, a new law was passed requiring the UOC-MP communities to change their names to ones that show their connection to the Russian Orthodox Church.

Moreover, starting in October 2018, a very important set of events happened when the Ecumenical Patriarch of Constantinople and the President of

Ukraine Poroshenko announced the new OCU that is independent of Russia and legitimate according to the canons of Orthodoxy. Debates over the nuances of the legal transition of other Orthodox churches into the body of the OCU are still in progress.

These actions were inspired to a large degree by the idea that a single united Orthodox Church will better serve as a religious pillar of society than a fragmented market of fiercely competing Orthodox jurisdictions. Moreover, the Russian church is seen as a threat to national security since it serves as one of the conduits of the Russian cultural policies in Ukraine. In terms of public opinion, in 2018, 31% of respondents answered in a survey that they support the idea of having one united independent Orthodox Church of Ukraine. At the same time, 20% were against it and 35% were indifferent (Stvorennya avtokefaliyi, 2018). Interestingly, this idea received equal support among the adherents of the Kyiv Patriarchate and Greek Catholics (48% and 48% respectively). This finding goes in line with previous literature which suggests that in Ukraine national and religious narratives are highly connected (Brik, 2018; Yelensky, 2010). Adherents of the latter two churches share pro-Ukrainian patriotic sentiments and are more likely to support a new church that is independent from Russia. In contrast, adherents of UOC-MP are less likely to support this idea.

While Ukraine has shown some evidence of state and local favoritism and social support for the politically pro-Ukrainian churches (i.e., UOC-KP), the territories of the self-proclaimed Donetsk and Luhansk "people's republics" have witnessed unprecedented levels of religious repression and hostilities. For example, a leader of the DPR publicly stated that he acknowledges only four religious groups: Orthodoxy, Roman Catholicism, Islam, and Judaism (Anna News, 2015). In the same interview, he promised to fight sectarianism and "pseudo-religions," clearly referencing Protestantism and Greek Catholicism.

According to a report from the Institute of Religious Freedom, militants of the DPR kidnapped parishioners of one of the Evangelical churches in the city of Sloviansk; some of parishioners' bodies were discovered later in a mass grave (Khronolohiya teroru, 2014). The same report includes information about some attacks on Protestant churches in the cities of Horlivka, Shakhtarsk, and Druzhkovka and an attack on a Protestant rehabilitation center in the city of Donetsk as well as information about a Greek Catholic priest who was temporarily imprisoned by the militants.

Religious regulations in Ukraine after the Euromaidan: registration and denials of registration

Religious groups across the globe often have to receive legal status in order to operate openly within their political states. However, states sometimes use registration requirements to increase restrictions on religions (Finke, Mataic, & Fox, 2017). This is not primarily the case in Ukraine, but registration is important for groups to enjoy all the benefits of legal entity status. We use our novel data regarding religious registration requirements in 2014 and

2017 in order to see the trends in grants and denials of registrations of religious communities in Ukraine.

The data on grants and denials of registrations for religious communities in Ukraine are different in magnitude. The total number of granted registrations of religious communities is relatively high and ranges from dozens to hundreds per year. At the same time, the incidence of registration denials is not very high. Furthermore, denials are entirely absent in some regions. Therefore, the distribution of these two metrics across regions will be discussed and presented in different formats for the sake of simplicity and readability. Finally, one has to keep in mind that the data are based on official registrations of local religious communities. It is possible that these data underestimate the total number of some religious communities that made a choice to avoid registration. For example, some Crimean Tatars could move to another region and maintain their old Crimean affiliation. Considering Donbas, our data for 2014 and 2017 are not comparable in the case of Donetsk and Luhansk oblasts. We have aggregated numbers only for those parts of Donetsk and Luhansk oblasts that are under the control of the Ukrainian government. Thus, any significant change between 2014 and 2017 in those regions could be attributed to the loss of territories.

Figure 8.3 shows rates of change from 2014 to 2017 in the numbers of registered Orthodox communities. For instance, there were 249 registered communities of the UOC-MP in the city of Kyiv in 2014. After 3 years, there were 269 communities of the same church. Twenty new communities were registered, which reflects an eight percent increase.

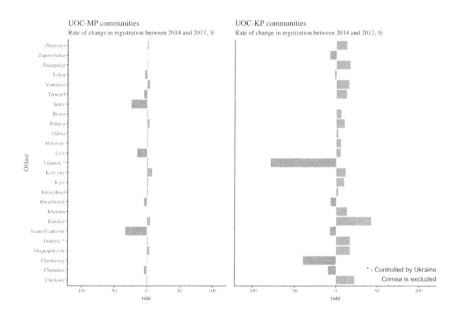

Figure 8.3 Rate of Change of Communities of the Orthodox Churches in Ukraine

Table 8.1 Rate of decline of communities of the Ukrainian Orthodox Church of the Moscow Patriarchate

	2014, absolute numbers	*2017, absolute numbers*	*Rate of change, %*
Ivano-Frankivsk Oblast	36	24	−33.3
Sumy Oblast	442	334	−24.4
Lviv Oblast	66	56	−15.5
Khmelnytskyi Oblast	960	916	−4.6
Ternopil Oblast	124	118	−4.8
Chernihiv Oblast	560	538	−3.9
Volyn Oblast	667	643	−3.6

Considering Figure 8.3., one observes that most of the regions witnessed stagnation in the number of UOC-MP communities, i.e., a small increase of about 1–3 percent per region. However, in several regions the numbers of the UOC-MP declined, including Chernihiv, Ivano-Frankivsk, Khmelnytskyi, Lviv, Sumy, Ternopil, and Volyn oblasts. While most of these regions are in western Ukraine, two of them – Sumy and Chernihiv oblasts – are in the northeast of Ukraine and are located very close to Russia. Thus, this decline is quite interesting. A careful investigation of the total numbers of registered religious communities in these regions shows that the largest rate of decline was observed in Ivano-Frankivsk due to the small total numbers of the UOC-MP (see Table 8.1). However, a decline in the Sumy oblast is significant in terms of both total numbers and rates of decline.

In sharp contrast to the UOC-MP, the UOC-KP increased in most of the regions. The outstanding rate of decline observed for the Luhansk Oblast can be explained by the fact that Ukraine lost a number of territories there due to the conflict with Russia. Interestingly, there was a small increase of the UOC-KP in another region that suffered from this war, the Donetsk Oblast. In other words, while Luhansk lost a significant number of religious communities of the UOC-KP and did not recover after this shock, the Donetsk communities of the UOC-KP managed to sustain their numbers.

Surprisingly, the Sumy Oblast appeared to be quite an outlier. We found that in addition to the UOC-MP, almost all other religious groups in our data declined in numbers as well (see Table 8.3 in the appendix). For instance, there were 33 Evangelical Baptist Union of Ukraine communities in the Sumy Oblast in 2014. In the course of four years, only seven of their communities remained (a 79% decline). Furthermore, four communities of the UGGC in 2014 were reduced to only one in 2017 (a 75% decline). In contrast, the numbers of the pro-Ukrainian UOC-KP in the Sumy Oblast did not change at all.

All in all, we see a stagnation of the UOC-MP communities with a significant increase of UOC-KP communities and a modest increase in the Greek Catholic communities. Given the backdrop of national events and public support for the UOC-KP, we assume that this could be indicative of state or local favoritism for these churches' patriotic position. While the state may not formally favor them (in the sense of classic state favoritism with public funding), it could possibly be discouraging other groups from even seeking to register.

Another interesting finding that we observe in our data is that traditionally regional religious groups increased their presence in other regions (see Table 8.3 in the appendix). For example, Muslim communities were typically organized by Crimean Tatars, but some of them left Crimea after the Russian annexation. Kyiv city and the Lviv, Dnipropetrovsk, and Mykolaiv oblasts have seen the largest increase in Muslim communities, which generally corresponds to the patterns of internal migration of Tatars (Dynamika mihratsiyi, 2019). The outlier is the Khmelnytskyi Oblast, where two registered communities in 2014 were reduced to only one in 2017 (i.e., a 50% decline due to the very small number of communities).

Considering denials of registration, Table 8.2 shows changes in total numbers of religious communities between 2014 and 2017.

In 2014, most of the regions presented in this table had zero instances of registration denials. In 2017 there were dozens of them. For example, there were 61 UOC-MP communities and 36 UOC-KP communities that were denied registration in the Khmelnytskyi Oblast in 2017, while 4 years previously (before the Euromaidan) neither of the churches had experienced any registration denials there. A similar pattern is observed for Chernihiv, Volyn, Ivano-Frankivsk, and Donetsk oblasts. All these regions display registration denials towards both UOC-MP and the UOC-KP.

We also observe some interesting and unexpected results. Surprisingly, the Ivano-Frankivsk Oblast, a region in Western Ukraine, has seen a sharp increase in denials of registration for more pro-Ukrainian communities, such as the UOC-KP and Greek Catholics (see Table 8.3). Furthermore, this particular oblast also displayed more denials of registration of Protestant communities as well. Interestingly, the Sumy Oblast is not among the regions with visible

Table 8.2 Changes in the numbers of denials of registration (absolute numbers) during 2014–2017

	UOC-MP	UOC-KP	Jehovah's Witnesses	Baptists	UGGC	Muslims
Khmelnytskyi Oblast	61	36	1	10	0	2
Chernihiv Oblast	35	25	1	3	0	1
Volyn Oblast	31	39	0	−2	0	0
Donetsk Oblast	28	34	0	5	10	0
Kirovohrad Oblast	18	8	10	−8	0	0
Lviv Oblast	15	0	1	0	22	0
Luhansk Oblast	0	21	0	0	0	1
Ivano-Frankivsk Oblast	12	45	8	3	55	0

registration denials. At the same time, we described this region as suspect for state or local favoritism in terms of growing communities of the UOC-KP. Thus, this favoritism may not always go hand in hand with state restrictions; these are two separate mechanisms. These findings open up room for debate about possible influences of local political elites in restricting some religious groups.

Registration denials for the Protestant communities and Jehovah's Witnesses groups followed another trajectory. In contrast to Orthodox and Greek Catholic groups, these groups (especially the Jehovah's Witnesses) did experience state registration denials before the Euromaidan. Thus, their denials after the Euromaidan cannot be indicative of a specific new wave of repression.

Conclusion

Sociologists have long argued that characteristics of religious markets can predict people's religious behaviors. In other words, the religious behavior of individuals can be modeled successfully once one knows whether a religious market is competitive or concentrated, regulated or unregulated, omnipresent or isolated. These variables are crucial because they tell us a lot about the incentives and capacities of religious organizations to be engaged with people and expand.

The structure of the religious market in Ukraine has changed dramatically since the Euromaidan. More regulation, state and local favoritism, and social regulation have been observed in Ukraine by pundits, journalists, and researchers. A number of Crimean Tatars have migrated from Crimea to other regions in Ukraine. Furthermore, new, previously unseen religious repression towards Protestants has emerged in the self-proclaimed republics of Donetsk and Luhansk during the hybrid war with Russia (Institute of Religious Freedom, 2018).

At the same time, the Ukrainian territories have witnessed an increase in religious regulations as well, mostly for Orthodox communities. While such regulations harm social legitimacy, they are far from full-fledged repression. Furthermore, a new independent OCU was announced by the Ecumenical Patriarch of Constantinople and the President of Ukraine, Poroshenko. This church is presented as a new, independent, and truly Ukrainian church. This status of national prestige and legitimacy could be seen as part of a social regulation of religion (Grim & Finke, 2006), meaning a type of cultural restraints that are not necessarily legally enforced by the state but create an overall image that some religious groups should be supported while others should be discouraged.

To what extent have these changes in legislation and public opinion influenced religious organizations in Ukrainian regions? While most of the previous studies have focused on the bottom-up narrative of religious organizations in Ukraine, we have employed the top-down approach and studied how state registration of religious communities changed after such major national events as the Euromaidan, the annexation of Crimea by Russia, and the hybrid war in Donbas. We have observed a profound change in the religious landscape of Ukraine.

Our novel data on religious communities in Ukraine since the Euromaidan largely support the above-mentioned narrative, however, with some clarifications. Considering Orthodox communities, we find evidence that the number of the UOC-KP communities increased after the Euromaidan, while the number of the UOC-MP communities remained almost unchanged from 2014 to 2017. We interpret this finding as evidence of state and/or local favoritism towards the UOC-KP. At the same time, we do not observe severe repression of the Moscow Patriarchate in terms of a sharp decline of their numbers.

We also observe a significant increase in denials of registration for the Orthodox communities in some regions of Ukraine. In some cases, registration denials were observed in those regions where no such action existed previously before the Euromaidan. This can be explained by local competition of religious groups that was stimulated by changes in legislation and public opinion. It is also possible that the registration denials we have observed in our data are merely a function of total growth of the quantity of communities that are trying to get registration. In other words, when more people apply to register a religious community, more people are denied the opportunity to register. The reasons for failure could be as trivial as lack of bureaucratic experience. It is also possible that some communities migrated from Crimea and/or eastern Ukraine and attempted to register their religious communities but were denied because of their ambivalent legal and social status of internally displaced persons. Unfortunately, we cannot investigate all these hypotheses with our data for now. Nevertheless, we clearly see three things. First, the rate of denials of registration increased dramatically. The situation has changed significantly since the Euromaidan, the Russian annexation of Crimea, and the hybrid war in Donbas. Second, there is regional variation. Finally, we observe that state favoritism in terms of "granted registrations" and state penalties in terms of "registration denials" do not always correlate at the local level.

For many years, researchers have observed a gap between religious demand and supply in Ukraine. According to surveys and polls, most Orthodox Ukrainians have identified themselves with the Kyiv Patriarchate. At the same time this religious organization has remained inferior in terms of the number of existing communities when compared to the Moscow Patriarchate. We observe that after the Euromaidan the gap has narrowed. Given that religious identities are tied to national identities in Ukraine, this shift in the religious landscape is likely to have consequences for a wide range of circumstances in Ukraine including elections, politics, and culture. Moreover, it seems that the lack of severe repression of the UOC-MP may pave the way for a gradual transition in the number of registered communities of the UOC-MP and the OCU to align more closely with popular opinion; so far there is no evidence of any violent polarization in the country at regional levels.

Appendix

Table 8.3 Rate of change of registration of the Ukrainian Religious Communities from 2014 to 2017, %

	UOC-MP	UOC-KP	Jehovah's Witnesses	Baptists	UGCC	Muslims
Vinnytsia Oblast	+4.6	+15.4	0	0	+11.8	+25
Volyn Oblast	−3.6	−1.9	0	−6.8	0	0
Dnipropetrovsk Oblast	+4.2	+16.7	−3.7	+8.8	+100**	+50**
Donetsk Oblast*	+1.6	+16.9	0	−4	−36.4	+11.4
Zhytomyr Oblast	+2.1	+12.8	−12.5	+12.1	+30.8	0
Zakarpattia Oblast	+1	+16.7	0	+1.1	+3.1	0
Zaporizhzhia Oblast	+0.8	−7.9	−12.9	+8.2	+21.4	+15.4
Ivano-Frankivsk Oblast	−33.3	−7.5	−11.6	−10	−7.4	0
Kyiv Oblast	+2	+9.6	0	+5.7	+26.3	+66.7**
Kirovohrad Oblast	+1.4	+2.6	−91.7**	+7.2	0	0
Luhansk Oblast*	+1.5	−78.6	0	0	+16.7	−8.3
Lviv Oblast	−15.2	+5.3	−4	+0.9	−0.4	+33.3
Mykolaiv Oblast	+1.4	+5.8	0	−13.5	0	+22.2
Odesa Oblast	+1.4	+2.4	0	−2.2	+5	0
Poltava Oblast	+3.8	+9.9	0	+4.1	+8.3	0
Rivne Oblast	+1.3	+6.1	0	+2.6	+22.2	0
Sumy Oblast	−24.4	0	−6.7	−78.8	−75	0
Ternopil Oblast	−4.8	+12.8	−5.6	+0.8	+1.3	0
Kharkiv Oblast	+5.2	+42.1	−10.3	0	+14.3	+11.1
Kherson Oblast	+0.3	+12.9	−63.2	+2.6	+11.5	+8.3
Khmelnytskyi Oblast	−4.6	−6.7	−7.1	−10	+10.1	−50**
Cherkasy Oblast	+1.3	+22.3	−11.1	+6.1	+16.7	0
Chernovtsy Oblast	+0.9	−39.9	0	+6.9	+4	0
Chernihiv Oblast	−3.9	−9.6	0	−8.7	0	0
Kyiv City	+8	+11.4	−20	+13.5	+7.1	+25

Source: *In 2017 the data are only for those regions that are under control of Ukraine.

**Extreme figures are due to the small numbers of communities.

Notes

1 We also offer our data and scripts (R-studio) online at http://bit.ly/sacred_maidan.
2 See more in Andriy Fert's chapter in this volume.
3 See Maria Kravchenko's interview in this volume for more information.
4 We see this discrepancy in our previous data for 1992–2012 as well as in the new edition of our data for 2012–2017. We will be happy to share our data by request.
5 See an unofficial map made by religious activists in Ukraine. The map shows the whole amount and location of UOC-MP communities that have switched to the OCU (RISU, 2019).
6 See also Dmytro Vovk's chapter in this volume.

References

Anna News. (2015, May 18). Aleksandr Zakharchenko otvechayet na vopros predstavitelya tserkvi [Aleksandr Zakharchenko responds to the question of a representative of a church]. [Video file]. Retrieved from www.youtube.com/watch?v=hIm_eqhkd38

Balakireva, O., & Sereda, I. (2013). Religion and civil society in Ukraine and Russia. In J. de Hart, P. Dekker, & L. Halman (Eds.), *Religion and civil society in Europe* (pp. 219–250). doi:10.1007/978-94-007-6815-4_12

Borowik, I. (2002). Between Orthodoxy and eclecticism: On the religious transformations of Russia, Belarus and Ukraine. *Social Compass, 49*(4), 497–508. doi:10.1177/0037768602049004002

Brik, T. (2018). When church competition matters? Intra-doctrinal competition in Ukraine, 1992–2012. *Sociology of Religion, 80*(1), 45–82. doi:10.1093/socrel/sry005

Brubaker, R. (2012). Religion and nationalism: Four approaches. *Nations and Nationalism, 18*(1), 2–20. doi:10.1111/j.1469-8129.2001.00486.x

Casanova, J. (1998). Ethno-linguistic and religious pluralism and democratic construction in Ukraine. In R. Barnett & J. Snyder (Eds.), *Post-Soviet political order* (pp. 81–103). doi:10.4324/9780203269046.

Democratic Initiatives Fund. (2015). Opytuvannya: Bil'shist' naselennya Ukrayiny vidnosyt' sebe perevazhno do Pravoslavnoyi tserkvy Kyyivs'koho Patriarkhatu [Public opinion poll: Most Ukrainians identify themselves with the Orthodox church of the Kyiv Patriarchate]. Retrieved from https://dif.org.ua/article/bilshist-naselennya-ukraini-vidnosit-sebe-perevazhno-do-pravoslavnoi-tserkvi-kiivskogo-patriarkhatu

Dynamika mihratsiyi v Ukrayini: De reyestruyet'sy naybil'she poselentsiv [The dynamics of migration in Ukraine: Where IDPs prefer to be registered]. (2019, January 22). *Slovo i Dilo*. Retrieved from www.slovoidilo.ua/2019/01/22/infografika/suspilstvo/dynamika-mihracziyi-ukrayini-reyestruyetsya-najbilshe-pereselencziv

Finke, R., Mataic, D. R., & Fox, J. (2017). Assessing the impact of religious registration. *Journal for the Scientific Study of Religion, 56*(4), 720–736. doi:10.1111/jssr.12485

Fox, J. (n.d.). *Religion and state dataset*. Retrieved from www.religionandstate.org

Fox, J. (2008). *A world survey of religion and the state*. doi:10.1017/cbo9780511993039

Fox, J. (2011). Building composite measures of religion and state. *Interdisciplinary Journal of Research on Religion, 7*(8), 1–39.

Fox, J. (2018). *An introduction to religion and politics*. doi:10.4324/9781315583787

Froese, P. (2004). After atheism: An analysis of religious monopolies in the post-Communist world. *Sociology of Religion, 65*(1), 57–75. doi:10.2307/3712507

Grim, B. J., & Finke, R. (2006). International religion indexes: Government regulation, government favoritism, and social regulation of religion. *Interdisciplinary Journal of Research on Religion, 2*(1), 1–40.

Institute of Religious Freedom. (2018). Religious freedom at gunpoint: Russian terror in the occupied territories of Eastern Ukraine. *Analytical report*. [Adobe Digital Editions version]. Retrieved from www.irf.in.ua/files/publications/2018.10.24-IRF-Report-ENG.pdf

Khronolohiya teroru: boyovyky DNR i LNR peresliduyut' khrystyyan Donbasu [A chronology of terror: DPR and LPR militants persecute the Christians of Donbas]. (2014, August 6). *Institute of Religious Freedom*. Retrieved from www.irs.in.ua/index.php?option=com_content&view=article&id=1456:1&catid=34:ua&Itemid=61&lang=uk

Krindatch, A. D. (2003). Religion in post-Soviet Ukraine as a factor in regional, ethno-cultural and political diversity. *Religion, State and Society, 31*(1), 37–73. doi:10.1080/0963749032000045846

Kyiv International Institute of Sociology. (2018). Sotsial'no-politychna sytuatsiya v Ukrayini: presentatsiya dannyh zvitu [Report on the social and political situation in Ukraine]. Retrieved from http://kiis.com.ua/?lang=ukr&cat=reports&id=783&page=1

Ministry of Culture of Ukraine. (2018). Dani departamentu u spavah relihiy i natsional'nostey pro relihiynu merezhu [Data of the Department of religious and nationalities affairs about religious landscape]. Retrieved from https://risu.org.ua/ua/index/resourses/statistics/ukr_2018/70440/

Mitrokhin, N. (2001). Aspects of the religious situation in Ukraine. *Religion, State and Society*, *29*(3), 173–196. doi:10.1080/09637490120093133

Pid Radoyu mitynhuyut' pryhyl'nyky UPTs-MP [UOC-MP adherents are protesting in front of the Parliament]. (2017, May 18). *Ukrayins'ka Pravda*. Retrieved from www.pravda.com.ua/news/2017/05/18/7144261/

RISU. (2019). Karta peryhodiv do Pravoslavnoyi Tserkvy Ukrainy [Map of communities' switches to the OCU]. Retrieved from www.google.com/maps/d/u/0/viewer?mid=1XQR0sfHFFiiXyGiVYqI1mNylJ9fFPdnh&ll=50.37875869902123

Stark, R., & Finke, R. (2000). *Acts of faith: Explaining the human side of religion*. Berkeley, CA: University of California Press.

Stvorennya avtokefaliyi: Choho bil'she zahroz chy zdobutkiv, dyskutuvaly eksperty [Establishment of autocephaly: Experts discuss threats and advantages]. (2018, June 30). *Democratic Initiative Fund*. Retrieved from https://dif.org.ua/article/zdobuttya-avtokefalii-chogo-bilshe-zagroz-chi-zdobutkiv-diskutuvali-eksperti

Titarenko, L. (2008). On the shifting nature of religion during the ongoing post-Communist transformation in Russia, Belarus and Ukraine. *Social Compass, 55*(2), 237–254. doi:10.1177/00377/0037768607089743

Yelensky, V. (2010). Religiosity in Ukraine according to sociological surveys. *Religion, State and Society, 38*(3), 213–227. doi:10.1080/09637494.2010.499280

9   Changes to religious life in Crimea since 2014

Roman Lunkin

Introduction

The annexation of Crimea as a part of the Russian-Ukrainian crisis has had a significant impact on religious life on the peninsula. Based on my field research in Crimea, including sociological interviews with religious leaders, officials, and public intellectuals, I argue that after annexation, Crimean religious organizations lost almost all of the religious freedom and freedom of association that they previously enjoyed in Ukraine because of the state's interference with internal operations and the external life of religious groups. In particular, the state denied several religious groups in registration, imposed additional, burdensome restrictions on religious minorities' missionary activities and social work, and forced some clerics and religious activists to leave Crimea. For example, the Russian state has interfered with inter-Muslim relations, has deported or forced some Protestant priests out of the peninsula, and has pressured the Ukrainian Orthodox Church of the Kyiv Patriarchate (UOC-KP) to leave the peninsula for its alleged disloyalty to the Russian regime.

This loss of freedom particularly resulted from draconian Russian legislation adopted during 2015–2016, which entrenched the tendency toward framing religious activity as a question of security and limitation of religious groups' activities. For example, the so-called Yarovaya Law, a set of amendments to several laws, implemented rules that severely restricted missionary activities and religious life as a whole (Clark, 2016). These rules are broad and vague, and courts and law enforcement agencies tend to interpret them harshly and arbitrarily against certain religious minorities. Lawmakers have claimed that the Yarovaya Law aimed to counteract threats of religious extremism, but, in reality, this law was an attempt to strengthen government control over religion and believers.

To support my argument, I start with analyzing recent changes to religious policy. I particularly demonstrate that the Yarovaya Law has become a powerful tool of the state to force religions into compliance and to persecute allegedly disloyal religious groups. I then explore how the political transformation in Crimea in 2014 has influenced the life of Protestant, Orthodox, Catholic, Muslim, and other religious communities operating in the region. I show that some religious groups that were considered "suspicious" by the authorities (for example, Catholics) succeeded in adapting to the new political circumstances, but others found it very difficult or impossible. Thus, the religious pluralism that had developed in Crimea after the collapse of the Soviet Union has significantly decreased.

Policies of the new authorities

After annexation, the new authorities dissolved the Ukraine-period Council of Religious Affairs and reformed the system of executive bodies that were responsible for religious issues. Though departments for interaction with religious associations remain in the Ministry of Culture and the Ministry of Internal Policy, Information, and Communication of Crimea, after the reform religious affairs have been also supervised by the State Committee for Inter-Ethnic Relations and Deported Citizens of the Republic of Crimea.

The local authorities developed their religious policy chaotically. Beyond security issues, where they have no real power, the leadership of the Republic of Crimea sought to preserve the status quo and the previous forms of interaction among the main religions and did not want to change state-religion relations significantly. In particular, the authorities continued to cooperate with the interreligious council "Peace – a Gift of God,"[1] which has been operating in Crimea since the early 1990s. The council did not support the Euromaidan and repeatedly called the inhabitants of the peninsula to solve conflicts peacefully (Religioznyye lidery, 2014).

The Russian authorities significantly changed registration procedures and prescribed that all religions be re-registered according to Russian legislation (though re-registration is still in progress). During the Ukrainian period in Crimea there were roughly 2,000 religious communities, whereas in 2014–2017, only about 800 associations were registered or re-registered by the Russian authorities. This difference can be explained by the fact that according to Russian legislation, most of the religious organizations that were registered during the Ukrainian period now operate without registration as religious groups.

The state also de facto banned all forms of religious minorities' social work in state-funded social institutions, such as support for orphanages and houses for retired people or humanitarian aid to hospitals. In Ukraine there were almost no rules regulating this kind of religious activity, but under Russian rule religion-based social services, except those of the Orthodox Church, nearly stopped completely even though there are no laws banning it.[2]

Missionary work, as well as any public religious manifestations and other activities (e.g., rallies, street fests and praying, performances, preaching, dissemination of religious literature, etc.) were essentially limited. Before the Yarovaya Law was approved in 2016, believers were punished for street missionary work on the ground of the Russian Law on Assemblies, Rallies, Manifestations, Marches, and Picketing No 54-FZ (2004). For example, in October 2015, three Baptists of the Council of Churches of Evangelical Christian Baptists were fined and sentenced to twenty hours of community service each because they refused to register but continued to distribute literature on the streets without notifying the authorities.

The Yarovaya Law brought public religious manifestations fully under the discretion of the state. Named after one of its authors, the Russian MP Irina Yarovaya, this law added a chapter to the Russian Law on Freedom of Conscience and Religious Associations (1997) and prescribed how, where, and by whom missionary activities (this term is interpreted very broadly) may be performed. Also, the Yarovaya Law amended the Russian Code of Administrative Offences to set fines for illegal missionary work.

If we summarize the provisions of the Yarovaya Law on missionary work, they are as follows:

(1) Every believer who speaks of God outside a religious property must have a document from their religious organization entitling him or her to do this. The police and courts have fined or detained everyone preaching on his or her own behalf.

(2) Religious groups operating without registration must also issue documents to their missionaries. But documents can be issued only by groups that have notified the state about their existence. Thus the Yarovaya Law de facto subjects religious groups to the obligatory quasi-registration procedure of notification in order to strengthen the state's control over religious groups that would like to preach in the streets. If a group does not notify the state, it and its believers could be punished for illegal missionary work.

(3) In private residences one can conduct worship services, but one cannot preach to or invite believers of other religions or non-believers. In addition, private residences cannot be transformed into houses of prayer. Those preaching their faith on the internet, in the media, or "by other legal means" must also have a document from a religious association or a group.

(4) A foreign missionary must conclude an employment contract with a religious organization, which means that he or she must obtain a humanitarian or religious visa and the group that invited the missionary must gain permission to employ him; this missionary is then allowed to preach only in the region where the initiating group operates according to its charter.

(5) Those violating these rules shall be fined up to 50,000 rubles (about $750) for individuals, and up to 1,000,000 rubles (about $15,200) for legal entities.

After the Yarovaya Law came into force, there were several cases where various religious minorities, such as the Society of Krishna Consciousness, Pentecostals, Muslims, Jehovah's Witnesses (before this association was totally banned in 2017), Baptists, Adventists, and their believers were fined for public manifestations without permission, for the absence of a sign on a church building with the full name of the religious association (in this instance, the sign omitted only one word from the group's full name), for illegal missionary activity during religious services, and for meetings of unregistered religious groups in private residences. A Crimean human rights group reported that there were more than twenty cases of this kind between 2016 and 2017 (Sedov & Skrypnik, 2018). Analysis of these cases proves that law enforcement bodies and courts often apply the Yarovaya Law arbitrarily and disproportionately.

Thus the Yarovaya Law, in concert with similarly vague Russian anti-extremist legislation, has caused chilling effect on the activities of religious minorities because these groups cannot afford to engage in street missionary work or evangelization at the risk of being fined or declared extremist. These laws could be employed by the state at any moment to persecute allegedly disloyal or unreliable religious groups, such as Protestant churches, Greek Catholics, the UOC-KP, parts of the Muslim community (such as those close to the Crimean-Tatar *Mejlis*, as well as the Salafi branch called "Wahhabis" or groups connected to the *Hizb ut-Tahrir*, which are all banned within the Russian Federation), and other minority religious organizations.

However, in the next sections I will show that despite these policies, the real situation is more complicated. Certainly the Russian authorities differentiate between loyal and disloyal or unreliable religious communities. Orthodox Christian communities under the Moscow Patriarchate mostly do not experience any troubles with registration, social work, or public events. Some of the groups belonging to "suspicious" religions have also adapted to the new circumstances, but others are targeted by the authorities and security forces and suffer from oppression, deportations, internal splits, and changes to religious jurisdiction.

Evangelical Protestantism

The Crimean transition to Russian rule strongly affected Protestant churches. The emigration of pastors and missionaries who led these churches caused a great psychological blow to many of these communities. Generally, ministers left Crimea voluntarily, not wanting to live under Russian rule and realizing that foreigners or people of pro-Ukrainian orientation would likely have problems in the new Crimea.

Due to the prevailing opinion about Pentecostals as active participants of the Orange Revolution of 2004 and Euromaidan in 2013–2014, they were subjected to mass intimidation by law enforcement. Pentecostal services were sometimes roughly interrupted by the police and the Federal Security Service's (FSB) officers to conduct searches and inspect private documents. Due to the wave of xenophobia and radical patriotism under the slogan "Crimea is ours!" all Protestant churches, along with Catholics, Greek Catholics, and the UOC-KP, became symbols of Western influence, which resulted in persecution of and suspicion towards these churches. Some communities were destroyed by this, while others have survived, but both their influence and the number of believers have drastically decreased. Protestants have lost their former social status, becoming in the eyes of the authorities "sectarians" and "second-class" believers.

In many Pentacostal communities during 2014 and 2015, pastors fled with most of their congregants, or believers stopped supporting their pastors, who later left the peninsula. For example, the pastor of the independent community of Evangelical Christians in Simferopol, Sergey Golovin, left almost immediately after it became clear that Crimea would come under Russian rule. One of the reasons for his departure was the disappointment in the pastor's pro-Ukrainian position felt on the part of his parishioners supporting Russia. In his interview, Pastor Golovin notes:

> There is a split in the community's attitude toward what is happening. And for me it is a sign of my failure as a pastor. For twenty years I've spread the biblical doctrine of righteousness and truth, but it was for nothing. The anticipation of a slightly larger pension [that Russia will pay] seems to be more attractive for many people. . . . Before the annexation, the question of Russian identity in churches was not raised at all. Problems with language did not exist. "Russian" or "Ukrainian" identities were just a marker. This division [between the parishioners regarding the annexation] is between those who would like to create the future and those who want to restore the past. We left the Egypt of communism for the desert of democracy, but. . . [some people] were happy that Pharaoh had overtaken them.[3]

Many churches have become targets of the Russian security services, particularly Pentecostal churches and charismatic movements that were connected with the "Embassy of God" movement in Kyiv, where pastors were supportive of the Euromaidan and conducted pro-Ukrainian sermons. As reported by Protestants themselves, authorities tried to deport their pastors with Ukrainian passports but no Crimean registration. Some pastors, however, have succeeded in avoiding deportation and continue to serve or visit Crimea from time to time. Some of the deported pastors still retain their ministry in churches and conduct sermons on the internet via Skype.

Pressure on Protestant pastors has been mostly politically motivated. Their pro-Ukrainian bent has served as a ground for expulsion. Among those deported from Crimea were the pastor of the New Generation Church, Oleg Trikozyuk (now serving in Henichesk), and the pastor of the Embassy of God, Anton Litvin (now the pastor of the Church of the Protection of God in Boryspil). Under pressure from the FSB, Ruslan Zuyev, an official of the Salvation Army in Simferopol, fled in June 2014 (now he is a major of the Salvation Army in Lviv). Zuyev's departure from Crimea was probably the result of his political activities within the organization "Euromaidan Crimea" (*Yevromaidan Krym*), which participated in anti-Russian rallies in concert with the Crimean Tatars. Further, in 2016, the authorities closed many houses of prayer of the Pentecostal church "The Voice of Hope" in Bakhchysarai because the church was a branch of the Kyiv church "Skinia."

Most Crimean Pentecostal communities entered the Russian Church of Evangelical Christians (RCEC), and many communities joined the centralized organization of the RCEC directly rather than any of its regional associations. In August 2016, the RCEC conducted a conference of its churches on the Crimean coast, which was approved by the authorities.

The Baptist Union in Crimea is split. One union of Evangelical Christian Baptist Churches (ECB) acts autonomously as a regional organization, and another union of churches has become part of the Russian Union of Baptists.[4] The ECB is much larger, and its leader, Bishop Veniamin Yukhimets, represents the ECB at the official level in the interreligious council "Peace – Gift of God."

In connection with the crisis within the Baptist community, Pastor Yuhimets points out:

> We disagree with the statement issued by the Russian Union of Evangelical Christians Baptists' on Ukraine in 2015, in which the [Euro]maidan was condemned. This statement has been made because of fear. We actively help refugees from the Donbas, but our principle is this: we do not work for war – the church helps people only. Not for the purpose that the war could be continued, but so that people can build a house for themselves, for example. In this case, it makes no difference where people who need it are from – from Ukraine or from Donetsk People's Republic and Luhansk People's Republic. The main thing is that the aid does not go to the Ukrainian army or the separatists. And this kind of help is provided by all – Orthodox, Baptists, charismatics.

After 2014, there were several Russian pastors to whom, as they claim, "God opened a new vision" to send them to the peninsula in order to establish new churches or take over religious communities whose previous pastors had left. For example, in Yevpatoria the pastor of the Church of Living Water, Vladimir Yeremeyev, who came from Siberia, told me that he had found all the church documents on the floor in the house of prayer after the former pastor left for Ukraine. Russian missionaries embraced the prospect of preaching in a new place, especially on land historically linked to Russia and now de facto included into Russia. However, some other Protestant church ministers, who remained in Crimea, have not experienced such hope. They are more skeptical of the legitimacy of Crimea's transition to Russia; it is psychologically difficult for them to change their patriotic identity from Ukrainian to Russian. This more negative perspective is fueled by some Ukrainian pastors who have emigrated from Crimea, for whom the peninsula is not a field for a new mission, but a land punished for its sins, a land that banished its shepherds: "For it is written, I will smite the shepherd, and the sheep of the flock will be scattered" (Matthew 26:31). However, all of the Crimean pastors that I interviewed considered this "accursed" Crimea theory offensive, regardless of their perception of the annexation.

There are some Crimean pastors who decided to remain in Crimea after the annexation and have changed their minds about the political situation. For example, Pentacostal pastor Dmitry Gula says in his interview that he "took off my orange tie [symbol of the Orange Revolution and pro-Ukrainian position in general] after one of the sermons. It was a mistake to bring politics into the Church." Moreover, the pastor appreciates the Yarovaya Law. He believes that the law will help believers be more careful in evangelism and encourage religious groups to prepare more qualified preachers.

Lutheranism was historically represented in Crimea by the German Evangelical-Lutheran Church, but over the last twenty years several other Lutheran jurisdictions have also appeared on the peninsula. After 2014, the number of Lutheran jurisdictions even increased. German Lutherans joined the Evangelical-Lutheran Church of Russia. Now they receive pastors from Russia and hope to obtain old Crimean Lutheran Church buildings, which they were not able to get during the Ukrainian period.

Orthodox churches in Crimea

Among all the religions operating in Crimea, the Ukrainian Orthodox Church of Moscow Patriarchate (UOC-MP) occupies a unique position as a religion that is favored by the federal and local authorities. The church has experienced no serious problems with conducting missionary and social work and organizing public events, and has taken part in programs funded by the Russian government and the local authorities. The Crimean UOC-MP monasteries have received some additional financial resources from the Russian government and new sponsors, who became involved in order to develop tourism and spiritual pilgrimage in Crimea.

The UOC-MP on the peninsula is divided into three separate eparchies – Simferopol and Crimean, Dzhankoy, and Theodosia. The lead role in fact belongs to Metropolitan Lazarus – the head of the Simferopol and Crimean eparchy. The status of the eparchies in Crimea has not been changed for ecclesiastical and political reasons. All of these eparchies are still part of the Ukrainian Orthodox Church of the Moscow Patriarchate. The Russian Orthodox Church of Moscow Patriarchate (ROC), which includes the UOC-MP, essentially preserves this state of affairs, emphasizing the inviolability of the canonical territory of the UOC-MP and non-interference in its internal affairs. However, the ROC has a direct influence in Crimea as well. In October 2015 the prominent Tikhon (Shevkunov), then-Bishop of Egoriev in Moscow and executive secretary of the Patriarchal Council for Culture, became a member of the Expert Advisory Council under the Head of the Republic of Crimea.

However, the Moscow Patriarchate's rival – the Crimean Eparchy of the UOC-KP headed by Archbishop Kliment – is tragically much worse off. Russian authorities and law enforcement agencies have chosen the tactic of gradually driving the church out of Crimea and forcing the UOC-KP communities to join the UOC-MP, though the latter is not directly involved in these actions. For example, the authorities have terminated rental agreements and revoked UOC-KP property contracts for government-owned buildings. The situation has worsened after the Kyiv Patriarchate refused to submit to re-registration in accordance with Russian legislation (Solonina, 2018).

In his interview, Archbishop Kliment noted that for now, only nine out of fifteen UOC-KP parishes function. Five of the ten priests left the peninsula in 2014; churches do not operate in Krasnoperekopsk, Kerch, Sevastopol, Perevalny and Saki. As of 2018, there are only nine religious premises owned by believers of the UOC-KP available for conducting religious services.

The situation of the Cathedral of Saints Prince Vladimir and Princess Olga in Simferopol is the most painful for the UOC-KP. During the Soviet era, the Officers' Club was housed in this building, but later the cathedral was given to the UOC-KP. Since 2014, local authorities have significantly raised the rent (previously rental payments were symbolic), and on June 14, 2016, the Sevastopol Court of Appeal ordered the Crimean Eparchy of the UOC-KP to vacate the cathedral. However, the church continues to conduct services on the first floor of the building. In my opinion, the high degree of confrontation between the UOC-KP and the authorities may result in the seizure of the UOC-KP Cathedral in Simferopol,[5] and the church itself may go underground.

Moreover, even if the UOC-KP communities submit an application for registration as communities of the newly established the Orthodox Church of Ukraine (OCU), there is a chance that they will not be registered. Moscow does not recognize the OCU and perceives it as a nationalistic anti-Russian structure established by the Ecumenical Patriarchate and inspired by American politicians and Ukrainian lobbying in the U.S. and Canada (Kuzmin, 2018).

It is also worth mentioning that contrary to expectations because of his criticism of Russia's policies, Archbishop Kliment himself has not been subjected to severe repressions. He continues to visit Ukrainian activists imprisoned in Crimea, regularly appeals to the UN and the OSCE to stop Russia's persecution of the UOC-KP, and constantly travels from Kyiv to Simferopol and back (see e.g., Kurmanova, 2018). However, in March 2019 he was prevented from visiting a Ukrainian political prisoner in Rostov-on-Don and detained for a half of a day by the police.

Catholics and Greek Catholics

Like the UOC-KP and Protestants, Catholics are considered pro-Western, unreliable religions after the Orange Revolution and the Euromaidan in Ukraine. Moreover, Crimean Catholic communities were under the jurisdiction of the bishop located in Odesa, which could be considered a signal of their unreliableness. This threat was most likely the main reason why after the annexation of Crimea, Catholic communities in the region gained a new status. On December 22, 2014 a new "pastoral district" of the Catholic Church was established and headed by Bishop Jacek Pyl, who was formerly the auxiliary bishop of the Odesa and Simferopol diocese of the Catholic Church. The status of the pastoral district means that these communities are directly subordinated to the Holy See, but not to Russian or Ukrainian dioceses. After negotiations between the Russian Foreign Ministry, the Russian Orthodox Church, and the Vatican, Moscow directly instructed the Crimean authorities to register Catholic parishes as autonomous organizations.

Greek Catholic communities were registered as Catholics of the Byzantine rite and became a part of the pastoral district.[6] The Ukrainian Greek Catholic Church (UGCC) in Crimea had experienced pressure from the Russian authorities because Greek Catholics actively participated in the Euromaidan and the head of the UGCC Archbishop Svyatoslav Shevchuck is an ardent critic of Russia. Also, in March 2014 the so-called peoples' militia in Crimea had found ten bulletproof vests during a search of the home of UGCC priest, father Nikolay Knych in Sevastopol (Klimonchuk, 2014). Thus registration as a part of the pastoral district seems a good solution for the UGCC. Due to the Church's decision to be registered as Catholics of the Byzantine rite, the head of the Kyiv Patriarchate in Crimea, Archbishop Kliment, accused UGCC communities of opportunism.

Once they obtained official status and the support of the Vatican, Crimean Catholics tried to bring their property demands before Russian authorities. In particular, they sought to obtain the inactive Catholic church of Saint Clement of Rome in Sevastopol, built at the beginning of the twentieth century. Conflict surrounding the church had continued for the last twenty years, but finally, in June 2018 the authorities decided to transfer the church to the Catholic community. However, as of February 2019 they have not yet been able to register their property rights to the church building.

Muslim communities

Within the Crimean Muslim population, Russian authorities developed a relationship with the Spiritual Administration of Muslims of Crimea and Sevastopol (SAMC) headed by Mufti Emirali Ablaev. The SAMC broke with and condemned the *Mejlis*, the representative body of Crimean Tatars that opposed the annexation and was subsequently banned in Russia (Karamanoglu, 2016; Skripunov, 2016). The SAMC began to actively cooperate with Russian Muslim associations, primarily with the Spiritual Administration of Muslims of the Russian Federation headed by Supreme Mufti Ravil Gainutdin. It has also maintained relations with the Spiritual Administrations of Muslims of the Republic of Tatarstan and Chechnya. In August 2016, a delegation of the SAMC participated in the World Islamic Conference in Grozny called "Who Are They – Alyus Sunna Wal Jama'a," where Emirali Ablaev signed a fatwa for the prohibition of Wahhabism[7] in Russia.

Deputy Mufti of the SAMC Aider Ismailov noted in his interview that the SAMC has been building relations with the authorities and other religious leaders since 1991, when it was registered. He also said that these relations had not been changed after the annexation, although Muslims had been deprived of the opportunity to openly criticize the Crimean eparchy of the UOC-MP as was the case previously. Now, he said, it is perceived as anti-patriotic.

The SAMC's new status has incurred both benefits and losses. The price that the SAMC paid for its political significance and special relations with the Russian state was the partial loss of sponsors (Turkish and Arab countries) and strict control over its financial flows and educational projects. Any social work and cultural events conducted by the SAMC must be approved by the authorities. Several projects conducted by the SAMC were canceled, and as a result, a large proportion of active Muslim youth left the organization. Ayder Ismailov notes that after 2014 there were several inspections and searches of Muslim youth organizations, and most of these organizations did not pass re-registration. Some Muslim activists left Crimea voluntarily or were forced to do so, as they could be accused, for example, of participating in the banned *Hizb ut-Tahrir* organization.[8]

Members of the SAMC also note that at the middle level of bureaucracy, they face more or less the same problems as they did before annexation because most bureaucrats kept their positions. In Ukraine, the process of allocating land for the mosque took eight years. The city authorities did not want to transfer the property, so the SAMC sued them for the land. The case reached the Supreme Court of Ukraine. Only in 2011, under pressure from the head of the Crimean Republic, did the city council approve the property transfer. However, construction only began three years later in 2014 after President Putin took the cathedral mosque under his patronage.

Stressing its exclusive monopoly position in Crimea and loyalty to the authorities, the SAMC promotes the idea that only centralized religious organizations like itself should be granted the right to own religious buildings built by religious associations or obtained by them from the state. Thus, for example, religious communities must not be entitled to sell their property if the centralized religious organization that they belong to does not sanction this. This position is supported by the UOC-MP, whose charter contains a similar rule, and the Karaites' Spiritual Administration, which lost its *kenesa* building in Simferopol when an independent community "Cholpan" was registered there. The SAMC leaders note that the authorities support them in this demand, and as of the present, title to approximately seventy older mosques has been transferred from the public authorities to the SAMC. The SAMC leaders' concern could alternatively be explained by the fact that they compete for some mosques with an alternative organization, the Central Spiritual Administration of Muslims – Tauride Muftiate, created in August of 2014 and headed by Mufti Ruslan Saitvaliev and chairman Enver Akhtemov. Many experts whom I interviewed think that the fate of the Tauride Muftiate was a matter of bargaining and mutual blackmailing between the SAMC and the authorities. In exchange for SAMC's loyalty to the Russian authorities, the state rejected the Tauride Muftiate registration as a regional association, though it still exists. Members of the Tauride Muftiat even succeeded in recapturing the historical Juma-Jami Mosque in Yevpatoria from the SAMC.

The Tauride Muftiate occupies the most pro-Russian position in Crimea. The Crimean Tatars' national problems (national autonomy, a strong national movement, promotion of language and culture) are not high priorities for the new Muftiate. Mufti Ruslan Saitvaliev believes that today there is no need for an intermediary organization (such as the *Mejlis*) between the Crimean Tatars and the authorities. Their main goal should be to counteract extremist organizations like *Hizb ut-Tahrir*. Sheikh Ruslan also believes: "We have a mess here in Crimea. For example, the association 'Creation (Ar-Raid)' is openly operating, though it is just a proxy of the Muslim Brotherhood [recognized as a terrorist organization in Russia]. We must isolate Wahhabis if we cannot fix them." Thus, because of the Tauride Muftiate's activities and its radically pro-Russian views, the SAMC has found itself in a controversial position where it must permanently prove its loyalty and the "traditionalism" of its ideology to the authorities.

Finally, it is worth mentioning that my field research did not focus on persecutions of Muslims and I was unable to identify any openly pro-Ukrainian Muslim communities in Crimea. The *Mejlis*, as the national Crimean Tatars body, was mostly displaced by Muslim leadership, but there are still people sympathizing with the *Mejlis* leaders Mustafa Dzhemlev and Refat Chubarov, who sustain the *Mejlis* and an alternative Crimean Muftiate working from Kyiv.

Conclusion

According to many Crimean clergymen in the peninsula, there is "more order" now when compared with the Ukrainian period, but there is less freedom in society, particularly religious freedom. Russian authorities have developed a more authoritarian framework of relations in Crimea than even in Russia through enacting vague rules, imposing additional restrictions on the activities of "non-traditional" religions, interfering with internal religious affairs, deporting disloyal Ukrainian pastors, and persecuting allegedly unreliable communities. Under this framework the state and the dominant Orthodox church are supposed to play the role of suzerain, and all others will have to accept the role of vassal. Due to various reasons leaders of major religious associations of the region explicitly or implicitly support the state in these attempts by obeying the officially recognized version of patriotism, avoiding any criticism of the state, and accepting any formal and informal rules of church-state relations, even if they violate religious freedom. In this way these leaders strive to demonstrate their loyalty and reliability because they fear the consequences that disloyalty and the status of being an unreliable religion would bring.

However, the Crimean example shows that, in spite of state attempts to closely control religious life, the authorities are unable to thoroughly destroy the religious pluralism that developed primarily during the Ukrainian period. Thanks to this pluralism, including inter- and intra-religious debates, many believers and middle- and low-level clergy belonging to Protestant, Orthodox, and Islamic communities are more active and inclined to promote religious freedom. This resistance makes the state's task of keeping religion subservient to the state more difficult.

Notes

1 "Peace – a Gift of God" is the informal council that includes representatives of all the large religious communities in Crimea. Their main activity is meeting with officials and making common appeals on different issues. The council includes Orthodox (Moscow Patriarchate), Catholic, Lutheran, Armenian Apostolic Church, Baptist, Adventist, Muslim, Jewish, and Karaite communities. For many faiths this council remains a channel for maintaining dialogue with the authorities.
2 The situation in Russia is pretty much the same. Only Orthodox priests enjoy open access to state-funded social institutions, such as medical institutions or orphanages. Others are prohibited from entering them. Moreover, now Catholics and Protestants face serious troubles with receiving humanitarian aid from abroad.
3 Here and below, if not mentioned specifically otherwise, I am quoting interviews and data from my field research. The data is available upon request.
4 The split between Crimean Baptist associations occurred in the 2010s because of financial issues, but political developments in 2014 deepened it.
5 Editorial note: Dr. Lunkin was right in assuming that the Russian authorities would seize the Cathedral in Simferopol from the UOC-KP and would continue to pressure the church from the peninsula. On February 9, 2019, Archbishop Kliment reported that he had received a writ issued by the Crimean ministry of property and land relations to leave the Cathedral (Coynash, 2019). In a later interview Kliment said that he was considering the option of registering the UOC-KP communities in accordance with Russian legislation (Samokhvalova, 2019).
6 There are twelve Greek Catholic parishes in the district and three churches in Yevpatoria, Yalta and Kerch.
7 The term "Wahhabism" in this chapter is used in the conventional sense, in the way in which it is used by representatives of the Russian authorities or among various Muslim movements. A more precise definition of Wahhabism is beyond the scope of the chapter. In the Russian context, not only followers of Muhammad ibn Abd al-Wahhab are called "Wahhabis," but also Salafis, or followers of "pure Islam."
8 As of 2018 four persons were imprisoned for participation in *Hizb ut-Tahrir*, and sixteen more were in Crimea under trial.

References

Clark, E. A. (2016, August 30). Russian anti-missionary law in context. *Religious Freedom Institute*. Retrieved from www.religiousfreedominstitute.org/cornerstone/2016/8/30/russias-new-anti-missionary-law-in-context

Coynash, H. (February 14, 2019). Russia moves to crush Orthodox Church of Ukraine in occupied Crimea. Human Rights in Ukraine. Retrieved from http://khpg.org/en/index.php?id=1550095831&fbclid=IwAR1cyQLliyTLBmCL9UVWRE9IC0uHCqyuase3mE3hZaPqWpkLcjY1ZkPNgYo

Karamanoglu, H. (2016, June 24). Pochemu Krymskiy muftiyat ushel v Rossiyu? [Why has the Crimean Muftiat taken Russia's side?]. *Krym.Realii*. Retrieved from https://ru.krymr.com/a/27817830.html

Klimonchuk, O. (2014, March 18). Otets Nikolay Kvich: 'Menya obvinili v tom, chto ya sponsiruyu Voenno-morskiye sily Ukrainy' [Father Nikolay Kvich: 'I was blamed for helping the Ukrainian Navy']. Retrieved from http://news.ugcc.ua/ru/articles/otets_nikolay_kvich_menya_obvinili_v_tom_chto_ya_sponsiruyu_voennomorskie_sili_ukraini_69744.html

Kurmanova, T. (2018, January 23). Arkhiepiskop Kliment: 'Ya okazyvayu Vladimiru Balukhu duhovnuyu, a ne politicheskuyu podderzhku' [Archbishop Kliment: 'I provide

Vladimir Baluh with spiritual, not political support']. Retrieved from https://ru.krymr. com/a/28992058.html

Kuzmin, Yu. (2018, December 12). Mitropolit Ilarion: Nad pomestnoy tserkov'yu net kakoy-libo inoy vlasti, krome vlasti samogo Boga [There is no authority over a local church, except the authority of God]. *BOSS*. Retrieved from www.bossmag.ru/hotnews/ mitropolit-ilarion-nad-pomestnoj-pravoslavnoj-tserkovyu-net-kakoj-libo-inoj-vlasti-krome-vlasti-samogo-boga.html

Religioznyye lidery prizvali k sohraneniyu tselostnosti Ukrainy [Religious leaders call for preserving the integrity of Ukraine]. (2014, January 30). Retrieved from www.religion. in.ua/news/ukrainian_news/25093-religioznye-lidery-kryma-prizvali-k-soxraneniyu-celostnosti-ukrainy.html

Samokhvalova, L. (March 21, 2019).Vladyka Kliment, arkhiyepiskop Simferopol'sky i Krym-sky Pravoslavnoy Tserkvi Ukrainy: Bez ukrainskogo gosudarstva ne budet tserkvi, a bez tserkvi – ne budet gosudarstva [His Grace Klement, Archbishop of Simferepol and Crimea of the Orthodox Church of Ukraine: There will be no church without the Ukrainian state, and there will be no state without the church]. *UKRINFORM*. Retrieved from www. ukrinform.ru/rubric-crimea/2664385-vladyka-kliment-arhiepiskop-simferopolskij-i-krymskij-pravoslavnoj-cerkvi-ukrainy.html

Sedov, A., & Skrypnik, O. (2018). Svoboda religii i ubezhdeniy v Krymy: Analiticheskiy obzor v sfere svobody religii i ubezhdeniy v usloviyah okkupatsii Kryma (aprel' 2014 – yanvar' 2018) [Freedom of religion and belief in Crimea: An analytical review of the situation in the sphere of freedom of religion and belief in occupied Crimea (April 2014 – January 2018)]. [Adobe Digital Editions version]. Retrieved from https://crimeahrg.org/wp-content/uploads/2018/03/Svoboda-religii-v-Kryimu.pdf?fbclid=IwAR3E26pFpXy_L8b3fb6iL55gkJtTlMJyRp0XxZLYhgARy7Gbir1WSWM0EqI

Skripunov, A. (2016, March 16). Zamglavy musul'man Kryma: My v polnoy mere pol'zuyemsya svoimi pravami [Vice-head of Crimean Muslims: We fully enjoy our rights]. *Ria Novosti*. Retrieved from https://ria.ru/20160316/1390804158.html

Solonina, Ye. (2018, October 10). 'Neanneksirovannaya' tserkov' v Krymu ['Not-annexed' church in Crimea]. *Krym.Realii*. Retrieved from https://ru.krymr.com/a/neanneksirovannaya-tserkov-v-krymu/29535969.html

Part 3

The Russian–Ukrainian conflict and inter-Orthodox relations

10 History, ecclesiology, canonicity, and power

Ukrainian and Russian Orthodoxy after the Euromaidan

Jerry G. Pankhurst

Introduction

Nearing the end of the third decade since the breakup of the Soviet Union, nostalgia for Soviet great power status is an active ingredient in Russian political and civic life, and dreams of western freedoms and prosperity animate Ukraine. These two great societies are heading in opposite directions, and Russia has put Ukraine in its crosshairs since the Euromaidan events of 2013–2014. It is no wonder that the one major institution that extends structurally across the Russia-Ukraine border – the Orthodox Church – should experience acute stress, being torn in both directions at once (Razumkov Center, 2014). Although both Ukraine and Russia are multi-confessional states with legal protection of freedom of religion, they each have an historic symbolic relationship with the Orthodox churches on their soil. Both countries see their Orthodox faith rooted in the conversion of the Grand Prince of Rus' near the end of the first millennium of the Christian era. Jumping to more recent history, for more than three centuries now the Orthodox Churches of both Russia and Ukraine have been linked together organizationally, with temporary variations during major political upheavals, under the Patriarchate of Moscow. Trying to adapt to state independence from Russia on the international stage, many Ukrainian Christians have pursued parallel independence of their church within the international community of Eastern Orthodox churches. The requisite systemic, structural adjustments and adaptations are most fully embodied in the creation of the autocephalous Orthodox Church of Ukraine (OCU), independent from the Moscow Patriarchate, which was finalized at the beginning of 2019 (Ponomariov, 2019). The creation of the separate OCU is emblematic of the vectors of influence and change that are found throughout the social order.

The examination of the religious situation in Ukraine at this time in history is essential because it opens to view the deep dynamics of international relations not only for Ukraine, but for all those who deal with the troublesome foreign policy of the Russian Federation with Vladimir Putin as its leader. One aspect of that policy is the use of the Russian Orthodox Church (ROC) as part of its "soft power" assets. As such, its primary role seems to be to support friendship with Russia and foster doubt about policies in the other countries that disagree with Russian interests and presumed prerogatives (Petro, 2015). Until the granting of autocephaly, Orthodox Ukrainians had only the Ukrainian Orthodox Church under the Moscow Patriarchate (UOC-MP) as their canonical faith home. The essential aim of making a fully independent autocephalous Orthodox church in Ukraine was to sever the control over Ukrainian Orthodox affairs from Moscow. However, one cannot stop with ecclesiology alone in understanding the changes going on. Ukraine with a majority church that was formally subordinate to the Moscow Patriarchate was Ukraine still in the Russian orbit. When Russia engaged in major aggressions against Ukraine in 2014, this kind of subordination of the foremost Ukrainian cultural institution to Russian power was no longer viable.

While the Moscow Patriarchate was part of soft power foreign policy for Russia, the church itself had a great stake in its domination of the Ukrainian Orthodox scene. The ROC prided itself in being the largest Eastern Orthodox Church in the world by number of adherents and by number of parishes, bishops, and the like, but a major concentration of its faithful was found in Ukraine. Using church data from 2011, Fagan (2013) calculated that more than one-third of ROC parishes worldwide were in Ukraine. This state of affairs has been longstanding, perhaps indicating a deep cultural religiosity among Ukrainians. It has also been seen as originating in the alienation of Ukrainians from Russia during the early Soviet period, especially in connection with the great famine in Ukraine of 1932–1933 (Holodomor) that was caused by Stalin's policies, and the greater success of the anti-religious program of the Communist Party of the Soviet Union in Russia than in Ukraine. In addition, it has been argued that German occupation of much of Ukraine during the course of the Second World War, during which period many churches that had been closed by the communists were re-opened, re-invigorated Ukrainians' religious sensibilities that were never quashed in later years under Soviet control (Fireside, 1971).

Although it is very difficult to count the number of adherents, and the number of parishes, bishops, or eparchies can be manipulated by multiplying administrative units (as has happened in Russia over the last several years), there seems little basis to think the proportion of the overall number of Orthodox believers under the Moscow Patriarchate in Ukraine would have changed to show greater ROC numbers inside Russia or a decline in numbers in Ukraine until recently.[1] Hence, the loss of Ukraine would mean a major diminution in the size of the Moscow Patriarchate's flock and, consequently, of the relative size of the ROC in comparison with other branches of Eastern Orthodoxy. The loss of Ukraine, depending upon how strongly the Orthodox faithful or their parishes move to acceptance of the OCU for leadership, diminishes the claim of the Moscow Patriarchate to be the leader of the Orthodox world. The historic honorific head of Eastern Orthodoxy is the Patriarch of Constantinople, commonly known as the Ecumenical Patriarch because of the notion that he represents universal Orthodoxy. As will become apparent, his role as a center of ecclesial power that is an alternative to the Patriarch of Moscow has provided an opening for the Ukrainian Orthodox to separate themselves in some sense from the Russians.

Factors underlying the promulgation of Ukrainian autocephaly

This paper explores the nature of the aspirations and claims of Orthodox believers in Russia[2] and Ukraine, and the impact on claims-making that the politics between Russia and Ukraine are having following the crisis identified with the Euromaidan protests of 2013–2014. The ouster of Viktor Yanukovych from the Ukrainian presidency was a rejection of Russian influence over Ukrainian affairs (Colton, 2016). The violations of Ukrainian sovereignty by Russia – namely, the annexation of Crimea in 2014, the aggressive incursions in the Donbas region in eastern Ukraine that began in 2014 and continue today, and the blockage in November 2018 of the Kerch Strait and the capture of 24 Ukrainian sailors and 3 ships (MacFarquhar, 2018) – have deeply alienated both sides from each other (Prokip, 2018). In the context of this estrangement, at issue are: (1) the status of the church units within state structures with regard to church canonical status and (2) the empirical markers of status, honor, and power for major actors in both Orthodox church circles and international relations among sovereign governments (cf. Yelensky, 2005).

The Orthodox people of Ukraine arrived at the point of achieving autocephaly for their church because of a confluence of factors. Each factor was a contingency that could have turned in a different direction. But their confluence opened the door to the imagination of Ukrainians that they might have their own church and permitted them to take the moves to detach from the Russian church. Sociologists might say that, under these changed circumstances, the Ukrainian Orthodox found the *agency* to act on their dreams.

Six factors

I state a complex hypothesis that identifies the major factors that led to the place at which Ukrainians would actually make the move to detach from the Russian Church and seek their own autonomy.

(1) New states like Ukraine, through a historical process, reach a level of maturity in national identity to begin to act with *agency* both domestically and internationally. All the fifteen post-Soviet states are new states, even though they were given statehood by separating the constituent republics of the USSR into independent states. Each has had to develop and institutionalize a national identity, and that requirement has opened up contestation in symbolic spheres and a debate about how to fit religion and national identity together. (Agadjanian, 2001; cf. Bremmer, 1994 on ethnicity in the early post-Soviet period). This process is not easy, as the example of the development of the OCU shows. The church is a cultural institution that is

interrelated with the rest of culture. Change in one part stimulates change in other parts.

(2) Continued and increasingly aggressive Russian meddling and domination – symbolic, cultural, diplomatic, and military – begs a response. The new state matures enough to give that response. The agreements that established fifteen sovereign states out of the previous "republics" of the Soviet Union have not stopped Russian re-assertion of domination. Russian interventions have left several "pseudo-states" under Russian control which were carved out of the territory of other former Soviet republics. Abkhazia and South Ossetia were carved out of Georgian land, and Transnistria was carved out of Moldova. The Russian incursions into Donbas are creating similar conditions for eastern Ukraine. With the exception of Crimea, the Russian Federation has not formally annexed territories that it controls beyond the previous Soviet republics' borders. Crimea marks a new stage of acquisitional aggression, a new form of foreign policy for Russia, and a form that has victimized Ukraine and may victimize it again.

(3) After early signs of a European orientation in Vladimir Putin's first presidential term from 2000, Russia has turned itself more eastward, opposite to the European-oriented new states like the Baltic countries and Ukraine. Ukraine and other new states along the western border of the old USSR encountered the alternative of EU and NATO affiliation, and saw it as a means to establish a position counterweighted against Russia's impulses to gather again the separated parts of the Soviet empire. The Baltic states gained full membership in the western institutions, and Western Europe and the United States provide them serious allied support against Russia. However, Ukraine has received only partial affiliation; the EU and NATO are reluctant to go all the way to offering inclusive membership, given the reciprocal obligations of military protection and economic support that are included in membership. Vladimir Putin's leadership of the Russian Federation has evolved from an orientation toward Europe to an anti-European, anti-Western framing. Most Ukrainian politicians have been enticed by the European Union, with its Eastern Partnership initiative, and by the possibility of expansion of the North Atlantic Treaty Organization to include Ukraine. In the 2013–2014 Euromaidan demonstrations, Ukraine opted to go west, seeking EU and possibly NATO membership and setting up the underlying rejection of Russian leadership and domination that so inflamed Moscow. The West has been aroused by the aggressions of Russia, and the serious sanctions policies give additional assurance to Ukrainians that they can move in ways that are not favorable to Russia. Included in the rejection of Russian superiority is the pursuit of Ukrainian autocephaly.

One caveat about seeing the Ukrainian motivations based in the seductions of Western culture and society: in her examination of Russian national identity entitled *Russia: Inventing the Nation*, Vera Tolz (2001) notes that Russians usually ignored the differences between Russian identity and Ukrainian identity, and they were stunned by the calls for independence for

Ukraine at the time of the breakup of the Soviet Union. "Russians tended to view the empire's nationality problems through the prism of Russia's relations with the West" (p. 232). Here we are reminded of Morozov's (2015) notion that Russian identity can only be understood as being in connection with reactions to Europe or the idea of Europe, a pattern that Tolz confirms is long standing. "This too often encouraged [Russians] to interpret manifestations of separatism on the part of the Ukrainians as the result of intrigues by European powers and/or the United States (i.e., the West)" (Tolz, 2001, p. 232). There is undoubtedly some truth to the value of seeing Western cultural attractiveness and protections as part of the desire for autonomous institutions for Ukraine. However, we should take Tolz's (2001) warning seriously not to accept unquestioningly the meme from Russian and some western media that the Ukrainians are responding to some illegitimate forms of seduction from the EU and NATO. Ukrainians undoubtedly want to be independent and free from Russian domination fundamentally because they want to be free, period, not just because of external interferences.

(4) Pushback against the Moscow Patriarchate by the Ecumenical Patriarchate has become more possible. The centuries-long competition between the Patriarchs of Constantinople and Moscow over leadership of the Orthodox Church globally showed some openings for both the Moscow Patriarchate and the Ecumenical Patriarchate as the twenty-first century began. The ROC came out from under Soviet communist control to take its place as the largest patriarchal jurisdiction in the world by far. Although the Ecumenical Patriarch held the title of *primus inter pares*, "first among equals" in the leadership of global Orthodoxy, the Moscow Patriarch believed real leadership of Orthodoxy should be in his hands (Bodin, 2014).

In the historical period when Constantinople was the center of the Byzantine Empire, the area of Kyivan Rus' had been under the jurisdiction of the Ecumenical Patriarch. However, in 1686, the Patriarch of Constantinople ceded authority over the Metropolis of Kyiv to the Russian Patriarchate. According to Brünning (2016) he was affirming a *fete accompli* rather than accepting defeat in anything like a direct competition for the Metropolis. The Byzantine Empire had crumbled in the face of Turkish conquest of Constantinople in 1453, leaving the Ecumenical Patriarchate in disarray. By contrast, the Moscow Patriarchate, created in 1598, found itself atop the church of the Russian state which was expanding and growing stronger after the crisis of the "Time of Troubles" ended in the early 1600s. Although Peter the Great eliminated the office of Patriarch in 1721, replacing it with a Holy Synod to manage the Church, the subordination of Ukrainians to Moscow remained intact. The Synodal arrangement ended in 1917 to the sound of revolutionary guns when a Patriarch of Moscow was once again appointed. With the collapse of the Russian Empire, Ukraine had a brief period of independence during which to form an autocephalous Orthodox church, and autocephaly was attempted again under Nazi occupation during World War II. However, with these exceptions, the Orthodox affairs of Ukrainians have been carried out under the authority of the ROC continuing through the Soviet period. The end of the Soviet Union opened up a new possibility for Ukrainian autocephaly, but it took another 27 years and the intervention of a re-invigorated Ecumenical Patriarchate to realize this potential. For now, the Ecumenical Patriarch has gained some room to move at the expense of Moscow.

(5)   Global Orthodoxy is a huge and unwieldly institution in any case, but under modern conditions, it cannot continue to be organized by patterns of administration that date back to the first days of the Christian church. During the twentieth and twenty-first centuries, Orthodox churches in diaspora settings have posed major jurisdictional conflicts as immigrants brought their own faiths to new lands and established jurisdictions based in ethno-national ties that crisscrossed and overlapped each other. Seeking to create "clean" structures of authority and geographic boundaries, the Ecumenical Patriarchate attempted to start a process of rationalizing diaspora structures to conform to Orthodox principles (Assembly of Canonical Orthodox Bishops of the United States, n.d.). In order to counter the Ecumenical Patriarch's symbolic status, however, the Moscow Patriarchate repeatedly intervened to manipulate leadership assignments and the like in diaspora churches. This situation exacerbated relations between Moscow and the Ecumenical Patriarchate, giving the Ecumenical Patriarch greater license to intervene in places like Ukraine. Subsequent to the Ecumenical Patriarch's intervention to support the autocephaly of the Ukrainian Orthodox Church, Moscow's Patriarch Kirill has declared the Ecumenical Patriarch to no longer be the leader of world Orthodoxy (Kirill: Bartholomew, 2019).

(6)   The 2016 Pan-Orthodox Council that had been planned by the Ecumenical Patriarch could not address major issues such as autocephaly, particularly because the Russian hierarchy pulled out of the conference at the last moment. The model *par excellence* for church life was always the historic Ecumenical Councils that defined what it means to be Christian. Starting with the 1961 Rhodes conference, the Ecumenical Patriarch (then Athenagoras) began a series of meetings of the Orthodox churches around the world with the goal to set out an agenda for a Great and Holy Council of the Orthodox Church that would renew the Christian faith (Brusanowski, 2016). Through the process of preparation for the council and then actually convening it, hierarchs and their churches hoped to settle festering differences and seek an ecumenical basis for further development of the Christian witness. One question that was to be on the agenda was that of defining the process by which a church could be designated to be autocephalous, that is independent and self-structuring, within the Eastern Orthodox communion. Representatives of the Moscow Patriarchate took part in all the preparatory meetings but, in the end, did not participate in the conference, which took place on the island of Crete in June 2016. The

ROC seems to have been threatened by the discussion of the question of autocephaly, one of the items on the agenda, with the clear call for auto-cephaly for the Ukrainian church in the air after the conflictual events of 2014.[3] The last-minute departure of the ROC hierarchs from the global process probably angered Patriarch Bartholomew in a way that made him more prone to move on his own on Ukrainian autocephaly.

In the balance of this paper, details of these factors will be explored to find some implications for the future of Ukrainian Orthodoxy.

Symbols and history

Ukraine and Russia share a long and profoundly important common history in economic and trade ties and in Christianity. Although their paths have diverged in certain important ways over the centuries, both Ukraine and Russia date their origin as nations or peoples to the period of the formation of the society of Rus' as a confederation of trading cities along the river routes of central Eurasia at the end of the first Christian millennium. The Christian "conversion" of Grand Prince Volodymyr (Ukrainian variant)/Vladimir (Russian variant) in 988 A.D. is understood as a shared source of blessing and culture. On July 28 2001, Vladimir Putin, at that time a year and one-half into his first term as President of Russia, made a special effort to emphasize the ties between Ukraine and Russia. He said that "values such as kindness, mercy and love are the true spiritual roots that tie our peoples together" as Russia and Ukraine have "entered a period of creative, restorative and constructive effort in the true sense of the word" (Russia, Ukraine leaders, 2001). He made this pronouncement at the consecration ceremonies of the newly restored Saint Vladimir Cathedral in Chersoneses, Crimea. Chersoneses is the place where Prince Volodymyr is said to have been baptized and then married to Byzantine Princess Anna. This marriage linked Rus' to the Byzantine imperial family, thus cementing the claim on Eastern Christian history for the societies and states that succeeded Rus', principally, Ukraine and Russia.[4]

No observer in 2001 would have thought that Putin knew then that he would lead the aggressions into Ukraine that his government has carried out by now. Some voices were calling for the "return" of Crimea to Russia, but the public politics did not predict the annexation that came later. The description and analysis of the reasons for the incursions into Eastern Ukraine and the annexation of Crimea that have occurred since 2014 are not the object of this chapter, but I can assert that their basic purpose has been to try to force Ukraine to remain in political, military, economic, and cultural subordination to Russia. Along with similar incursions in Georgia and threats all along the borders that were internal to the USSR but are now international, Russian leaders seek to regain some of the old glory of the Soviet empire.

From the mid-1990s until the present, there has been a major project to rebuild and re-sacralize Moscow as the fulcrum of Russian history and the heart of its cultural heritage. Its mayor Luzhkov once carried out a major marketing/branding campaign for the city centered on the idea of Moscow as the heart of Russia, and he devoted great resources to rebuilding the environs of Red Square and the churches of the city to reflect the fairytale image that the folktales of old Russia spread in the popular imagination (Grant, 2001; Stanley, 1997). The building of the massive Cathedral of the Savior, which Orthodox Church leaders had deeply yearned for, was carried out under his guidance – alongside the support of President Yeltsin and other major secular political leaders.

While public sculptures of political and military figures were common during the Soviet period and many were retained after 1991, now the historical religious figures of the capital's statuary are taking on a distinctly political meaning. The newest monumental addition is the statue of Saint Vladimir (nearly 60 feet high) that graces a main intersection near the Kremlin walls (Walker, 2016). Besides glorifying the Grand Prince of Kyiv who converted ancient Rus', the precursor of both Ukraine and Russia, to Christianity, it also provides the public reference for the naming of President Putin. Put up in 2016 following major controversy about its location and style (MacFarquhar, 2015), the statue seems to mimic (in a rather pathetic way) the large statue of Saint Volodymyr that stands on the ridge over the Dnipro River in Kyiv. Could this be a move in a game of symbolic one-upmanship being pursued by Moscow and the Russian Federation leadership to undermine Ukraine's claims to historic authenticity and national identity linked to the ancient roots of the Eastern Slavic religion and culture?

History is, as most social science scholars understand, a malleable thing. It can be seen as a kind of set of resources that one uses to justify oneself or denigrate the "other." Although I suspect that there is some concrete and absolute history, we are allowed only to see glimpses of that version. Most of the time we see history in the accounts of those mortals who have only partial access to it or in the manipulations of those wielding power. Especially in the context of massive digital information exchange, we are subject to the distortions of power-wielders and power-seekers who shape our vision of the past. Thus, we see in the arguments about the true nature of history not truth-seeking, but power manipulation. "Controlling the narrative" has become the objective rather than understanding the reality. Machiavelli mentored his prince to show himself as a religiously pious person so that he would receive the loving self-subjugation of the population, culture-based subjugation being more desirable than the costly use of force or coercion to control the people. Later, Max Weber wrote about the masking of motives of power with the creation of legitimation strategies that avoided the pitfalls of force or coercion to get done what power pursues. More modern theorists argue similarly that shared understandings of the past often cover up power grabs. And religion proves a major means of manipulating the past for the use of the powerful. The manipulation of the historical narrative and the symbolic one-upmanship that Vladimir Putin has been gaming as a means to justify ex post facto the political strategies that he pursues.

The cultural level

The role of religion in these circumstances must be seen on at least two levels, the cultural and the organizational or institutional. First, there is the level of the religious culture of the people (cf. Pankhurst, 1996). One can appeal to many aspects of the general culture to support one's case as one weaves a narrative of domination and power. And one may appeal to ethnocentric sensibilities. Russians argue that the alleged late emergence of a unique Ukrainian culture is evidence of Ukraine's backwardness. Ukraine's language is seen as derivative of the Russian tongue. The heritage of "Little Russia" is considered variously less authentic than that of "Russia" or less developed or less sophisticated or less civilized or . . . fill in the blank. Kravchenko (2015–2016) emphasizes that much of the task of nation-building for Ukraine involves "fighting Soviet myths" that biased thinking about Ukraine and limited its ability to construct the national narrative that would allow it to move forward. Under a broad cultural criticism of Ukraine emanating from Russian circles, the ROC can argue for the necessity of Ukraine to have mentoring from a senior institution or from a more developed culture like that of Russia. Even with autocephaly, we can expect these memes to continue to emanate from Russian writers and, *inter alia*, anger Ukrainians.

Moreover, the church of Imperial Russia, which included Ukraine, and the continuation of that church under the government of the Soviet Union, has had long-established privileges for demarcating the boundaries and borders of institutional structures. Now that Ukraine has become a separate and sovereign state, the principles of Orthodox jurisdictional structuring would seem to justify autocephaly for the Ukrainian Church. On the other hand, under long-recognized traditions, such autocephaly, it would seem, would have to be granted by the Russian Church. Such a contradictory situation caused Ukrainian frustration to rise to a high boil.

The year 2018 was the turning point for the debates on autocephaly for the Ukrainian Orthodox Church, and it was also the year in which both Russia and Ukraine celebrated the work of Grand Prince Volodymyr in converting their peoples to Christianity 1030 years before. On July 28, Patriarch Kirill celebrated the divine liturgy in the Moscow Kremlin, together with Patriarch Theodoros of Alexandria[5] who was paying a fraternal visit to Moscow. In his remarks following the prayer service at the new monument to Vladimir in the square outside the Kremlin, Kirill emphasized that "Vladimir wished his people to share with him the joy of life in Christ and the light of the Gospel truth to shine in the Russian land . . . The Day of Baptism [of Rus'] is celebrated today in Moscow, Kiev, Minsk and other cities. Millions of people offer up their prayers to the Equal-to-the-Apostles Prince for prosperity and peace in **the countries of historical Rus'**" (His Beatitude Patriarch, 2018, emphasis added).

A few paragraphs later, Kirill added, "as we commemorate Grand Prince Vladimir, we pray for our President Vladimir Putin named after him. There are no coincidences especially when we consider those people whose activity changes the world. On behalf of the Russian Orthodox Church I congratulate you, dear Vladimir Vladimirovich on your name day and wish you God's aid in your work and spiritual and physical strength. May the Lord keep you" (His Beatitude Patriarch, 2018[6]).

Organizational level

The ROC is one of the many national churches of the Eastern Orthodox global communion. Although heavily restricted and persecuted in many ways under communist atheist governance during the Soviet period, the structure and boundaries of the ROC were fairly clear as they were contiguous with the boundaries of the Soviet state. Since the collapse of the Soviet Union in 1991, the jurisdictional issues surrounding the creation of fifteen independent states in its place have vexed Orthodox believers and their leaders. With the special case of Estonia[7] alongside Ukraine, all the remaining states that emerged from the breakup of the USSR have retained ROC control of the Orthodox churches for virtually all the ethnic Russian, Belarusian, and most of the Ukrainian Christian Orthodox populations.[8] Ukraine, however, has experienced a more complex ongoing relationship with the ROC than the other post-Soviet states even though the UOC-MP, according to the Charter of the Russian Orthodox Church, is "self-governing with rights of broad autonomy . . . [and] shall enjoy independence and self-determination." However, the UOC-MP acts under "the Charter of the Patriarch of Moscow and All Russia of 1990," and the ROC charter directs that after election, the Primate of the Ukrainian Orthodox Church shall be "blessed by His Holiness the Patriarch of Moscow and All Russia" (Department for External Church Relations of the ROC, n.d.).[9] Clearly, under this arrangement, ultimate control of the Ukrainian Orthodox Church is held by the Moscow Patriarch. Lacking other irritants, this structure of authority between fraternal Christians might not have been problematic.

Difficulties have arisen, in the first place, because the Ukrainian Orthodox faithful have been considerably more committed and pious than the Orthodox in Russia, and second, because the number of Ukrainian Orthodox Church adherents within the UOC-MP, which is headed by Metropolitan Onufry, had provided a large contingent of the total of ROC adherents counted under the jurisdiction of the Moscow Patriarchate. As conflicts between Russia and Ukraine have increased over the last few years, so have disagreements about this church structure. According to Church canons, the UOC-MP had been the only ecclesiologically legitimate church in Ukraine, which meant it was the only Orthodox church to represent Ukrainians in relations with other Orthodox churches around the world. Nevertheless, two additional Orthodox churches have contended for the allegiance of the Ukrainian faithful. This challenging situation became more complicated in 2014 subsequent to the annexation of Crimea by the Russian Federation and with the changing and ambiguous national identities of those involved in the Russian-Ukrainian conflict in eastern Ukraine. Not only are the natural conflicts and disagreements over jurisdictional allegiance among the Orthodox churches at play; also, now weighing in heavily are problems related to the boundaries that would normally define canonical territories.

International politics

The conditions for Eastern Orthodox Christians in Ukraine have been affected profoundly by international politics. On one level, the gradual buildup of relations between Ukraine and the European Union over the last decade or so and the Ukraine government's open aspiration to ally with or join NATO (Zaremba, 2019) have driven a political wedge deeply between the Russian and the Ukrainian states. The Euromaidan events, with their obvious participation by Orthodox believers and clergy, emphasized and increased the differences between the Russian and the Ukrainian Orthodox Christians, and they also identified international allies for each side, a process that crystallized further the sides in the conflict. In current political and social parlance, this means that there has been a significant pattern of growth of "othering" on the part of both the Ukrainians and the Russians. Although the ties between Russian and Ukrainian people remain quite strong on many levels, and the interactions between them in commerce and trade continue, the general political respect and respect for the two governments in the eyes of each other have been lost.

Within this international context, while government authorities in Ukraine struggle with giving one or the other of its Orthodox churches appropriate privileges and rights, the world Eastern Orthodox communion struggles to acknowledge appropriate national church identities and privileges, and to untangle jurisdictions in diasporas and new states in appropriate and canonical ways.

Meanwhile, the depth of disquiet among leaders of the Russian Church concerning problems in Ukraine is reflected in speeches and interviews given during 2018. A review of the websites of the Moscow Patriarchate demonstrates increasing concern about the splits within Ukrainian Orthodox groups over their allegiance to Moscow. The political authorities of Ukraine have also taken a role in threatening the place of the Moscow Patriarchate in Ukrainian affairs. The issue of who possesses many parishes tops the agenda as the allegiances of Ukrainian believers change.

Further setting the stage

The role of Russian politics for the events in Ukraine has been subject to extensive evaluation, but less clear is the nature of the debate *within* the Moscow Patriarchate about (1) how the ROC should relate to the Ukrainian conflict and the related Putin government activities, and (2) how the ROC should exercise its authority over the UOC-MP, which is a "self-governing" church under the authority of the Moscow Patriarchate within the world Eastern Orthodox communion of churches. Changing personnel assignments and statements of some former insiders may be the tip of a bigger iceberg of dispute (Chapnin, 2015; Chernykh, 2015). As both Russian and Ukrainian national identities are being re-constructed, the church is challenged to adapt to such changes.[10]

The interaction of Russian governmental politics, the ROC internal politics, and the status of Russian speakers in Ukraine is of great importance. Ukraine is the "competitive marketplace" for Catholic, Orthodox, and Protestant faiths, as well as Muslims and other smaller groups. Each group has a legitimate claim for its location in Ukraine, but there had been three Eastern Orthodox churches as "competitors for adherents" in Ukraine, each of which had a unique connection with Ukrainian national identity. Following the December 2018 Unifying Council (*Ob"yednavchy Sobor*) of these churches, there are now two Orthodox Churches in the competition, the UOC-MP and the autocephalous Orthodox Church of Ukraine. The UOC-MP, as a "self-governing" church under the Moscow Patriarchate, encompasses Ukrainian historical ties with Russia that are now strongly contested. Both factors that are internal to Russian policy-making and external factors that are related to Russia's quest for international recognition and legitimacy shape the image of the UOC-MP and influence its attractiveness for Ukrainians as compared to the pull of the OCU. In addition, factors internal to Ukraine make the choice of adherence to one or another Orthodox church complex for Ukrainian believers.

As described above, the nature of the authority of the ROC over Orthodox believers in the countries formerly part of the USSR has been at issue since the 1991 breakup of the Soviet Union. Early on, there arose major disputes within the international Eastern Orthodox community about the division of ecclesiastical authority between the Moscow Patriarch and the Patriarch of Constantinople (most acutely in Estonia) and the Romanian Patriarch (in Moldova and Transnistria). Since 2000, the entry of the ROC more directly into shaping the political culture and supporting the political authority of the central Russian regime with the ascendency of Vladimir Putin has given such jurisdictional questions within Orthodoxy considerable relevance for serious political conflicts in the region. The 2008 war between Georgia and Russia elevated these questions dramatically, but the mutual decisions of the Georgian Patriarch and the Moscow Patriarch kept the church largely to the side. Georgia has had its own ancient Orthodox church and its own autocephalous Patriarch. Although absorbed into the ROC during the Soviet period, its long separation makes it different in important ways, and Patriarch Kirill honored that canonical difference of the two patriarchates and the essential differences in history and culture between Russia and Georgia. On the other hand, Ukraine was dominated by Russian imperial designs for most of modern history, and Kirill does not honor the cultural differences between Russia and Ukraine as having the same degree of authority as in Georgia. The conflict in Eastern Ukraine and the annexation of Crimea have placed the church jurisdictional question at center stage and left the Ukrainian Orthodox believers in a difficult quandary.

Borders and boundaries

Physical state borders are not the defining boundaries of faith under the "new" Russian Orthodox theology of Russian civilization that has been articulated by Patriarch Kirill (Chapnin, 2015;Verkhovsky, 2014). Nevertheless, changing state boundaries creates challenges in the places where it occurs. These challenges have been massive in the adjustments that were necessitated by the end of the USSR (Bodin, 2014).

Russian civilization and Ukrainian territory

Not being an official state church but nevertheless having a great deal of nostalgic capital among the population of Russia – but not being able to get the Russian population truly "churched" in this secular age, – the ROC has developed a social and political theology of ROC leadership of "Russian Civilization." This civilization is not contained within state political boundaries but is a cultural agglomeration that encompasses all Russian speakers and extends across adherents of all Eastern Slavic cultures, including the Ukrainian culture. Thus, the political theology of Russian Civilization or Russian World (*Russkiy mir*) has become the platform for the debate about the relationship between Russia and Ukraine and between the role of the ROC in Ukrainian affairs, both broadly cultural affairs and ecclesiological affairs (Chapnin, 2015; Zhurzhenko, 2014).

President Putin has clearly taken up the ideas of Russian civilization – which may have emanated in their present form more from his direction than the church – and his use of the notion points to the political functions of the idea and the likelihood of manipulation of the idea for political purposes in Russian-Ukrainian international relations.

East Slavic civilization?

Since the establishment of new state borders following the ending of the USSR in 1990–1991, the question of the unity or separation of the three Eastern Slavic nations of Russia, Belarus, and Ukraine has been on the table. One could argue that several developments since 1991 point to the lack of finality of the border arrangements in the region: several attempts to unite Belarus and Russia in some form of state entity, the creation and then rocky continuation of the Commonwealth of Independent States – which Ukraine helped found, then never finally joined, but continued to participate in until 2014 – and the several smaller and more temporary economic and customs organizations of the former Soviet states.

Some observers have argued that President Vladimir Putin, in particular, has been pushing to create a new USSR-like state under his leadership, and, again, the core of such an expanded state would be Russia, Belarus, and Ukraine, if these states would be willing to unite for this purpose.

Union of Belarus and the Russian Federation in some form may be possible, but I shall leave that question aside here. The Russia-Ukraine dyad is another matter, however. We used to say that Ukraine and Russia were the only two countries to devolve from the non-Baltic USSR that have a chance to become stable and successful states on their own in global affairs. Putting them together would have made a truly formidable political force. Russia may have had some misgivings related to the weak economy of Ukraine in the 1990s, but the bigger problem, I would assert, was the cultural differences between the two entities, that is, cultural differences that have deep and significant historical foundations, and which permeate the very national identities of both countries.

Discounting for present purposes the great diversity of Russia in the north Caucasus and the Asian side of Eurasia, Russia has always had difficulties with the adjectives "European" and "Western", and some of the most dangerous Europeanization threats have historically come from or via Ukraine (Tread-gold, 1985). Ukraine itself is culturally divided, as it long has been, between the western provinces, which include substantial Catholic and Greek Catholic populations, and the eastern regions, which are strongly Eastern Orthodox and Russian-speaking. With a long border with Poland, Ukraine was often a path-way of influence from Catholic Europe into the Russian Empire itself. In the late sixteenth century, when the Reformation was afire in Germany and fur-ther west in Europe, the Ukrainian borderlands became a unique meeting place of Protestant, Roman Catholic, and Eastern Orthodox faiths, and the result was the Union of Brest (1595–1596) where a Byzantium-oriented Catholic faith was institutionalized. The "Uniate" church that was formed then has been a national church of Ukraine ever since. From the sixteenth century forward, the Kyiv-Mohyla Academy, located in the very birthplace of the Rus'-Ukraine nation, was a conduit of Roman Catholic thinking and practice into the Rus-sian Orthodox Church. The memory of the "Time of Troubles" (1598–1613), when a Polish imposter temporarily took over the rule of Russia, has been cultivated over the centuries to demonstrate the differences between the Polish and Roman Catholic West and the Orthodox East. The western boundaries of Belarus and Ukraine, which run along the eastern borders of Poland, have had great significance in forming the Soviet and the Russian national identity, the ideological factor that has determined their differentness.

The conflict in Ukraine has always had a religious side. Whether today that is just a theme adjunct to the economic, political, national, and linguistic differ-ences between "Russians" and "Ukrainians" or whether it is a master theme of the confrontation between Russia and Ukraine over the eastern territories of Ukraine is, then, a core question for analysis.

Russian national identity and religion: passive revolution and transnational Eastern Orthodoxy

The national identity of Russia has historically been problematized by its rulers and intelligentsia, and a critical issue has long been whether Russia is Euro-pean by nature, or whether it has a unique identity of its own. The East-West divide of the Christian churches has provided much of the cause and context for the question, and, in the post-Soviet world, continues to animate the ongoing debate. Ukraine, as part of the Russian Empire or as a new state, has been at the vortex of the debate for historical cultural reasons and as a result of its geographical position. Thus, the broader debate has profound implications for Ukraine itself. Political leaders from Peter I to Vladimir Putin have taken a side in the debate, and Mr. Putin, within the periods of his presidency, has taken both sides, that is, that Russia is European and that Russia is a non-European unique civilization. The ROC plays a critical role in defining the terms for the quest to define national identity and in providing ideas of what is central and what is peripheral to that identity. Morozov (2015) has recently argued, using concepts taken from Antonio Gramsci, that Russia is a "subaltern empire" that is characterized by "passive revolution" under the leadership of Vladimir Putin. In this situation the Russian Church plays a significant role alongside the state in keeping the population's dissatisfaction *passive* and, in addition, in articulating a position of being universal, transnational, and "European" in values while at the same time demanding a unique perspective on human rights and values that is not simply subsumed in European materialism and secularity.

Ukraine – geographically, historically, culturally – is at the nexus of a series of forces and its future is very much going to be shaped by how these forces intersect and interact. The role of the UOC-MP, with its cross-cutting administrative and theological subordination to the ROC, is a critical force with which Ukrainians are contending today. As both the Russian state and the ROC have taken up a "values project" to extend their conceptions and, hence, their identity boundaries beyond those of the boundaries of the Russian Federation, Ukrainians must respond to the "traditional values" campaign, the anti-European Union politics of the Russian Federation, and the formal canonical subordination to the Moscow Patriarchate. Ukrainian Orthodox believers must respond to the strategies of the ROC in its role as, on the one hand, definer of the Russian national spirit and, on the other, leader of Eastern Christianity. Based on statements of Russian Church leaders and documents of the ROC, the political implications of notions of *Russkiy mir* and similar conceptions articulated by the Church, and, conversely, the implications of its position as a European and global Christian faith present major challenges for Ukrainians. The church's position must be compared and contrasted with the position of Putin and other political leaders on "Russian civilization" (Makarychev, 2017), a supposedly unique Slavic worldview that is pursued while also claiming to uphold universal values of human rights and democracy. How can seemingly contradictory positions of ideology and values be put together in the work of state and church? How can we interpret these dynamics in the light of sociological theory and research? Does the notion of subaltern empire as applied to Russia provide useful insights that move us forward conceptually and theoretically? What are the aspects of this condition that elucidate the religious sphere in Ukraine as it is developing in the post-Euromaidan period?

Finally, for present purposes, to understand the relationship of Orthodoxy to the Ukrainian people, one also must assess the impact of both general

Europeanization and the politics of the EU, NATO, and other related agencies on the international stage. These are the present embodiment of the European-ness that may be seen as differentiating Russia from Ukraine, Poland, and so forth. Orthodoxy has several national homes in the EU – Greece, Bulgaria, Cyprus, Romania – and many parishes and communities not in these national homes. The politics of Europeanization for Ukraine, which were at the base of the Euromaidan uprising and the beginning of the current conflictual stage, have their reflection in the aspirations and patterns of support and neglect originating in the broader European setting.

Six factors become seven

Earlier in this article I described six factors that have led up to the situation where the push for Ukrainian Orthodox autocephaly was attempted and gained success. There is one other factor that I have left until the end of my argument here. Noting that Ukrainian President Petro Poroshenko has been very active in recent years in pushing for and facilitating the processes leading up to the decision of the Ecumenical Patriarch to go ahead with the proposal to grant autocephaly and to carry out the local council that established the new Ortho-dox Church of Ukraine, several observers have speculated that Poroshenko has been motivated in his actions by the impending presidential election, hoping to improve his popularity in the polls and win votes before then (Ukrainian President announces, 2019). There is no question but that Poroshenko seemed to be in every gathering related to the autocephaly process and even chaired the local council that wrote up the charter of the OCU in December 2018. Likewise, Yulia Tymoshenko is including religion in the set of assets she will use for her candidacy. At the meeting of her Batkivshchyna Party when she formally announced her intention to run for president, the first speaker on the rostrum was former Patriarch of the Kyiv Patriarchate, Filaret, the leader of the now replaced UOC-KP (Ex-PM Tymoshenko, 2019).

However the appeal to voters favoring religious concerns plays in the March 31, 2019 election, the energy in the system of civil society contem-plating the election may, indeed, have contributed to the energy that took Poroshenko to Constantinople to start the current process off in earnest. And when there are so many aspiring candidates for the presidency, the religious issue is bound to get more attention. It will be interesting to see if anyone can gain votes on this basis.

Conclusion

As the Orthodox Church of Ukraine gets comfortable with its role as an important cultural institution and stabilizes its pastoral ministry to the people, and as it joins with the ecumenical community which is well developed in Ukraine, it should be troubled by important social problems that the church, as a prime cultural actor, should target to fulfill its social responsibility. The greater development of the national identity of the new Ukraine would encompass initiatives like those suggested here.

Surely, addressing the war in Donbas, helping to heal wounds, and seeking avenues for peace must be the church's first task. Seeking to facilitate a greater social and cultural consensus against extremism (Likhachev, 2018) together with forthrightly addressing the problem of corruption in the system should be next in line. Freedom House (2019b) scores Ukraine as only "partly free" in its comparative evaluations of countries, and it cites it for declining democracy scores and ongoing problems with corruption (Freedom House, 2019a). Transparency International's Corruption Perceptions Index scores Ukraine a fairly low 32 out of 100, which puts it at the rank of 120 out of 180 countries scored on the index. The organization states that Ukraine demonstrates a very low level of social trust, but "an active and independent civil society could help control corruption and improve confidence in government institutions" (Transparency International, 2018). Supporting trust-building efforts and engaging actively in civil society initiatives can be a social mission for the OCU. If such initiatives are not taken forthrightly, the OCU itself is likely to be co-opted by the political actors who are speaking so positively about it and to be drawn into the political system of corruption itself. Above that fray, the OCU can make a signal contribution to Ukraine's future.

Some observers have warned that the creation of the autocephalous Orthodox Church of Ukraine, with its struggles to convert parishes and people from the UOC-MP, will likely cause increased civil strife, including violence. The OCU must be cautious as it grows; it must guard against overstepping its own prerogatives as defined by free and democratic social principles.

In a critique of American historians' treatment of U.S. history, Jill Lapore (2019) notes that "one way to turn a state into a nation is to write its history" (p. 13). At this point, approaching thirty years since the creation of the post-Soviet state of Ukraine as a political structure, Ukrainians are faced with writing the history that both accurately encapsulates their past – both in the *longue durée* and the more recent post-Soviet experience – and fairly represents their best aspirations for the future. The state political structure needs to gain the protective cultural shielding of a strong national identity, one that is neither narrowly nationalistic nor so formless as to be unable to address legitimate national interests. The conflictual conditions in Ukraine need to be healed culturally not only by building defensive morale to face off Russian aggression, but also to foster deep national consensus as well.

In the long debates about the nature of Ukrainian and Russian Orthodoxy, popular historical understanding has clearly been shaped too much by elites with special and often corrupt interests to safeguard. With the new Orthodox Church of Ukraine, there has arisen a great opening for the Church to write Ukraine's history – honestly and fairly, in the first place – in service to the greater good, acknowledging the diversity of the Ukrainian population and its many voices (Elsner, 2019). With the recent intertwining of religious and political motives in the creation of the OCU, the danger is that one or another political faction will drive Church affairs rather than facilitate the autonomous development of the Church in its new role as a national cultural institution. The OCU must eschew the role of political insider and seek the role of public defender and representative of public will. Its forthright demands for such a role as an independent social body will undergird the further development of Ukrainian democracy and freedom. For the Church to support open democracy and to overcome long-held grievances in a just way will take many acts of moral courage and a commitment to participate in civil society in ways that balance the Church's essential religious mission of pastoral care for the people of Ukraine with its obligation as a national church in the Orthodox tradition to contribute to Ukraine's future well-being. The ecclesiastical status as an autocephalous church is not just an honor to be relished in its particularity; it profoundly embodies an obligation to nurture the nation that it embraces in its independent status. In short, the OCU, if it is to succeed as a truly autocephalous Eastern Orthodox Church, must clearly face the challenge of spinning the political and cultural threads that can "stitch together" the seams of the diverse and complex nation-state[11] into one social organism that is Ukraine for the twenty-first century.

Notes

1 But the number of adherents of the Moscow Patriarchate's churches is declining as Orthodox Ukrainians have moved to one of the alternative Orthodox churches. Before December 2018, the alternatives were the Ukrainian Orthodox Church of the Kyiv Patriarchate or the Ukrainian Autocephalous Orthodox Church. These two churches have now formally joined into the Orthodox Church of Ukraine.
2 The overall issues of Russians are explored more fully in Pankhurst and Kilp (2013).
3 In connection with the question of autocephaly the related issue of cross-cutting and overlapping jurisdictional structures in countries with varied Orthodox diaspora communities was also on the conference agenda. In the U.S. and elsewhere, this problem entailed major conflicts between Moscow's and Constantinople's authority. It added to the threat that the ROC faced at the conference.
4 We set aside from this analysis the case of Belarus, which can also claim provenance from the Rus' city states. It has special issues that merit treatment in a separate paper. So far, the question of church independence for Belarus has not led to mass movements as in Ukraine.
5 The Patriarchate of Alexandria is one of the four ancient patriarchates that have the greatest prestige among the Orthodox patriarchates and head the list of the fourteen (now fifteen with Ukraine added) canonical autocephalous churches of Eastern Orthodoxy.
6 I have translated the quoted passage slightly differently from the website's English version after comparing it with the Russian original.
7 For complicated historical reasons, Estonia has churches that exist under the Moscow Patriarchate's authority and others that fall under the special care of the Ecumenical Patriarch.
8 As there is within the Russian Federation, there may be some attempts to co-opt Moscow Patriarchate's control among Orthodox Christians by splinter Orthodox groups. Orthodox Christians living in the central Asian states that are dominated by Islam are within the jurisdictional territory of the ROC without challenge. By and large, the Belarusian Orthodox Christians are at peace with membership in the Belarusian Exarchate of the

ROC (at least I am not ready to argue otherwise here). Armenia and Georgia have their own national churches, but Russians there are likely to consider themselves Russian Orthodox. The two parts of the former Moldovan SSR, Moldova and Transnistria, are experiencing a jurisdictional dispute between two patriarchal claimants – the Moscow Patriarchate versus the Metropolitan Church of Bessarabia which was created under the Romanian Patriarch – but, again, Russians in these regions would also likely consider themselves to be Russian Orthodox.

9 Notably, the Metropolitan of Kyiv and all Ukraine is a permanent member of the Holy Synod of the ROC as well as Primate of the Ukrainian Orthodox Church. Part X of the ROC Charter clarifies that "the name of the Primate shall be commemorated in all churches of the Ukrainian Orthodox Church after the name of the Patriarch of Moscow and All Russia."

10 On aspects of Russian efforts, see Epplee (2019).

11 This imagery is taken from the article by Lapore (2019).

References

Agadjanian, A. (2001). Revising Pandora's gifts: Religious and national identity in the post-Soviet societal fabric. *Europe-Asia Studies, 53*(3), 473–488. doi:10.1080/09668130120004545898

Assembly of Canonical Orthodox Bishops of the United States of America. (n.d.). Fourth pre-conciliar pan-Orthodox conference in Chambesy. Retrieved from http://assemblyof-bishops.org/about/chambesy

Bodin, P.-A. (2014). The enthronement of Patriarch Kirill: A liturgical event. In K. Tolstaya (Ed.), *Orthodox paradoxes: Heterogeneities and complexities in contemporary Russian Orthodoxy* (pp. 56–70). doi:10.1163/9789004269552_005

Bremmer, I. (1994). The politics of ethnicity: Russians in the new Ukraine. *Europe-Asia Studies, 46*(2), 261–283. doi:1080/09668139408412161

Brünning, A. (2016). Orthodox autocephaly in Ukraine: The historical dimension. In A. Krawchuk & T. Bremer (Eds.), *Churches in the Ukrainian crisis* (pp. 79–101). doi:10.1007/978-3-319-34144-6_4

Brusanowski, P. (2016). Autocephaly in Ukraine: The canonical dimension. In A. Krawchuk & T. Bremer (Eds.), *Churches in the Ukrainian crisis* (pp. 47–77). doi:10.1007/978-3-319-34144-6_3

Chapnin, S. (2015, November). A church of empire: Why the Russian Orthodox Church chose to bless empire. *First Things.* Retrieved from www.firstthings.com/article/2015/11/a-church-of-empire

Chernykh, A. (2015, December 22). Sergey Chapnin: Zapros na sviashchennuyu voynu na Ukraine v RPTs uzhe est' [Sergey Chapnin: Within the ROC there has been a demand for a holy war in Ukraine]. *Republic.* Retrieved from https://republic.ru/posts/61598

Colton, T. J. (2016). *Russia: What everyone needs to know.* New York, NY: Oxford University Press.

Department for External Church Relations of the ROC. (n.d.). Statute of the Russian Orthodox Church. Retrieved from https://mospat.ru/en/documents/ustav/

Elsner, R. (2019, January 6). Orthodox Church of Ukraine: Challenges and risks of a new beginning. *Russian Analytical Digest, 231.* Retrieved from www.css.ethz.ch/content/specialinterest/gess/cis/center-for-securities-studies/en/publications/rad/details.html?id=/n/o/2/3/no_231_orthodox_church

Epplee, N. (2019, February 1). Inventorying the past: Russia refreshes its historical memory. *The Russia File: A Blog of the Kennan Institute.* Retrieved from www.wilsoncenter.org/blog-post/inventorying-the-past-russia-refreshes-its-historical-memory

Ex-PM Tymoshenko launches bid for Ukrainian presidency. (2019, January 22). *RFE/RL*. Retrieved from www.rferl.org/a/ex-pm-tymoshenko-launches-bid-for-ukrainian-presidency/29724626.html

Fagan, G. (2013). *Believing in Russia – Religious policy after Communism*. doi:10.4324/9780203095379

Fireside, H. (1971). *Icon and swastika: The Russian Orthodox Church under Nazi and Soviet control*. doi:10.4159/harvard.9780674333963

Freedom House. (2019a). *Freedom in the world 2019: Ukraine*. Retrieved from https://freedomhouse.org/report/freedom-world/2019/ukraine

Freedom House. (2019b). *Nations in transit 2018: Confronting illiberalism*. Retrieved from https://freedomhouse.org/report/nations-transit/nations-transit-2018

Grant, B. (2001). New Moscow monuments, or, states of innocence. *American Ethnologist, 28*(2), 332–362. doi:10.1525/ae.2001.28.2.332

His Beatitude Patriarch Theodoros of Alexandria and His Holiness Patriarch Kirill celebrated prayer service at the monument to Prince Vladimir Equal-to-the-Apostles. (2018, July 28). Retrieved from https://mospat.ru/en/2018/07/28/news162561/

Kirill: Bartholomew no longer the Ecumenical Patriarch of all Orthodoxy. (2019, January 3). Retrieved from www.religiousfreedomnews.com/2019/01/03/kirill-bartholomew-no-longer-the-ecumenical-patriarch-of-all-orthodoxy/

Kravchenko, V. (2015–2016). Fighting Soviet myths: The Ukrainian experience. *Harvard Ukrainian Studies, 34*(1-4), 447–484.

Lapore, J. (2019, March-April). The new American nationalism: Why a nation needs a national story. *Foreign Affairs, 98*(2), 10–19.

Likhachev, V. (2018). Far-right extremism as a threat to Ukrainian democracy. *Freedom House website*. Retrieved from https://freedomhouse.org/report/special-reports/far-right-extremism-threat-ukrainian-democracy

MacFarquhar, N. (2015, May 28). Another huge statue in Russia? Not rare, but hugely divisive. *The New York Times*. Retrieved from www.nytimes.com/2015/05/29/world/europe/another-huge-statue-in-russia-not-rare-but-hugely-divisive.html

MacFarquhar, N. (2018, November 26). Russia-Ukraine fight over narrow sea passage risks wider war. *The New York Times*. Retrieved from www.nytimes.com/2018/11/26/world/europe/russia-ukraine-kerch-strait.html

Makarychev, A. (2017, June). The Russian world, post-truth, and Europe. *PONARS Eurasia*. Retrieved from www.ponarseurasia.org/memo/russian-world-post-truth-and-europe

Morozov, V. (2015). *Russia's postcolonial identity: A subaltern empire in a Eurocentric world*. doi:10.1057/9781137409300

Pankhurst, J. G. (1996). Religious culture. In D. N. Shalin (Ed.), *Russian culture at the crossroads: Paradoxes of postcommunist consciousness* (pp. 127–156). doi:10.4324/9780429497506–5

Pankhurst, J. G., & Kilp, A. (2013). Religion, the Russian nation and the state: Domestic and international dimensions: An introduction. *Religion, State and Society, 41*(3), 226–243. doi: 10.1080/09637494.2013.844592

Petro, N. N. (2015, March 23). Russia's Orthodox soft power. *Carnegie Council for Ethics in International Affairs*. Retrieved from www.carnegiecouncil.org/publications/articles_papers_reports/727/

Ponomariov, A. (2019, January 25). Ukrainian church autocephaly: The redrawing of the religious borders and political identities in the conflict between Ukraine and Russia. *Russian Analytical Digest, 231*. Retrieved from www.css.ethz.ch/content/specialinterest/gess/cis/center-for-securities-studies/en/publications/rad/details.html?id=/n/o/2/3/no_231_orthodox_church

Prokip, A. (2018, April–June). *Ukraine Quarterly Digest.* Retrieved from www.wilsoncenter.org/blog-post/ukraine-quarterly-digest-april-june-2018*Razumkov Center.* (2014). Ukraine-2014: Socio-political conflict and the church (positions of religious figures, experts, and citizens): Nationwide sociological survey. Retrieved from www.razumkov.org.ua/upload/1403784774_file.pdf

Russia, Ukraine leaders sing church praises. (2001, July 28). *BBC News.* Retrieved from http://news.bbc.co.uk/2/hi/world/monitoring/media_reports/1462322.stm

Stanley, A. (1997, August 31). The power broker. *The New York Times.* Retrieved from www.nytimes.com/1997/08/31/magazine/the-power-broker.html

Tolz, V. (2001). *Russia: Inventing the nation.* New York, NY: Oxford University Press.

Transparency International. (2018). *Corruption perception index 2018.* Retrieved from www.transparency.org/cpi2018

Treadgold, D. W. (1985). *The West in Russia and China: Vol. 1: Russia: 1472–1917.* Boulder, CO; and London, UK: Westview Press.

Ukrainian President announces reelection bid, aims for EU membership. (2019, January 29). *RFE/RL.* Retrieved from www.rferl.org/a/ukrainian-president-petro-poroshenko-seek-reelection-march/29739846.html

Verkhovsky, A. (2014). 'Kirill's Doctrine' and the potential transformation of Russian Orthodox Christianity. In K. Tolstaya (Ed.), *Orthodox paradoxes: Heterogeneities and complexities in contemporary Russian Orthodoxy* (pp. 71–84). doi:10.1163/9789004269552_006

Walker, S. (2016, November 4). From one Vladimir to another: Putin unveils huge statue in Moscow. *The Guardian.* Retrieved from www.theguardian.com/world/2016/nov/04/vladimir-great-statue-unveiled-putin-moscow

Yelensky, V. (2005). Globalization, nationalism, and Orthodoxy: The case of Ukrainian nation building. In V. Roudometof, A. Agadjanian, & J. Pankhurst (Eds.), *Eastern Orthodoxy in a global age: Tradition faces the twenty-first century* (pp. 29–57). Walnut Creek, CA: AltaMira Press.

Zaremba, A. (2019, February 8). Ukraine's path toward EU and NATO: Point of no return. *UNIAN.* Retrieved from www.unian.info/multimedia/photo/10005939-rada-prinyala-izmeneniya-v-konstituciyu-o-kurse-v-es.html

Zhurzhenko, T. (2014). A divided nation? Reconsidering the role of identity politics in the Ukraine crisis. *Die Friedens-Warte, 89*(1-2), 249–267. Retrieved from www.jstor.org/stable/24868495

11 The cause of Ukrainian autocephaly

Cyril Hovorun

Introduction

The Russian aggression against Ukraine, which began after the Revolution of Dignity in 2014, placed the cause of autocephaly for the Ukrainian Orthodox church at the center of security concerns. This cause ceased to be only religious and turned social, political, and military. It became a reaction to another religious cause that had turned political and military – that of the "Russian World." The doctrine of the "Russian World" (*Russkiy mir*) has been elaborated by the Russian Orthodox Church (ROC) and became weaponized by Russia in its aggression against Ukraine. The dependence of the largest part of the Ukrainian Orthodoxy on Moscow also became an instrument in the hands of the Kremlin.

Seeking independence of the Ukrainian church from Moscow, therefore, has become part of a survival strategy for the Ukrainian state. The Ukrainian political establishment, including the President and Parliament, have found support for this cause from the Ecumenical Patriarchate. Claiming its right to manage church matters beyond its direct jurisdiction, the Patriarch of Constantinople contested the exclusive rights of Moscow over Ukraine, causing tensions in the global Orthodox church. These tensions can be interpreted as a conflict between two visions of the Orthodox church: one appreciating and the other detesting neo-imperial political projects.

The cause of the Ukrainian autocephaly is not a recent one. It goes back one hundred years. It emerged after the collapse of the Russian Empire and from its beginning was anti-imperial and anti-colonial. Recently, it has had three distinguishable stages: in the period of the Ukrainian People's Republic in the late 1910s and early 1920s, during World War II, and after Ukraine gained its independence in 1991. All these stages are explored in this chapter. To understand how autocephaly became the focus of Russian and Ukrainian geopolitical tensions and a fault line in inter-Orthodox relations, a detailed review of Orthodox jurisdictions is necessary. This will not only lay out the arguments advanced for and historical attempts at autocephaly, but also reinforce how closely tied autocephaly is historically with the fate of Ukraine as a nation.

The church of Kyiv under Constantinople

When the people of Rus' were baptized in 988, they became members of the church, which was immediately shaped as a structure typical for Eastern Christianity. This was a structure of a *Metropolia* or Metropolis – a large administrative unit, which included smaller units of dioceses or eparchies. A Metropolis, however, is not an independent unit, but is included in an independent church. In the case of the Metropolis of Kyiv, it was the Patriarchate of Constantinople, which arranged the baptism of the Kyivans after the relevant agreements between the Byzantine emperor and the grand prince (*knyaz*) of Kyiv were made. The Metropolis had to follow certain rules in its relations with Constantinople, which were established by Constantinople. These rules defined mainly the way in which new Metropolitans of Kyiv had to be installed. According to these rules, the rulers of Kyiv had either to send their own candidates to Constantinople for approval or to receive appointees of the patriarch.

During the tenth and eleventh centuries, the Rus' was one of the most powerful states of Europe, which covered vast territories from the Black to White Seas. However, it was unstable and began rapidly declining in the twelfth century. Prince Andrey Bogolyubsky pillaged Kyiv in 1169. In 1240, the city was captured and burned down by the Mongols. It did not reemerge as a significant center of political power until early modernity. The dramatic political decline of Kyiv incurred dramatic changes to the church connected with it. The Kyiv Metropolis was divided in two parts. While formally these parts were still regarded as structures under the Ecumenical Patriarchate with their center in Kyiv, they became detached from Kyiv as a practical matter. Later on, they became detached also from the Ecumenical Patriarchate.

Two states emerged from the Kyivan Rus' and claimed their succession to it. In the southwest, it was the principality of Galicia-Volhynia, and in the northeast, the principality of Vladimir-Suzdal. The grand duchy of Lithuania and the kingdom of Poland absorbed the former in the fourteenth century. The grand duchy of Moscow did the same to the principality of Vladimir-Suzdal. These two duchies became rivals and tried to appropriate the Metropolis of Kyiv. What happened to this Metropolis as a result can be seen as a "cloning" of the Kyiv See. One clone emigrated to the southwestern Rus'. Halych, Novgorodok, and Vilno became new residences of the Kyiv metropolitans. The Primates of the other clone were first hosted in Vladimir-on-Klyazma and then ended up in Moscow.

With the growth of the political and military strength of Moscow, it began seeking its own autocephalous church, i.e., independent from Constantinople. Eventually it considered an opportunity to proclaim ecclesiastical independence after the church of Constantinople participated in the Council of Basel-Ferrara-Florence (1431–1445). The delegation of Constantinople at the council included Isidore (1380/90–1463), who was promoted to be the Metropolitan of Kyiv, to reside in Moscow. Moscow did not accept the choice of Constantinople and eventually expelled Isidore from its realm. The grand princes of Moscow instead promoted in 1448 the Bishop of Ryazan Jonas to the Metropolitan's See, without seeking the consent of Constantinople. This was a de facto proclamation of independence, but only affected only a part of the original Kyiv church.

The independence of a part of the church of Kyiv, which had its center in Moscow, was a political step initiated and conducted by civil authorities and was attempted to be theologically justified after the fact. They accused Constantinople of apostasy from Orthodoxy and falling to maintain uniatism (Golubinsky, 1900, p. 459). When Constantinople denounced the union, this did not help, because Moscow found another excuse to accuse Constantinople and thus to justify its self-proclaimed autocephaly. In 1453, the capital of what remained of the Byzantine Empire fell to the hands of the Turkish Ottoman dynasty. In the eyes of Moscow, this meant that the Orthodox Christian empire ceased to exist, and its church lost legitimacy. Ivan the Terrible (reigned 1547–1584) offered the following apologetics to save the legitimacy of the otherwise schismatic church: "The Turkish tsar turned God's large churches to mosques; and those churches, which were left to the patriarch, have no crosses on them and bells . . . the Orthodoxy of the Greeks has been corrupted" (Golubinsky, 1900, p. 511).

Whatever excuses and accusations were designed by Moscow, Constantinople did not recognize its unilateral proclamation of autocephaly, leading to the schism between Moscow and Constantinople. This schism was resolved only in 1589, when the Patriarch of Constantinople Jeremiah II (1572–1579, 1580–1584, 1587–1595) visited Moscow. There, he recognized the autocephaly of the Russian church (as it became known) and gave it patriarchal status. Constantinople proclaimed autocephaly and granted patriarchal status to only one of the two parts of the original Metropolis of Kyiv. The other part remained faithful to Constantinople. It was contained mostly within the confines of the Polish-Lithuanian state (*Rzeczpospolita*).

The Kyiv church under Moscow's management

In the meantime, at the end of the sixteenth century the Polish-Lithuanian state in collaboration with Rome initiated the process of *unia* (the unification of the Catholic and Orthodox churches). A third clone of the Metropolis of Kyiv was created, this time in unity with Rome at the Council in Brest (now in Belarus) in 1595–1596. The advance of *unia* urged the autonomous Ukrainian state, ruled by hetmans and subordinate to the *Rzeczpospolita*, to seek solutions to the church issue in Moscow and Constantinople. Constantinople, in addition to this, was motivated by the ongoing war between the Polish-Lithuanian kings with the Ottoman sultans, and by Moscow's generous donations. Moscow, after signing a political union with the Ukrainian Hetmanate in Pereyaslav in 1654, sought more dependence of Ukraine in both political and ecclesiastical terms. A conflation of the interests of Ukrainian hetmans, Moscow tsars, and the Ecumenical patriarchs led to the decision of the latter to transfer to the Moscow Patriarchate some rights over that part of the Kyiv Metropolis, which remained faithful to Constantinople.

This decision materialized under Dionysius IV Mouselimes, who was tenured as the Patriarch of Constantinople five times: in 1671–1673, 1676–1679, 1682–1684, 1686–1687, and 1693–1694. With the consent of his Synod, he issued two letters in 1686 that transferred to Moscow rights to install the Metropolitans of Kyiv. Constantinople would remain the kyriarchal (mother) church for Kyiv, for which reason the Metropolitans there were obliged to commemorate the Ecumenical Patriarch. Moscow, however, interpreted the decision of Constantinople as a complete inclusion of the Kyiv Metropolis in the Moscow Patriarchate. For this reason, the commemoration of the Ecumenical Patriarch in Kyiv was soon abolished, and the Metropolis was completely absorbed by the Russian church.

The Metropolis of Kyiv not only lost its connection with the Patriarchate of Constantinople, but was also cleansed of Ukrainian ethnic elements. For example, in 1915, according to the statistics of the Holy Synod of the ROC, only one of nine eparchial bishops and two of fifteen vicar bishops in Ukraine were Ukrainians (Partykevich, 1998, p. XV). It was forbidden to use the Ukrainian language to print spiritual literature or for the liturgy.

The Russian revolution in February 1917 changed the situation radically. The tsar abdicated, the empire collapsed, and new nations emerged from it, including the Ukrainian state. The Ukrainians established their own republic, which lasted until 1921, when it was replaced by the Soviet Union. The Ukrainian republic was democratic in its nature and cultivated both ethnic identity and social change. It also opened a window of possibilities for the Ukrainian church to become more sensitive to people's identity and their thrust for social justice.

The rise of national self-awareness among the Ukrainians brought back their historical memory that they once belonged to the Ecumenical Patriarchate. In 1917, to promote the independence of the Ukrainian church, the All-Ukrainian Church Board was founded. Its first president, the Archbishop of Vladimir and Suzdal Oleksiy (Dorodnitsyn) (1859–1919) suggested engaging Constantinople in the Ukrainian cause. Although the Ukrainian government did not support the idea at first, eventually it commissioned its minister of religious affairs and later the ambassador to Turkey Oleksandr Lototsky (1870–1939) to accomplish this mission. Lototsky repeatedly visited the Phanar and urged it to support the Ukrainian ecclesiastical cause. The Ecumenical Patriarchate then, however, remained irresponsive, which made Lototsky confess with bitterness in 1922:

> When the spirit of God once again renewed church life in Ukraine, and when the daughter turned her eyes in supplication to her Mother, and fate assigned my unworthy person to deliver these supplications and I unceasingly knocked at the door of the Ecumenical Patriarchate, that door did not open and the prayer went unanswered.
>
> (Partykevich, 1998, p. XVI)

Reluctance of the Ecumenical Patriarchate to support the cause of an independent church for Ukraine did not stop the autocephalist movement. The All-Ukrainian Church Board proceeded to convene a council – a traditional

eastern Christian form of decision-making with the highest legislative authority. The All-Ukrainian Church Council gathered in January 1918. It failed,
however, to agree that autocephaly was what the Ukrainian church needed.
Instead, it endorsed autonomy in a form of the semi-independence of the
Ukrainian church from the Russian church. Another church council, which
was convened in October 1921, proclaimed autocephaly and established the
Ukrainian Autocephalous Orthodox Church (UAOC).

This church, however, did not receive support from any bishops. As a result, it
was unable to promote any bishop to its leadership. It decided to elect instead a
married priest, Vasyl Lypkivsky (1864–1937), who was consecrated not by other
bishops, but by clergy. The bishops and priests who received their ordination
from these consecrations became known as *samosviaty* – the ones that consecrated
themselves. This method of consecration of bishops and clergy put a "stigma of
ecclesial illegitimacy" (Denysenko, 2018, p. 8) on the entire autocephalist movement for decades to come. This movement continued in the first years of the
Soviet regime, which tolerated it because it served the purpose of the Soviets to
challenge the Russian church under Patriarch Tikhon (Bellavin). Only in 1930
was the Ukrainian autocephalous church abolished by the Communist state.

The case of the Polish autocephaly

Although the Ecumenical Patriarchate remained irresponsive to the appeals
of the independent Ukrainian government and the Orthodox community in
Ukraine, it responded to similar requests from the government of the Polish
republic after it achieved independence from the Russian Empire. The number of Orthodox Christians in the predominantly Catholic Poland was much
smaller than in Ukraine. In contrast to Ukraine, however, the cause of Polish autocephaly was supported by bishops. Metropolitan Georgy (Yaroshevsky)
agreed to become a Primate of the independent Orthodox Church in Poland.
However, he was assassinated in 1923 by a priest of the ROC.

Metropolitan Dionizy (Waledyński) (1876–1960) was elected to replace
Georgy. The Ecumenical Patriarchate confirmed the election of Dionizy and
the next year, in 1924, granted autocephaly to the Orthodox Church of Poland.
This decision was contested by the ROC, which recognized Polish autocephaly
only in 1948.

The document of the Ecumenical Patriarchate that granted independence to
the Polish church (*Tomos*) is important for Ukrainian history. It presented the
Polish church as a part of the ancient Metropolis of Kyiv, which was transferred
to the administration of Moscow. In 1924 the Ecumenical Patriarchate revoked
its decision regarding this part of the Kyiv Metropolis and reinstated it in its
own jurisdiction, and then granted autocephaly to the Polish church. Here is
the rationale of Constantinople's decision from its *Tomos* of 1924:

> Having listened to the loud voice of canonical duty, which has imposed on
> our Holy Ecumenical See to take care of the Holy Orthodox Churches in

distress; having taken into consideration that history also testifies in favor of the above (because it has been written that the alienation from our Throne of the Metropolis of Kyiv and of the Orthodox Churches of Lithuania and Poland as dependent on it, as well as their insertion to the Holy Church of Moscow, from the very beginning were not carried out at all in compliance with the lawful canonical requirements; nor was it followed what had been jointly declared with regard to the complete ecclesiastical self-sufficiency of the Kyiv Metropolitan, who had the title of the exarch of the Ecumenical See), our Modesty together with holy Metropolitans – our respected and beloved in the Holy Spirit brothers and concelebrants – decided to readily accept the request, which was sent to us by the Holy Orthodox Church in Poland, and to grant our blessing and approval of its autocephalous and independent status.

(Tzortzatos, 1975/1926–1927)

The recognized independent Church of Poland played an important role during the revival of the Orthodox Church on the Ukrainian territories occupied by Nazis during 1941–1944. It helped establish a second UAOC there in 1942. Polish bishops supplemented the doubtful consecrations of the Ukrainian bishops and thus made the UAOC hierarchy legitimate. The proponents of the UAOC based their arguments in its favor on the same references that the Ecumenical Patriarchate made in its *Tomos* of Polish autocephaly in 1924. The renewed UAOC, however, was not favored by Germans, because it supported the cause of the Ukrainian Insurgence Army, which fought against both Communists and Nazis. The Nazis were more in favor of the autonomous church, which wanted to preserve unity with the Russian church in the spirit of the All-Ukrainian Church Council of 1918.

After Nazis were expelled from Ukraine and the Bolsheviks reinstalled their rule there, the activists of the autocephalous church had to flee the country. They emigrated mostly to Canada and the United States, where they continued as an autocephalous church. In the meantime, the correction of its hierarchy was finalized, with its Primate Archbishop John (Teodorovych) being re-consecrated in 1949 by two canonical bishops. As an administrative structure, however, the UAOC remained unrecognized by other local Orthodox churches. Only in 1990 did the Ecumenical Patriarchate embrace the UAOC in Canada, and in 1995, the UAOC in the United States.

The autocephalous movement in independent Ukraine

In 1991, Ukraine became an independent state and the Ukrainian republic was restored. Simultaneously, just like when it was established in 1917, it began promoting an autocephalous church. This time, however, the Ukrainians did not have to establish a new autocephalous church, but also had the option to invite back the church that existed in North America. The UAOC was replanted in Ukraine under the leadership of Mstyslav (Skrypnyk) (1898–1993).

Mstyslav was proclaimed the first UAOC Patriarch of Kyiv in 1990 and enthroned at Saint Sophia Cathedral. This proclamation, however, was not recognized by other local Orthodox churches. In 1992, Mstyslav allowed the merger of his church with the structures created by the former ROC Metropolitan of Kyiv Filaret (Denysenko). Filaret occupied the Episcopal See of Kyiv from 1966 as an exarch. This title presupposed some degree of formal autonomy for the church. It did not, however, translate to more Ukrainian features in the exarchate, as Filaret personally opposed them. He grew to be one of the most influential hierarchs of the Moscow Patriarchate. In 1990, after the death of Patriarch Pimen (Izvekov), Filaret was elected the *locum tenens* of the See of Moscow. He was not, however, elected Patriarch and lost the elections to Aleksy (Ridiger) (1929–2008).

Filaret returned to Kyiv, where he continued as an exarch. Having observed how Ukraine was rapidly heading towards independence from Russia, Filaret initiated a similar process in the church. He urged the Ukrainian bishops to sign a petition to Patriarch Aleksy with a request to grant the Ukrainian church more independence. The request was satisfied when the council of bishops of the ROC on October 25–27, 1990 granted "independence in management" to the Ukrainian Orthodox Church. This status, however, did not mean autocephaly or even autonomy. After Ukraine was proclaimed independent on August 24, 1991, Filaret convened on November 1–3 of the same year a council that requested that Moscow grant full independence (autocephaly) to the Ukrainian church.

This time Moscow did not accept the request, but postponed this question to the next Local Council of the ROC. At the council of bishops of the Moscow Patriarchate, which was held on April 1–2, 1992, Filaret promised that he would resign as the Metropolitan of Kyiv. When he came back to Ukraine, however, he declared that he made his promise under duress and therefore would not keep it. The council of Russian bishops on June 11 of the same year defrocked Filaret accusing him of breaking his promises and inappropriate behavior.

Two weeks before that, on May 27–28, the council of bishops of the Ukrainian Orthodox Church met in Kharkiv, without Filaret. It decided to remove him from the see of Kyiv. A new Metropolitan of Kyiv, Volodymyr (Sabodan) (1935–2014), was elected to replace him. Filaret did not recognize the decisions of either of the councils of the Russian and Ukrainian churches. Instead, he initiated an All-Ukrainian Orthodox Council, which was held on June 25, 1992. At this council, the UAOC under Mstyslav (Skrypnyk) agreed to merge with the group that remained with Filaret. Together they established the Ukrainian Orthodox Church of the Kyiv Patriarchate (UOC-KP). Mstyslav became the formal leader of this church, as its patriarch, while Filaret was his deputy and informal leader. After Mstyslav died in 1993, Volodymyr (Romanyuk) became his successor as the Patriarch of Kyiv. Filaret remained a deputy of Volodymyr and the real leader of the church. In 1995, after Volodymyr passed away, Filaret was elected the UOC-KP Patriarch of Kyiv.

Although the UAOC in 1992 agreed to unite with the group of Filaret, a part of this church soon decided to stay away from the UOC-KP, which was formed as a result of the merger. This part proceeded with electing its own patriarch Dmytro (Yarema) in 1993, who stayed in the office until he died in 2000. After his death, the UAOC decided to not elect a new patriarch, but instead to be headed by a Metropolitan. Metropolitan Mefodiy (Kudryakov) became the new Primate of this church. In 2015, after his death, he was succeeded by Metropolitan Makariy (Maletych).

Moscow, in the meantime, did not recognize the UOC-KP and the UAOC. Other canonical Orthodox churches also regarded them as schismatic groups. In 1997, the council of bishops of the ROC anathematized Filaret. This anathema was accepted by other Orthodox churches as well. Under pressure from Moscow, even non-Orthodox churches and ecumenical organizations refused to have any formal contact with the Kyiv Patriarchate. It became completely isolated.

On the one hand, Moscow did not want the Ukrainian church to go and did everything possible to keep it under its jurisdiction. The unrecognized Ukrainian churches, on the other hand, did not want to compromise their independence from Moscow, even if this would mean remaining in complete isolation from global Orthodoxy. As a result, the Ukrainian Orthodoxy became fragmented, with little hope for reconciliation. This fragmentation, it seems, satisfied all the churches.

The Ukrainian state, however, did not give up on the reconciliation of the Ukrainian churches. To my knowledge every president of Ukraine, regardless of his political orientation, wanted the Orthodox church in Ukraine to be united and independent. The Ukrainian governments endorsed contacts between the separated Ukrainian churches and systematically contacted both Moscow and Constantinople in this regard.

The attempt at autocephaly in 2008

In 2008, the Ukrainian state came closer than ever before to fostering the unification of the Ukrainian Orthodoxy. This was under the presidency of Victor Yushchenko (2005–2010), who initiated and supported the process. He used the celebrations of the 1020th anniversary of the Baptism of Kyiv as an opportunity towards reunification.

For this reason, he invited the Patriarch of Constantinople Bartholomew to attend the celebrations in Kyiv, and encouraged him to proceed in granting autocephaly to a united Ukrainian church. President Yushchenko envisaged a single Ukrainian church, which would comprise all existent Orthodox jurisdictions. He also saw Filaret as the patriarch of this church. This vision, however, was not realistic, as many Ukrainian Orthodox, especially from the UOC-MP, did not want to belong to the autocephalous church and instead cherished their membership in the ROC. Additionally, many had reservations concerning the figure of Patriarch Filaret, particularly because of the anathema against him by Moscow.

This made Patriarch Bartholomew hesitant about the plans of President Yushchenko. While in Kyiv, he declined to implement them. Nevertheless, he made some important statements regarding Ukrainian Orthodoxy. In particular, he confirmed the historical rights of Constantinople in Ukraine. He also doubted that Moscow continued to have the same rights because it did not keep the conditions of the Synodal decision of 1686 (Bartholomew, n.d.).

To neutralize the efforts of Constantinople to grant autocephaly to the Ukrainian church, Patriarch of Moscow Aleksy hastily organized his own visit to Kyiv for the celebrations of the 1020th anniversary of the baptism of Rus'. There was a risk of a split between the churches of Moscow and Constantinople at that time, but it was averted. The two Primates peacefully concelebrated in Kyiv and sent irenic messages to their flocks.

The peaceful resolution of the imminent conflict became possible, among other things, owing to the standpoint of the then-head of the UOC-MP, Metropolitan Volodymyr (Sabodan). The UOC-MP was not happy about the plans of President Yushchenko to unify all Orthodox in the country against their will. It also opposed the idea of using the UOC-KP as a platform for such unification. The UOC-MP, under the leadership of Volodymyr, promoted itself as a platform for unification. After 2008, it began seeking more independence from Moscow.

In particular, the UOC-MP tried to engage in dialogue with other Orthodox churches in Ukraine. There were several attempts at such dialogue, and all of them failed. This happened because the Moscow Patriarchate and some influential hierarchs of the UOC-MP did not want the dialogue to become something more than just an imitation. The UOC-MP became uninterested in the dialogues after it elected Metropolitan Onufry (Berezovsky) as its new Primate as he embraced an agenda of isolationism.

His policies prepared ground for the second attempt at granting autocephaly to the Ukrainian church by the Ecumenical Patriarchate. This time, the UOC-MP could not even pretend to serve as a platform of unification for the Ukrainian Orthodoxy, as it chose a path of isolation and self-sufficiency. Another difference between the model of unity in 2018 and the model of unity in 2008 was that the former presupposed not one, but two canonical Orthodox churches in Ukraine: autocephalous and the Moscow Patriarchate.

Granting autocephaly in 2018–2019

In spring 2018, the Ecumenical Patriarchate decided to proceed to grant the Ukrainian church autocephaly. It announced this to President Poroshenko while he was visiting the Phanar during the week after Orthodox Easter (April 8). Upon his return to Ukraine, President Poroshenko met with the hierarchs of all the Orthodox churches in Ukraine and asked for their support for his initiative. The Kyiv Patriarchate and the UAOC unanimously endorsed the President and promulgated official requests to the Ecumenical Patriarchate. The Primate of the UOC-MP Metropolitan Onyfry refused to endorse the initiative. Nevertheless, some bishops from his church agreed to participate in the process, even though their names were not disclosed. Poroshenko also sent his own official request to the Phanar to proceed in granting autocephaly. On April 19, the President asked the Parliament to support his request, and the Verkhovna Rada passed a relevant decision with the majority of votes.

Petro Poroshenko thus became the chief facilitator for the Ukrainian churches and political bodies in their communication with the Ecumenical Patriarchate. He swiftly secured formal support from the Ukrainian parliament and most Ukrainian churches, with the UOC-MP predictably abstaining from this.

On September 7 the Secretariat of the Holy Synod of the Ecumenical Patriarchate issued a statement about the appointment of two patriarchal exarchs to Ukraine, Archbishop Daniel of Pamphilon from the United States and Bishop Ilarion of Edmonton from Canada. The mission of exarchs in the Ecumenical Patriarchate is similar to the mission of legates in the Catholic Church. They represent the patriarch and give an account to him. They cannot act by their own authority and do not exercise the power of a diocesan bishop in the places where they have been sent. The particular mission of the exarchs in Ukraine was to prepare a unifying council of the church, which would then be granted autocephaly.

On October 9–11, 2018, there was a session of the Holy Synod of the Ecumenical Patriarchate in Istanbul. According to its communique (Chief Secretariat of the Holy and Sacred Synod, 2018), it decided to declare that the faithful of the non-canonical churches "have been restored to communion with the Church." This declaration meant the end of the schism that existed in Ukraine from 1992. The Phanar, however, did not recognize the Kyiv Patriarchate and the UAOC as canonical churches in Ukraine. Only their faithful were reconciled with global Orthodoxy, while their bishops were included in the Ecumenical Patriarchate. They were supposed to establish a new ecclesial group, which would receive recognition and independence from Constantinople. The new church would be established on the basis of the Metropolis of Kyiv under the jurisdiction of Constantinople.

The new church was founded at the council held in Saint Sophia of Kyiv on December 15, 2018. Two churches that existed prior to that, the Kyiv Patriarchate and the UAOC, annulled themselves and all their bishops joined the new church, called the Orthodox Church of Ukraine (OCU). As for the existing UOC-MP, only two of its bishops joined the new church. At the Unifying Council in Saint Sophia, the delegates adopted a statute for the new church and elected its Primate, Metropolitan Epiphany. On January 6, 2019, Epiphany paid his first, irenic, visit to the Ecumenical Patriarchate in Istanbul. During a solemn ceremony, he received from the Patriarch of Constantinople Bartholomew a *Tomos* that granted autocephaly to the OCU. On February 3, Metropolitan Epiphany was enthroned as the Primate of the new church.

The UOC-MP treated the new church in the same way as it earlier treated the Kyiv Patriarchate and the UAOC, i.e., as schismatics. It not only refused to recognize the OCU, but also excommunicated those bishops and priests who decided to join it. Although the Ecumenical Patriarchate did not recognize these excommunications, they still prevented many in the UOC-MP from switching to the OCU. The UOC-MP followed the line of the Moscow Patriarchate, which unilaterally broke relations with the Ecumenical Patriarchate. In particular, the ROC at the session of its Synod on September 14, 2018 decided (1) to suspend the liturgical prayerful commemoration of Patriarch Bartholomew of Constantinople; (2) to suspend the concelebration with hierarchs of the Patriarchate of Constantinople; and (3) to suspend the participation of the ROC in all Episcopal Assemblies, theological dialogues, multilateral commissions, and other structures chaired or co-chaired by representatives of the Patriarchate of Constantinople (Patriarchal Press Service, 2018). The decision of the ROC was unilateral, which meant that the church of Constantinople did not reciprocate it. From the perspective of Constantinople, there was no break in relations between Constantinople and Moscow, a view adopted by most other Orthodox churches.

Most churches, however, initially hesitated to recognize the new Ukrainian church. Some of them issued statements with explicit support for the UOC-MP and Metropolitan Onufry, while others called on Constantinople and Moscow to dialogue. The positive side of the churches' hesitation was that they also refused to endorse the unilateral withdrawal of Moscow from relations with Constantinople. Most Orthodox churches thus chose to smooth over the conflict within the global Orthodoxy, rather than to contribute to it. The establishment of the independent OCU shook the order of global Orthodox churches to its foundations, but did not break it. It demonstrated some pre-existent weak points in this order, such as lack of inter-Orthodox solidarity.

Conclusion

Tensions with long historical roots within Ukrainian Orthodoxy, as well as between Constantinople and Moscow reflect the power of the idea of autocephaly in the Orthodox tradition to legitimize and reinforce political sovereignty. The almost-mythic nature of autocephaly has prompted multiple efforts over time to create an autocephalous Ukrainian church. The social and political factors that autocephaly reinforces have only become more salient with the Russian Orthodox Church's use of the *Russkiy mir* doctrine and the Russian aggression against Ukraine. This political, social, and military conflict, with its competing views of neo-imperialism, formed the background for the 2018 creation of the Orthodox Church of Ukraine, which also revealed the weakness in inter-Orthodox unity in the split between the Moscow and Ecumenical patriarchates. Hopefully, after being diagnosed, these weak points can be addressed accordingly so that the unity of the Orthodox world can be renewed and enhanced.

References

Bartholomew, Ecumenical Patriarch. (n.d.). Speech of His Holiness the Ecumenical Patriarch Bartholomew I to the Ukrainian nation on July 26, 2008. Retrieved from www.ec-patr.org/docdisplay.php?lang=en&id=963&tla=en

Chief Secretariat of the Holy and Sacred Synod. (2018, October 11). Announcement (October 11, 2018). Retrieved from www.patriarchate.org/-/communiq-1

Denysenko, N. (2018). *The Orthodox Church in Ukraine: A century of separation*. DeKalb, IL: Northern Illinois University Press.

Golubinsky, E. (1900). *Istoriya Russkoy Tserkvi* [History of the Russian Church] (Vol. 2). Moscow, the Russian Empire: Universitetskaya Tipographiya.

Partykevich, A. (1998). *Between Kyiv and Constantinople: Oleksander Lototsky and the quest for Ukrainian autocephaly*. Edmonton, Canada: Canadian Institute of Ukrainian Studies.

Patriarchal Press Service. (2018, September 14). Minutes of the Holy Synod's held on 14 September 2018. Retrieved from www.patriarchia.ru/en/db/text/5268268.html

Tzortzatos, V. (1975). I vasiki tehsmi diikiseos tis Avtokefalu Orthodoxu Ekklisias tis Polonias meta istorikis anaskopisis [The basic administrative institutions of the autocephalous church of Poland, with historical excursus]. *Theologia, 46*(1), 67–69 (Original work published in 1926–1927).

12 Equivocal memory

What does the Ukrainian Orthodox church of the Moscow Patriarchate remember?

Andriy Fert

Introduction

The collapse of the Soviet Union and the emergence of nation states out of its wreckage became a real challenge for the Russian Orthodox Church (ROC), whose jurisdiction covered most of the Soviet republics. The break-up of former Soviet republics with Moscow undermined the legitimacy of then-existing church ties.

In Ukraine, where a large number of ROC parishes were located, there was the Ukrainian Orthodox Church under the Moscow Patriarchate (UOC-MP). Following Ukraine's proclamation of independence, UOC-MP then-head, Metropolitan Filaret (Denysenko) attempted to obtain autocephaly (independence) for his church, but failed.

During the post-Soviet period the UOC-MP repeatedly found itself under pressure from Ukrainian public opinion urging it to break ties with Russia, its former imperial center. This began right after Ukrainian independence, when a substantial part of its clergy left to create the Kyiv Patriarchate; and continued during the presidency of Victor Yushchenko (2005–2010), with his undertaking to unite major Orthodox churches in Ukraine into a national church. Finally, the UOC-MP has been facing difficulties in recent years with the conflict between Russia and Ukraine, especially in 2018–2019, when the Ukrainian state, together with many Ukrainian Orthodox leaders, managed to convince the Patriarch of Constantinople – *primus inter pares* of the Orthodox world – to grant autocephaly to the Orthodox Church in Ukraine.

As these events suggest, the UOC-MP leaders have been forced to legitimize the very existence of their Church. I outline two main objectives the UOC-MP has been forced to address. First, the UOC-MP has needed to show that subordination to Moscow is historically justified and does not prevent the UOC-MP from being truly Ukrainian, which has often been questioned by rival Orthodox churches and part of the political elite. Second, the UOC-MP has needed to build a representation of itself that would take into account the different and contradictory historical memory of its believers.

In this chapter, I will demonstrate that by drawing upon specific historical narratives, the UOC-MP has managed to shape a memory regime which allowed it to complete both of the abovementioned objectives. In other words, the chapter analyzes the UOC-MP's official memory developments and the structure of historical narratives through which this church has represented itself.

Hence the main focus of this research has been on the discourse produced by the ecclesiastical authorities (the Kyiv Metropolitan, the Holy Synod, and the Synodal departments). The material for this research has been drawn from UOC-MP publications such as the official press (the *Tserkovna Pravoslavna Hazeta* (Church Orthodox Newspaper), the *Pravoslavny Visnyk* (Orthodox Bulletin) journal, and its official website), books, movies, lives of the saints, history textbooks for seminaries, as well as from open reports about the UOC-MP's editorial activities, decisions on canonization, etc.

To some extent, my research can be described in terms of the politics of memory. After all, it is about how Church leadership creates a cohesive narrative about its past, establishes its own pantheon of heroes (saints), and through these elements forms its own value system. However, considering the fact that my sources are exclusively open materials designed for clergymen and parishioners, it is necessary to make a reservation that this study is devoted to *the implementation* of the politics of memory. Given the lack of access to the internal documents of the UOC-MP, it is not possible to investigate the actual goals the ecclesiastical authorities were trying to pursue. The focus of this chapter is, therefore, on the analysis of public discourse.

Consequently, I approach the implementation of politics of memory/public discourse about the past with help of Jan Kubik and Michael Bernhard's concept of a memory regime. They define it as "a set of cultural and institutional practices that are designed to publicly commemorate and/or remember a single event, a relatively clearly delineated and interrelated set of events, or a distinguishable past process" (Kubik & Bernhard, 2014, p. 11). Following Kubik and Bernhard (2014), a memory regime arises out of specific cultural constraints – a historically formed repertoire of cultural (mnemonic) forms and themes in a given time and space. It means here that the church has shaped its memory regime out of existing narratives. In simpler terms, the way churches see and interpret the past and the way they consider some individuals as traitors and the others as heroes is related to the existing set of beliefs, stereotypes, and views of different groups in society. This process is examined by Rogers Brubaker, who demonstrated how religion supplies myths, metaphors, and symbols that are central to the discursive or iconic representation of the nation and also the reverse process, when national narratives inflect religious discourse (Brubaker, 2011).

Finally, it is quite important to note the relationship between religious identity and national identity in Eastern Europe. As a study conducted by the Pew Research Center (2017) reports, they "are closely entwined . . . in former communist states, such as the Russian Federation and Poland. . . . Majorities say that being Orthodox or Catholic is important to being 'truly Russian' or 'truly Polish.'" Being Orthodox, thus, means associating oneself with a certain cultural, historical, and religious tradition, rather than just practicing a faith.

This chapter is divided into several parts. The first part is dedicated to the late-Soviet attempts of the Kyiv Metropolitan Filaret to assimilate within the Ukrainian Exarchate of the ROC the former Greek Catholic and autocephalous parishes, forcibly affiliated with the ROC during earlier Soviet times. These parishes were formally Russian Orthodox, but existed as a kind of separate church within the Ukrainian Exarchate and had strong Ukrainian nationalistic sentiments. For this reason, Filaret created a historical representation of the Exarchate that explained why Ukrainian churches should be subordinate to the patriarch in Moscow. It is important to start with this, since the narratives formed at that time became a basis for the historical imagination of UOC-MP. These narratives can be designated as the "History of Orthodoxy in Ukraine."

The next part demonstrates how the collapse of the USSR and the emergence of rival Orthodox Churches in Ukraine in the 1990s caused those making this representation to pay more attention to the struggle between the "genuine Ukrainian Church" – namely the UOC-MP – and "nationalistic schismatics."

After that I will analyze the period of the gradual departure from Moscow attempted by Kyiv Metropolitan Volodymyr from 2007–2014. During this period, the idea of a long history of the Ukrainian Orthodox Church appeared in the official discourse of the UOC-MP. Written without concepts that legitimized the leading role of Moscow, the history of a separate Ukrainian Church implicitly undermined unity with the Moscow Patriarchate. At the same time the UOC-MP leadership continued to employ historical narratives that, on the contrary, emphasized the "canonical unity of the Russian Church." Thus the UOC-MP constructed two opposing narratives, which I refer to as the "History of the Ukrainian Orthodox Church" and the "History of Orthodoxy in Rus'."

At the end of the chapter I will offer my explanation of the divided historical narratives of Ukrainians as a whole and why ecclesiastical authorities have simultaneously used narratives that contradicted each other. I argue that coexistence of these representations reflects the UOC-MP's attempts to appeal to its believers in different parts of the country and their distinctive historical narratives.

History of "Orthodoxy in Ukraine"

The modern memory regime of the UOC-MP draws heavily from how the Moscow Patriarchate, faced with national challenges in Soviet Ukraine after WWII, created a historical narrative about Ukrainian Orthodoxy as a unique, but unalienable part of the Russian Church. The need for the Ukrainian exarchate of the ROC to present itself as a Ukrainian Church arose back in the 1950s. At that time, the Moscow Patriarchate was attempting to integrate Greek Catholic parishes in the western regions of the Ukrainian SSR (Shlikhta, 2015), as well as the remnants of the Ukrainian Autocephalous Orthodox Church that existed during the Nazi occupation. A second reason for emphasizing the Ukrainian nature of the UOC-MP was the existence of Orthodox churches independent from the Moscow Patriarch in the Ukrainian diaspora that needed to be persuaded that there was a Ukrainian Orthodox Church in the USSR with which they could reunite (Markus, 1989). One of the ways to do so was through the usage of historical narrative.

For these reasons the Exarch (Metropolitan of Kyiv) was allowed to start publishing a monthly Ukrainian-language magazine, *Pravoslavny Visnyk*, and an annual calendar in Ukrainian in the 1960s. These publications featured numerous articles devoted to local history: stories of monasteries located on the territory of Ukraine, of saints who lived there, about the first Ukrainian printed books, etc.

All these local-history episodes were built around the same discursive scheme. First, Ukrainians and Russians were represented as fraternal peoples who emerged from the "common cradle of baptism" of Prince Volodymyr the Great (Romanchuk, 1976, p. 19). Accordingly, any division of these peoples would be unnatural. The Greek Catholics are "anti-national," since they destroy the fraternal unity between Ukrainians and Russians (Zatovsky, 1988, pp. 21–22). Second, the period prior to the "reunification of Ukraine with Russia" in 1654 was depicted as a time of suffering. Orthodox Ukrainians had suffered under "national and religious oppression" of "Catholic Poland" (Marochkin, 1988, p. 23); this oppression reached its peak when Ukrainian Orthodox Christians were forced to unify with Papal Rome (Protsyuk, 1976, p. 21). Finally, the Orthodox people of Ukraine had always wanted to reunite with the fraternal people in Russia. And as soon as they reunited, the narrative suggests, the suffering changed to times of flourishing for the Church (Zatovsky, 1988).

Employing this approach, during the 1960s – 1980s the authors of the *Pravoslavny Visnyk* created a series of articles about the history of particular territorial units and holy places of the Ukrainian Exarchate. But the history of the Exarchate itself, or the history of some imagined Ukrainian Church, did not appear on its pages, since the construction of such a narrative would be impossible without the deconstruction of the narrative of a common history of the Moscow Patriarchate, which was clearly not in the interest of the Soviet state.

In addition, these episodes of local history created a strict hierarchy of the events and places of the past. There were more important events for the *Pravoslavny Visnyk* authors, such as the reunification of Ukraine with Russia; these topics appeared in every episode and shaped the storyline of national religious oppression. And there were also less important things – those that happened at the local level. This approach established discursive unity of the Russian Church under the leadership of Moscow.

Local-history narrative was redesigned during *perestroika* when the nationalist movement in Soviet Ukraine entailed a revival of the Greek Catholic and Autocephalous Orthodox Churches. Both of them, once absorbed by the ROC in the 1940s with the help of Soviet regime, represented themselves as truly national Ukrainian Churches as opposed to the one affiliated with Moscow (Ukrainian Exarchate of the ROC). Under these conditions, in 1990, the Ukrainian Exarchate was renamed the "Ukrainian Orthodox Church." The ecclesiastical authorities of the church started looking for ways to explain why they retained their unity with Moscow and how this did not prevent their Church from being truly Ukrainian. These explanations were usually built on the refutation of the "nationalistic schismatics," i.e., other Orthodox groups and Greek Catholics.

In 1991, then-Kyiv-Metropolitan Filaret wrote an article titled "On the issue of the Kyiv Metropolis' history" (Filaret, 1991a, 1991b, 1991c). However, its content was dedicated to schisms within the Kyiv Metropolis rather than to the Metropolis itself. The article consists of several structural blocks, each focused on one or another schism which happened to "Orthodoxy in Ukraine." To demonstrate the untenable nature of the schisms, Filaret used the same discursive approaches as before. Among them he placed an emphasis on the fact that Ukrainians and Russians have a common history and a common church, suggesting that all the schisms occurred for political reasons during times of national-religious oppression and political crises, as he called them.

But besides this, Filaret's narrative questioned the very idea that the "schismatics" could create a Ukrainian Orthodox Church since, after all, this church had already existed for many years. Filaret argued that in 1918 the eparchies of the Orthodox Church in Ukraine were named the "Ukrainian Church" by the Local Council of the ROC (Filaret, 1991a). This church received autonomy from Saint Patriarch Tikhon in 1921, "and it was exactly the path of Saint Tikhon that the Patriarch Alexy [II of Moscow] decided to take" when giving the UOC-MP "independence and self-governance" in 1990. "Radical clergy" were not satisfied either by the decision in 1918, or in 1990, and therefore split "the unity of Ukrainian Church" (Filaret, 1991c).

Throughout the 1990s and the early 2000s the narrative of Filaret's article was used by the UOC-MP in various publications and films dedicated to church history. An excellent example is the film *Anatomy of a Schism* (*Anatomiya raskola*) produced by the Synodal department for information and the Kyiv-Pechersk Lavra in 2002 (Kievo-Pecherskaya Lavra, 2012a, 2012b, 2012c, 2012d). The film explains that "when Ukraine was under the oppression of Poland" a reunion with Papal Rome was signed in 1596 and people were driven to the Uniate Church "by sticks and clubs." The "Orthodox Cossacks" revolted against these actions. Cossacks triumphed over the Polish Catholic king and united with Russia because of its Orthodoxy. With the Orthodox eparchies "left under Poland, the outrage continued." Eventually during World War II, the Uniate Church actively collaborated with the Nazis and therefore was banned and dissolved.

With regard to the autocephalous movement, the film stresses that the Autocephalous Church in Ukraine was created with the support of the Soviet authorities in 1921, who did so to split and destroy the Orthodox Church. Then during WWII, like the Uniate Church, the Autocephalous Church continued its existence in the territories occupied by the Nazis (which hints at the alleged cooperation between autocephalists and Nazis). The way the state established the Uniate Church and the Autocephalous Church is directly associated in the film with the events of the 1990s, when Ukrainian President Leonid Kravchuk in concert with Metropolitan Filaret, "obedient to the authorities," established the Ukrainian Orthodox Church of the Kyiv Patriarchate. The emphasis on the collaboration between Nazis and "nationalist-minded clergy and intelligentsia" appealed to the Soviet associative link between nationalism and Nazism still widespread at the time.

It is important to note that both Filaret's article and the film focus on "Orthodox Ukrainian people" or "Orthodox Cossacks," but not "the Ukrainian Church" itself as the key actors in the events that happened prior to 1990. However, in the 1990s, a new actor appeared – the Ukrainian Orthodox Church of the Moscow Patriarchate.

History of "the Ukrainian church"

The anti-schismatic narrative about struggling Ukrainian Orthodoxy employed during the 1990s gradually transformed into another one – less aggressive and more pro-Ukrainian – in the second half of the 2000s. This shift was by and large connected with the evolving views of the Kyiv Metropolitan Volodymyr (Sabodan), head of the UOC-MP. Strengthening his own position in the UOC-MP by the end of the 1990s, Metropolitan Volodymyr aimed at making his Church (1) truly Ukrainian and (2) truly autonomous (Shlikhta, 2016). He emphasized in every possible way that the Ukrainian Church under his leadership was independent and the decisions of the ROC were merely advisory in nature (Yelensky, 2013). During the presidency of Viktor Yushchenko, the Metropolitan even attempted to start a dialogue with other Orthodox churches in Ukraine (Kirill, 2009), which from the perspective of Moscow were "nationalistic schismatics." These actions could not help but influence the historical narratives voiced by the Church.

In 2008, the UOC-MP celebrated the 1020th anniversary of the Baptism of Rus'. This jubilee was presented as a definite milestone, commemorating the religious revival in the twenty years since 1988. Addressing the flock on the eve of the celebrations, Metropolitan Volodymyr stressed that the Baptism of Rus' in 988 "gave birth to Ukraine as we know it" and "since that time **the Ukrainian Orthodox Church** has always been with its people" (Volodymyr, 2007, p. 19, emphasis added). Thus, he introduced into the discourse the new idea of a specifically Ukrainian Church, which was said to have existed since the tenth century. In the following years this church would appear in popular UOC-MP literature under two different names: the "Ukrainian Church" and the "Kyiv Church." Allegedly, it was born during the reign of Prince Volodymyr in the tenth century and continuously functioned up to the present day.

In the autumn of 2009, Metropolitan Volodymyr gave a speech laying out his vision of a "specific path of Ukrainian Orthodoxy" (Yelensky, 2013). According to him, Kyiv was a bridge between East and West. As an example of how this bridge worked, he recalled Kyiv Metropolitan Petro Mohyla's times in the seventeenth century, when the "Kyiv theological tradition" synthesized the experiences of Orthodox East and Catholic West to create a unique social and cultural space. Moreover, this bridge preserved the legacy of the Kyivan Rus', i.e., Orthodox culture. Thus, the contemporary UOC–MP, as Volodymyr argued, had inherited both the bridge and the legacy which needed to be used to unite Ukrainian society (Volodymyr, 2009).

Shortly after this, the official newspaper of the UOC–MP published the article "The Ukrainian Church is the cradle of Orthodox Rus'" (Dyatlov, 2009b, 2009c, 2009d), which reflected on key messages from the Metropolitan's speech. One can call the contents of this article a long history because it builds a narrative linking the modern UOC–MP with apostolic times, and according to this new narrative both the "Orthodox Ukrainian people" and the "Ukrainian Church" have been important actors throughout the whole history.

This long history, according to the article, began in Crimea. It was "the first pulpit . . . the Gospel Truth had been proclaimed from in the lands of the future Ukraine" (Dyatlov, 2009b). From there apostle Andrew went to the North to bless the mountains on which the city of Kyiv would be founded a few centuries later. It is interesting that the article mentioned not a word about Andrew visiting the place of the future Novgorod in modern Russia, even though this part of his trip has been seen as an important detail legitimating the apostolate of the Rus' Church (Vlodek, 1989).

The narrative further led the reader to the Baptism of Rus' and the era of Prince Yaroslav the Wise, emphasizing the unity of Rus', both the North (the future Russia) and the South (the future Ukraine) in every possible way. The narrative, however, brought up no episodes from the North, even when it came to the fragmentation of the Rus' after the death of Yaroslav the Wise; all the described events took place on the territory of the future Ukraine. The North emerged in the narrative with the Mongol yoke, which was immediately followed by the story of Saint Alexander Nevsky, a "ruler of North-East Rus'." His alliance with the Mongols to preserve Orthodoxy was set against Prince Danylo of Galicia's "South-West Rus'," which allied with the Catholics.

The appearance of two separate Metropolitans "in the lands of Rus'" (Moscow and Kyiv) is presented as a consequence of the struggle for "obtaining the Rus' lands" between the Grand Duchy of Muscovy and the Grand Duchy of Lithuania. The author of the article neither mentions that a separate metropolis was established in the Principality of Galicia-Volhynia in the fourteenth century, nor that Lithuania also managed to establish a separate metropolis in due time. Instead, according to the author, a separate Kyiv metropolis in the fifteenth century was created by the Greek schismatic bishops, who in 1438 adopted a union with Rome. At the time when "the Grand Duchy of Muscovy finally threw off the Mongol yoke and became the only independent Orthodox state in the world," a schismatic Kyiv Metropolitan "moved to the ethnic lands of Lithuania" (Dyatlov, 2009c), the article states, i.e., the lands inhabited by the non-Orthodox population. This metropolis in Lithuania, separate from Moscow, became legitimate in the eyes of readers through the figure of the martyr Makariy, Metropolitan of Kyiv, whose cult has been widespread among contemporary Orthodox believers in Ukraine. The article does not mention him until he unexpectedly appears in the story, collecting money for the restoration of the Saint Sophia Cathedral in Kyiv and perishing at the hands of the Tatars.

At this point of the article the legitimate metropolis of Kyiv had to face the "planting of Catholicism" and Greek Catholics. But here the narrative focuses the reader's attention not so much on Ukrainians' previous suffering, but on victories, such as the appearance of brotherhoods (lay societies) or the foundation of the Orthodox monastery in Pochaiv. The greatest triumph in this series is the "epoch of Saint Petro Mohyla" when the "ancient shrines of Kyiv" were restored, and the academy was established to "defend the truth of the Orthodox faith." However, despite the "efforts of Saint Petro . . . the attitude of the Orthodox inhabitants of South Rus' to the government remained tense," which led to Bohdan Khmelnytsky's uprising, and then to the "oath of the Cossacks to the Moscow Tsar" (Dyatlov, 2009d) – the term Ukrainian national historiography uses in lieu of the Soviet phrase "the reunification of Ukraine with Russia."

Moreover, there was no "reunification of the Rus' Church" in this narrative. Instead, "the Kyiv Metropolis became part of the Moscow Patriarchate." "Mazepa's betrayal," an episode central to Imperial and Soviet history is hardly touched upon. Instead, the narrative focuses on the ill-conceived policy of Russian tsar Peter I causing "a decline of the resurgent economy in Ukraine" and pushing Mazepa, a "patron of Orthodox Churches," into an alliance with the tsar's enemy – Charles XII of Sweden (Dyatlov, 2009d).

The article also repeats the thesis from the article of Metropolitan Filaret that Saint Patriarch Tikhon established the "autonomous Ukrainian Exarchate" in 1918 and then Patriarch Alexy II granted this exarchate "independence and self-governance" in 1990. However, these events were not presented as the creation of a church as Filaret did, but rather as the restoration of genuine rights that a pre-existing Ukrainian Church had "prior to becoming a part of the Moscow Patriarchate" (Dyatlov, 2009d).

In addition, the article avoids talking about the "reunification of Greek Catholics" with the ROC in 1946, which in the Ukrainian national narrative of history is typically presented as an element of the Stalinist repressions against Ukrainians. Moreover, there is not a word of condemnation of the schisms of the 1920s, 1940s, and 1990s that led to the emergence of the Ukrainian Autocephalous Orthodox Church.

This long history, unlike the previous narratives, turns out to be a continuous story, where the main character is the Ukrainian Church with its "special path." The narrative dates this church back to the apostolic times and also describes it as a "cradle" from which Christianity spread to the rest of the lands of the Rus'. Certain concepts, such as the "reunification of Ukraine with Russia" or "national-religious oppression" were abandoned while the Moscow Patriarch and Russia were implicitly represented as those who violated the rights of the Kyiv Metropolitans by taking away their broad autonomy.

"It is necessary not only to know the names of saints, but also to read their lives"

This gradual invention of the long history in the 2000s was accompanied by the Church's own creation of a pantheon of specifically Ukrainian saints. This process consisted of two interrelated approaches: the canonization of Ukrainian saints, that is, those who were born or lived in the territory of modern Ukraine; and the nationalization of already-existing saints from the Rus' pantheon.

A vivid example is Saint Dmitry of Rostov. The official newspaper of the UOC-MP devoted more than a dozen publications to this saint in the 2000s. The description of his life usually began with this argument:

> Saint Dmitry is called "of Rostov" after the ancient Rus' city of Rostov, which is in the present Yaroslavl Oblast of Russia. In Rostov [he] occupied the episcopal see for eight years, until his death. . . . However, the saint of God spent the previous half-century, from the moment of his birth, in his native Ukraine – the spiritual heir of the ancient South Rus'.
>
> (Dyatlov, 2009a)

Further, the narratives built up in such a way as to maximize Saint Dmitry's life in his "native Ukraine" and to minimize his life in Russian Rostov. One of the most striking examples is an article published in 2012 which, after a long description of Saint Dmitry's life in Ukraine, abruptly finished with the following phrase: "The last place of service of Saint Dmitry was Rostov Veliky (Yaroslavl Oblast, Russia)" (Zozulenko, 2012). Beyond publicizing his life the Synod of the UOC-MP established the Order of Saint Dmitry in 2009, making the nationalization official (Svyatyteliu otche Dimitrie, 2009).

Similarly, Saint John of Tobolsk was also Ukrainianized. The official UOC-MP newspaper published the story of his life under the title "The Lantern of the Siberian Land." However, judging by the content of this article, Saint John, having spent his whole life "in the lands of Ukraine," brought his books to Siberian Tobolsk and died almost immediately (Hor, 2012).

In 2011, the Synod of the UOC-MP established the Synaxis of Kyiv Saints – the day of all Kyiv Saints (Holy Synod of the UOC [Holy Synod], 2011). The bishops of the Holy Synod included in this Synaxis traditionally Russian characters such as Theophan the Recluse and Joasaph of Belgorod. This step, apparently, caused such an ambiguous reaction among believers that in less than a year the Church authorities had to explain their decision: "Although many names in this Synaxis may seem unexpected, each of them was justifiably included in this list" since all of these saints were born, studied, or served for a long time in Kyiv (Holy Synod, 2012).

Following this principle, the Synaxis of Volhynia Saints, for instance, included "natives of Volhynia"; the Chernihiv Synaxis – apart from natives – included the above-mentioned Russian John of Tobolsk, because after all, he brought the "traditions of the of Chernihiv's theological schools" alongside his books to Tobolsk (Holy Synod, 2012).

Nationalization was presented to believers as a correction which revealed forgotten things about the saints:

> If the ascetic spent less time in the last place of his earthly ministry than in other places, and this last place subsequently became associated with (his) works . . . people usually add this place to ascetic name, "overshadowing" other places of his life and ministry. Is it not a kind of "limitation"? **It is necessary not only to know the names of saints, but also to read their lives.**
>
> (Dyatlov, 2009a, emphasis added)

In addition to nationalization, the UOC-MP has canonized more than 300 local saints during the post-Soviet period (Local Council of the UOC, 2011). Many of these saints were heroes from the national discourse of Ukraine. Among them are several figures of the Ukrainian clergy, including Metropolitan Petro Mohyla (recalling the revival of Ukrainian Orthodoxy and a vivid example of how to use Western and Eastern traditions to unify the Church) (Drabinko, 2015), and Metropolitan Volodymyr Bogoyavlensky (a martyr of the twentieth century, as the Church claims, the first churchman persecuted by Bolsheviks). The list also includes Ukrainian statesmen, such as Prince Yaroslav the Wise (builder of Saint Sophia's Cathedral in Kyiv) and Petro Kalnyshevsky (the last Koshovy *Otaman*, a chief officer of the Zaporozhian Host, and an opponent of the Russian imperial government).

"History of Orthodoxy in Rus'"

Along with the process of constructing a long-history narrative and appropriation of saints, another narrative has been developing. This one is aimed at legitimating the unity with Moscow. This section identifies the roots and schema of this narrative, as well as its key messages.

In order to explain the ties with the ROC and undermine claims of schismatics to establish a separate Ukrainian Church, the UOC-MP leadership employed the historical narratives from the Soviet times, which emphasized the common origin and common historical fate of Russians and Ukrainians. Turning again to the case of the 2002 film *Anatomy of a Schism* one could observe strong anti-schismatic sentiments strengthened by the appeals to the alleged unity of the Rus' people or fraternal peoples – which in other words were nothing but a mere repetition of the narrative schema from *Pravoslavny Visnyk*.

The textbook for the theological seminaries of the UOC-MP, titled "History of Orthodoxy in Rus'," is yet another example of this scheme remaining in the official discourse. It opens with the phrase: "The history of the Rus' Church as an academic study . . . depicts the course of the gradual development of Christ's Church in Rus'. . . . It also finds out . . . how the Rus' Church guided the people of Rus' toward moral progress" (Vlodek, 1989, p. 1). This textbook, compiled as early as 1989 and republished several times since then with the imprimatur of the Kyiv Metropolis, offers students the history of a common Rus' Church. The narrative is built in such a way that most of the events take place in the north – Moscow and Saint Petersburg.

The textbook history is divided into four periods. The first, the Kyivan period of the "common cradle," was before the Mongol invasion. Following that was the Moscow period, when the Metropolitan moved to the north and the Metropolis was subsequently divided in two. The authors emphasize that during this period "for the Moscow Metropolis a time of internal prosperity had come . . . and the Kyiv Metropolis suffered disasters from hands of non-Orthodox" (Vlodek, 1989, pp. 1–2). The third period was in Saint Petersburg, when "the Rus' Church was under the strong pressure and influence of the state," and the final one was the Soviet era.

Like the Soviet articles from *Pravoslavny Visnyk*, "History of Orthodoxy in Rus'" tells the readers about sufferings of "people from South-West Rus'" (Ukrainians) before the reunification with Russia, and condemns Greek Catholics and so on. Above all, this narrative used the concept of "one people" (*odin narod*) defined by their location in Rus' and affiliation with the Orthodox church. And this people had only one true Church – the Russian Orthodox Church. Both the people and the Church could have been divided either by different states or metropolises, but against all odds they remained unified, albeit temporarily separated by state or administrative borders.

The cornerstone of this narrative was the commemoration of Kyivan Rus' as the "cradle of the Ukrainian, Belarusian and Russian nations." The present-day unity of UOC-MP with Moscow was explained by appealing to the Kyivan Rus'. In 2008, leaders of the ROC came up with the idea of "Holy Rus'," which brought together narratives from the Soviet period and the seminary textbook. This idea was founded on the formula of Lavrentiy Chernihivsky (1898–1950), a monk canonized by the UOC-MP in 1993: "Ukraine, Russia and Belarus are together the Holy Rus'" (Suslov, 2014). Beginning in 2008, then-Metropolitan of the ROC Kirill (Gundyayev) made several trips to Ukraine, addressing the flock with this formula and starting public debates about it. The Holy Rus' project considered the period of the Kyivan Rus' a golden age when the Orthodox people lived in an Orthodox state created by Saint Prince Volodymyr the Great. The Prince's legacy, allegedly, lasted until now in the form of a common Orthodox-based culture shared by Ukrainians, Russians, and Belarusians. The key actor of the Holy Rus' narrative – "the people of the Rus'" – despite "being divided by the borders of the different states and certain inconsistencies in politics" remained spiritually united (Kirill, 2009).

The narrative from the seminary textbook apparently influenced by the Holy Rus' concept would also appear in the public discourse of the UOC-MP alongside the above-mentioned long history. For example, in 2010 the publishing department of the UOC-MP issued a book titled *The Law of God* – a textbook on Orthodox faith and liturgy and biblical and Church history designed for laymen and clergy alike. Among other things, it contained two chapters on the history of the Orthodox Church in Ukrainian lands, which present a narrative in tension with that of the long history.

The first chapter, "History of Orthodoxy in Rus'," covered events from the apostle Andrew's trip to the present day. The storyline of the second chapter, "The History of the Ukrainian Orthodox Church," started in the 1990s, when, amidst schisms and revival of Greek Catholics, an institution entitled the "Ukrainian Orthodox Church" was established.

In this book, the history was told exactly the same way as in the textbook for seminaries: after the Mongol invasion in the thirteenth century, the Metropolis, being the heart of the Rus' lands, moved up to the North and all the main events took place there. The reader returns to "South-West Rus'" only when the "Orthodox people suffer" at the hands of Catholics, or when they "reunite with Russia" and the "Rus' Church."

Unlike the long-history narrative, here the Ukrainian Church as an actor appeared in the narrative no earlier than 1990, when the Moscow Patriarch granted the Kyiv Metropolis "independence and self-governance" (Drabinko, 2010). But the real birth of this church was in 1992, when Metropolitan Filaret was deposed from his see; the whole history after that consisted of just a struggle against the schisms of Filaret and others.

Moreover, this type of narrative employs the familiar approach of inscribing specific historical episodes into the common historical narrative of the Rus' Church used by Filaret (Filaret, 1991a, 1991b, 1991c). Many of such episodes were published by the *Tserkovna* newspaper after 2009. In them, apostle Andrew usually did reach the North Rus' or Novgorod. The Kyiv prince Volodymyr necessarily baptized "all of the lands of Rus'" (together with its northern parts, namely, where Russia subsequently appeared) (Moiseyenko, 2010c).

Returning to the narratives of schismatics and suffering, the *Tserkovna* newspaper also describes how, after the oppression of the Orthodox people in Lithuania, the Constantinople "pseudo-Patriarch Gregory Mammis" divided the single Rus' Church into two Metropolises – one in Moscow and the other, schismatic, in Kyiv (Moiseyenko, 2010b). This division caused all subsequent troubles: greater oppression, the planting of Catholicism, and the union of Brest in 1596 (Moiseyenko, 2010a). Metropolitans of a separate Kyiv Metropolis "did not have much of any credibility and their moral fiber was low" (Moiseyenko, 2010b), and "the Polish lords, wishing to tear Orthodox Ukrainians away from their brother in faith in the Russian state, acquired Jesuits and other Catholic orders ... to discredit the Orthodox hierarchy" (Moiseyenko, 2010d). The Union of Brest apace with "national and religious oppression" caused "the national liberation war of the Ukrainian people" and "the reunification of Ukraine with Russia", as well as "the reunification of the once unified Rus' Church" (Moiseyenko, 2011). In eparchies not reunited with Russia, as, for example, in Volhynia, "persecutions continued ... fanatic crowds thundered churches and even killed Orthodox priests"; "only with the accession of most of the Ukrainian lands to Russia, things began to gradually improve" (Moiseyenko, 2010e).

The narrative, of course, included references to autocephalous schisms, which became possible due to nationalistic rule or Nazi occupation. In 1946, the Greek Catholics "returned to Orthodoxy" for a short while until the 1990s, when together with the *Filaretovtsy* (Metropolitan Filaret's followers) they started to take over Orthodox churches "everywhere . . . accompanied by violence" (Moiseyenko, 2010e, 2010f). The revival of Orthodoxy began after 1992, and all these stories concluded with a common summary, claiming the need to overcome schisms and "firmly cherish the spiritual heritage of three fraternal peoples, growing from the same root, the Kyivan Rus'" (Moiseyenko, 2011).

Thus the narrative, which can be called the "History of Orthodoxy in Rus'," was supposed to emphasize the unity of Ukrainian Orthodoxy with the Rus' Church. It exploited the memory of a common past (the Kyivan Rus') as a starting point and employed discursive approaches of the Soviet-period suffering of Orthodox Ukrainians before reunification with Russia, dangers of separation, etc.

"Ukraine is a divided country"

In a recent study, Ukrainian historian Georgy Kasyanov has outlined two narratives of collective memory in post-Soviet Ukraine – national/nationalist and Soviet-nostalgic. According to Kasyanov, the national narrative is a set of ideas about the "uniqueness, distinctiveness and independence of the community, which is called a nation," while the Soviet-nostalgic narrative is built around the "elements associated with the 'leading' role of Russian culture . . . and [this narrative] insists on a supranational unity of historical experience" (Kasyanov, 2018, p. 29). The peculiarity of the coexistence of these two narratives in the collective memory is that they are in some way regionalized. The national/nationalist narrative has dominated in the western regions of Ukraine and the Soviet-nostalgic narrative has been dominant primarily in the eastern regions (above all in Donbas) and in Crimea (Kasyanov, 2018, p. 31).

Despite the regional variations of Ukrainian collective memory, the UOC-MP, according to statistics, throughout the entire post-Soviet period has been comprised of parishes and monasteries in all regions of Ukraine – both in the west and in the east. Moreover, in most areas it was and still remains the dominant church and thus had to speak to bearers of each of these narratives. Hence the need for both the long history of "the Ukrainian Orthodox Church" and the "History of Orthodoxy in Rus'" narrative in the UOC-MP. In 2008, Kyiv Metropolitan Volodymyr described the phenomenon this way: "The Church must consider that Ukraine is a divided country with two different cultures . . . two civilizational orbits:'Eastern' and 'Western'" (Ukrayins'ka Pravoslavna Tserkva, 2017). In practice, this means that in order to belong to these different "civilizational orbits," the Church had to use historical narratives that those in each of these "orbits" could have identified as "theirs."

This resonates with Kubik and Bernhard's concept of cultural constraints, which "define actors' understanding of the world." They point out:

> Mnemonic entrepreneurs are free to construct their narratives out of the available . . . repertoire but are limited in their choices by its boundaries. If they choose elements outside this repertoire, they appear to be alien and not credible to their potential constituents.
>
> (Kubik & Bernhard, 2014, p. 22)

In other words, to be adopted by the bearers of the Soviet-nostalgic memory narrative, the Church must use a repertoire that emphasizes the unity of the "fraternal peoples," demonstrates the negative consequences of separation, the leading role of Russian culture, and so on, that is, all those elements that we find in the narrative that can be called the "History of Orthodoxy in the Rus'" after the name of the seminary textbook. At the same time, to be able to talk with the bearers of the narrative of memory focused on nationalism, the Church needs to apply concepts representing a separate and distinctive Ukrainian Church that has existed since the times of Kyivan Rus' and follows "its own special path." This also could be seen in the narrative, which we can call the "History of the Ukrainian Church."

Interestingly, both of these narratives have been given the same weight and the same authority: they appeared on the pages of the same official newspaper, *Tserkovna*. The same commemorative practices and sites of memory have also been used to simultaneously legitimize them both. The historical memories of the Council in Kharkiv of 1992 and the Baptism of Rus' serve as excellent examples of the bifurcated narratives of the UOC-MP.

Kharkiv council

On May 27, 1992, the bishops of the UOC-MP gathered in Kharkiv and elected Volodymyr as the new Kyiv Metropolitan, who later contributed the long-history narrative, while the incumbent Metropolitan Filaret was trying his very best to achieve autocephaly for the UOC-MP from the Moscow Patriarchate. Most of the bishops, once willing to establish an independent church, changed their minds and withdrew their support from Filaret's undertaking. As a consequence, Filaret found himself "in schism" with the ROC, and Volodymyr "preserved the unity (of the UOC-MP) with the mother church" (Kievo-Pecherskaya Lavra, 2012d).

This event was memorized in a series of annual commemorations and festivities which reflected the developing imagination of the UOC-MP about itself: unity with the Moscow Patriarchate, preservation of grace (canonicity) and apostolic succession through this unity, as well as a revival of the spiritual life of Ukraine under the UOC-MP guidance and UOC-MP's status of an independent and self-governed church. The Council marked the victory of the conciliar mind (*soborny razum*) of the Church (Kievo-Pecherskaya Lavra, 2012d). It also laid the foundation for a separation of the Church and politics. "This council is famous for electing a brand-new way of Church service in the new social and political conditions," said Kyiv Metropolitan Onufry (Berezovsky) (Ukrayins'ka Pravoslavna Tserkva, 2017). The Council also became a unifying factor. Metropolitan Volodymyr in his interview stressed that "by liberating the Church from the rough interference of the state and politicians, the council had spiritually united the East, the West, the North, and the South of Ukraine" (Anisimov, 2007), emphasizing the uniquely Ukrainian nature of the Church. Moreover, due to the Council, "the spiritual revival of our Church has begun," as Metropolitan Volodymyr would repeatedly recall (Drabinko, 2015). The period after the council was a time of "unprecedented flourishing in **Ukrainian Orthodoxy**," echoed the authors of the film *Council of Kharkiv – 25 years* (Press Service of the Kyiv Theologian Academy and Seminary, 2017, emphasis added). Memories of the Kharkiv Council were also used to legitimize the unity with the ROC: "By retaining a spiritual connection with the Russian Orthodox Church, [the UOC-MP] has become a true Church of the Ukrainian people. . . (that) respects the national history and traditions" (Volodymyr, 2008).

Baptism of the Kyivan Rus'

The UOC-MP celebrated the 1020th, the 1025th, and 1030th anniversary of the Baptism of the Kyivan Rus' in 2008, 2013, and 2018 respectively. In addition, on July 27–28 every year since 2007, Saint Volodymyr's Day and the Baptism of Rus' Day have been celebrated.

The symbolic meaning of these festivities before 2014 was related to the UOC-MP's attempts to construct a long-history narrative. The Baptism of Rus' Day, reported the official newspaper of the UOC-MP, was the first holiday of the Motherland (Darpinyants, 2008). The Holy Synod (2008a) noted in their addresses: "When the Kyiv Church was established, a people was born with its own consciousness and noble spirit." The Synod (2013) also added that "the celebration . . . will encourage the Ukrainian people to realize their historical roots". The large-scale celebration of the jubilee in 2008 in Kyiv was evidently an attempt to legitimize claims of the heritage of Kyivan Rus' and thus to declare a special path of Ukrainian Christianity. The UOC-MP Synod noted on the eve of festivities: "The Ukrainian Orthodox Church is the successor of Volodymyr the Great's baptism, the guardian of the centuries-old spiritual tradition connecting the East Slavic nations with the Orthodox East" (Holy Synod, 2008b).

At the same time, the Baptism of Rus' has been used by the History of Orthodoxy in Rus' narrative to promote the ideas of the Holy Rus' (Suslov, 2014). For this reason, the Moscow Patriarch or his representatives have tried to take part in all the celebrations of Saint Volodymyr's Day and the Baptism Day starting in 2007. For them it was important to convey the idea that the Rus' Church was the heir of Saint Volodymyr's baptism. Different nations may have sprung from this baptism, but all of them were nevertheless united by a common culture – or even further – that they were "spiritually one people."

After Metropolitan Volodymyr's death the ecclesiastical leadership of the UOC-MP changed the symbolic meaning of these festivities in accordance with the History of Orthodoxy in Rus' narrative. In 2017, they even merged celebrations of the Council in Kharkiv and the Baptism of Rus' into one, further legitimizing the subordination to Moscow rooted in the "common cradle of baptism" and preserved by the Council in Kharkiv. Metropolitan Onufry wrote in his annual address: "Do not call us the Moscow Church simply because we guard the millennial spiritual tradition beginning with Baptism of Rus'" (Holy Synod, 2017).

Conclusion

In telling about its own past, the UOC-MP now employs two basic narratives. The one, which could be called the "History of Orthodoxy in Rus'," is based on the concepts of the common history of "fraternal peoples" – Ukrainians, Russians, and Belarusians – united by the common Rus' Orthodoxy-based culture. The lineage of events in this narrative is built around Moscow and Saint Petersburg. Events on the periphery, that is in Ukrainian Orthodoxy, are described with the help of tropes of suffering and struggle for unity with the "fraternal Russian people."

Another narrative (which I call the "History of the Ukrainian Church") grew out of the intention of ecclesiastical leaders to make their Church more Ukrainian. Initially reflecting the attempts of Kyiv Metropolitan Volodymyr to decrease Moscow's influence and to start a dialogue with rival Orthodox churches in 2007–2014, this narrative gradually transformed into a long history of the Ukrainian Church. This long history claims that the Ukrainian Church was created by Prince Volodymyr in the tenth century and since then has "always been with its people." It avoids direct condemnation of nationalistic schisms and does not use concepts legitimizing the unity of the Russian Church.

Simultaneous employment of these two narratives can be explained by the fact that the UOC-MP unites communities with different collective memories. Accordingly, attempting to remain acceptable to all its members, the Church maintains both narratives. However, after the death of Metropolitan Volodymyr and the beginning of the Russian-Ukrainian conflict in 2014, usage of the "History of the Ukrainian Church" narrative in its latest version has been increasingly relinquished. The new Church leadership is paying much more attention to legitimizing its unity with the ROC and, following the recognition of the "schismatic" Orthodox Church of Ukraine in 2018 by the Ecumenical Patriarchate, also to the condemnation of schisms.

References

Anisimov, V. (2007, May). Boh ne v syli, a v pravdi (interv"yu z mytropolytom Kyivs'kym i vsiyeyi Ukrayiny Volodymyrom) [God is not in might but in truth (Interview with Metropolitan of Kyiv and all Ukraine Volodymyr)]. *Tserkovna Pravoslavna Hazeta, 12*(188), 2–3.

Brubaker, R. (2011). Religion and nationalism: Four approaches. *Nations and Nationalism*, *18*(1), 2–20. doi:10.1111/j.1469–8129.2011.00486.x

Darpinyants, V. (2008, April). Pershe svyato Vitchyzny [The first holiday of the Motherland]. *Tserkovna Pravoslavna Hazeta*, 7(209), 1–2.

Drabinko, A. (Ed.). (2010). *Zakon bozhiy* [The law of God]. Kyiv, Ukraine: Izdatel'skiy otdel Ukrainskoy Pravoslavnoy Tserkvi.

Drabinko, A. (Ed.). (2015). *Metropolit Vladimir: Mysli raznyh let* [Metropolitan Vladimir: Reflections of different years]. Kyiv, Ukraine: Laurus.

Dyatlov, V. (2009a, October). Shliakhy Rus'koho Zlatousta v Ukrayini [The paths of Russian Zlatoust (Chrysostom) in Ukraine]. *Tserkovna Pravoslavna Hazeta*, 20(246), 6–7.

Dyatlov, V. (2009b, November). Ukrayins'ka Tserkva – Kolyska Pravoslavnoyi Rusi (Chastyna 1) [The Ukrainian Church is the cradle of Orthodox Rus' (Part 1)]. *Tserkovna Pravoslavna Hazeta*, 21(247), 8–9.

Dyatlov, V. (2009c, November). Ukrayins'ka Tserkva – Kolyska Pravoslavnoyi Rusi (Chastyna 2) [The Ukrainian Church is the cradle of Orthodox Rus' (Part 2)]. *Tserkovna Pravoslavna Hazeta*, 22(248), 8–9.

Dyatlov, V. (2009d, December). Ukrainska Tserkva – Kolyska Pravoslavnoi Rusi (Chastyna 3) [The Ukrainian Church is the cradle of Orthodox Rus' (Part 3)]. *Tserkovna Pravoslavna Hazeta*, 23(249), 8–9.

Filaret, Metropolitan of Kyiv. (1991a). K voprosu ob istorii Kievskoy Mitropolii (Chast' 1) [On the issue of the Kyiv Metropolis history (Part 1)]. *Pravoslavnyi Visnyk*, 2, 39–47.

Filaret, Metropolitan of Kyiv. (1991b). K voprosu ob istorii Kievskoy Mitropolii (Chast' 2) [On the issue of the Kyiv Metropolis history (Part 2)]. *Pravoslavnyi Visnyk*, 3, 38–50.

Filaret, Metropolitan of Kyiv. (1991c). K voprosu ob istorii Kievskoy Mitropolii (Chast' 3) [On the issue of the Kyiv Metropolis history (Part 3)]. *Pravoslavnyi Visnyk*, 4, 44–50.

Holy Synod of the UOC. (2008a, April). Zvernennya Svyashchennoho Synodu Ukrayinskoyi Pravoslavnoyi Tserkvy z pryvodu 1020-littya Khreshchennya Rusi [Address of the Holy Synod of the Ukrainian Orthodox Church on the occasion of the 1020th Anniversary of the Baptism of Rus']. *Tserkovna Pravoslavna Hazeta*, 8(210), 3.

Holy Synod of the UOC. (2008b, July). Zvernennya Svyashchennoho Synodu do virnykh chad Ukrainskoyi Pravoslavnoyi Tserkvy z nahody vizytu v Ukrayinu predstoiateliv ta predstavnykiv Pomisnykh Pravoslavnykh Tserkov [Address of the Holy Synod to committed believers on the occasion of the visit of the heads and representatives of the local Orthodox churches to Ukraine]. *Tserkovna Pravoslavna Hazeta*, 14(216), 2.

Holy Synod of the UOC. (2011, February). Zasidannya Svyashchennoho Synodu UPTs: Zhurnal 1 [Session of the Holy Synod of the UOC. Protocol No 1]. *Tserkovna Pravoslavna Hazeta*, 4(278), 2.

Holy Synod of the UOC. (2012, July). Zasidannya Svyashchennoho Synodu UPTs: Zhurnal 52 [Session of the Holy Synod of the UOC: Protocol No 52]. *Tserkovna Pravoslavna Hazeta*, 14(312), 4–5.

Holy Synod of the UOC. (2013, May). Zvernennya Svyashchennoho Synodu UPTs do yepyskopatu, dukhovenstva, chernetstva ta myryan z nahody 1025-richchya Khreshchennia Kyivs'koyi Rusi [Address of the Holy Synod of the UOC to episcopacy, clergymen, monastics and laypeople on the occasion of 1025th Anniversary of the Baptism of Rus']. *Tserkovna Pravoslavna Hazeta*, 9(331), 4.

Holy Synod of UOC. (2017, June). Poslannia Sviashchennoho Synodu do yepyskopatu, dukhovenstva, chernetstva ta myrian z nahody 25-yi richnytsi Kharkivskoho Arkhiyereis'koho Soboru Ukrayinskoyi Pravoslavnoyi Tserkvy [Address of the Holy Synod to episcopacy, clergymen, monastics and laypeople on the occasion of twenty-fifth anniversary of the Bishops' Council in Kharkiv]. *Tserkovna Pravoslavna Hazeta*, 11(429), 5.

Hor, A. (2012, June). Svityl'nyk blahochestya Sybirs'koyi zemli [The lantern of the Siberian land]. *Tserkovna Pravoslavna Hazeta, 12*(310), 3.

Kasyanov, G. (2018). *Past continuous: Istorychna polityka 1980–2000: Ukraina ta susidy* [Past continuous: Politics of history 1980–2005: Ukraine and neighbors]. Kyiv, Ukraine: Laurus.

Kievo-Pecherskaya Lavra. (2012a, May 24). Anatomiya raskola, fil'm 1, seriya 1 [Anatomy of a schism, film 1, episode 1]. [Video file]. Retrieved from www.youtube.com/watch?v=PEOL9E_NTeA&t=5s

Kievo-Pecherskaya Lavra. (2012b, May 24). Anatomiya raskola, fil'm 1, seriya 2 [Anatomy of a schism, film 1, episode 2]. [Video file]. Retrieved from www.youtube.com/watch?v=lII8Zq_RXa4

Kievo-Pecherskaya Lavra. (2012c, May 25). Anatomiya raskola: Filaretovskiy raskol: Seriya 1 [Anatomy of a schism: Filaret's schism: Episode 1]. [Video file]. Retrieved from www.youtube.com/watch?v=fsVVojZWEQ8

Kievo-Pecherskaya Lavra. (2012d, May 25). Anatomiya raskola: Filaretovskiy raskol: Seriya 2 [Anatomy of a schism: Filaret's schism: Episode 2]. [Video file]. Retrieved from www.youtube.com/watch?v=h3VMxPMqbM0&t=4s

Kirill (Gundayev), Patriarch of Moscow. (2009, November 3). Vystup Sviatishoho Patriarkha Kyryla na urochystomu vidkrytti III Asambleyi fondu 'Ruskyi svit' [Speech of His Holiness Patriarch Kirill to the solemn opening of the III Assembly of the Russkiy Mir Foundation]. Retrieved from http://archive.orthodox.org.ua/uk/node/6030

Kirill (Hovorun), Archpriest. (2009, September 11). Komentar do rishennya Synodu UPTs pro dialoh z Tserkvamy [Commentary on the decision of the Synod of the UOC on dialogue with the Churches]. Retrieved from https://religions.unian.ua/holidays/264773-komentar-do-rishennya-sinodu-upts-pro-dialog-z-tserkvami.html

Kubik, J., & Bernhard, M. (2014). A theory of the politics of memory. In M. Bernhard & J. Kubik (Eds.), *Twenty years after communism* (pp. 7–34). doi:10.1093/acprof:oso/9780199375134.003.0001

Local Council of the UOC-MP. (2011, July). Ukhvala Sobory UPTs [Ruling of the Council of the UOC]. *Tserkovna Pravoslavna Hazeta, 14*(288), 9.

Markus, V. (1989). Religion and nationalism in Soviet Ukraine after 1945. In P. Ramet (Ed.), *Religion and nationalism in Soviet and East European politics* (pp. 138–170). Durham, NC: Duke University Press.

Marochkin, V. (1988). Posylennya ekonomichnoho ta natsional'no-relihiynoho hnitu pravoslavnoho narodu Ukrayiny na pochatku 17 stolittya [Strengthening of economic and national-religious oppression against the Orthodox Ukrainians in the beginning of the seventeenth century]. *Pravoslavnyi Visnyk, 3,* 23–27.

Moiseyenko, V. (2010a, May). Podibnoho do n'oho ne bulo na vsiyi pivnichniy zemli vid skhodu do zakhodu. . . [There was nothing of his kind in all the northern lands from corner to corner. . .]. *Tserkovna Pravoslavna Hazeta, 9*(259), 8–9.

Moiseyenko, V. (2010b, July). Khrystova Blahodat' usyu zemlyu opovyla . . . Istoriya eparkhiy 'korinnoyi' Rusi (Chatyna 1) [The grace of Christ descended upon the lands . . . A history of eparchies of native Rus' (Part 1)]. *Tserkovna Pravoslavna Hazeta, 13*(263), 8–9.

Moiseyenko, V. (2010c, July). Vin khrestyv usyu Rus'ku zemlyu vid kraiyu do krayu [He baptized all the lands of Rus' from corner to corner]. *Tserkovna Pravoslavna Hazeta, 14*(264), 8.

Moiseyienko, V. (2010d, August). Khrystova Blahodat' usyu zemlyu opovyla . . . Istoriya eparkhiy 'korinnoyi' Rusi (Chatyna 2) [The grace of Christ descended upon the lands . . . A history of eparchies of native Rus' (Part 2)]. *Tserkovna Pravoslavna Hazeta, 15–16*(265–266), 12–13.

Moiseyenko, V. (2010e, September). Trymaisya tverdo viry tvoyeyi i Tserkvy: Istoriya Pravoslav'ya na Volyni [Stay strong in your faith: History of Orthodoxy in Volhynia]. *Tserkovna Pravoslavna Hazeta, 18*(268), 8–9.

Moiseyenko, V. (2010f, Novermber). Viruyte tverdo i nepokhytno i bud'te yedyni u viri: Istoriya Pravoslav'ya v Halychyni [Believe firmly and unwaveringly and be united in faith: History of Orthodoxy in Halychyna]. *Tserkovna Pravoslavna Hazeta, 21*(271), 8–9.

Moiseyenko, V. (2011, February). 'Pokladaysya na Boha, bo virysh u N'oho': Istoriya Pravoslav'ya na Slobozhanshchyni, u Donets'komu krayu ta nyzhn'omu Podniprov''yi ['Trust God, for you believe in Him': A history of Orthodoxy in Sloboda Ukraine, the Donetsk region, and in the lower Dnipro lands]. *Tserkovna Pravoslavna Hazeta, 4*(278), 8–9.

Pew Research Center. (2017, May 10). Religious belief and national belonging in central and eastern Europe. Retrieved from www.pewforum.org/2017/05/10/religious-belief-and-national-belonging-in-central-and-eastern-europe/

Press Service of the Kyiv Theologian Academy and Seminary. (2017, May 16). *Kharkiv'skyi Sobor – 25 rokiv* [Council of Kharkiv – 25 years]. [Video file]. Retrieved from www. youtube.com/watch?v=rARqtMDWfZM

Protsyuk, Yu. (1976). Peremoha pravoslav'ya [The victory of Orthodoxy]. *Pravoslavnyi Visnyk, 9*, 20–24.

Romancuk, V. (1976). Radist' sviatoho yednannya [The joy of a sacred unification]. *Pravoslavnyi Visnyk, 10*, 19–21.

Shlikhta, N. (2015). 'Ukrainian' as 'Non-Orthodox': How Greek Catholics were 'reunited' with the Russian Orthodox Church, 1940s – 1960s. *State, Religion and Church, 2*(2), 77–98.

Shlikhta, N. (2016). Eastern Christian Churches between state and society: An overview of the religious landscape in Ukraine (1989–2014). *Kyiv-Mohyla Humanities Journal, 3*(3), 123–142. doi:10.18523/kmhj73945.2016–3.123–142

Suslov, M. (2014). 'Holy Rus': The geopolitical imagination in the contemporary Russian Orthodox Church. *Russian Politics & Law, 52*(3), 67–86. doi:10.2753/rup1061–1940520303

Ukrayins'ka Pravoslavna Tserkva. (2017, June 22). Ukrayins'ka Pravoslavna Tserkva u viri ta istyni [Ukrainian Orthodox Church in faith and truth]. [Video file]. Retrieved from www.youtube.com/watch?v=d7w2YwmGySU

Vlodek, P. (Ed.). (1989). *Konspekt po istorii Russkoy Tserkvi dlya uchashchihsya 1 i 2 klassov duhovnoy seminarii* [Textbook on history of Russian Church for students of the first and the second classes of seminary]. Kyiv, USSR: (n.p.).

Volodymyr, Metropolitan of Kyiv. (2007, September). Zvernennya Predstoyatelya Ukrayins'koyi Pravoslavnoyi Tserkvy Blazhennishoho Volodymyra, Mytropolyta Kyivs'koho i vsiyeyi Ukrayiny do ukrayins'koho narodu z nahody Dnia nezalezhnosti [Address of the Primate of the Ukrainian Orthodox Church His Beatitude Volodymyr of Kyiv and all Ukraine to the Ukrainian people on the occasion of Independence Day]. *Tserkovna Pravoslavna hazeta, 19*(195), 4.

Volodymyr, Metropolitan of Kyiv. (2008, June–July). Dopivid' Volodymyra, Mytropolyta Kyivs'koho i vsiyeyi Ukrayiny, na Arkhiyereys'komu Sobori Rosiys'koyi Pravoslavnoyi Tserkvy [Address of Volodymyr, Metropolitan of Kyiv and all Ukraine, to the Bishop's Council of the Russian Orthodox Church]. *Tserkovna Pravoslavna Hazeta, 12–13*(214–215), 14–15.

Volodymyr, Metropolitan of Kyiv. (2009, October). Pam''yat' pro novyy Yerusalym: Kyivs'ka tradytsiya [A memory about New Jerusalem: The Kyiv tradition]. *Tserkovna Pravoslavna Hazeta, 19*(245), 4.

Yelensky, V. (2013). Ukrainskoe pravoslavie i ukrainskiy proekt [Ukrainian Orthodoxy and the Ukrainian project]. *Pro Et Contra, 17*(3–4), 27–44.

Zatovsky, L. (1988). Pravoslavna Tserkva u vyzvol'niy borot'bi za vozz'yednannia Ukrayiny z Rosiyeyu [Orthodox Church in the liberation struggle of Ukraine for reunification with Russia]. *Pravoslavnyi Visnyk, 5*, 21–25.

Zozulenko, T. (2012, November). Svyatyni Chernihivshchyny [Saints of Chernihiv land]. *Tserkovna Pravoslavna Hazeta, 22*(320), 8.

Part 4

Interviews

13 "The Orthodox identification of militants is an element of their understanding of the *Russkiy mir*"

Interview with Dr. Ihor Kozlovsky[1]

Dr. Ihor Kozlovsky is a senior researcher at the Hrihoriy Skovoroda Institute of Philosophy of the Ukrainian National Academy of Science in Kyiv. He has written several books and articles in the fields of religious studies, interfaith dialogue, and freedom of religion. Until 2001 he directed the Department for Religious Affairs within the Donetsk State Oblast Administration. Then he worked as a Professor of Religious Studies at several universities in Donetsk. From 2016 to 2017, he was detained and imprisoned by the authorities of the self-proclaimed Donetsk People's Republic for political reasons. On December 27, 2017 he was freed in a prisoner exchange between the Ukrainian government and the Russia-backed "people's republics."

Q: Can you describe the development of religious freedom in the so-called Donetsk People's Republic (DPR) since 2014?

IK: There were three different periods in the DPR with respect to religion and religious freedom.

The first period lasted from the spring of 2014 through the spring of 2015. During this period the cruelest acts of violence against religious believers took place. Only the Ukrainian Orthodox Church of the Moscow Patriarchate (UOC-MP) escaped persecution. These acts of violence included seizures of churches, houses of prayer, religious schools, and other property for religious worship in addition to brutal violations of human rights such as arbitrary arrests, illegal detentions, kidnapping, torture, extrajudicial executions, etc. The worst acts of violence were committed by the Cossacks of the All-Powerful Don Army, a battalion of neo-Cossacks from the Rostov Oblast and other regions of Russia; militants of the Russian Orthodox Army; the military group founded and led by Russian army veteran Igor Girkin (Strelkov); the Vostok Batalion; the Oplot Brigade; and the military group headed by Horlivka insurgent Igor Bezler (aka Bes). All of these groups share ideals of the Russian World (*Russkiy mir*) and loyalty to the Moscow Patriarchate as the canonical Orthodox church, as well as strong anti-Western and anti-Ukrainian sentiment.

These radical groups inspired by a grim cocktail of extremist ideologies committed persecution and unpunished violence in the name of God. As a result, during this period the majority of religious leaders and activists left the region, and a significant proportion of religious communities stopped their activities or went underground.

The second period started in the summer of 2015 and lasted through the summer of 2016. During this time, the DPR Ministry of State Security (MSS) sought to control religious communities. The separatist authorities developed a network of informants and a system of surveillance over believers and other suspect individuals, restricted or fully banned evangelizing and missionary activities, and initiated a series of "anti-cult" protests targeted at religious minorities.

During this period, many priests, religious leaders, and non-UOC-MP believers were arrested and persecuted. On January 27, 2016, I was arrested by the MSS and detained together with many others. Among them were political prisoners imprisoned for their convictions, believers detained because of their religion, businessmen whose property or business was seized by the separatists, and ordinary people who were reported by their neighbors or the authorities or even those who the military simply did not like.

The third period started in the summer of 2016. During this period, the MSS has further limited religious freedom by prohibiting the establishment of "cults" and the dissemination of "sectarianism." The authorities continue to arrest religious leaders and believers and to seize religious property. The separatist authorities' main targets include Jehovah's Witnesses, Protestants, Ukrainian Greek Catholics, and adherents of the Ukrainian Orthodox Church of the Kyiv Patriarchate (UOC-KP). Evangelizing and proselytizing are still banned. In DPR, there are now only three priests of the UOC-KP, although there were 40 before the military conflict with Russia. Similarly, the Ukrainian Greek Catholics Church (UGCC) is now represented by only two priests, and the Roman Catholic Church by only one. Several religious organizations, such as the Church of Jesus Christ of Latter-day Saints, the Church of Christ, the Jehovah's Witnesses, Buddhists, and all new religious movements, are forced to operate underground or leave the territory.

Thus, from 2014 to 2018, the DPR has developed a totalitarian system of control over religious groups. The courts are completely at the will of law enforcement; and the MSS, the police, and the public prosecutors' office have succeeded in persecuting individuals for their religious convictions, beliefs, or worldview. In blatant violation of human rights, the MSS maintains several illegal detention centers that Ukrainian and international humanitarian missions are prohibited from entering or investigating. Prisoners and detainees can be held captive for years without court orders and are subjected to moral pressure and torture, including physical abuse, forced suffocation, extraction of teeth, fingernail pulling, the use of electric shock, mock executions, etc. I also know of incidents of sexual assault.

Q: **Can you share any concrete examples with our readers of the persecution of clergy and believers?**

IK: As an example, I can tell you about several incidents that occurred in 2014, which, in my view, clearly show what is going on with religious freedom in the DPR. (In compiling this list, I am particularly indebted to the Institute of Religious Freedom website,[2] which correlates with my own memory.)

On May 16 in Sloviansk, separatists kidnapped Pentecostal Bishop Olexiy Demydovych and detained him for seven hours. They broke into the property of the Good News Pentacostal church, where Bishop Demydovych served as a senior pastor, several times and used the building for a sniper's nest. Later, on June 7, separatists deployed artillery in the church property. They blindfolded members of the church and used them as human shields to prevent backfire from Ukrainian government troops.

On May 25, DPR *boeviks* (militants) confiscated a Protestant church in Horlivka. On that same day, separatists established their headquarters at a location that was formerly occupied by the Church of Christ and the biblical institute Bear Valley.

On May 27, pro-Russian separatists kidnapped the Polish Catholic priest Father Pavel Vitek while he was leading a public street prayer. The next day, he was released after the intervention of the coadjutor bishop of the Roman Catholic Diocese of Kharkiv-Zaporizhya and Polish diplomats.

On June 2, separatists arrested the Pentecostal priest Henady Lysenko from Sloviansk on charges of providing support to the Ukrainian military forces, tortured him, and confiscated his car.

On June 6, pro-Russian militants attacked the Christian children's shelter Canvas of Hope located in Sloviansk and took mattresses, pillows, and blankets from the residents of the shelter. On June 13 the shelter was destroyed.

On June 8, *boeviks* under the command of Igor Strelkov arrested Albert and Rouvim Pavlenko (sons of Olexandr Pavlenko, pastor of the Evangelical church Transfiguration of the Lord) and Volodymyr Velichko and Viktor Brodarsky (deacons of that church) for supporting the Ukrainian army. The separatists also stole their cars. It was reported that the victims were tortured by members of the military group Russian Orthodox Army and then executed.

On June 15, DPR militants trashed the office of the Evangelical church New Generation in Horlivka. They stole computers, documents, and other office equipment of the charity foundations established by the church. On the same day a group of separatists attacked the Christian radio station Valentina.

On June 16, DPR separatists seized the Protestant church "Word of Life" and its affiliated drug rehabilitation center located in Horlivka. The separatists claimed that not only would the church become a new DPR headquarters and be considered part of the Republic's assets, but also that they would no longer allow Protestant churches in the city at all.

On June 21, pro-Russian militants captured the "Word of Life" church in Shakhtarsk and detained its pastor Mykola Kalinichenko. Later he was freed, but his car was confiscated. Local media reported that separatists used the house of prayer as a detention center where 20 to 40-year-old men were held captive and threatened with continued detainment unless they agreed to join separatist military forces.

On June 25, DPR *boeviks* captured the religiously sponsored rehabilitation center Rock of Escape in Donetsk and relocated their military unit there.

On June 26, armed separatists broke into the Evangelical Church of Winners in Druzhkivka and took pastor Pavlo Lisko and his wife to their headquarters. Later the pastor reported that *boeviks* took his money, documents, and computer and held him and his wife in separate prison cells. The pastor also said that he and his wife were accused of collaborating with Americans and supporting the people who left Donbas after the beginning of the war.

On July 3, DPR separatists arrested and detained the Greek Catholic priest Tikhon (Serhiy) Kulbaka. Before the arrest Kulbaka was repeatedly threatened, and his car was covered with Nazi swastikas. The priest was tortured and forced to leave DPR territory.

On July 8 in Donetsk, separatists arrested Yury Ivanov, a priest of the UOC-KP. He was released on July 30.

On July 9, armed *boeviks* seized the privately-funded Donetsk Christian University and converted the university's property and equipment into the headquarters of a pro-Russian paramilitary group.

On July 15, separatists kidnapped Father Viktor Vonsovych, a Roman Catholic priest. He was the parish priest in the Sacred Heart of Jesus parish in Horlivka. The priest was arrested at a DPR checkpoint and freed after 10 days. Boeviks warned Father Viktor that if he tried to come back to Horlivka, he would be executed.

On August 8, after a public prayer in Donetsk, separatists arrested Protestant pastors Olexandr Khomchenko and Valeriy Yakubenko and an UOC-KP activist Roxolana Shvayka. Pastor Khromchenko was charged with holding illegal rallies, helping the Ukrainian army, and enlisting people into his "cult." *Boeviks* repeatedly physically tortured him and simulated his execution as a means to psychologically torture him. He was told that "on this land there will be only one religion."

On August 13, pro-Russian militants seized the Word of Life church building in Donetsk.

On August 15, *boeviks* captured the UGCC female monastery building in Donetsk.

On September 27, armed separatists captured the Seventh-Day Adventist house of prayer in Horlivka during a religious service and forced congregants to leave the premises. Pastor Serhiy Litovchenko was arrested and detained for 20 days.

Q: What was the role of religion in spreading or de-escalating the conflict in Donbas in 2014?

IK: In February 2014 religious leaders and activists of the Christian denominations of the region (except the UOC-MP) established the Council of Churches and Religious Organizations in the Donetsk Oblast, which became a platform for dialogue among religious associations, civil society, and public authorities in the face of the escalating conflict. On March 6, 2014, the Council adopted a statement of peace, unity, and mutual understanding for the people of Ukraine. In the statement the Council condemned the aggressive actions committed by the Russian government, provoking war and division in Ukraine, and emphasized that Ukrainians may be diverse but are still one people. Specifically the Council said: "We have different worldviews and belong to various religions. We are diverse in culture and ethnicity. We speak different languages. There are Ukrainians and Russians, Jews and Crimean Tatars, Greeks and Armenians, and many other ethnic groups among us. But we all want the same: peace, national accord, and freedom in one unitary Ukraine! We have one homeland – Ukraine!"

In addition, the Council organized the Interdenominational Marathon for unity, peace, and reconciliation in Ukraine, called "Pray for Ukraine," which started on March 4, 2014. Orthodox Christians of the Kyiv Patriarchate, Greek Catholics, Roman Catholics, and various Protestant denominations participated in the Marathon. Every day from 18:00 till 19:00 in the evening people gathered together at the Constitutional Square in Donetsk and prayed. At first there were 30–40 people participating in the prayer, but after a while there were hundreds of people who came to pray.

In August 2014, DPR authorities prohibited these public prayers and threatened executions, so the Marathon went underground. At the end of 2014, DPR police identified the Marathon's secret meeting place, forced participants to disperse, and arrested 15 of the Marathon organizers, including myself, at different times. During detention all of them were tortured. I personally spent 700 days in detention.

The biggest church of the region, the UOC-MP, did not participate in either the Marathon or the other joint initiatives. DPR authorities recognize this church as the main religion of the Republic. Militant groups, such as the All-Powerful Don Army, the Russian Orthodox Army, and others identifying themselves as part of Russian Orthodox Christianity, launched a crusade against "cults" and "alien" religions. I know that in some ways many local UOC-MP priests supported militant groups in their campaigns against Protestants, Evangelicals, Catholics, and Orthodox Christians that do not belong to the Moscow Patriarchate.

Q: How did DPR authorities and paramilitary groups react to the peaceful initiatives of the churches?

IK: The Interdenominational Marathon irritated both DPR authorities and militant groups operating in Donbas. On March 22, 2014, after public prayer, unknown persons shot a car of Marathon participants. On March 30, the Greek Catholic priest Tiknon (Serhiy) Kulbaka reported on his Facebook page that approximately 100 participants in a pro-Russia rally taking place nearby attacked a one-hour Marathon public prayer. They demanded that the Marathon participants stop praying and take down their tent and the Ukrainian flag because, so they said, the Marathon "gave [them] serious problems" and they "would no longer tolerate it."

The most serious attack took place on May 23. Approximately 15 armed and masked persons came to the place of the Marathon. They dismantled the tent and threw it into the river. They violently stole equipment including microphones, speakers, and batteries, and threatened that everyone who came to pray again would be executed. One of the organizers of the Marathon, Serhiy Kosyak, was arrested that day.

And, of course, DPR authorities did not try to prevent attacks and violence against the Marathon. Instead, they were engaged in putting permanent pressure on the participants.

Q: **You told us about Russian and pro-Russian paramilitary groups identifying themselves with Russian Orthodox Christianity. What were their goals? Do you think they really believed that they fought for Russian Orthodoxy or did they simply employ religious rhetoric in order to justify some military or political ends?**

IK: I would identify the majority of them as Orthodox Christians only conditionally. I mean that they belong or associate themselves with the Russian Orthodox Church. However, they know almost nothing about Orthodox canons or the Church's polity and life. Their Orthodox identification is an element of their understanding of the *Russkiy mir*, and their ultimate goal was to carry out this revanchist project through the seizure of Ukrainian territory by military force.

Q: **How would you describe the political and religious views of the UOC-MP communities operating on territory that the Ukrainian government does not control? Do they politically associate themselves with Ukraine?**

IK: In my opinion, there are almost no pro-Ukrainian priests in the UOC-MP in those territories. Those who did not agree with the Russian aggression and the establishment of the "people's republics" left those areas during 2014–2015. The situation with believers is almost the same. Orthodox believers in those areas are mostly part of the older generations whose minds and views are very often determined by Russian and local pro-Russian media, and they have very limited access, if any at all, to alternative Ukrainian sources of information. Thus, they lack access to objective knowledge about what is really going on and the only thing they have is hope that something will change for the better.

Notes

1 This and the following two interviews were conducted by Elizabeth A. Clark and Dmytro Vovk in 2018–2019.
2 See: Khronolohiya teroru: boyovyky DNR i LNR peresliduyut' khrystyyan Donbasu [Chronology of terror: Militants of DPR and LPR persecute Christians of Donbas] (August 6, 2014). *Institute of Religious Freedom*. Retrieved from www.irs.in.ua/index.php?option=com_content &view=article&id=1456:1&catid=34:ua&Itemid=61&lang=uk

14 "The militants used the Bibles to keep fires going and to cook food"

Interview with Rev. Dr. Vitaly Sorokun

Rev. Dr Vitaly Sorokun works as an Associate Professor of Public International Law at Yaroslav the Wise National Law University in Kharkiv, Ukraine. He received his PhD in 2009, and published a monograph *International Protection of the Freedom of Conscience and Belief* in 2010. Dr. Sorokun is also an ordained Christian minister having received his ordination in 2002. He is a founding pastor of New Hope Church in Kharkiv, and currently serves as the Head of the Foreign Missions Committee of the Baptist Union of Ukraine.

Q: **It is reported that Protestant communities suffer from severe persecution and discrimination in the occupied territories. Why are they among the main targets of the regime in the so-called Donetsk People's Republic/Luhansk People's Republic (DPR/LPR)?**

VS: Perhaps it would be better to start with a brief description of Protestantism in Ukraine. It will aid in understanding better the reason why the Protestant communities are under attack in the occupied territories.

Protestants are considered a tiny minority in Ukraine largely due to the stereotypes created in the past by Soviet antireligious propaganda and sustained by the mass media. The Protestants are still often called a "sect," a word with a clear negative connotation in Ukrainian and Russian. But this popular belief is open for debate. According to the official data published by the Ministry of Culture of Ukraine, as of January 2018, there were 9,877 Protestant churches in the country altogether. The largest Protestant group is the Baptist Union of Ukraine with over 2,680 churches and more than 300,000 attendees.

The Protestants thus represent quite a large segment of the Ukrainian society, and the number of believers and churches continues to grow. For example, the celebration of Reformation Day in Kyiv in September 2017 was attended by several hundred thousand Protestants.

Q: How many Protestants were in the DPR/LPR region before the conflict?

VS: According to official statistics, at the beginning of 2014 (before the Russian occupation), there were 1,797 religious organizations in the Donetsk region.

Of these, there were 762 Orthodox parishes of the Moscow Patriarchate, 366 Evangelical Christian communities (Pentecostals, Charismatics, etc.), 186 Christian Baptist churches, 86 Orthodox parishes of the Kyiv Patriarchate, 83 Jehovah's Witnesses organizations, 49 Seventh-day Adventist churches, 38 Muslim communities, 36 Greek Catholic parishes, 19 Jewish communities, 14 Catholic parishes, 14 Buddhist communities, and 8 Hare Krishna communities.

There were 835 religious organizations in the Luhansk Oblast. These organizations included 423 Moscow Patriarchate Orthodox parishes, 131 Evangelical Christian communities, 99 Baptist churches, 35 Kyiv Patriarchate's Orthodox parishes, 39 Seventh-day Adventist churches, 28 Jehovah's Witnesses organizations, 14 Jewish communities, 13 Muslim communities, 6 Greek Catholic parishes, and 6 Buddhist communities.

Thus Protestant communities are one of the biggest religious minorities in the region.

Q: How many communities have left the region? Can you give estimates of the numbers of Protestants and Protestant ministers left in the DPR/LPR region?

VS: It is very difficult to give such numbers, as there is no exact official data. However, according to a recent report by the United States Commission on International Religious Freedom, over 50 church buildings were confiscated. As I know the religious communities decreased by between 30 and 80% as believers have left the occupied territories.

Q: Why are Protestants targeted in the occupied territories of eastern Ukraine?

VS: I think Protestants are targeted because of one characteristic – their emphasis on individual faith in the gospel, which is the deity, death, and resurrection of Jesus Christ. What we emphasize, however, is not a mere agreement with some biblical facts, but a transformed life of devotion and obedience to Jesus Christ as the Lord and the King over one's life. It is this transformed life which motivates Protestant believers to be very active members of the society.

Evidently, no totalitarian or authoritarian regime appreciates a large group of people who pledge allegiance not to the country's leader, or the leader's ideology, but to the Kingdom of God, and who are not afraid to lay down their lives for their allegiance. This is the very reason why faithful Christians have historically been and currently are under persecution in many countries. The brutal militant regime of the occupied territories of eastern Ukraine is no exception.

When the war came to eastern Ukraine, the local Protestant communities immediately took a very active role in humanitarian work. They helped evacuate people to safety, provided shelter, distributed food and clothes, assisted with paperwork, and gave out medication. They actively raised money locally and abroad to support humanitarian and volunteer relief efforts on both sides of the line of conflict. Even today, four years into the war, the Protestant communities are very active in this relief work both in Ukraine and Russia.

In addition to those I've already mentioned, there are several more factors which contribute to the persecution. For example, one can say that the Protestant communities in general have a strong sense of identity and unity among themselves. We have a large and effective network of people and churches with access to resources both in the mainland Ukraine and abroad. We also have ties with the West.

Q: What kind of violations of freedom of religion are the Protestant communities experiencing in the occupied territories?

VS: Such violations are too many to count. For our purposes, we could break these violations down to at least eight types and provide a brief description of each.

1. Discrimination

According to the U.N. Declaration on the Elimination of All Forms of Intolerance and of Discrimination Based on Religion or Belief (1981), discrimination means any distinction, exclusion, restriction, or preference based on religion or belief and having as its purpose or as its effect nullification or impairment of the recognition, enjoyment, or exercise of human rights and fundamental freedoms on an equal basis.

The authorities of the so-called people's republics give preferences to the Ukrainian Orthodox Church of the Moscow Patriarchate (UOC-MP). This is not surprising, because similar cases happen even in many regions of the rest of Ukraine. However, they are more evident in the eastern territories where the Protestant communities are simply removed from the picture. According to the recent Law on the Freedom of Religion and Religious Associations, adopted in the DPR last summer, every religious organization was forced to re-register. However, this requirement did not apply to the communities of the Moscow Patriarchate. A similar law with similar implications was adopted in the LPR.

2. Hatred and hate speech against the Protestants due to their connections to the West

Olexandr Turchynov – a Baptist – was the Interim President of Ukraine after the ousting of President Yanukovych. A Baptist as the Interim President was used as a negative image of the West forcefully removing the "legitimate regime" of Yanukovych in Ukraine. The DPR/LPR authorities stigmatize the Protestant communities as sects or cults which bless the war. There are new popular slogans such as "DPR is a cult-free territory," or "There is no room for cults in DPR." The local media organizes propaganda campaigns against the Protestants with outright incitement to hatred, disinformation, and hate speech.

3. Creating pressure, unpredictability, uncertainty, and fear

Religious communities and their representatives must be able to function and perform their duties in a predictable and safe environment. This is a clear implication of the freedom to manifest one's religion or belief in worship, teaching, practice, and observance provided for the internationally recognized human rights instruments.

There have been numerous cases of armed individuals in camouflage uniforms walking into church buildings, interrupting church services, and arbitrarily detaining ministers.

On May 23, 2014, gunmen from a local pro-Russian paramilitary group destroyed a prayer tent in Donetsk, took all the equipment, and threatened to shoot anyone who came to pray there. Serhiy Kosyak, a pastor from the local Assembly of God Church and one of the organizers of the Interdenominational Prayer Marathon, was detained and brutally beaten.

In addition, most of the Protestant pastors in the occupied territories report that they believe their phones are tapped.

4. Deliberate destruction of religious literature

Protestant Christians base their daily living on the teachings of the Bible and believe that the Bible is the inspired, authoritative word of God. There have been numerous cases when printed Bibles and New Testaments were destroyed by the militants in a way that was insulting to the religious sentiments of Christians. One such example out of many took place in Krasny Luch, in the Luhansk Oblast. After the church building, which had been taken over and robbed by the militants, was finally returned to the local Protestant community, the members of the community found charred remains of New Testaments and Bibles. The militants had used the books to keep fires going and to cook food.

5. Confiscation of church buildings and of objects for sacred use

Multiple cases of this kind have been documented. A recent case which received much attention over the internet, and which was confirmed by the OSCE monitoring group, happened on March 27, 2018, in Kadyyivka, the Luhansk Oblast. A group of camouflaged individuals robbed the church building and took out absolutely everything, including even the light switches. They drove away in two trucks full of the stolen goods. Furthermore, many church buildings, or houses of prayer, were also confiscated by the militant regime and converted into police stations and other such buildings.

6. Imprisonment, torture, and murder of Christian ministers and missionaries

On August 8, 2014, pastor Oleksander Khomchenko was kidnapped in Donetsk. He spent four days in captivity and sustained excessive injuries from brutal beatings and torture by suffocation. He passed away on February 14, 2018 because of the injuries received during this detention.

Additionally, on June 8, 2014, after the Sunday service at the Transfiguration Church in Sloviansk, pro-Russian gunmen detained four members of the church: the pastor's adult sons, Rouvim Pavenko and Albert Pavenko, and two of the church's deacons, Viktor Bradarsky and Volodymyr Velichko. They were brutally beaten and killed. Their bodies were found in a mass grave after the pro-Russian fighters had left the city and the Ukrainian armed forces took over.

According to the report made by the Institute of Religious Freedom, a Ukrainian human rights organization, LPR militants arrested all the clergymen of the Christian Pentecostal Community in the Luhansk region who had gathered at a joint church meeting in August 2018. The militants identified each of the clergymen, rewrote their personal data, and imposed a fine on them up to $100 USD for unregistered religious activities.

7. Travel ban

Several Christian ministers have not been allowed to re-enter the occupied territories. In 2017 at different times, two pastors – Olexander and Mykhaylo Nagirnyak – were not allowed to re-enter DPR from the rest of Ukraine. No explanations were given other than that the ministry of security of DPR did not allow them to return. As of today, such cases are numerous.

Several other Protestant ministers who live and minister in Ukraine have been given persona non grata status by the authorities of the DPR and LPR. No official explanations have been provided. These men were advised by the members of local Protestant communities not to try to enter the so-called republics.

8. New legislation

The republics passed legislation regulating the activity of religious organizations. Even a brief look at the provisions of these "laws" reveals that they were passed with the purpose to ban the ministry and terminate the existence of all religious groups except those of the UOC-MP. These laws on freedom of conscience and religious associations are available on the DPR and LPR websites.

The laws stipulate that a religious scholarly examination is obligatory for the re-registration of existing religious organizations. These requirements for obligatory re-registration and religious scholarly examination, however, are not applied to the UOC-MP.

To illustrate, the re-registration process begins with the authorities of DPR and LPR requiring the Protestant communities and other non-UOC-MP to re-register within an unreasonably short period of time. This registration requirement was nothing else but the collection of information on the members, leaders, property, and activities of such communities. Once the communities submitted the necessary documents, all of them were denied the new registration in both DPR and LPR. Now these communities have been totally outlawed and are forced to function illegally.

The law adopted by the LPR goes even further. It prohibits any activity of religious groups (which refers to any five-person organization that is not directly related to any of the "traditional denominations"). At the same time there is no list of such denominations, which allows the LPR power structures to act arbitrarily.

In addition, the LPR authorities ruled the All-Ukrainian Union of Churches of Evangelical Christian-Baptists to be an extremist organization. According to Serhiy Moroz, the vice-president of the Baptist Union, many Baptist communities have now ceased to conduct worship or any activity, even in their own houses of worship, for fear of persecution of their now unregistered activities.

Q: Is there an official explanation of the reasons for outlawing the Protestant communities?

VS: Yes, but what should raise a red flag is that none of the reasons for outlawing Protestant communities are officially motivated by religious preference. There is always another official reason such as that the church, as an organization, did not sign a particular contract on time, or failed to submit a document in a given term, etc. This is a sign of a true totalitarian regime being formed on the occupied territories.

Unfortunately, the number of documented violations of freedom of religion in the occupied territories only continues to grow. Such violations are unthinkable in the twenty-first century in the territory of Ukraine, especially in such a sharp contrast to Ukraine's past legislation and practice of the freedom of religion as one of the most liberal in the former USSR.

Q: How has the Russian-Ukrainian military conflict influenced relations between Protestant groups in both countries?

VS: I think the military conflict has negatively affected relations between Protestant groups in Russia and Ukraine. I need to clarify from the start, however, that there remain ongoing unofficial individual contacts and relationships. Those have not been interrupted. The groups also coordinate relief work in the occupied territories because it is much easier for the Russian churches to send relief support to the churches across the Russian border. It is next to impossible to do so through the Ukrainian border.

However, official relationships have been put on hold. There is a disagreement in the way the Ukrainian and Russian groups evaluate the root cause of the conflict. It is a very serious issue, and a deep partnership is not possible until this disagreement is resolved.

Q: **How do the Ukrainian government and law enforcement agencies address all these violations of the religious and other human rights of Protestants in the occupied territory?**

VS: We know that the Ukrainian authorities regularly raise the issue at international conferences of the OSCE. We also know that the authorities keep track of the violations and notify international partners through available channels. I do not know if there have been complaints filed in the European Court of Human Rights yet.

15 Persecutions of Jehovah's witnesses in Russia

Interview with Maria Kravchenko

Maria Kravchenko is a researcher at the SOVA Center for Information and Analysis, a Russian-based nonprofit organization in Moscow founded in 2002. The organization monitors relations between religious organizations, the state, and secular society in Russia as well as the misuse of anti-extremist policies by the authorities, and analyzes these as well as other issues arising in relation to racism and xenophobia. Maria is the author of the report *Inventing Extremists: The Impact of Russian Anti-Extremism Policies on Freedom of Religion or Belief* created for the U.S. Commission on International Religious Freedom in 2018.

Q: **Where and how did the repression against Jehovah's Witnesses (JW) start in post-Soviet Russia? What were the first steps?**

MK: After the end of the Soviet rule in 1991 the Administrative Center of JW in Russia was officially registered. JW were rehabilitated and deemed victims of unjustified repression against believers after Boris Yeltsin's decree in 1996. However, in the same year a series of complaints against JW filed by the Moscow Committee for the Salvation of Youth from Pseudo-Religions and Totalitarian Sects (an organization created by activists and relatives of members of minor religious groups) encouraged one of the Moscow prosecutor's offices to launch an investigation. In 1998, the prosecutor's office filed a case seeking to dissolve the JW Moscow branch. The claim was denied. However, the JW Moscow community was nonetheless dissolved – not for extremism but for violating the 1997 Russian Law on Freedom of Conscience and Religious Associations. The branch was charged with forceful disintegration of families, infringement on the personal rights and freedoms of citizens, refusal of medical aid on religious grounds, and inciting citizens to refuse to fulfil their civil duties. In 2010, the Moscow branch won its case challenging this dissolution in the European Court of Human Rights and was registered again in 2015, two years prior to a complete ban of JW organizations in Russia. By 2010, when the European Court of Human Rights (ECtHR) granted their complaint, the persecution of JW in Russia had reached its first peak. The pressure grew step by step, from occasional registration hurdles, refusals to allow the construction of Kingdom Halls or holding congresses in the early 2000s, to declaring JW's publications extremist, attempts of banning JW local communities, and prosecution of believers at the end of the decade. The pressure by the authorities was accompanied by a wave of vandalism and pogroms against JW inspired by defamation campaigns in the press. Early in the second decade, the wave of repression receded for some time and then increased manifold, finally bringing the total ban on Jehovah's Witnesses activities and mass criminal prosecution for violation of such ban.

Q: What were the main arguments the courts employed to declare JW's activities extremist?

MK: Russian legislation on extremist groups and religious associations provides the state with a set of tools to interfere in the religious realm. The Russian Law on Combating Extremist Activity (2002) defines extremist activity as propaganda of exclusivity, superiority, or inferiority of a person on the basis of their religious affiliation or attitude toward religion. In its 2011 resolution on the implementation of anti-extremist laws, the Supreme Court of Russia pointed out that criticism of political, religious, and ideological associations and beliefs, as well as national and religious customs in and of themselves that are not followed by statements that justify or affirm the need for "genocide, mass repressions, deportations, and other unlawful actions, such as the use of violence, against members of a ethnicity, race, adherents of a particular religion and other groups of persons" should not be regarded as an incitement to hatred. However, Russian courts hearing extremism-related criminal cases have usually ignored this clarification.

The above-mentioned definition of extremism, often seen simply as the propaganda of the superiority of one's religion, which is, in fact, inherent in any religion, provided Russian law enforcement agencies with a way to suppress any unwelcome religious group regardless of whether it poses any actual danger to society.

Law enforcement agencies usually use the same simple scheme. The first step is a prohibition of materials, such as books, magazines, and brochures in the case of JW, on the grounds that they promote the superiority of one religion over others. On these grounds, a prosecutor's office applies to the court, using an expert opinion as an evidence. As a rule, such an opinion is provided by experts from research institutions affiliated with law enforcement agencies. These experts usually have expertise in linguistics or psychology, though in their opinions they analyze religious texts, which requires some level of expertise in theology and religious studies. However, religious scholars are very rarely engaged. Contrary to procedural norms and the Supreme Court's special directive, experts have often been asked questions of law (such as "Does the material contain signs of inciting hatred?"), which only courts have the power to answer.

As a rule, courts have relied on the opinion of prosecutors and experts and have not tried to review or challenge them. Banned materials have been placed in the Federal List of Extremist Materials administered by the Ministry of Justice.

The bans have been followed by fines for believers and local communities for distribution of (or even possession "with the intent to distribute") prohibited literature under Article 20.29 of the Russian Code of Administrative Offenses. After documenting occurrences of the distribution of banned materials by believers and communities, local prosecutor's offices issue warnings to relevant local JW religious organizations about the impermissibility of their extremist activities. If after the warning a religious organization continues to violate the anti-extremist law, it can be dissolved, and its believers can be prosecuted under Article 282.2 of the Russian Criminal Code, which penalizes activities of a religious organization banned as extremist. This is what happened with a number of JW local communities and eventually with the entire JW organization in Russia. Besides anti-extremist legislative tools, a wide range of other measures have been employed against Jehovah's Witnesses, including administrative punishments for violating legislation on religious associations, tightened in 2016 under its anti-missionary amendments (known as the Yarovaya Law). There have been attempts to sanction local communities for the violation of sanitary or fire regulations and attempts to accuse them of failing to provide proper paperwork. Some believers were also investigated for their involvement in non-extremist crimes or offenses without any legal grounds for such inquiries.

Q: What about bans on JW materials?

MK: The first court decision banning JW materials was issued by the Rostov Oblast Court in 2009. Thirty-four brochures, including the most important treatise for JW believers, *What the Bible Really Teaches*, were declared extremist as "religious literature, which contained statements that degraded human dignity on the basis of attitude towards religion and elements of propaganda of the exclusivity of one religion over another, thus indicating the presence of signs of incitement of interreligious hostility, religious exclusivity, and human rights violations." In 2012, the *Awake!* and *Watchtower* magazines were also banned by courts. In total, the Federal List of Extremist Materials included at least 119 JW materials as of October 2018, among them being the retranslated Bible of the JW (*The New World Translation of the Holy Scriptures*, published in 2015), banned in 2017 by the Vyborg City Court.

In fact, the experts engaged for the case of *The New World Translation of the Holy Scriptures* employed quite absurd and weak arguments to meet the needs of the prosecutor's office. They cited the Old and New Testaments on original sin, the destruction of Babylon and the Canaanites as well as Sodom and Gomorrah, Israel's apostasy at the time of Joshua, and the divine favor resting upon Christians to prove that JW promote the superiority of their religion and incite religious hatred. The experts also had to find a way to circumvent the law prohibiting recognition of the scriptures of the major religions as extremist.[1] In order to do this, they pointed out that *The New World Translation of the Holy Scriptures* used the concept of Jehovah instead of the concept of God, but also that the texts of the New Testament were changed by JW to misrepresent the idea of oneness of the Father and Son, and that the name of the Holy Spirit was written with small letters "to depersonalize Him." They also noted that the book was divided into different parts than in the canonical translation, which is the Russian Orthodox Church's Synodal translation, and that there was no indication in the book that it in fact is the Bible. Thus, the experts concluded that the JW version of the Bible was not the "real" Bible and that it did not even cite the "real" Bible. In spite of the inconsistencies in the experts' opinion, the court granted the claim and the JW Bible was declared extremist.

Many online JW resources were also declared extremist and blocked over the many years of persecution, including their official website, www.jw.org, banned in 2014, and www.jw-russia.org, blocked in 2018. JW have either been charged with publishing banned materials or, after the complete ban on JW organizations, such online resources have been prohibited because of their affiliation with the extremist religious association.

Q: How was the complete ban on the JW imposed and what were its legal and social ramifications?

MK: From 2007 to 2017, JW communities received 18 warnings about the impermissibility of violating anti-extremist laws, most of them during the last 4 years. In 2009, the first JW community was banned by a court in Taganrog. Following this ban, seven other local religious organizations were dissolved as a result of their extremist characterization by the courts: in Samara in 2014, in Abinsk in 2015, and in Stary Oskol, Belgorod, Elista, Oryol and Birobidzhan in 2016. The above-mentioned standard scheme was used in all these cases: they were fined under Article 20.29 of the Code of Administrative Offences, followed by the issuance of warnings, and the subsequent claims to the courts by the prosecutor's offices for dissolution of the communities.

In 2016, the authorities initiated a full-scale ban on the activities of JW communities in Russia. A warning was issued to the umbrella organization – the Administrative Center of JW in Russia. The Administrative Center appealed the warning, but failed. In March 2017, the Ministry of Justice applied to the Supreme Court of Russia with a claim to dissolve the Administrative Center and its constituent local organizations for reasons of extremism, seeking to prohibit their activities and confiscate their property on behalf of the state. The claimant asked the Supreme Court to ban both the Administrative Center and all 395 local organizations of JW. The Ministry argued that the Administrative Center had funded local JW communities, including those that were later banned, and was, therefore, involved in financing extremist activities. The Ministry also pointed out that the Administrative Center imported literature that was later recognized as extremist, as well as reprints of prohibited materials to Russia. The Supreme Court ruled in favor of the Ministry on April 20, 2017. The JW appealed to the Appellate Chamber, but their appeal was rejected and the lower decision came into force. Notably, the Supreme Court stressed in its decision that while their organizations were banned believers could still enjoy religious freedom in accordance with the Constitution of the Russian Federation. In fact, however, the law enforcement bodies fail to distinguish between the continuation of activities of a banned religious organization and the religious practice of its believers.

The JW subsequently applied to the ECtHR. In December 2017, the Court promised to consider as a matter of priority the complaint of the Administrative Center and its chairman Vasily Kalin, challenging the warning issued in 2016 and the subsequent ban of the Administrative Center. In May 2018, the t - ECtHR accepted a complaint of 395 JW communities, their chairmen, and rank-and-file members, claiming that the state deprived the JW communities of their property at a cost of €79,215,679 (approximately $89,000,000).

It is also worth noting that in May 2017, when the ban was not yet in force, JW places of worship and residences suffered from a series of break-ins – either by law enforcement officers performing inspections, by pro-government or Orthodox activist volunteers, or by autonomous vandals. Incidents of vandalism and pogroms were reported in a number of Russian regions. JW premises were pelted with rocks to the windows and fences were broken; there were also cases of arson of private residences.

Also, a number of illegal layoffs targeting JW have also been registered along with incidents in which believers have been denied a lawful alternative to military service. JW children also face pressure in educational institutions: school administrations interrogate them on their families and press them to abandon their parents' faith. Notably, in 2017, the Supreme Court expanded the list of conduct which can be used as grounds for termination of parental rights under the Family Code as to include the involvement of children in extremist organizations. According to the JW, as of February 2019, nearly 5,000 believers left Russia following the ban of their communities.

Q: When did criminal prosecution of the JW start and what is the current situation?

MK: The first criminal trial against a follower of the JW in post-Soviet Russia was that of Alexander Kalistratov in the Altai Republic in 2010. Kalistratov was accused of inciting religious hatred by distributing JW literature. None of the 40 witnesses called by the prosecutor's office could confirm the accusations. The lower court found him guilty, but the case was overturned by the Supreme Court of the Altai Republic. From 2011 to 2018, at least 11 similar criminal cases were opened against two dozen believers in the Astrakhan, Orenburg, Tyumen, and Moscow oblasts, as well as in the republics of Kabardino-Balkaria, Chuvashia, and Mari El and the Transbaikal Krai. Two of those cases were abandoned before they reached the courts; in eight others, the defendants were finally acquitted. Among these cases, the case of Vyacheslav Stepanov and Andrei Sivak stands out. It started in the Sergiev-Posad district of the Moscow region in 2013 and lasted over four years. Stepanov and Sivak were charged with inciting hatred or enmity committed by an organized group. Having found no evidence of hatred in their statements, the court found them not guilty in 2016, but the regional court remanded the case for a retrial. In 2017, both of the believers were acquitted. There were other cases of this kind.

Although criminal prosecution of the JW did not happen on a large scale between 2011 and 2017, there were many administrative fines and warnings issued to organizations. Thus, in 2016, at least two dozen fines were imposed for distributing JW banned literature.

The first criminal case based on the prohibition of the JW Administrative Center and their 395 local communities was reported in August 2017. The prosecutor's office in Kursk brought before the court a case against a local woman who distributed JW leaflets at a marketplace. As of the beginning of February 2019, the JW reported 115 believers ranging aged 23–84 became defendants in 50 criminal cases instigated in 33 regions of Russia; 24 of these defendants were in custody. The commencement of criminal cases has usually been followed by house searches with confiscation of equipment (computers, tablets, smartphones, etc.) and nighttime interrogations of believers, including elderly people and children. In total, nearly 270 searches were carried out in 2018. Law enforcement representatives often break into homes, kicking down doors, and engage in rough treatment of the residents. Some believers have reported that law enforcement officials planted banned brochures in their homes.

Q: **Is it possible to compare post-Soviet repressions against JW to the situation during the Soviet era? What is the difference?**

MK: Of course, in Russia, we do not have mass deportations of JW to Siberia as it was common in 1949 and in 1951, and none of the believers have been sentenced to 25-year prison terms as was the case in the 1940s. It should be noted, however, that at the moment dozens of JW are being prosecuted and hundreds have applied for asylum abroad. Obviously, the causes of the persecution are much the same as in Soviet times, including JW pacifism and conscientious objection to military service, rejection of state ideology, active proselytism, certain isolation of communities, and ties abroad. All of these features have been irritating for authorities and law enforcement agencies of both regimes.

Q: Does the Russian Orthodox Church (ROC) play any role in the persecution of JW?

MK: There is no clear evidence of the ROC's active participation in the process of banning JW organizations. Metropolitan Hilarion (Alfeyev), chairman of the ROC Department of External Church Relations argued that the church had nothing to do with the ban. He said that nobody requested their opinion and emphasized that the ban was issued for the purpose of banning extremism and not as a result of theological divergence. Still, he appreciated the Supreme Court decision. Hilarion said that the JW organization was a very harmful and dangerous totalitarian sect, presenting itself as part of Christianity. "Now this product won't be available on the market of denominations, and it's for the best," he added. This view was widely shared by the Orthodox clergy and only a few clergymen mentioned a possible negative impact of persecution based on religious grounds. Furthermore, the role of "anti-sectarians" or "ant-cultists" (people struggling against "harmful sects") should also be taken into account. The Russian state's suspicions against religious minorities are reflected in the use of the adjective "non-traditional" and the terms "cult" or "totalitarian sect" entrenched in its official language. The terms refer to religious communities other than those that are "traditional" within Russia, namely Orthodox Christianity, official Islam, Judaism, and Buddhism. This approach was largely borrowed from prominent representatives of the anti-sectarian movement: Orthodox theologian Alexander Dvorkin, religious philosopher Alexander Savin, religious expert and former staff member of the ROC Department of External Church Relations Roman Silantyev, and some others closely connected with the ROC, who serve as members of the Expert Council on State Religious Examination in the Russian Ministry of Justice. It is also worth mentioning that Alexander Konovalov, chief of this Ministry since 2008, received a theological education at Saint Tikhon's Orthodox University; he has also received two medals from the ROC.

Q: What is the political context of the situation with the JW? Why have persecutions become more severe in the past four years?

MK: It should be noted that whomever the stakeholders have been in the past, the current situation involves combined efforts by the prosecutor's offices and the Ministry of Justice, which have been filing claims against JW literature and organizations, the Federal Security Service (FSB) and the Investigative Committee, which have been investigating criminal cases against JW believers. A large-scale campaign like this would be impossible to execute without a collective decision by the authorities to engage in it. A number of factors had to come together for such a collective decision to be made, among them the recent anti-Western turn of Russian policies and the state's general commitment to the suppression of religious minorities.

Q: Why has it happened to the JW? Are there any other groups in Russia which face the same level of state persecutions and hostility?

One may assume that the JW are an easy target for persecution because of popular prejudices against them based on their rejection of blood transfusions, active proselytism, and denying certain popular traditions, as well as the relatively closed nature of their communities, which is commonly believed amongst the general Russian population to cause a disruption of families. These prejudices have been actively stirred up by the mass media during the defamation campaigns undoubtedly sponsored by the authorities.

However, the JW are not alone in facing prosecution for their religious practices in Russia. Scientologists in particular have been accused of violating registration rules, engaging in illegal entrepreneurship, collecting personal data, and using surveillance devices illegally. A number of Ron Hubbard's works, including his book *What is Scientology*, have been banned as extremist, exposing Hubbard's adherents to prosecution for their distribution. Now, in Saint Petersburg a group of Scientologists faces criminal charges, including incitement to hatred. There is a chance that if they are found guilty, their conviction may lead to the banning of Scientology centers as extremist organizations. Moreover, Baptists and Pentecostals have increasingly experienced various problems with registration and facilities as well as missionary restrictions. However, the pressure against religious groups of Western origin is still not as intense as against certain Islamic movements, such as Said Nursi followers or Tablighi Jamaat. Adherents of these movements, banned as extremist at the end of the 2000s, have been systematically sentenced to long-term imprisonment.

Q: Are there any signs that state policies towards the JW could change and the ban could be overruled? It is reported that President Putin pledged to look into persecution of JW in December 2018. Has this had any impact?

MK: Putin commented on the situation concerning JW during a meeting with the Presidential Council on Civil Society Development and Human Rights in December 2018. He said: "We should treat the representatives of all religions equally. This is true, but still, it is also necessary to take into account the country and the society in which we live. For sure, this does not mean at all that we should classify followers of religious communities as [members of] destructive or even terrorist organizations. Of course, this is complete nonsense."[2]

This statement raised certain expectations for a reduction of pressure of religious organizations. They were nurtured by the fact that some believers were being released from custody. However, the same month as Putin and his press secretary's promises to handle the situation, Arkadiy Akopian – a Jehovah's

Witness from the Kabardino–Balkaria Republic – was sentenced to community service for incitement to hatred through the distribution of banned brochures.[3] Also, in February 2019 Danish citizen Dennis Christensen was sentenced to six years imprisonment as an organizer of activities of a banned community in Orel. Christensen's sentence received wide publicity and international responses. Among others, the UN High Commissioner for Human Rights expressed deep concern about the sentencing of Christensen and called for the release of all JW prosecuted for exercising their right to freedom of religion, freedom of expression, and freedom of peaceful assembly. Although the national legislation provides certain possibilities for repealing the ban on JW organizations, it is more likely that such a repeal will follow a possible ECtHR decision in the cases brought before the court by Russian Jehovah's Witnesses. Still, even the ECtHR decision will not guarantee that pressure on the JW in Russia will lessen.

Notes

1 In 2015, a series of scandals related to bans against religious materials in Russia led President Putin's proposal of a bill that was adopted immediately. The law prohibited banning fundamental religious texts, amending the federal Law on Combating Extremist Activity to include the provision which read as follows: "The Bible, the Koran, the Tanakh, and the Kangyur, their contents, and quotations from them cannot be recognized as extremist materials." The amendment, however, failed to clarify whether various versions and translations of the scriptures can be subject to a ban, in whole or in part.

2 Putin, V. (2018, December 11). Presidential Council for Civil Society and Human Rights' meeting with the President [Transcript]. Retrieved from: http://president-sovet.ru/events/meetings/read/15/

3 Editorial note: his conviction was later overturned by the Supreme Court of the Kabardino-Balkaria Republic.

Index

Aleksy, patriarch 186, 188
All-Ukrainian Council of Churches and
    Religious Organizations 37, 41, 47,
    48n3, 121
anti-cult ideology in Russia 76–79

Bartholomew, patriarch 37, 139

Chersoneses 59, 165
church-state relations in Ukraine: before
    Russian-Ukrainian conflict 32–34;
    dynamics of 45–46, 123, 129, 134–135; and
    European integration policies 38, 125n2;
    and religious autonomy 28n1, 39–40, 49n9
civil religion: tensions with religious
    freedom 17–18; thick and thin version of
    16; in Ukraine 24, 114, 121; in wartime
    19–21
Crimea: annexation of 2, 59, 161, 162,
    168; Catholics in 151–152; Muslims in
    152–154; Protestants in 147–150;
    religious freedom in 4, 144–146, 154

Donetsk People's Republic/Luhansk
    People's Republic (DPR/LPR):
    Orthodox-self-identified military
    groups in 2, 213–214, 217, 218; religious
    minorities in 92, 216–217, 220; and
    Russian Christian Orthodoxy 2;
    violations of religious freedom in 4, 22,
    93, 100, 135, 213–215, 218, 220–224
Dvorkin, A. 76–78

Ecumenical Patriarchate 163, 164, 184,
    188, 192
Epiphany, metropolitan 36, 39, 123, 189
Euromaidan 70, 78, 115, 119, 120; and
    European integration policies 162, 169;
    role of religions in 122; and Russian-
    Ukrainian relations 161

Filaret: anathema imposed by Russian
    Orthodox Church on 187; as
    metropolitan of Russian Orthodox
    Church and Ukrainian Orthodox
    Church of Moscow Patriarchate 192,
    195–196, 205; as patriarch of Ukrainian
    Orthodox Church of Kyiv Patriarchate
    38, 39, 174, 186, 197

global Orthodoxy 164, 174

Heaven's Hundred 24, 121
Hilarion, metropolitan 56, 232
historical memory in Ukraine
    204–205
Hizb ut-Tahrir 147, 153, 154

inter-religious council "Peace – a Gift of
    God" in Crimea 145, 149, 155n1

Jehovah's Witnesses: objection to military
    service 19–20, 36; persecutions and
    ban in Russia 79, 229–231, 233–234;
    persecutions in DPR/LPR 132, 214;
    and Russian Orthodox Church 232; in
    Ukraine 132

Karaites' Spiritual Administration of
    Crimea 153
Kharkiv Council 186, 205–206
Kirill, patriarch 71, 171; on contemporary
    Europe 62, 63; and Putin, V. 22,
    167–168; on Russia and Ukraine
    56, 59, 170, 202
Kravchuk, L. 196

Mejlis 152, 147, 154
military chaplaincy 20, 25–26, 35–37

Nebesna Sotnya see Heaven's Hundred

Onufry, metropolitan 123, 189, 190, 207
Orthodox Church of Ukraine: creation of
39, 159, 160; historical attempts to obtain
autocephaly 163, 185, 187–188, 192;
relations with Ecumenical Patriarchate
183; relations with Ukrainian Orthodox
Church of Moscow Patriarchate 190;
Tomos for 37, 60, 117, 189; and Ukrainian
civil society 117, 173–174; and Ukrainian
state 47, 175–176

Pan-Orthodox Council in Crete 164
Poroshenko, P. 25, 37, 39, 42, 139, 174, 189
prayer breakfasts in Ukraine 42
Prilepin, Z. 62
Putin, V. 57–58, 83, 165

religion and violent conflicts 1–3
religious landscape of Ukraine 115–116,
118, 130–135, 139, 170
Revolution of Dignity *see* Euromaidan
Russian-Georgian war of 2008 170
Russian Orthodox Army 2, 213
Russian Orthodox Church: in DPR/LPR
95; perception of Orthodox Church of
Ukraine 60–61, 151, 190; perception of
Russian-Ukrainian conflict 123, 169–
170; in post-Soviet area 43, 176–177n8;
in pre-Soviet times 163; role in Global
Orthodoxy 160, 168, 190; and Russian
state 23, 83, 159–160, 170; in Soviet
times 19, 74–75
Russian World: concept and ideology of
23, 39, 55–57, 61–63, 171; and Russia's
influence in Ukraine 3, 181; and
Ukrainian Orthodox Church of Moscow
Patriarchate 131
Russkiy mir see Russian World
Russkiy Mir Foundation 55–56

Spiritual Administration of Muslims of
Crimea 152–154

Tauride Muftiate 153–154
Tsvigun, M. 79–82

Ukrainian Autocephalous Orthodox
Church 45, 115, 131, 184–185,
188–189
Ukrainian Greek Catholic Church 37,
70, 117, 120, 122, 172; in Crimea 152,
155n1; in DPR/LPR 214; and Orthodox
Church of Ukraine 27–28, 135; and
Russian-Ukrainian conflict 122
Ukrainian Orthodox Church of Kyiv
Patriarchate: as basis of Ukrainian
autocephaly 39; in Crimea 151; and
Ecumenical Patriarchate 189; perception
in Russia 70, 78, 117; and Ukrainian state
37, 39
Ukrainian Orthodox Church of Moscow
Patriarchate: ambiguity of historical
memory of 194, 201, 205, 207; in
Crimea 150, 153; in the DPR/LPR 135,
213, 215, 218; and separatism in Ukraine
3, 218; ties with Russian Orthodox
Church 24, 48n5, 123, 168–169, 170,
173, 177n9, 197, 205; and Ukrainian state
24, 26, 37, 39–40, 47
Ukrainian Orthodox Unifying Council of
2018 39, 117, 170
U.S. Commission on International
Religious Freedom 86–88, 94–97,
99–100

Volodymyr, metropolitan 186, 197, 207

Yarovaya Law 144, 146–147, 228
Yushchenko, V. 192

Made in the USA
Middletown, DE
30 October 2023

41654302R00139